JSP AND JAVA

The Complete Guide to Website Development

ART TAYLOR

PH
PTR

Prentice Hall PTR
Upper Saddle River, NJ 07458
www.phptr.com

Library of Congress Cataloging-in-Publication Data

Taylor, Art.
  JSP and Java: the complete guide to Web site development/Art Taylor.
    p.   cm.
  Includes index.
  ISBN 0-13-091813-X
  1. Java (Computer program language) 2. Web sites—Design. I. Title.

  QA76.73.J38 T39 2002
  005.2'762—dc21   2001053110

Editorial/production supervision: Kerry Reardon
Acquisitions editor: Karen McLean
Production coordinator: Anne R. Garcia
Manufacturing manager: Alexis Heydt-Long
Editorial assistant: Richard Winkler
Cover design director: Jerry Votta
Cover designer: Nina Scuderi
Art director: Gail Cocker-Bogusz

© 2002 Prentice Hall PTR
Prentice-Hall, Inc.
Upper Saddle River, NJ 07458

Prentice Hall books are widely used by corporations and government agencies
for training, marketing, and resale.

The publisher offers discounts on this book when ordered in bulk quantities.
For more information, contact: Corporate Sales Department, Phone: 800-382-3419;
Fax: 201-236-7141; E-mail: corpsales@prenhall.com; or write: Prentice Hall PTR,
Corp. Sales Dept., One Lake Street, Upper Saddle River, NJ 07458.

Printed in the United States of America

10 9 8 7 6 5 4 3 2 1

ISBN 0-13-091813-X

Pearson Education LTD.
Pearson Education Australia PTY, Limited
Pearson Education Singapore, Pte. Ltd.
Pearson Education North Asia Ltd.
Pearson Education Canada, Ltd.
Pearson Educación de Mexico, S.A. de C.V.
Pearson Education Japan
Pearson Education Malaysia, Pte. Ltd.
Pearson Education, Upper Saddle River, New Jersey

To my daughter, Hannah, a most intriguing young woman,
and
to my son, Eric, an excellent young man.

CONTENTS

CHAPTER 5   **MAKING THE PIECES WORK: INTEGRATING THE TOMCAT SERVER WITH APACHE   129**

CHAPTER 6   **JAVA SERVER PAGES   151**

CHAPTER 11   DATABASE ACCESS WITH JAVABEANS   325

PREFACE

Purpose of Book

This book is intended to provide instruction on the various tools and servers required to develop a Web site using Java technologies. The infrastructure or technical architecture with which these tools will be demonstrated will be a Linux server, the Apache HTTP server, the Tomcat Java server for JSP and servlet processing, and the PostgreSQL relational database. All of these tools are freely available on the Web though there may be licensing requirements for sale and distribution of some of the tools.While Linux will be the development environment for the purposes of this book, the installation and deployment on the NT platform are not significantly different.

The first section of the book will detail the installation and configuration of these technologies; the process of creating the infrastructure for development. While installation is generally not that involved, configuration for something as complex and variable as a Web site can be complex and dependent on the application being developed. The process of configuration will be revisited in later sections of the book that detail the development and deployment process.

The second section of the book will present several JSP examples and then present the code involved in the creation of a sample discussion group application using static HTML, JSPs, JavaBeans and JSP custom tags. These chapters will also provide some discussion of various design strategies for Java web development and then detail the Java code necessary to develop these applications.

Design patterns are, in a nutshell, proven solutions to recurring problems. Several design patterns have been identified for development with Java Web sites. The use of these design patterns are presented, discussed and then demonstrated in this text.

After reading this book, the reader will understand the benefits of Web development using JSPs and will have the knowledge to begin building such a site. The book will demonstrate tips and techniques for Java development on the Web and in many cases, will drill down into several of the more interesting features of Java.

Intended Audience

The intended audience for this book is the web site developer, technology architect or technical manager interested in Web site development and curious about the technical aspects of a Java web site. The reader should be familiar with the various Web technologies: the HTTP server, the database, the browser, HTML and the Java programming language. But familiarity does not imply expertise. The reader is not expected to be an expert in these technologies; the purpose of this book is to fill in the various holes in the reader's knowledge and make them aware of what technologies are needed to create a Java web site.

After reading this book the reader will understand the requirements for building a Java web site and using the information provided in the book and using the examples as a guide, can begin building the site. This book includes directions on developing a sound architecture for a Java web site and provides examples for the design and development of the site. Several sample applications demonstrate best practices for Java web site development.

While this book strives to provide detailed information on the various technologies involved in Web site creation (Apache, JSP, servlets, the Java language) it does not purport to be a complete reference on all of these technologies. Many books could be written (and have been written) on the components of a web site and on Java development. These books provide excellent complements to this text and, if I've done my job well, should rest comfortably on the shelf next to a well-worn copy of this text.

ACKNOWLEDGMENTS

A special thanks to the technical editors who helped me put this together: Michael Dailous and Randy Layman. Though at times I know it seemed like it would never end, it did and their fine work has helped make this a better book.

Appreciation also goes to my patient editor Karen McLean and the production team at Prentice Hall, including Kerry Reardon who, as always, manages to produce an excellent final product.

And thanks to Mark Taub, the senior editor at Prentice Hall—a supportive and informed advisor and the person responsible for getting me started on this road many years ago.

Last, but in no way least, a heartfelt thanks to my wife Carolyn, whose support (and patience) is always appreciated.

THE WEB TAKES OVER

Introduction

If there is any trend that is obvious in the information technology IT industry in the last five years, it is the movement toward the Web—everything is, or soon will be *on the Web*. Client–server has been superseded as the development model of choice. Development activity is now focused on the Web, where applications can be easily deployed and shared among multiple users at a fraction of the expense and effort of client–server deployment.

Initially, Web development was difficult, requiring a paradigm markedly different from the simplified client–server development it was in the process of replacing. The components used to develop Web pages [HyperText Markup Language (HTML), Web browsers] were never intended to provide a full-featured set of programming tools. Database access was difficult and security was an ever-present issue.

Over time, many of these issues were overcome, primarily through server-side scripting solutions, where a script language is executed on the server and ultimately outputs a Web page to the browser. The most notable and popular of these was Active Server Pages (ASP) from Microsoft. Microsoft realized that the HTML Web page was the primary user interface design component of the Web and that any attempt to add procedural logic to this (a significant reason for server-side scripting such as ASP) must integrate easily with

1

HTML. Toward this goal, ASP was designed to be an integral part of the HTML page, using special tags that can be located anywhere on the page, thus allowing procedural logic in the form of VBScript anywhere within the HTML Web page. At the time, other server-side scripting solutions were more complicated and restrictive.

Borrowing a *page* from Microsoft's book, Java Server Pages (JSP) allows Java code to be interspersed liberally anywhere on an HTML page, just as VBScript can be integrated into a page using ASP. This JSP code has access to all the Java language syntax, and since it is run on the server and not the client (the browser), it can easily access any Java components installed on the server (e. g., JavaBeans components). Using this approach, the robust power of Java, including database access and a rich set of APIs, is available using JSP.

In conjunction with the availability of JSP, the release of a firm Java 2 Enterprise Edition (J2EE) specification with a robust remote component model in Enterprise JavaBeans and various other tools that provide excellent support for this environment creates a powerful platform for Web development and deployment. The ability to use Java-based tools to develop a Web environment allows development and deployment to span multiple platforms, from low-end, inexpensive Windows-NT or Linux machines, to high-end Unix platforms from Sun Microsystems, IBM, and Hewlett-Packard. This provides an attractive value proposition for developers, allowing Web development to proceed regardless of platform availability, and avoiding the platform *lock-in* of Windows-based tools. Using Java-based Web development tools, a system could be developed and potentially deployed on Windows-NT using MS-SQL-Server, and if the Web site outgrows the NT platform, the migration path to a Unix-variant platform with an Oracle or Informix database back end would be smooth and relatively painless.

Open Source Solutions

The availability of good, production-ready open-source solutions adds to the value proposition of a Java-based Web site. First and foremost, the Apache Web server provides a solid backbone for any Web site, proven through years of use at some of the busiest sites on the Web. Given the large number of Apache sites, there are an ample number of Web administrators available to help develop and maintain an Apache Web site (although hiring a qualified technical administrator is not easy, by any means).

The Tomcat server follows in the open-source footsteps of Apache. The code for this application server is open source and is managed by the Apache.org organization. Installation and setup are simple and straightforward and the configuration allows for a great deal of flexibility. Although the Tomcat server is still in the early stages of development, it offers a great deal of functionality and scalability and is in production use at numerous small- to medium-sized Web sites.

The Apache Organization

The Apache organization is a loosely knit group of developers spread over the globe. This divergent and diligent group has created some of the most significant software of the past decade. Their core product, the Apache Web server, serves a majority of the pages delivered over the Internet (over 60 percent as of November 2000 according to *Netcraft*).

Aware of the importance of Java on the Web, the Apache organization has spawned a project known as Jakarta, which has grown to include a large number Java subprojects (`http://jakarta.apache.org`). The Jakarta project represents this effort and includes a number of subprojects. One of these subprojects is the Tomcat server, which as of this writing includes an implementation of Java servlet 2.2 and JSP 1.1. (Other subprojects under Jakarta include Ant, Slide, Struts, Taglibs, Velocity, and Watchdog.)

One of the more significant of these subprojects is the Tomcat server. The Tomcat server provides the ability to use JSP and servlets on a Web site. This ability can either be used standalone, with the Tomcat server managing all Web site pages, either HTML, JSP, or servlets, or the server can be used in conjunction with the Apache HTTP server.

In the time since the project's inception, the Tomcat server has met with a great deal of interest. Although technically a reference implementation, it is increasingly being used for low- to moderate-use production systems. (Sun currently distributes the Tomcat server as part of its J2EE distribution.)

To understand server-side Java, we need to understand the history of Java, from its creation at Sun to the vast array of technologies and APIs that now constitute Java. It is more than just a language; it is a technology, an environment, and a platform as the following section will explain.

History of Java

Java had its beginnings at Sun Microsystems in the early 1990s. James Gosling, laboring at Sun, needed a language that was small and CPU-independent. One of the privileged engineers fortunate enough to have a window office, the Oak tree outside his window formed the inspiration for the initial name of the language: *Oak*.

The development team Gosling worked with considered UCSD Pascal as the syntactical basis for the language but, instead, opted for a syntax that would be more familiar to the ubiquitous C language programmer, so C formed the basis for the language syntax. And no doubt inspired by the ever-present cup of coffee in Sun's development labs, the language was named *Java* instead of Oak.

Realizing the importance of the then nascent Web, the developers designed Java to work well in a networked environment. To demonstrate some of the capabilities of Java, they created a Web browser using the language and demonstrated the browser, dubbed the HotJava browser, at SunWorld '95. This browser generated a great deal of interest in the Java language. Then, in the fall of 1995, Netscape announced that the next version of Web browser would support Java applets (small Java applications designed to run in a browser environment). This, in turn, furthered interest in the Java language.

In the years since its inception, Sun has continued to improve Java. Application programmer interfaces (APIs) have been added at what at times has seemed a frenetic pace. Lacking a database interface, the Java Database Connectivity (JDBC) API was added soon after the initial release of Java. More recently, the Java 2 release has bundled a number of features and APIs together. Enterprise JavaBeans (EJBs) provide a rich set of software component programming facilities. Servlets initially provided a Java solution for Web development. But the JSP standard extends servlets and provides a more natural development environment than that provided by servlets alone.

Benefits of Java

Central to all of these developments has been the Java tenet of "write-once, run-anywhere," the promise of seamless cross-platform development. This may be the most important draw of Java, but it is not the only draw. Java removes many of the features of C and C++ that allowed problems to creep into applications. Language pointers are the most notable deletion. Loved by many developers as a convenient means of abstraction, their implementation in C allowed them to ignore proper data boundaries and subtly corrupt a program. Pointer errors would often not be discovered until long after a program was in production, at which time it is often horrendously expensive to fix.

Pointers in C were often used to allow the application to manage memory. Java removes the chore of memory management from the programmer and performs its own periodic garbage collection. (When and how effectively this garbage collection is performed are sometimes a matter of debate.) Unlike

C++, Java forces an object-oriented design on the application. Every program is a `class` with at least one method. All of the important object-oriented features are present in Java: polymorphism; public, private, and protected variable scope; and interfaces.

Web Infrastructure

Unlike client–server or character-based application development where a single executable program may have controlled all aspects of the application, from the control of the user interface to database interaction, Web applications represent a set of programs executing and communicating in tandem, a multitiered approach (see Figure 1.1). To understand this infrastructure it is important to understand the background of the technologies used on the World Wide Web, their purpose, and how they have matured into the technologies that we use today.

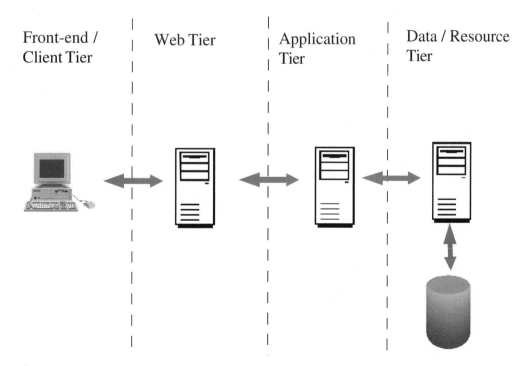

Front-end / Client Tier   Web Tier   Application Tier   Data / Resource Tier

Figure 1.1 Multitiered Web Applications

HTML has it roots in the late 1980s at CERN. Tim Berners-Lee and his associates developed a set of technologies to make it easier to find information on the Internet. The system would help to simplify the access of documents on the array of computers that were connected to the Internet. As part of the effort to manage the collection of documents on the Internet, a *hypertext* approach to document rendering was chosen. This involved creating documents that contained links to other documents, which themselves could contain links to other documents.

This approach to document presentation allowed users to drill down into a document to get more detail or find related information. Since the documents were to reside on the Internet, the document links could point to documents on the local machine or on any machine connected to the Internet. Not only could documents be linked in this manner, but any number of document elements and other resources could be inserted into a document using links.

To provide communication between the servers that would serve these documents, a protocol was devised, appropriately named HyperText Transport Protocol (HTTP). This protocol provided a handshaking mechanism that used a *request/response* protocol, where the client would request a resource (document/page) and the server would respond in some fashion. A *resource* could be a document, a graphic image, or virtually any other *object* on the network.

To simplify the process of resource location, a *uniform resource identifier* (URI) or uniform resource locator (URL) was created. This convention allowed the location of the document to be represented in a platform-neutral method. This combined approach of links and URLs, HTML, and HTTP proved to be extremely flexible. Within a few years of its inception, this simple but elegant solution had spawned a major paradigm shift in the computer industry. The firmly entrenched world of client–server software was forced to take notice, and even the giant Microsoft had made a major shift toward Web software.

The Web infrastructure involves not one tool but a set of tools and components. It is important to understand the part played by these tools and the standards that apply to them. The primary components of the Web infrastructure are shown Figure 1.2.

Collectively, these components represent what is known as *a multitiered application environment* or *infrastructure*. One of the hallmarks of this infrastructure is the extremely low cost of deployment and the flexibility derived from the component design of the middle tier.

On one end of this infrastructure model lies the *client tier* with the ubiquitous Web browser. The browser is effectively a small, focused operating environment that navigates the Web and retrieves *resources*. Once a resource has been retrieved, it either renders the resource or performs some action required to manage the resource (as defined by the MIME type). If the resource is an HTML document, the browser will render it or display the page. This would involve rendering the text correctly and retrieving any images that may be contained on the page (which are also resources). For some resources the browser may need help; this could involve loading a plug-in module or executing an external program. The browser can also send documents and/or data to another point on the Web.

The browser can communicate only with certain types of servers. It can communicate with an HTTP server using HTTP. It can also communicate with an FTP server using File Transmission Protocol (FTP). The HTTP server represents the backbone of the Web infrastructure. It monitors the server port for connections and then attempts to perform whatever HTTP transaction is requested at the port.

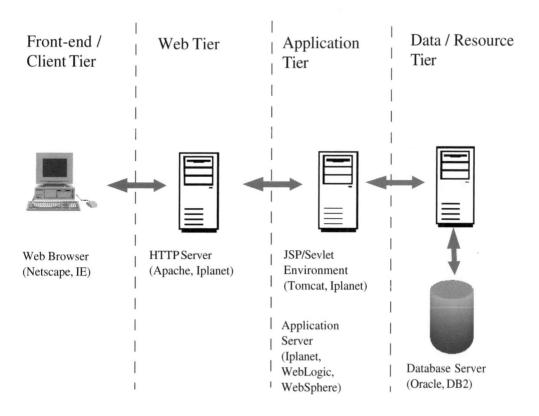

Figure 1.2 The Web Infrastructure

If necessary, the HTTP server will pass the request to another application, a container or application server, for processing. It will then become the job of the container to process the resource and send a response back to the client that requested the resource. This container or application server performs an important role. It can process the business logic of the application, enforcing business rules and managing data. To manage the data required for the site, the container must communicate with the third component of this infrastructure, the database.

The database will manage the data for the site. The container will request data from the database server when it is needed to complete a page and it will send data to the database server when an update is being performed. The database is an important part of this infrastructure. Although technically it is not needed to produce dynamic content, it is almost always present and provides a much cleaner means of managing a site than do nondatabase alternatives.

The glue that holds all of this together is the network. Although these components could all be placed together on a single machine running under multiple services (a narrowly deployed distributed application), that would not serve the purpose of creating a distributed application. Specifically, by spreading the application over multiple machines, the risk of having a single point of failure is eliminated, and if properly deployed, performance and scalability of the application can be increased.

The Network: TCP/IP

The foundation of Web development is the network. The network is the *wire* through which the application operates, and if it were not present, the Web application that requires remote users to connect to a Web server would not run. (A Web application can be run locally on a machine and not use a physical network, but it will nevertheless be using local network loopback mechanisms to mimic operation of the network on the local machine.)

Networks are composed of a series of *nodes* or points on the network. Networks provide high-speed data communications between the nodes using a *protocol*, a predetermined language for communication, and a predetermined format for a *data buffer* or information *packet*. The protocol is used by the two nodes in the communication process to determine what information is being conveyed. The data buffer or packet is what is transmitted between the two nodes and is a combination of the actual data being transmitted and information about the data packet contained in the packet header. To transmit a packet, a node may set a flag in the packet header indicating that the packet is being transmitted to a specific target; the target address will also be included in the header. The packet will then be transmitted and may travel to a number of different nodes until it is received at the node to which it was sent. The source and destination nodes may exchange additional packets of data to ensure delivery of the data packet; this exchange of additional packets is part of a handshaking protocol used to provide some control over the transmission process.

At any given point a large number of data packets may be coursing through a network. These packets are sent to their correct destination via *routers*. The routers examine the packet and try to make a determination about where the packet is bound (see Figure 1.3).

The World Wide Web uses the Transmission Control Protocol/Internet Protocol (TCP/IP) for communication and represents one of the most common protocols for network communication. TCP/IP is actually two protocols: TCP and IP. The IP protocol stands for Internet Protocol and provides routing information, information on how to find the address of the resource being requested. IP splits the data into packets and attaches a source and destination address. This information is then used to route the packet from the source to the destination.

TCP uses the IP layer to provide routing services. TCP establishes the connection and provides a handshaking mechanism to ensure that data get to their destination. TCP provides guaranteed delivery of data (unlike other protocols, which do not) and for this reason provides some level of error correction and integrity for data transmission.

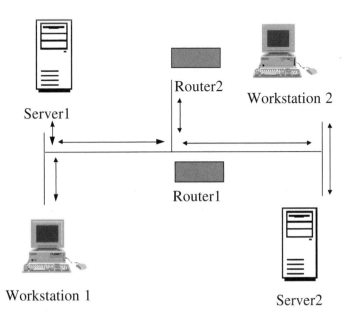

Figure 1.3 The Data Network

But TCP/IP communication alone does not make the Web. As mentioned previously, the HTTP protocol provides a layer of communication above the TCP/IP layers. This protocol uses a small number of handshaking directives to transmit resources from the server to the client. In respect to the World Wide Web infrastructure, TCP/IP and HTTP are part of a network protocol layer framework known as the Open Systems Interconnection (OSI) developed by the International Standards Organization (ISO). The framework provides for seven layers, and although vendors have implemented parts of this framework, rarely is the entire standard adhered to in a product. TCP/IP combined with HTTP comprises the part of this layer model used in this book (see Table 1.1).

Table 1.1 Open Systems Interconnection Framework

OSI Layer	Type	Description
HTTP	Application	HyperText Transport Protocol
TCP	Transport	Transport Control Protocol
IP	Internet	Internet Protocol
Ethernet, ISDN, PPP, SLIP	Data Link	Network packet transmission

At the lowest level, a layer exists to move the network packets from one point to another. This layer has only rudimentary knowledge of the contents of the packets; higher-level protocols such as IP provide the routing of the packets. Above IP, the TCP layer provides for the communication between network nodes and ensures accuracy, using the IP layer for routing. Above all other layers, the HTTP layer executes the handshaking between client and server with some knowledge of the information being transmitted.

HTML and the Web

A standard that resides separate from the other portions of the Web infrastructure is that of the HyperText Markup Language. Although separate, it is by no means unimportant, and its origin and purpose speak directly to the need for server-side scripting in Web development. HTML is a markup language not a programming language and as such has been sorely stretched to perform the work necessary to create complete applications on the Web. HTML is a *presentation language* derived from Standard Generalized Markup Language (SGML) and is comprised of tags that define how the text they surround will be rendered. But these tags, combined with links, the ability to input data into data entry forms, and the ability to execute external programs with Common Gateway Interface (CGI) provide some level of functionality and thus provide the ability to create working applications that operate over the Web.

But this combination of tools and components (HTML, links, and CGI) has distinct limitations. To implement business logic is difficult and clumsy and the performance of CGI solutions has generally been poor. The logical solution to this problem was to somehow extend HTML to provide for many of the shortcomings of the original presentation language. Vendors originally did this in such a way as to address the shortcomings of HTML and CGI and to provide a proprietary solution that would lock the user into their product. These solutions generally used tag extensions that would be embedded into the HTML page and would be executed at the server (not the browser client), providing a server-side scripting solution. To implement these solutions, the infrastructure of the Web was also extended, often adding an application server to manage the execution of the vendor's server-side script. This application server would work together with the HTTP server to parse, execute, and serve the HTML page to the browser.

Originally, server-side scripting solutions provided for limited functionality in their scripting languages. Complex programming constructs were not available. Database access was either not available or limited, and the ability to access software components was nonexistent. Microsoft addressed some of these issues with Active Server Pages (ASP), which provided a subset of their popular Visual Basic programming language and allowed cross-vendor database access using Active-X Data Objects (ADOs).

Active Server Pages also provided a very natural method of programming a Web application. Procedural ASP (VBScript) code could be interspersed with the HTML on Web pages, and programming loops and conditional statements could be executed to provide for dynamic content with HTML. But ASP had its limitations. Originally it ran only on the Windows-NT platform (although there are now vendors who support ASP on Unix platforms). Communicating with software components (COM objects) could be done but required some effort. One of the most limiting factors of ASP was the Visual Basic syntax for the language. VBScript was not an object-oriented language, and many of the more interesting benefits of an object-oriented language (inheritance, encapsulation, aggregation) were not directly available in ASP.

An alternative server-side scripting solution offered by Sun Microsystems was Java *servlets*. Written in Java, servlets were portions of Java code that would be executed at the server. The output of these servlets would be a completed HTML page that would be sent to client browsers. With servlets, the output stream needed to describe the page completely, unlike ASP or other solutions that embedded tags into an HTML page; servlets needed to use a series of output statements to assemble the page.

Many users found the servlet server-side scripting solution to be tedious compared to the ASP approach, which they found to be a more natural approach. Taking note of developer response, Sun developed a specification for JSP that married servlets with embedded HTML tags to create a simple, yet powerful server-side scripting solution. This development model was extended further by adding extensibility in the form of JavaBeans, components that can be invoked from within the Web page. Using JavaBeans, components require very little effort to create and have few restrictions.

JSP makes extensive use of the servlet development model. Special tags in the Web page denote Java scriplets. Java scriplets can use the full Java syntax, API, and JavaBean components. At runtime, when a JSP is processed, it is converted into a Java servlet, compiled, and then executed in the servlet container and its output stream (a completed HTML page) is directed to the client browser. All of this takes place within a *server* (see Figure 1.4). (JSP processing is covered in more detail in later chapters.)

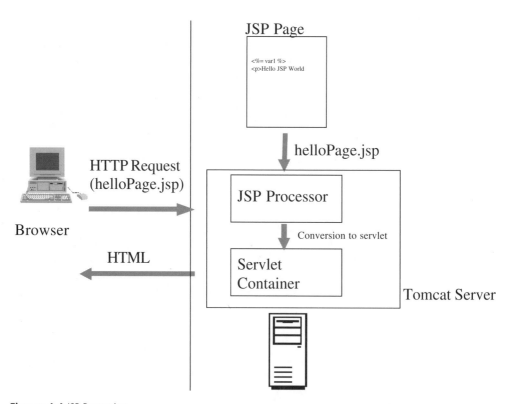

Figures 1.4 JSP Processing

The Middle Tier

If we consider our Web application to be a series of *tiers*, we are creating a *multitiered* application, with the client tier represented by the Web browser and the data tier represented by the database server. The portion of this application that connects the client tier to the database tier is the *middle tier*. This tier is effectively the glue that connects the client to the database. But we expect this tier to provide more than just simple database access. Good Web architecture and design recommends that business logic be pushed back to this middle tier. With this design strategy, the client tier encapsulates *presentation logic* and the middle tier encapsulates the *business logic* of the enterprise.

Since the middle tier must interact with a Web browser for a client, it will need to produce Web pages as output. The middle tier must execute business logic and dynamically build Web pages to be presented on the client tier. Java technologies are the logical choice for the middle tier. Their primary attraction to many is their platform independence. Not only can Java applications be moved freely from one Unix variant to another across multiple hardware platforms, but Java application code can easily be moved from various NT platforms to Unix with no code changes required.

J2EE offers a variety of server-side technologies for Web applications: Java Server Pages, Java servlets, JavaBeans, and Enterprise JavaBeans. As discussed previously, Java servlets represent a Java class that is extended and uses certain methods to receive and process HTTP requests. A servlet is composed of Java code and must be written by someone who understands the Java programming language.

JSP is a more user friendly approach to using Java with Web development. Using JSP, Java `scriplets` can be embedded directly into the HTML page. The scriplets are then converted into a Java servlet by the JSP/servlet container (running either as a thread within the Web browser or as an external process). The JSP server/container converts the JSP code and HTML code into a Java servlet. The servlet is then compiled (if necessary) and executed and the results are returned to the client that initiated the request.

JavaBeans are a server-side component that can be executed and invoked using JSP pages (JSPs) and servlets. As used in JSP, JavaBeans are Java classes coded with methods that allow them to be invoked from within the JSP using special JSP tags. (The expectation is that when using JSP, a great deal of the business logic will be pushed back into JavaBeans.)

EJBs are a more robust and complex Java component. EJBs run within a container that provides a number of features to the component. EJBs can be invoked locally or remotely and provide features such as transactions, persistence, and scalability for large transaction volumes. In general, the more advanced features of EJBs are applied to the more complex and busy applications that require the additional scalability and reliability offered by their containers.

The focus in this book is on applications that can benefit from the JSP and JavaBean technologies. These Java tools are relatively easy to use and do not require expending a large sum of money for a high-end application server. (In fact, the examples shown throughout this book use freely available, open-source software.)

Java Servlets versus JSPs

The ability to use servlets goes hand-in-glove with the ability to use JSPs, since JSP technology is built on servlet technology. But using servlets is not the focus of this book. Both servlets and JSPs provide a means of executing business logic at the server using the full Java language and thus share many of the same capabilities. The difference lies in where and how the Java code is written. The servlet is essentially a Java application component which requires Java developers to write and then maintain the application code. But a well-designed JSP could be developed by a team of Java and HTML developers, with HTML developers focusing on the look and feel of the page and the Java developer creating the code (and tags) to provide the dynamic content of the page. Once complete, the page could be left to HTML developers alone to maintain.

The benefit of this approach is that, in general, HTML developers represent a less expensive resource (i.e., lower hourly consulting rate) than Java developers. The maintenance of well-written JSP is a significantly simpler and safer process than the maintenance of servlets. This is not to say that there is never a case where servlets may represent a better choice than JSPs. If the application component requires extensive decision logic and requires little or no output for the client, or requires the use of an extensive number of Java language API calls, a servlet may be the better choice. (This is an issue that will be revisited several times in the coming chapters.)

The Application Server

In general, an *application server* is considered to be a program that provides a number of services needed for an application, a computer program, to run. The computer program is considered in this case to be a set of components or multiple parts that when combined create a complete application. Originally, the term *application server* was used relative to multitier application, applications with three or more tiers. The application server would reside between the front-end client portion of the application and the back-end portion of the application usually responsible for management of application data. Since the application server was in the middle of these two tiers, the term *middleware* was often applied to these servers. The job of the application server was to apply the business logic of the application to access the data from the back-end tier. To provide this service in an active, volatile environment, application server vendors developed a complex set of capabilities and now on the whole provide much more than simple execution of business logic and data access.

The current set of application servers provide scalability, fail-over, transactions, and connectivity to legacy systems in addition to management of distributed components such as Enterprise JavaBeans. Since it is not uncommon for access to legacy data sources to involve connecting to mainframe systems or even to nondatabase sources, the complexity of the application server moves beyond simple database access and could include connections to mainframe systems or remote software components such as CORBA or Enterprise JavaBeans.

In addition to providing connections to legacy data sources, the application server may also provide some reliability, fail-over capabilities, and scalability features to provide extremely high, reliable throughput for simultaneous Web clients, which may number in the tens of thousands. In an Internet/intranet environment, the application server provides the connection between the Web clients and the information they need. They must communicate with both the HTTP server and the components of the back end, the resource tier. Communication with the HTTP server is usually conducted using a *dispatch module*, an add-on component that runs in the Web server and dispatches requests that must be handled by an application server or some other service. If there are multiple instances of the application server running, the dispatch module can spread incoming requests across multiple servers using a *load-balancing* technique to distribute the workload. Since these multiple instances are usually running on more than one machine, this distribution of work has the effect of spreading the workload for the site across several machines and providing scalability for the site (see Figure 1.5). Additionally, this feature can provide some degree of reliability and high availability. If the Web server module is aware that one of the machines in its distribution list has failed, it can stop sending output to the machine and send the incoming requests to the remaining server instances.

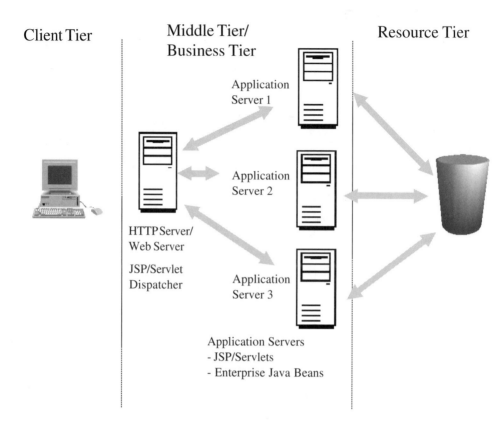

Figure 1.5 Web Server Workload Distribution over Multiple Application Servers

The High-End Application Server and Alternatives

As we have seen, the term *application server* has come to mean more than just the execution of business logic. High-end application servers of today are robust, scalable, feature-rich, complex, and, not surprising given the amount of technology they contain, expensive. But the complex technology of the high-end application servers is by no means a requirement for all applications. Several distinct groups of Web applications can be identified based on the complexity of the application being created, the reliability required, and the number of concurrent users expected. Table 1.2 shows the relation between these three criteria and the toolset required to deliver the application.

Table 1.2 Web Site Solution Criteria[a]

Level	Complexity	Concurrent Users	Dynamic Content	Security	Availability	Toolset
1	Low	Small to medium	None	Moderate	Moderate	Web server with static HTML pages
2	Medium	Small to medium	Moderate (half of an application)	Moderate	Moderate	Web server for static HTML; low- to midrange application server or Web server container for dynamic content; JSP, servlets, HTML; low- to midrange database
3	Medium to high	Medium to high	Moderate to high	Moderate to high	Moderate to high	Web server (one or more); high-end application server with scalability and fail-over features; JSP, servlets, EJB

[a]What is important to note in this table is that a large number of sites fit the second level: medium complexity, small to medium user load, and a moderate number of dynamic pages. This is a site with between 50 and 150 pages. Approximately 20 to 50 percent of these pages are static and the remainder are dynamic pages. It is assumed that these sites do not have high availability or high security demands. Although it is, of course, desirable to keep the site available as much as possible, if the site were down for several hours this failure would not represent a multimillion-dollar loss for the enterprise, so some downtime is tolerable. It is also assumed that the site does not have high security demands. Although some of the low-range solutions provide sophisticated encryption security such as Secure Socket Layer (SSL), more complex requirements with many layers of security may require a mid- to high-range solution. Given the requirements for these level 2 sites, a low- to midrange application server solution is possible, with the low-end being an open-source solution such as Tomcat (which, nevertheless, provides many of the features of the midrange solutions), and the midrange solution being WebSphere, BEA WebLogic, and others.

Web Site Comparisons

In this table, the column on complexity tries to establish some measure of complexity. A low-complexity Web application would be an application that is composed of a relatively small number of static HTML pages. The page flow between pages would be simple and straightforward, using only hypertext links to move between one page and another. An application of medium complexity would include a larger number of static pages, from 50 to several hundred, and the relationship between these pages could be complex, requiring some level of logic to be executed to move between pages. A highly complex application would include a larger number of pages, many of which would be dynamically generated pages requiring the execution of business logic to create.

For the purposes of this table, a small number of concurrent users would be between 10 and several hundred page hits per day. A medium number of concurrent users would be between 100 and several thousand page hits per day, up to around 20,000 hits per day, and a large number of concurrent users would be between upward of 20,000 hits per day. Note that these are guidelines—the actual performance of an application under a user load depends on the application being run. If the application has 250 users who execute simple logic with very few database accesses, it would require much less system resource than an application that executed complex logic and required a large number of database accesses on each page. The prudent developer will test the application under various workloads to determine performance expectations.

Using the guidelines laid out in Table 1.2, the recommended toolset requirements for a level 2 application would involve the use of JSPs or servlets; the features of EJBs (extensive scalability, fail-over, connectivity to legacy systems, and data) are not necessarily needed at this level. These level 2 Web applications are the focus of this book.

Dynamic Content and Resource Use

Note that the use of dynamic content also exacts a toll on CPU resources. The more dynamic the pages being processed at a site, and the more those pages are hit by users, the more CPU resources that will be used on that platform. Additionally, if these dynamic pages require database data (which is most likely the case), additional CPU resources will be used to operate the database engine that will be responsible for retrieving the data.

The amount of CPU resource required by an application depends, of course, on the application. Applications that perform a large number of database access operations and perform complex logic will exact more CPU usage than those that perform few database operations and have simple logic. (These factors should be considered when developing the application; perhaps data can be cached in a session object or stored in a cookie on the client PC, thus reducing the database load of the server.)

The Java Server

Using JSPs and servlets extends HTTP in a significant way; the HTTP server alone cannot provide this capability. JSP services are built on and therefore rely on the services of Java servlets. JSPs are *preprocessed* by a server technology that outputs a Java servlet. This servlet is then executed by a servlet *container* in the same manner as a servlet developed without JSPs. Both the servlet container and the JSP preprocessor are part of what we define as a *Java server*. (Note that for purposes of our discussion we do not include EJB capabilities.)

The JSP preprocessor does not actually compile the Java source code—that is handled by the servlet processing portion of this technology. The preprocessor merely reads the JSP containing both HTML tags and embedded Java scriplet, and produces an output stream of Java servlet code that, when executed, will produce the output defined in the JSP page. (While the terminology for this JSP preprocessor service currently varies somewhat, for our purposes we refer to this as the *JSP preprocessor*.)

The technology that provides the capability for servlets to execute is referred to as a *container*. The container is a conception that encompasses the services required to provide for execution of the servlet. Java servlet specifications define the capabilities of the container but do not specify the implementation, leaving it to vendors and developers to implement this technology as they see fit.

There are primarily three implementations of Java servers: *in-process*, *standalone*, and *out-of-process*. The distinction between *in-process* and *out-of-process* is where the Java server will run. The in-process Java server will run as a separate thread within an HTTP server. As the HTTP server intercepts pages that require JSP preprocessing or servlet execution, these pages are passed to the Java server thread for processing. Alternatively, if the Java server is an out-of-process server, as the HTTP server encounters these pages they are passed to the standalone server for processing.

The *standalone* Java server is an integral part of the HTTP server and runs in the same code space as the HTTP server. This would essentially be a server that manages both static HTML and JSP pages and servlets. Although this would be efficient for small user loads, this solution would encounter scalability issues as the user load increased. Additionally, the HTTP servers of these implementations do not have the capabilities of the more robust Web servers such as Apache.

The *in-process* server opens a Java virtual machine as a separate thread of the HTTP server. The advantage of an in-process Java server is that it will require less overhead and be more efficient at processing a small to moderate number of user requests. The disadvantage is that as the user load increases, the in-process Java server will not scale as well as will an out-of-process server. Additionally, an in-process Java server cannot provide fail-over capabilities. If the hardware platform or the HTTP server were to fail, the entire Web site would be down due to the single point of failure being used—the HTTP server with its Java server processing thread.

Using an *out-of-process* server, fail-over, and load-balancing capabilities can optionally be implemented. With this approach, a distribution module (or plug-in) within the HTTP server is responsible for distributing Java processing requests (servlets or JSPs) to the various Java servers available. This means that multiple instances of the Java server can be started and the distribution module within the HTTP server can dispatch JSP/servlet requests in such a way that the user load is spread across the multiple Java servers (which can be running on multiple machines). With more than one Java server running on more than one machine, the user load for the site is spread over multiple servers (see Figure 1.6). Should one Java server fail in this configuration, the dispatch module would recognize this failure and cease dispatch of work to that Java server but would continue dispatching work to the remaining servers. Thus operation of the Web site could continue even with the failure of one or more Java servers at the site as long as additional servers are available to continue servicing the Java workload.

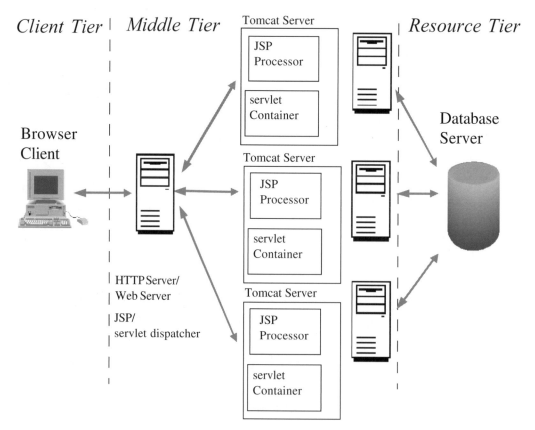

Figure 1.6 HTTP Server Dispatches JSP/Servlet Work to Multiple Servers

Java Web Site Overview

As defined for purposes of this book, the *Java Web site* is essentially a Web site where Java is the technology of choice for server-side scripting. Such a site would require an HTTP server, a JSP/servlet container, and a database engine. An example of a complete Java Web site could therefore include an Apache HTTP server, a Java JSP/servlet container, and a relational database in the form of PostgreSQL; these are the tools that will be used as examples in this book.

Execution of a page at this sample site would involve the interaction of these three applications. The first attempt to access a page would involve the client's Web browser communicating with the HTTP server, in this case Apache, to request a page (using an HTTP GET request). If the page being requested is an HTML page, the Apache server would process the request and return the page to the browser requesting the page as part of an HTTP RESPONSE. If, however, the page was a JSP, the request would be passed to the JSP/servlet container, in this case Tomcat. The JSP container would then perform one of two actions.

If the page requested had already been compiled after the container had started, the compiled page would be retrieved, executed, and the resulting output stream sent back to the client browser. If, however, the page being requested had not been compiled since the container had been started, the page would be compiled and then executed, with the resulting output stream being sent back to the client browser.

If the page being requested is a JSP (as indicated by the .jsp file extension), the HTTP server effectively acts as a broker, merely passing the connection off to the JSP container for processing. In this case, the JSP container acts as a container and an HTTP server. The simple presence of a .jsp file extension on a page is not enough to have the page be parsed and executed by the JSP container. The Tomcat server requires that a number of configuration parameters be set before it will process a JSP. These are covered in more detail in the following chapters.

Using Tomcat as an HTTP Server

Since the Tomcat server understands HTTP protocol, it could serve HTML pages (in fact, it can be configured to do just that). But this is a function that Apache is much better suited to fit. Apache can serve pages more quickly, and provides a number of additional features, such as server-side includes (SSIs) and authentication. Additionally, it is useful to spread the system load for the site amongst multiple servers, having Apache handle the HTML pages and Tomcat manage the JSPs.

Summary

As this chapter indicated and as anyone who has not been living in a cave the last few years knows, the Web has revolutionized computer use. From a technical standpoint, this means that the preferred means of delivering any application is via the Web. For the development team, this requires the creation of a Web infrastructure, a multitiered architecture that includes a client front end, usually a Web browser, a back end or resource tier that will maintain the data for the application, and a middle tier that will provide the communication between the front-end client and the resource tier and will execute the business logic of the application.

The term *application server*, although still a somewhat nebulous and weakly defined term, has come to be applied to a very specific set of tools. Originally, application servers were middleware, any set of applications that resided between the front-end client and the back-end data. Over time, these tools developed a complex set of features that greatly enhanced reliability and performance.

Although relatively young, the Java language has grown to provide an extremely useful seat of powerful technologies. The most important of these technologies for the purposes of Web development are JSP and servlets. These tools provide access to the complete Java language in the process of creating dynamic Web pages. Given the capabilities of Java, these technologies are the solution of choice for dynamic Web sites.

Under the strict sense of the term, the Tomcat server is not an application server. It provides some of the features of an application server (and over time may encompass all of the features), but does not yet provide enough features to be considered a true application server. What Tomcat does provide is a JSP processing environment and a servlet container. These two features provide the ability to produce dynamic Web content using Java. When combined with access to a relational database, they create a powerful arsenal for midrange Web application development.

A number of IT tools are available to create this Web infrastructure depending on the requirements of the application. The more complex and dynamic an application and the more stringent the requirements for uptime and extensive reliability, the more likely the application will require a high-end application server solution. But for many applications, this expense is not necessary. A lower-cost solution, one that uses open-source tools, may be perfectly satisfactory.

Coming Up Next

Now that we have some sense of what the requirements are for our Java Web site, we will examine each of the architecture components in detail: the HTTP server or the Web server; the Java server (Tomcat), which processes JSP and servlets; and the relational database for storage of data. We also provide details on the installation and configuration of these tools.

Once the installation and configuration of our infrastructure has been covered, the JSP syntax is explained, since this is the tool we use for creating dynamic content. This review covers the JSP facility for the creation of custom tags. In the final portion of the book we examine a series of examples of Web development with server-side Java. Issues of security and data management are covered in these examples.

CREATING THE WEB INFRASTRUCTURE: THE APACHE SERVER

Introduction

As we discussed in Chapter 1, a Web application involves the interaction of a client application, usually a Web browser, and one or more other applications running on one or more servers (see Figure 2.1). In this book our focus is on the server-side of the Web application, where most of the work is performed. On this server side there are a number of applications that perform the processing of the requests sent from browser clients.

In this chapter we focus on one of the server-side applications, the HTTP server. For some Web sites, this may be the only application running to support the site. But today this is the exception more than the rule. To develop and manage an effective and sophisticated site, more robust tools than just an HTTP server are needed. Nevertheless, the HTTP server is an important cornerstone for any Web site. In this chapter we present one of the most popular HTTP servers on the Internet: the open-source Apache server. First, we review the function of the Web server so that we are comfortable with operation of the server. Next we discuss installation of the server, and finally, we cover the process of configuring the server.

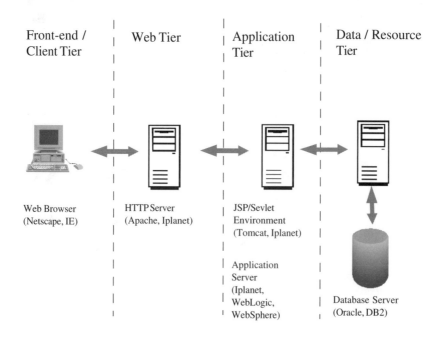

Figure 2.1 Web Application

The Operation of the Web Server

When a Web browser requests a page, it makes this request in the form of a URL, a uniform resource locator. The URL contains valuable information about the resource being requested, using the following syntax:

```
<protocol>://<server name>[:<port number>]/<location>
```

The *protocol* requested can be one of many different protocols, but most commonly is either HTTP for *Hypertext Transport Protocol*, ftp for *File Transfer Protocol*, or file for a file on the local machine. Table 2.1 provides a list of protocols that most browsers will accept.

The server name can, alternatively, be an IP address. This identifies for the browser the server that will manage the request it is going to submit. Optionally, this designation of the server can include a network port number. If the URL designates the protocol as http and the server name portion of the URL contains a port number, the browser will attempt a connection for HTTP services on the designated server at the port number specified. If no port number is specified, the browser will attempt communication with the server at the default port for HTTP communications, port 80.

Table 2.1 Web Protocols

Protocol	Description
http://	World Wide Web server
ftp://	FTP server (file transfer)
https//	Secure HTTP
news://	Usenet newsgroups
mailto://	e-mail
wais://	Wide Area Information Server
gopher://	Gopher server
file://	File on local system
ldap://	Directory server request
telnet://	Applications on network server
rlogin://	Applications on network server
tn3270://	Applications on mainframe

Name Resolution

When a server name is specified in a URL, this name alone is not adequate to achieve a connection to the server. The name must be resolved to an IP address. Resolution of the server name involves either retrieving the name from a local `hosts` file which contains a list of server names and their IP addresses or more commonly, the use of a *name server* or *domain name server*.

The job of the name server, which usually resides on the local network, is to take a query for a server name and return an IP address. Since the Internet is large and dynamic, the process of determining the correct IP address for an Internet domain name can involve querying several name servers on the Internet. To avoid the overhead of Internet name resolution, local name servers will often make an effort to *cache* Internet domain names so that the name can be resolved on the local network rather than the external Internet. Note that if the use of a name server is required, the network software where the browser is running must be configured to use the domain name server, or else the request for the URL will fail (assuming that the entry doesn't reside in the local `hosts` file). This is where good working relations with network administrators become an important element of the development process.

Once the HTTP request is sent, it will course through the network, whether it be an internal intranet or the Internet, and ultimately arrive at a server (see Figure 2.2). At this point in the request handling process, the program running on the server known as the HTTP server will be listening for connections on the appropriate port. This program will accept the connection and then retrieve the referenced resource for processing.

In its simplest form, processing a request involves little more than retrieving the HTML page and returning it to the client prepending HTTP headers in the process. But the HTTP server can provide a number of different services in the process. It can provide some level of application security by authorizing the user to access a page (through directory authorization). An HTTP server can also resolve short names for directories into full directory paths. It can provide the capability to include other documents in an HTML page (server-side includes). Most important for a Java-based Web site, it can determine that a page requires processing by an external program before being returned to the client. It is this process that is used to manage a JSP, passing the request to process the page to a JSP/servlet container (an external program), which must then return the page to the client.

In this chapter we discuss the functions of the HTTP server. The installation and configuration of the server are detailed as well as the configuration of the server. Given the features and extensibility of the Apache server, configuration of the server is not a trivial task. But by discussing the configuration of

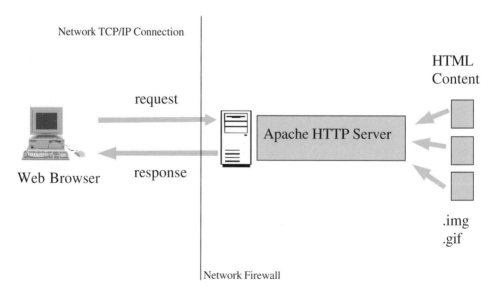

Figure 2.2 The HTTP Communication Protocol

the server in detail, it is easy to note the capabilities and applications of the Apache server and how they might complement the features of Java server-side scripting.

Background on Apache

The Apache Software Foundation is an incorporated nonprofit corporation that supports Apache open-source software projects. The support provided for these efforts is organizational, legal, and financial. The most notable product of the Apache Foundation is the Apache Web server. The Apache Web server operates on a variety of platforms and supports a significant percentage of Internet Web sites. The effort to develop the Apache server began prior to 1995 with the HTTP server developed by Rob McCool and others at the National Center for Supercomputing Applications (NCSA). A group of webmasters and developers continued to work with Rob's code base, adding modifications and bug fixes. A number of prerelease versions of Apache were released, and in December 1995, version 1.0 of the Apache HTTP server was released.

In December 2000 a survey by NetCraft (`http://www.netcraft.com`) surveyed 25,675,581 Internet sites. As a result of this survey, Apache was determined to be serving the majority of Internet sites, with about 59 percent of the active sites polled (the next most common was Microsoft Internet Information Server, with approximately 20 percent).

Installing Apache

Since Apache has become the dominant HTTP server, most major distributions of Linux and other Unix variants include Apache. If Apache is not on the distribution, it is generally easy to obtain via a download from the Apache.org Web site (approximately 10 megabytes in size), which now includes an NT version of Apache. For the more technically inclined, a source code distribution may be obtained and compiled on the target platform. Since Apache is highly configurable, compiling a version does not necessarily increase the flexibility of the server, but it can improve the performance of the engine on some platforms.

How Apache Runs

Apache runs as a Unix *daemon* (or in the NT world, as a *service*). This means that Apache starts, detaches itself from an terminal session that may have been used to start it, and then begins its work, effectively running in the background on the machine on which it was started. But before Apache begins its work, it must know something about the environment in which it will run. This is where Apache shines, in the ability to be tuned to the task at hand. Apache determines its configuration by reading one or more configuration files. These files contain very detailed instructions on how Apache should operate, containing information on the server listener port, valid host connections, document directories, virtual hosts, and other pertinent parameters.

What's in a Name?

Interestingly enough, Apache does not run as a program named *Apache*. (In fact, the distribution does not contain any binaries with the name Apache.) It runs as a binary program named `httpd` (the ending "d" is a common Unix designation for a daemon program).

Apache Installation Formats

Apache installations come in a variety of flavors. On the Linux platform, the most common distribution format is the `.rpm` file (for Red Hat Package Manager). Installation of Apache from an `.rpm` file is fairly straightforward. Running the `rpm` installation with the standard flags (`rpm -i`) will place the installation binaries, configuration, log files, and modules (shared object files) in the `/etc/httpd` directory. The standard directory structure for Apache on Unix is as shown in Table 2.2.

Table 2.2 Apache Directory Structure for Unix

Directory	Description
`/etc/httpd`	Root directory; all relevant directories lie below this directory
`/etc/httpd/conf`	Configuration files are located in this directory
`/etc/httpd/modules`	Modules directory; on Unix, this is a soft link to the `/usr/lib/apache;` may also be `/etc/httpd/libexec`
`/etc/httpd/logs`	Log file directory; on Unix this is a soft link to the `/var/log/httpd` directory

Configuration File: httpd.conf

As of version 1.3.4, all Apache configuration parameters are contained in one file named `httpd.conf`. It is possible, however, to override some parameters with configuration files placed in local directories. Since Apache is a highly flexible application, it comes as no surprise that there are a large number of configuration parameters in this file. The format of these parameters is usually a parameter name placed at the start of the line followed by the value of the parameter on the remainder of the line:

```
Parameter_Name parameter_value1, parameter_value2 ...
```

A line can optionally contain a comment which is indicated by a # character at the start of the line. Although Apache seems tolerant about having white space appear before the parameter name, the configuration file is more readable if no white space precedes the parameter name. The Apache configuration file also contains parameters denoted by HTML-like tags. These tags are used to form blocks referred to as *containers,* with specific parameters contained within the container blocks. All parameter entries in the container block apply to the container. For example, a container entry that details the security to be applied to a directory would contain the following:

```
<Directory /mydir>
    order deny, allow
    deny nyhost
    allow njhost
</Directory>
```

For those familiar with HTML, the structure of these container tags should look very familiar. As with many HTML tags, the < character denotes the start of the tag name and any attributes to be associated directly with the tag name. The > character then denotes the end of the tag name and attributes entry, and the tag entry that begins with a / character denotes the end of the container block.

Apache must understand each of the parameters in the configuration file or it will not start. The server is very specific about where parsing errors occur in the configuration file, providing a reason why the server wouldn't start and the line number in the configuration file where the error occurred. In the following sections we discuss the configuration of the Apache server by detailing the contents of the configuration file, the values to which configuration parameters could be set, and the reason for the settings. To be complete, all entries in the configuration file are identified. In practice, only a few of these entries may be changed for any particular site, but knowledge of all the capabilities of the Apache server will be useful, since the server could perhaps provide a solution to a problem that would otherwise require developer effort to create a programmatic solution.

Loading Apache Modules

Apache is an extremely extensible server. These extensions are provided in the form of modules that are loaded when the server starts. These modules are referenced in the configuration file as shown in the following annotated example.

```
LoadModule autoindex_module
/etc/httpd/modules/mod_autoindex.so
LoadModule dir_module          /etc/httpd/modules/mod_dir.so
LoadModule cgi_module          /etc/httpd/modules/mod_cgi.so
...
LoadModule includes_module
/etc/httpd/modules/mod_include.so
#LoadModule includes_module
/etc/httpd/modules/mod_include_xssi.so
```

The general rule of thumb with modules is not to load the modules that are not being used. The Apache server is shipped with a configuration file that loads a default set of modules, which are usually adequate. In this book we recommend a number of additional modules that are not loaded by default, including the module that allows Apache to work with the Tomcat server container.

Identifying the ServerRoot Directory

The `ServerRoot` directory is the directory below which all Apache-related files are contained. The default is `/etc/httpd` for Unix and `c:\Program Files\Apache Group\Apache` for Windows-NT. By altering this parameter you can effectively change the location of the Apache server installation. Alternatively, Apache provides a command line parameter which indicates the configuration file to use for startup; by passing the appropriate configuration file to Apache on startup, it can be directed to a specific installation directory. Following is an example of this parameter:

```
ServerRoot   /etc/httpd
```

This example sets the `ServerRoot` directory to `/etc/httpd`, the default directory for Unix installations.

There are few compelling reasons to set this parameter to something other than the default. Local system administration may have reasons for using a different directory, thus making this a site-specific setting. Note that changing this parameter to a directory that is under an NFS-mounted disk can create issues with some locking files.

Identifying the Document Root Directory

The `DocumentRoot` directory parameter identifies which directory is to be used as the root directory for documents to be served by Apache. When the Web server is referenced as the primary server (and not one of the virtual hosts), the value of this parameter is used as the root directory. A full path name must be specified.

It is not uncommon to move this to a directory separate from the rest of the Apache installation. The files in these directories tend to be more volatile and require access by a different set of users (e.g., developers and content managers) than the users who need access to the Apache configuration and administration files. All document directories are assumed to be relative to the `DocumentRoot` directory. But the Apache server is not limited to reading documents from the `DocumentRoot` directory and its subdirectories. The `Alias` and `Rewrite` parameters allow other directories to be specified for document retrieval; more about these directives later. An example of the `DocumentRoot` directive is

```
DocumentRoot   /part1/wwwroot
```

This example sets the `DocumentRoot` directory to the directory `/part1/wwwroot`. All references to the Apache location will now be assumed to start at `/part1/wwwroot` (the exception being directories that are referenced using the `Alias` parameter). For example, a reference to the URL of `myhost://mysite/index.html` would have the Apache server attempt to serve the file `/part1/wwwroot/index.html`.

ServerName Directive

The `ServerName` parameter is the name that will be associated with this server and is returned by the server to the client. This should be set to the host name of the server on which Apache is running; that is, this should be a valid host that can be resolved by a domain name server (DNS). This is not necessarily the host name Apache will use to listen but the name that Apache will return to clients. An example of this entry is

```
ServerName myhost
```

Server Listening IP Address and Port

The server listening parameter identifies the TCP/IP port that the server will use to listen for connections. By default, this entry is 80. The `Listen` directive specifies the port number and alternatively, the IP address and port number for the server to listen. The Apache server will make a TCP/IP socket connection to a specified port and listen for connections. When it detects a connection, it will confirm the connection and then attempt to read from the port and interpret the results of the read as an HTTP protocol message. The `Listen` parameter has two formats; one format can specify only the port number to listen to:

```
Listen 80
```

This setting would have the Apache server listen on port 80 of the host machine. If the host name were `myhost`, the server would listen on the port `myhost:80`.

If only one Apache server is running on a machine, the default is probably fine. If more than one server is running on a machine, then since the servers cannot share a port, a different listening port would need to be used by each server. Another reason to use a port other than the default is for security. Many hackers attempt to gain entry to sites using the IP address and several well-known ports. If a hacker had an IP address (which could be arrived at in some random fashion), he or she could then begin cycling through the well-known ports at that address trying to detect a connection and a protocol that he or she could use to gain access to the site.

Alternatively, a separate IP address and/or port can be specified using the `Listen` directive:

```
Listen 192.132.31.2:80
```

In this example the IP address and the port are specified, separated by a colon. This would have the Apache server listen on the IP address specified at the port specified. (Note that the IP address must be assigned to the Ethernet card before Apache is started.)

The `Listen` directive will take an IP address only as a parameter, not as a host name. There may be a reason to have Apache listen to multiple IP addresses and/or ports: for example, to manage secure Web sites in conjunction with nonsecure sites or to provide proxy services. The `Listen` directive provides this capability, as shown below.

```
Listen 80   # non-secure web site
Listen 352  # secure web site
Listen 8080 # proxy server
```

In this example, Apache will listen on several distinct ports and process connections, using separate ports for nonsecure connections, secure connections, and proxy services. Alternatively, distinct IP addresses could be used as follows.

```
Listen 192.3.35.32:80   # non-secure web site
Listen 192.3.44.21:235  # secure web site
```

The `BindAddress` directive can also be used to direct Apache to listen on a specific IP address. But `BindAddress` can appear only once in the configuration file, since each entry effectively overwrites the preceding entry.

By default, Apache will listen to all IP addresses assigned to all of the interfaces defined on the host machine. This is reflected in the configuration defined by the `BindAddress` directive below.

```
BindAddress *
```

The `BindAddress` parameter could also supply an IP address or a host name to the `BindAddress` parameter:

```
BindAddress 192.3.33.44
Port 80
```

Although the `BindAddress` directive can accept a host name, this is not recommended, due to the expense of the DNS lookups required to support this.

Many platforms now support the ability to identify virtual network interfaces, essentially creating multiple IP addresses on one network interface. This allows a host IP interface to manage TCP/IP packets for multiple IP addresses without the configuration overhead (and cost) of multiple hardware interfaces. A host file on a particular machine could contain the following entries:

```
204.133.23.1    BigWidgets.BigCompany.com
204.133.23.2    LittleWidgets.BigCompany.com
204.133.23.3    Accounting.BigCompany.com
204.133.23.4    HR.BigCompany.com
```

The configuration above could be used in conjunction with IP-based virtual hosting to create distinct Web sites for the domains defined. (In the section on virtual hosting later in this chapter we explain how to accomplish this task.)

Using the Alias Directive

The directory `Alias` parameter is a very useful function of the Apache server that allows the administrator to create a shorthand entry for a directory. This alias is resolved with the URL being referenced to the full path name of the resource. This capability serves several purposes. One is that it allows simpler URLs to be used on the site, ultimately making it easier for end-users to access the site. This feature also creates a form of redirection for file locations, allowing an administrator to change the physical location of a file without having to make major changes to pages at the site. (For example, moving a set of documents that are referenced in numerous pages on the site would involve changing every reference in every document, or making a soft link at the disk directory level, instead of merely changing a single configuration parameter as allowed by this feature.)

Another benefit of a directory alias is that it conceals the actual physical location of the directory, thus making it more difficult for hackers to find the location of the site content. An example of a directory entry is:

```
Alias /img /part12/acctgSite/content/img
```

This example makes the HTTP directory reference `/img` the alias for the physical directory `/part12/acctgSite/content/img`; therefore, any references to `/img`, such as `//myhost/img`, would be resolved to `/part12/acctgSite/content/img`.

Note that Apache assumes that the directory referenced is relative to `DocumentRoot` unless the reference contains a leading `/`, in which case it is assumed to reference a full path name for the directory. The following example maps the directory `JSPexample` to the full path name, `/lin/local/jakarta/webapps/examples`.

```
Alias /JSPexamples /lin/local/jakarta/webapps/examples
```

Alternatively, this example assumes a path relative to the `DocumentRoot` directory.

```
DocumentRoot /part1/webapps
...
Alias /JSPexamples jsp/examples
```

In this example, the `/JSPexamples` directory would map to the full path name, which would be a concatenation of `DocumentRoot` plus the alias mapping, which in this case would be `/part1/webapps/jsp/examples`.

Often, the `Alias` directive is followed by a `Directory` directive (and its container) which defines the options and permissions for access to the directory that has just been mapped, as shown in the following example.

```
Alias /ArtWork   "/lin1/content/ArtDocs"

<Directory "/lin1/content/ArtDocs">
Options Indexes FollowSymLinks MultiViews
Order allow,deny
allow from all
</Directory>
```

In this example, the `Alias` directive is used to associate the directory `/ArtWork` with the directory `/lin1/content/ArtDocs`. The `Directory` directive is then used to create a `Directory` container that assigns various options to the `/lin1/content/ArtDocs` directory (not to the `Alias` directive `/ArtWork`). Permissions are also set to allow access to this directory from all hosts using the `allow` directive to assign `allow from all` permissions to the directory.

Alternatively, instead of using a fixed string match for the source of the `Alias` directive, you can use pattern matching with the `AliasMatch` directive:

```
AliasMatch /ArtWork/(.*)\.gif$   "/lin1/content/img/$1.gif"
```

The `AliasMatch` directive makes use of extremely useful regular expression pattern matching. This example maps all content requests under the directory `ArtWork` with the `.gif` extension to the directory `/lin1/content/img` using the file name as part of the new location.

Alias Is Not a Location

The `Alias` directive allows a directory within a URL location to be mapped to another directory. It is completely transparent to the client, which requests a resource, and when all mapping is completed by the HTTP server, the client will receive the resource it has requested.

Alias mapping does not map a complete URL location to a new URL location (e.g., another Web site) but, instead, maps just the directory part of the location, essentially the disk directory reference within the URL and potentially, using regular expression matching with `AliasMatch`, some portion of the file name.

The `Redirect` directive allows a complete URL location to be mapped to a new URL location, as explained later in this chapter.

Defining Redirection with the Redirect Directive

There are times when it may be necessary to move the contents of a directory. In some cases, this effort may be a type of load balancing where the contents of a directory tree (which could represent an entire site or application) are taking a large number of hits. The contents of a directory can be moved and the `Redirect` directive can be used to map any requests for that URL to the new URL. The `Redirect` directive supports a parameter which indicates how the redirection should be cached on the client, as shown in the example

```
Redirect permanent /SunStuff "http://www.sun.com"
```

This example directs the location `/<Your Host Name>/SunStuff` to the URL `http://www.sun.com`. The first parameter to the directive is a string that provides information about the duration of the redirection. In this example, the string `permanent` is provided for this parameter, which indicates that this redirection is, appropriately enough, a *permanent* redirection, and therefore the client may cache this URL as it sees fit. So, for this example, if the Apache server at the host `MyHost` received the URL `http://MyHost/SunStuff`, the request would be redirected to `http://www.sun.com`. (Note that the entire URL presented in the request is completely mapped to the new URL.)

The first parameter is an HTTP client request return code. Apache has assigned a symbolic name for four of these return codes as indicated in Table 2.3. Either the symbolic name or the status code could be used for the first parameter, as shown in the example

Table 2.3 Apache Return Codes

Symbolic Name	HTTP Status Code
permanent	301
temp	302
seeother	303
gone	410

```
Redirect 305 /Archive http://ArchiveServer/HereDoc/
```

Specifically, the 305 status code directs the client to use a proxy server, so that in the example above, the client would resubmit the request to the proxy server and complete the name of the resource in the process.

Since the temporary redirection is the most common type of redirection, if the redirection type is not included, the redirection is assumed to be temporary redirection (status code 302) as follows:

```
# assume this is status code 302
Redirect /DocStuff "http://www.ourdocs.com/docs"
```

This example assumes a temporary redirection between the `/DocStuff` location on the current server (where Apache is installed) and the target location. Other valid duration values that may be used for this first parameter are `not cached`, `seeother`, and `gone`. With the `not cached` parameter, the redirection specifically directs the client not to cache the URL.

The `gone` parameter is used when a URL no longer exists (the resource has been deleted from the site; the use of the directive with this parameter will not perform a redirection but instead will return an error 303, indicating that the resource is no longer available. Since there is no forwarding URL, this use of the directive does not require a third parameter, as shown in the example

```
Redirect gone /VeryOldStuff
```

The `seeother` value for this parameter also indicates to the client browser that the value of the URL should not be cached and should be retrieved using the `get` method.

(Note that moving directory contents at a site would also involve changing any relevant links in the documents on the site to point to the new URL. The `Redirect` parameter is used because client browsers may have recorded the old directory in bookmarks stored on the local machines. Since the bookmarks will obviously not be affected by changing links on the site, the redirection mechanism is used to take the user to the correct URL.)

Defining Directory Properties

Using the `Directory` directive, access and options related to a specific directory hierarchy can be controlled. A number of parameters can be set within this container and would apply only to the directory being referenced. The following entry creates restrictive permissions at the root directory level:

```
<Directory />
Options Includes FollowSymLinks
AllowOverride None
</Directory>
```

This entry is a common approach to maintaining directory-level security. By setting the root directory ("/") to restrictive permissions, since the permissions of the parent directory are inherited by the subdirectories, all subordinate directories will have the same set of permissions. These permissions must then explicitly be altered in the subdirectory, where more open permissions are needed.

The following entry defines less restrictive permissions on the /lin/www-root directory (which we assume would be where the documents would be located):

```
<Directory /lin/wwwroot>
Options None
AllowOverride All
order allow,deny
allow from all
</Directory>
```

Defining a Location

Location definitions are made using Location containers. A number of directives can be set for the location within the container. These directives are then applied to the location when the location appears in a URL presented in a request to the Apache server. Within the container, settings can be made for authorization and handlers which are to be applied by the server for that location. The Location container is often used to set authorizations for a URL (just as the Directory container is used to set authorizations for a directory). An example of a location definition is

```
<Location /local-use>
order deny,allow
deny from all
allow from localhost, 127.0.0.1
</Location>
```

In this example, the Location container is used to assign access permissions to the URL /local-use. Note that the directory referenced by /local-use is assumed to be relative to the `DocumentRoot` directory—it is *not* interpreted as a full path name.

The `Location` container can reference a directory that is not under the `DocumentRoot` directory by using the `Alias` parameter in conjunction with the `Location` directive:

```
Alias /controlled_content   /local/content/controlled
...
<Location /controlled_content/SysAdmin/ >
    AllowOverride None
    order deny,allow
    deny from all
    allow from 127.0.0.1
</Location>
```

In this example, the directory `controlled_content` is mapped to the full path name `/local/content/controlled`. The HTTP directory reference for the alias `controlled_content` is then used in the `Location` directive and appended with a subdirectory as `/controlled_content/SysAdmin`. This URL reference is mapped *internally* by Apache as `/local/content_controlled/SysAdmin`, effectively mapping the location reference (in the URL) to a directory other than one under `DocumentRoot`.

Note that many of the directives that apply to the `Directory` directive can also be used within the `Location` directives, for example, the `Allow` and `Deny` directives.

Directory and Location Properties

The `Directory` container contains a number of properties that control access to the directory. These properties can also be used for `Location` containers. A `Directory` container referenced in a `Location` container will be merged with the `Location` container with properties in the `Location` container potentially overridding `Directory` properties.

The Option Directive

A number of optional properties can be defined for Apache `Directory` and `Location` containers using the `Option` directive. These options are listed in the table below.

Option	Description
All	Enables all options; the default setting.
ExecCGI	Allows the execution of CGI scripts.
FollowSymLinks	Allows symbolic links to be followed; not recognized in Location containers.
Includes	Allows server-side includes in this container; not used in Location containers.
IncludesNOEXEC	Permits server-side includes; disallows execution of CGI scripts.
Indexes	Apache creates a formatted listing of the directory contents.
MultiViews	Content negotiated MultiViews are allowed.
None	Disables all options; specific options can then be enabled when needed.

The allow and deny Directives

The allow and deny directives are used to perform authentication of the request to the directory or location based on the origin on the request. The use of these directives requires the mod_access module to be loaded.

The allow and deny directives can accept a full or partial host name or a full or partial IP address as an argument as in

```
. . .
     deny from all
   allow from myhost.net, ourhost.net
. . .
```

The keyword all applies to all hostnames and IP addresses and thus, when used with the deny directive, creates a very restrictive access policy. A good practice is as shown in the previous example where a very restrictive policy is applied with the deny directive and then specific domains are permitted access to the site. (For a site exposed to the Internet, this type of restrictive authentication would **not** be useful and some other form of authentication based on user logins would be used as shown later in this book.)

The order Directive

If both deny and allow are directives are defined, Apache must resolve the possible conflicts between the two. The order directive allows the order in which the two directives will be interpreted, with the directive listed last potentially overridding what was listed in the previous directive.

The AllowOverride Directive

The `AllowOverride` directive allows a local `.htaccess` file in a directory to override a restriction placed on the directory in the Apache configuration file.

Authorization and Directories

When used in conjunction with the `mod_auth.o,` the `Location` directive can be used to set authorizations for particular users to access a given location. This module provides for user authorization using passwords and can optionally assign the user to a group. The following example demonstrates the `Location` container used with one form of Apache authorization.

```
<Location /Admin>
AuthName "Admin Realm"
AuthType Basic
AuthGroupFile /home/admin/SecurityGroups
AuthUserFile /home/admin/SecurityUser
AuthAuthoritative on
require valid-user
</Location>
```

In this example, the location `/Admin` is assigned security based on the directive settings within the container. Any user attempting to access this directory with a browser will be presented with a password prompt requesting a user name and password, which are then checked against entries in the `SecurityUser` file. Optionally, the user could be assigned to a group in the `SecurityGroups` file. The directive entry `require    valid-user` requires that the user be validated before they can read any document in that directory.

This approach does provide some security, but there are issues that should still be addressed. The World Wide Web was designed as an open system. Information traveling around the Web travels in packets that contain *plain text*; that is, the data are unencrypted. If the packets are unencrypted, any user name and password traveling around the Internet could be read by someone so inclined (and with sufficient technical know-how) and the user name and password could then be used by them to access the site.

Secure Transmissions over the Internet

A better approach would be to use Secure Socket Language (SSL) encryption before accessing the location. SSL encryption uses an encryption scheme that is virtually impossible for hackers to decode. Once SSL is in place, all communication between the browser accessing the site and the Apache server will be encrypted. With SSL, transmission of the user name and password would be encrypted and therefore virtually hackproof.

The ServerType Directive

The `ServerType` directive is available only on Unix platforms and is used to control the way in which the Apache server process is run. With Unix, there is an option to run the Apache server as a service under the `inetd` daemon. With this option, Apache is started and run as needed, and if it is not needed, if there is no activity on the port it listens to, the server will not be running. The default setting is that Apache will manage itself as a `standalone` server (and not under `inetd`). The following is an example of the default for this setting:

```
ServerType standalone
```

The parameter provided in this example is `standalone`, thus identifying to Apache that it will start as a standalone process. Alternatively, had this parameter been set to `indetd`, the Apache process would be started by the `inetd` daemon.

Running Apache under `inetd` may be appropriate for a site that has very little traffic, but for most sites, this setting is not recommended for performance reasons and in fact is rarely used. The most common setting for this parameter is `standalone`.

HostNameLookups Logging Option

The `HostNameLookups` option controls the logging of client accesses to the server. By default, the IP addresses of the client (the *host* accessing our Apache server) is written to the log. In fact, Apache does not necessarily know the name of the client once the HTTP transaction has begun. Therefore, to log the host name of the client host, Apache will be required to perform a DNS lookup for the host name. The following is the default entry for this setting, to turn this feature off.

Unfortunately, host name lookups using DNS can be an expensive operation. For this reason, the use of `HostNameLookups` is not recommended. If the host name of the IP addresses in the log file is desired, utilities are available that will perform this function (e.g., the `logresolve` utility in the Apache distribution). The default setting for the directive is

```
HostnameLookups off
```

User/Group Directives

Apache is often started as user `root`, the Unix superuser, but then for security reasons switches to another user id. The user and group directives control the user that Apache will run as. The default setting for these parameters is

```
User            nobody
Group           nobody
```

ServerAdmin Email Address

The `ServerAdmin` parameter identifies the email address of the Web site administrator who will monitor the Apache system. When Apache has a problem, it will send an email to this address. The default setting for this parameter is

```
ServerAdmin root@localhost
```

Since the user root is most likely *not* the user id of the site administrator, this should be changed to an email address that is meaningful, preferably an email address that is read on a regular basis (e.g., `webadmin@myhost`).

ErrorLog Directive

The `ErrorLog` directive allows the error log to be moved to a location other than the default. Note that if the leading character of this string is not a forward slash (/), then the directory is assumed to be a subdirectory of the `ServerRoot` directory (see the section on the `ServerRoot` directive). Following is an example of this directive:

```
ErrorLog logs/error_log
```

Since the entry above does not include a leading / character, the entry is relative to the `ServerRoot` directory. In this example, if the `ServerRoot` directory were `/var/apache/root`, the error log file would be located in the directory `/var/apache/root/logs`. If a leading / character is provided, the entry is considered a full path name:

```
ErrorLog /lin/local/sysadmin/logs/Apache_error_log
```

This example would place the error log in the directory specified in the path name parameter. Additionally, error logging could be turned off using the entry

```
ErrorLog /dev/null
```

LogLevel Directive

The `LogLevel` parameter controls the output of the Apache message logs. Apache treats error levels as a hierarchy, where each level of logging used includes all levels previous to it. Table 2.4 shows the various settings for this directive.

Table 2.4 LogLevel Directive Settings

Number	LogLevel	Description
1	emerg	System is unstable
2	alert	Immediate action required
3	crit	Critical error
4	error	Noncritical error
5	warn	Warning
6	notice	Normal but significant
7	info	Informational message about the system's operation
8	debug	Debug level; copious information on the operation of the system

Note that an error level of error number 5 in the table would include the output messages for `error` (4), `crit` (3), `alert` (2), and `emerg` (1).

The following example sets the `LogLevel` for this site to the `warn` level. This default setting is appropriate for most sites.

```
LogLevel warn
```

Note that levels such as debug output a large amount of information and could have a significant impact on performance.

Transfer Logs and Log Formatting

Apache provides for the creation of an access log which provides a summary of HTTP transfers to and from the server. Transfer logs are not required and Apache must be explicitly directed to create one. On busy servers, creation of these logs should probably be omitted. The transfer log can be created with the TransferLog directive, which takes the name of the log file as an argument:

```
TransferLog /var/log/httpd/access_log
```

Two directives that can be used to create custom access logs are LogFormat and CustomLog. The LogFormat parameter can be used to set the format for the log output, and the CustomLog parameter can be used to identify the location and file name of the custom log as shown in the following examples.

```
LogFormat "%h %l %u %t \"%r\" %>s %b \"%{Referer}i\"
   \"%{User-Agent}i\"" combined
LogFormat "%h %l %u %t \"%r\" %>s %b" common
LogFormat "%{Referer}i -> %U" referer
LogFormat "%{User-agent}i" agent
```

The referrer (URL of link page, if any) and user agent (the browser) information can be placed in separate logs:

```
CustomLog logs/referrer_log referrer
CustomLog logs/agent_log agent
```

Alternatively, a combined log can be specified with the entry

```
CustomLog logs/access_log combined
```

The string argument to the LogFormat parameter identifies the format for the log file entry.

Note that if the value specifying the directory does not contain a / at the start of the directory specification, the directory is considered to be a subdirectory of ServerRoot. Leaving these lines commented out will turn off the custom access logging of the Apache server.

PidFile Directive

The `PidFile` directive contains the process id of the Apache master server process. The default entry for this is

```
PidFile /var/run/httpd.pid
```

This entry is useful to control the Apache server process; terminating process with this PID will shut down the Apache server. It is now easier, however, to use the `apachectl` program to start and stop the server, as shown in Chapter 3.

The ScoreBoardFile Directive

The `ScoreBoardFile` directive contains information which, with some ports of Apache, is used by the server master to communicate with its child processes. Since many platforms provide an alternative method of tracking server processes (such as shared memory), this file is not always needed. The format for this parameter is

```
ScoreBoardFile /etc/httpd/httpd.scoreboard
```

If this file is *not* created when Apache is being run on your machine, the architecture of your platform does not require it. If it is created, however, it is important that no two instances of the server share the same file. In other words, if there are multiple instances of the Apache server running on a platform that uses the `ScoreBoard file`, each separate instance must have its own `ScoreBoard file`. That being said, if there is only one instance of Apache running on the machine, there is no reason to change this from the default value.

LockFile Directive

The `LockFile` directive is set to the file to be used, in certain instances, to manage certain transactions. The following entry sets this parameter to its default value:

```
LockFile /etc/httpd/httpd.lock
```

If the directory in which Apache keeps its logs resides on an NFS-mounted disk, this directive should be set to a disk directory that is local to the Apache server. Otherwise, this directive should be left set to its default value.

UseCanonicalName Directive

The `UseCanonical Name` directive affects the manner in which the Apache server will construct a self-referencing URL, a URL that refers to the server that is sending the response. If this directive is set, the canonical name is used, constructed from the the value of the configuration file `ServerName` parameter and the `Port` parameter (see `ServerName` and `Port` parameter descriptions). If this parameter is set off, then if it can, the canonical name will be constructed based on the values sent by the client for the server name and port.

This parameter is useful at sites using virtual hosting. Since with virtual hosting we have a single Apache server pretending to be many servers with different *virtual* host names, supplying a canonical host name of the `ServerName` parameter would have each virtual host supplying the same self-referencing host name; this would obviously be incorrect. To solve this problem, virtual hosting schemes within Apache (as supported by add-on modules) allow the default canonical name to be turned off and either have the client supply the host name in the HOST header (`UseCanonicalName off`) or have DNS perform the lookup (`UseCanonicalName DNS`). (Note that there are performance and security problems associated with using DNS in this fashion.) The following entry sets `UseCanonicalName` on, the default value for this parameter:

```
UseCanonicalName on
```

CacheNegotiatedDocs Directive

The `CacheNegotiatedDocs` directive controls the behavior of document caching for HTTP 1.0 clients (HTTP/1.1 clients handle caching differently) . By default, Apache attempts not to cache negotiated documents. Since this is effective only for HTTP/1.0 clients, its level of use is in most cases very small and the default value is appropriate. The following sets this parameter to its default value of off by commenting the line in the configuration file:

```
#CacheNegotiatedDocs
```

Timeout Directive

The `Timeout` directive identifies the number of seconds the server will wait for a response from a connection. Most HTTP actions do not require connections to remain open (persistent connections). In fact, there are only certain periods in which the server will look for a timeout condition. During a PUSH or PUT HTTP request a series of packets will be moved over the network (by the network TCP layer). During the period in which these packets are being moved, the server will track the time required to return packets. If the time spent waiting for a packet to return is greater than the `Timeout` parameter, an error is returned by the server and the transaction is aborted.

The HTTP protocol first makes a connection to a resource and then expects a `GET` method to be received. If the time between which the connection is made and the `GET` request is received is greater than the `Timeout` parameter value, the connection is closed and the transaction is aborted. If the time between which the last ACK is received exceeds the `Timeout` parameter value, an error is generated and the transaction is aborted.

In the following example, the `Timeout` parameter is set to 300 seconds (5 minutes), the default value for this parameter.

```
Timeout 300
```

This setting will most likely be adequate for most installations. At sites where timeouts occur, the problem lies not with the `Timeout` parameter but with the network or server problem most likely that leads to the failure.

KeepAlive Directive

Initially, HTTP was not intended to use persistent connections. Maintaining connections can be expensive, consuming resources on both the client and database server. At the time the Internet was growing and being developed, using a protocol without persistent connections was considered an attractive approach to the rendering of discrete documents using HTTP. With HTTP, a document would be requested, a connection would be made, the HTML page would be copied over the network, and the connection would be closed. The server did not need to be concerned about an excessively large number of dormant connections which could quickly consume all its resources on large, highly active Web sites because the connections would be dropped immediately after each page was served.

Although this approach requires fewer server resources, it also slows page access. In many cases, persistent connections could improve client access. The World Wide Web has also changed dramatically since its inception. The types of operations being performed on the Web now go well beyond the delivery of simple text documents. A number of Web applications could benefit from the ability to maintain persistent connections. These types of connections have officially been available since the HTTP 1.1 standard.

To enable persistent connections in Apache, the KeepAlive parameter needs to be set to a value of "on." This will allow multiple sequential HTTP requests to be made by the client on the same connection. The default value for this parameter is for the service to be turned on:

```
KeepAlive On
```

It makes sense to leave this parameter at its default setting and allow client browsers that are capable of using this feature to use it. Note that if the client does not request this feature, they will not be provided with it.

Several other parameters are also used to control the behavior of this feature, as described below.

MaxKeepAliveRequests Directive

The server can optionally limit the number of persistent requests it will allow. If this parameter is set to 0, an unlimited number of persistent requests will be allowed. The default value for the MaxKeepAliveRequests parameter is 100:

```
MaxKeepAliveRequests 100
```

Allowing unlimited persistent requests is risky, since some network attacks could try to exploit these connections. The correct number depends on the number of simultaneous users on the site and the hardware resources available to the Apache server. A value of 100 would probably be adequate for most small to medium-sized sites.

KeepAliveTimeout Parameter

The KeepAliveTimeout parameter is used to set the number of seconds the server will wait for the next requests in a persistent transaction. This value should not be set too large, since the expectation is that any client requesting persistent connections should make constant use of the connections in a rapid, serial fashion. The default for this parameter is 15 seconds, as shown below.

```
KeepAliveTimeout 15
```

Server Pool Size Regulation

The Apache server attempts to balance the load on the server dynamically by adding new processes as needed. It does this by maintaining spare servers. The parameters `MinSpareServers` and `MaxSpareServers` control server spawning behavior. Apache starts by forking a number of processes (see the section on the `StartServer` parameter). Requests are passed to these processes as needed on a round-robin basis. Apache then monitors how many requests each server has pending. If Apache determines that more servers are needed (based on what it determines to be an excessively large server wait queue), Apache will begin using its spare servers. When the number of spare servers reaches the `MinSpareServers` count, Apache will begin spawning additional spare servers until it reaches the `MaxSpareServers` number. The `MaxSpareServers` number also represents the maximum number of idle servers Apache will allow. If the number of idle servers exceeds this number, Apache will begin killing the excess number of servers until the `MaxSpareServers` number is reached. Common settings for a small to medium-sized site are as follows.

```
MinSpareServers 8
MaxSpareServers 20
```

For a large, busy site with around 1 million hits per day, the following entries may be appropriate:

```
MinSpareServers 32
MaxSpareServers 64
```

The number of servers to start initially is set with the `StartServers` parameter. The following example starts 10 servers, a setting adequate for most small to medium-sized sites:

```
StartServers 10
```

These server settings can have a significant impact on the performance of the site. Assuming that adequate CPU resources are available, the number of servers active will make more CPU cycles available to perform Apache's operations.

Maximum Client Connections

The maximum number of concurrent clients who can connect to a site is set with the `MaxClients` parameter. If Apache is managing this number of connections, and additional connection requests are received, those requests will be refused. The following sets the maximum number of concurrent client connections to 150:

```
MaxClients 150
```

It is best not to set this parameter too low, since requests will be refused once this limit is reached. With HTTP servers, the number of active connections is often very transitory, changing quickly as Apache completes serving pages. The default value of 150 is probably good for most sites.

Maximum Requests per Child Process

The maximum number of requests per child process limits the number of requests an Apache child server can process. Once this number is reached,the child process will die and another process will serve the request. The following examples set the number of child requests to 500.

```
MaxRequestsPerChild 500
```

The purpose of this parameter is largely to control the resources utilized by long-running Apache processes. On some systems, the Apache process may load dynamic libraries that leak memory (continue to acquire more memory resources without freeing any previous resources). By killing the process and restarting another, the resources used by the process that has been killed will be freed.

Directory Structure Definition for Apache

The directory structure for Apache includes a directory for the configuration files, a directory for the log files, and a directory for the modules that are dynamically loaded. All of the directories defined for configuration and system maintenance are considered to be subordinate to the `ServerRoot` directory. Table 2.5 summarizes this structure.

Table 2.5 Apache Configuration Files Directory

Directory	Purpose
Conf	Contains the configuration files for Apache. Distribution includes `httpd.conf`. This directory may also include any configuration files that are "included" in `httpd.conf`.
Modules	Contains the dynamically loaded modules included in the Apache runtime server. On Unix this is a link to `/usr/lib/apache`. (This also appears as `libexec`, but is changed by the RPM installation process.)
Logs	Contains the error logs used by Apache. Various directives allow logs to be written to other directories.

Virtual Hosts

The ability to manage multiple hosts through a single Web server installation provides a powerful capability. This allows a single Apache installation to serve as an HTTP host for separate, distinct Web sites. Distinctive sites supporting different groups or departments within an organization can operate independently, yet be supported by the same Web server environment.

The Apache Web server supports this capability through *virtual hosts*. With virtual hosting, Apache allows distinct host locations to be defined using the `VirtualHost` container in the `httpd.conf` file. Within this container, a number of attributes that apply to the virtual host can be declared. The following provides an example of creating a virtual host.

```
<VirtualHost 192.3.6.1>
ServerAdmin vhostmaster@host.some_domain.com
DocumentRoot /lin1/Apache
ServerName VhostServer
ServerPath /VhostServer
ErrorLog logs/VhostServer-error_log
TransferLog logs/VhostServer-access_log
</VirtualHost>
```

In this example, the IP address 192.3.6.1 represents a virtual host for this Apache installation. When the Apache server encounters this IP address in a URL, it will immediately switch to the configuration defined in the container for this virtual host.

Within the container for this virtual host, important site-specific parameters are redefined for this virtual host. Almost any Apache directive can be placed in a virtual host container, allowing the virtual host to have a great deal of autonomy. The example above demonstrates the setting of the most common directives applied to virtual hosting. In this example, the `DocumentRoot` directory for the virtual host is set to `/lin1/Apache`, effectively creating a new document tree for this virtual site.

Since the activity for this virtual host will be tracked separately, separate log files are declared for this site. These log files will be located in the same directory as the log files for the main Apache site, but will be named using the designations in the `ErrorLog` and `TransferLog` directives defined in the virtual host container. This allows the log administration to be shared among the virtual hosts (by using the same log directory) but still manages to maintain separate logs for the virtual hosts. For the same reason, the `ServerAdmin` directive denotes a specific email address to be used for administrative email concerning the virtual site.

Table 2.6 Directives Not Usable in VirtualHost

Directive	Description
ServerType	Identifies how the server will operate; relevant to general server operation, not to virtual hosts
StartServers	Identifies the number of server processes to start; applies to the main Apache server process
MaxSpareServers	Number of spare server processes to start; applies to the main Apache server process
MinSpareServers	Minimum number of spare server processes to maintain; applies to the main Apache server process
MaxRequestsPerChild	Maximum number of requests per child (Apache process) to allow before the child will be restarted; applies to the main Apache server processing
BindAddress, Listen	Address for the server to listen; pertains to the main server, not to virtual hosts
PidFile	Process ID (PID) of the main server
TypesConfig	Name of the file for MIME definition for the main Apache server
NameVirtualHost	IP address for virtual hosting; applies to the IP address for all virtual hosts that will use named virtual hosting

Virtually any directive can be used in the VirtualHost container, with the exception of a few that don't necessarily make sense. These exceptions are listed in Table 2.6.

Using name-based virtual hosting, the domain name as supplied by the DNS server identifies the virtual host to the Apache server (via the Host: header sent to the server). Although multiple domain names are used for the various virtual Web sites, the multiple domains resolve to the same IP address. It is up to the Apache server to map these domain names internally to the appropriate virtual hosts.

```
NameVirtualHost 192.3.6.5
<VirtualHost 192.3.6.5>
     ServerName HRHost.WidgetsRUS.com
ServerAdmin HRAdmin@Websites.WidgetsRUS.com
```

```
DocumentRoot /lin1/Apache/MyHost1/docs
ServerPath /HR
ErrorLog logs/HR-error_log
TransferLog logs/HR-access_log
</VirtualHost>

# Another named virtual host on the same IP address
<VirtualHost 192.3.6.5>
     ServerName Accounting.WidgetsRUS.com
ServerAdmin AcctgAdmin@Websites.WidgetsRUS.com
DocumentRoot /lin1/Apache/Accounting/docs
ServerName Accounting
ServerPath /Accounting
ErrorLog logs/Accounting-error_log
TransferLog logs/Accounting-access_log
</VirtualHost>
```

AddModule Directive

The AddModule directive is used to specify the order in which modules are loaded by Apache. The load order of modules can be an issue, since there are cases where you may want one module to specify a certain order in which module use would be triggered, a set of if/else/if conditions.

The syntax for the AddModule directive is as follows:

```
ClearModuleList
#AddModule mod_mmap_static.c
AddModule mod_env.c
AddModule mod_log_config.c
. . .
```

In this example, the ClearModuleList directive clears any load order that may currently be specified. A series of AddModule statements then specifies the load order of the modules.

UserDir Directive

The UseDir parameter specifies the directory that will be identified as the user's home directory when a URL with a "~user" pattern is received. The following example sets the user's home directory (UserDir) to public_html:

```
UserDir public_html
```

With this example, if a URL is received for `//myhost/`
`~fred/index.html`, it will be resolved to the home directory for the user
`fred` (this assumes, of course, that the user has an account on that machine).
The reference resulting from this example would be the user's home directory
appended with the directory name parameter to the `UserDir` directory. For
the example above, if the user's home directory is `/home/fred`, the resulting
URL would reference `/home/fred/public_html/index.html`.

Controlling Directory Listings

A number of directives describe how Apache will list the contents of a directory. If the URL that Apache is processing does not specify a particular document file, Apache will usually look for a file of a specific name (this can also be
controlled using an Apache directive). If Apache cannot find this file, Apache
will attempt to list the contents of the directory.

The `DirectoryIndex` parameter specifies the name of the document
that contains the index for the directory. The following example identifies
`index.html` and several alternative names that can be used as the index file
for directory listings.

```
DirectoryIndex index.html index.htm index.shtml
index.cgi  Default.htm default.htm index.php3
```

Apache asserts that the entries in this document are correct and merely pre-
sents the file to the client (parsing it first, if necessary).

Using Automatic Indexing

If Apache does not find an index file in the directory, it can create one automatically. The manner in which it does this is flexible. The `FancyIndexing`
parameter can be used to instruct Apache to create and index as needed using
icons and text to indicate the type of files in the directory. To turn
`FancyIndexing` on, the following entry would be made:

```
FancyIndexing on
```

Using the `FancyIndexing` feature, various icons can be used to indicate
the data type of the file in the directory. Two parameters can be used to indi-

cate the icon type: `AddIconByEncoding`, which sets the icon by the encoded type, and `AddIconByType`, which sets the icon based on the type of file.

The following entry specifies icons to be used based on the encoding of the file. If the file is of **MIME** type x-compress, the `compressed.gif` icon is displayed next to the name of the file.

```
AddIconByEncoding (CMP,/icons/compressed.gif) x-compress x-gzip
```

The following entries set the icon by the type of file:

```
AddIconByType (TXT,/icons/text.gif) text/*
AddIconByType (IMG,/icons/image2.gif) image/*
AddIconByType (SND,/icons/sound2.gif) audio/*
AddIconByType (VID,/icons/movie.gif) video/*
```

The `AddIcon` parameter can alternatively be used to set the icon type based on the extension of the file, as shown in the following example.

```
AddIcon /icons/binary.gif .bin .exe
```

This `AddIcon` entry is used to set the icon type based on the name of the file:

```
AddIcon /icons/bomb.gif core
AddIcon /icons/back.gif ..
AddIcon /icons/hand.right.gif README
AddIcon /icons/folder.gif ^^DIRECTORY^^
AddIcon /icons/blank.gif ^^BLANKICON^^
```

Note that entries for individual files are also made for files named README and then for files of type DIRECTORY and for empty files.

A default icon can be specified for unknown objects in the directory, as shown in the entry

```
DefaultIcon /icons/unknown.gif
```

An `AddDescription` parameter allows a short text description of a file to be placed in the server-generated directory listing. The format for this entry is

```
AddDescription "The following file contains information
on the download" DownloadInfo
```

The `ReadmeName` allows the name of the informational *readme* file for the directory to be specified in the directory as shown below. The `HeaderName` file allows the name of the header file for the directory to be specified. Examples of both entries are

```
ReadmeName README
HeaderName HEADER
```

The `IndexIgnore` parameter identifies the files that the automatic index generation feature should ignore. The format of this entry is

```
IndexIgnore .??* *~ *# HEADER* README* RCS
```

Directory-Specific Access Configuration

The `AccessFileName` parameter can be used to identify the name of the file containing the directory-specific access configuration for the directory in which it is contained. The following entry sets the name of this file to `.htaccess`, the default name for this file.

```
AccessFileName .htaccess
```

This file contains information on the hosts and, potentially, the users that are allowed to access the contents of the directory in which the file is located. This information would override the access information entered in the `httpd.conf` file unless the `IgnoreOverride` parameter has been set for that directory. Note that use of this directive is recommended for critical directories since it limits the ability of hackers to infiltrate a site.

Specifying MIME Types

The `TypesConfig` parameter specifies the MIME types file for the Apache installation. The default setting for this parameter is

```
TypesConfig /etc/httpd/conf/apache-mime.types
```

If the MIME type of a file cannot be determined, the default type of the file can be specified with the `DefaultType` parameter.

```
DefaultType text/plain
```

Some browsers can decompress the contents of a file on the fly. The AddEncoding parameter allows the encoding for these files to be specified as follows:

```
AddEncoding x-compress Z
AddEncoding x-gzip gz
```

Specifying the Language Type of a Document

The AddLanguage parameter allows the language of a document to be specified (based on its extension). The following parameters specify the document language for a number of languages.

```
AddLanguage en .en
AddLanguage fr .fr
AddLanguage de .de
AddLanguage da .da
AddLanguage el .el
AddLanguage it .it
```

The language definition generally relates to ISO two-letter country codes. The priority of the language to use in negotiation with the browser can be specified. This entry can be used to specify the preference to be given to some languages, as in

```
LanguagePriority en fr de
```

Redirection for Missing Documents

It is not uncommon for documents to be moved from one server to another. The Redirect parameter allows the new location for a missing document to be specified as shown in the following example.

```
Redirect oldDoc.html http://newserver/newfiles/oldDoc.html
```

Specifying the CGI Directory

The Apache server provides the ability to execute CGI (Common Gateway Interface) scripts. The ScriptAlias parameter allows the CGI directory to be specified. This is the directory from which server CGI scripts will be executed.

```
ScriptAlias /cgi-bin/ /home/httpd/cgi-bin/
ScriptAlias /protected-cgi-bin/ /home/httpd/protected-cgi-bin/
```

The `ScriptAlias` directory is used in conjunction with the `AddHandler` directive, which will add the appropriate handler for the script.

(Although CGI does provide a means of managing dynamic content and Apache has a number of facilities for working with CGI, it can be cumbersome to develop, difficult to manage, and prone to security holes. Server-side Java provides a much more flexible, scalable, and secure alternative to CGI and is the focus of this book. For this reason, our discussion of CGI and Apache is intentionally limited.)

Using Server-Side Includes

Apache provides a module that allows special tags to be used in the HTML pages served by that server. Among other features, these tags allow documents to be included where the tag appears. This very important feature allows standard headers and footers to be included on HTML pages without the overhead of using a scripting language. The following tag inserts a header into an HTML page:

```
<html>
<body>
<h1>
<!- include file="header.html" ->
</h1>
. . .
```

To use server-side includes, several parameters need to be inserted into the configuration file. The `mod_include` module must be loaded into the server (using an `AddModule` parameter). Additionally, the `AddType` parameter must be used to specify the new type for the file type that will contain the server-side includes, and the `AddHandler` parameter specifies the handler for the file type (the handler that has been loaded using the `AddModule` parameter).

```
AddType text/html .shtml
AddHandler server-parsed .shtml
```

Adding MIME Types and Handlers

As shown in the preceding example, the `AddType` parameter allows additional MIME types to be added to Apache in the configuration file. For example, to add the JSP type to the server, the following entry would be made:

```
AddType test/jsp .jsp
```

This entry is most often used in conjunction with handlers to map the types added to specific handlers which convert the contents of the file to a form that can be returned to the browser. An `AddHandler` parameter entry to process files with a .cgi extension is

```
AddHandler cgi-script .cgi
```

Customizable Errors

Apache can be configured using the `ErrorDocument` parameter to process errors in three different ways: as a plain text file, as a local redirect to an HTML file, or as an external redirect to a specific URL. The format for specifying a plain text file is

```
ErrorDocument 500 "Server Failure"
```

This entry directs the server to display a page with the text message "Server Failure" when the server encounters error 500. Note that the double quotes are not closed; this directs Apache to treat the string with the value "Server Failure" as a text string.

Alternatively, the `ErrorDocument` parameter can be set to direct Apache to a local URL to display an error page for a particular error, as shown in the entry

```
ErrorDocument 404 /missing.html
```

which will direct Apache to display the page missing.html when error 404 is encountered. The local redirect could also be a script, as in

```
ErrorDocument 404 /cgi-bin/missing_handler.pl
```

This entry directs error 404 to the Perl script missing_handler.pl. It is assumed that Apache will have a handler for .pl files and will process the file using that handler.

Apache can also direct the user to an external URL, as shown in the example

```
ErrorDocument 402 http://otherserver.com/subscription_info.html
```

This entry will direct error 402 to the URL provided as an argument to the parameter.

Browser-Specific Capabilities

The `BrowserMatch` parameter can be used to specify browser-specific behavior, depending on the browser with which it is communicating.

```
BrowserMatch "Mozilla/2" nokeepalive
BrowserMatch "MSIE 4\.0b2;" nokeepalive downgrade-1.0
   force-response-1.0
```

The `BrowserMatch` capability is used to change certain features based on the browser with which the server is communicating.

Apache can also communicate with applications other than browsers. The following entries change the behavior of the server when it communicates with other applications.

```
BrowserMatch "RealPlayer 4\.0" force-response-1.0
BrowserMatch "Java/1\.0" force-response-1.0
BrowserMatch "JDK/1\.0" force-response-1.0
```

Obtaining Status and Server Information with Apache

Apache provides two modules that can be used to provide information on the status of the server: the `mod_info` (the `server-info` handler) module and the `mod_status` (the `server-status` handler) modules. The `ExtendedStatus` parameter can be used to describe how to use the output of the server-status module.

```
ExtendedStatus on
<Location /server-status>
SetHandler server-status
order deny,allow
deny from all
allow from localhost, 127.0.0.1
allow from .BestSite.com
</Location>
```

To use this module, the `ExtendedStatus` directive is supplied with the on parameter (effectively turning this feature on) and a `Location` container is created for the `/server-status` location. Within this location, a handler is *set* (not added, since that is done previously) for that location. Within the location container, access to all hosts except the `localhost`, thereby limiting users to those whose client is running on the `localhost` (presumably, system administrators). Additionally, adding an additional `allow` parameter to the `Location` container could be used to enable access from the local domain, thus allowing server status to be queried from the local network. This is shown with the final entry in the `Location` container above, which allows access from clients within the `.BestSite.com` domain.

To access the server status using this module, the URL `http://MyServer/server-status` (where `MyServer` is the name of your server) would be entered in the browser and the return value would be a page providing the status of the local server. Two versions of the status page are available: a standard status page and an extended status page. The standard status page returns information on the server uptime and the processes being run by the server, as shown in Figure 2.3.

A slightly more detailed report is available by setting the `ExtendedStatus` directive on (as shown in Figure 2.3). The results of this output shown in Figure 2.4, include additional information on the processes that are running under Apache.
Because of the additional overhead involved in the collection of extended status information, this option is usually not used continuously at busier sites (although it may be used periodically for site evaluation or debugging purposes).

The `mod_info` module provides information on the configuration status of the server. Although some status information is provided by this module, the focus is more on the configuration of the server: the modules that have been loaded, the containers that have been declared, the directives the server recognizes, and additional information (including some rudimentary documentation on the directives and parameters). Since this information is useful only to administrators of the server, access to this module is usually set to access from the the `localhost` only.

The parameters used to access this module are similar to those shown for the `server-status` module. A `Location` container is defined and a handler set for the location. Authorization is made restrictive and in this example is limited to users from the `localhost`.

```
<Location /server-info>
SetHandler server-info

order deny,allow
deny from all
allow from localhost, 127.0.0.1
</Location>
```

The server information provided by this module can be accessed by presenting the URL `http://MyServer/server-info` to the Apache server from a client on the `localhost` (using the configuration defined above).

```
Apache Server Status for ataylor.edu

Server Version: Apache-AdvancedExtranetServer/1.3.14 (Linux-
Mandrake/2mdk)
Server Built: Oct 24 2000 10:55:49

Current Time: Wednesday, 07-Feb-2001 07:35:34 EST
Restart Time: Wednesday, 07-Feb-2001 07:10:37 EST
Parent Server Generation: 4
Server uptime: 24 minutes 57 seconds
1 requests currently being processed, 9 idle servers
_____W........................................
....................................................
....................................................
....................................................

Scoreboard Key:
"_" Waiting for Connection, "S" Starting up, "R" Reading
Request, "W" Sending Reply, "K" Keepalive (read),
"D" DNS Lookup, "L" Logging, "G" Gracefully finishing,
"." Open slot with no current process

PID Key:
   1263 in state: _ ,    1264 in state: _ ,    1265 in state: _
   1266 in state: _ ,    1267 in state: _ ,    1268 in state: _
   1269 in state: _ ,    1272 in state: _ ,    1273 in state: _
   1274 in state: W ,

To obtain a full report with current status information you
need to use the ExtendedStatus On directive.

Quick Shortcut Cache (QSC) Status:
QSC disabled
```

Figure 2.3 Standard Status Page

Directory Authorization with the Apache

Authorization or security with Web documents is usually implemented using directories; documents in a specific directory are subject to the security restrictions of that directory. Therefore, any request to retrieve a document from a secure directory requires a user to meet the authorization require-

```
Apache Server Status for ataylor.edu

Server Version: Apache-AdvancedExtranetServer/1.3.14 (Linux-
Mandrake/2mdk)
Server Built: Oct 24 2000 10:55:49
──────────────────────────────────────────────────────────────
Current Time: Wednesday, 07-Feb-2001 07:44:58 EST
Restart Time: Wednesday, 07-Feb-2001 07:39:29 EST
Parent Server Generation: 0
Server uptime: 5 minutes 29 seconds
Total accesses: 2 - Total Traffic: 6 kB
CPU Usage: u0 s0 cu0 cs0
.00608 requests/sec - 18 B/second - 3072 B/request
1 requests currently being processed, 9 idle servers
W_____.....................................................
................................................................
................................................................
................................................................

Scoreboard Key:
"_" Waiting for Connection, "S" Starting up, "R" Reading
Request, "W" Sending Reply, "K" Keepalive (read), "D" DNS
Lookup, "L" Logging, "G" Gracefully finishing, "." Open slot
with no current process

Srv  PID   Acc    M  CPU   SS   Req  Conn Child Slot  Host       VHost      Request
0-0  7601  0/1/1  W  0.00  292  0    0.0  0.00  0.00  127.0.0.1  ataylor.edu GET
                                                                            /server-
                                                                            status
                                                                            HTTP/1.0

4-0  7605  0/1/1  _  0.00  77   113  0.0  0.00  0.00  localhost.ataylor.edu GET
                                                      localdomain           /server-
                                                                            status
                                                                            HTTP/1.0

Srv Child Server number - generation  PID OS process ID   Acc
Number of accesses this connection / this child / this slot   M
Mode of operation  CPU CPU usage, number of seconds   SS
Seconds since beginning of most recent request   Req
Milliseconds required to process most recent request   Conn
Kilobytes transferred this connection   Child Megabytes trans-
ferred this child   Slot Total megabytes transferred this slot
Quick Shortcut Cache (QSC) Status:
QSC disabled
```

Figure 2.4 Extended Status Page

ments of that directory. Apache provides several methods of directory authorization, using the modules listed in Table 2.7.

Basic authentication as implemented using the mod_auth module works by a series of HTTP transactions. When a browser requests a document in a directory secured with basic authentication, the Apache server returns an unauthorized message error (error 401) with a `WWW-Authenticate` header and the name of the realm configured by the AuthName parameter in the httpd.conf file. Upon receiving this response, the browser will display a dialog and have the user enter a user name and password. The browser will then repeat the request to the Apache server, adding the user name and password entered by the user in an Authorization header. The user name and password are encoded in a base 64 encoded string. This authorization would be configured using a set of httpd.conf entries as follows:

```
<Location /secureDir>
AuthName "My Realm"
AuthType Basic
AuthGroupFile /security/SecurityGroups
AuthUserFile /security/SecurityUser
AuthAuthoritative on
require valid-user
</Location>
```

This would create basic authentication security for a location named `/secureDir`. Entries for the implementation of security would be contained in the files `/security/SecurityUser` and `/security/SecurityGroups`. The contents of the user file must be administered with one of the Apache utility programs: `htpasswd` for basic authentication, `htdigest` for digest authentication, and `dbmanage` for `dbm` authentication. To create a password file, the `htpasswd` command is executed with the format

```
htpasswd -c <file_name> <user_name>
```

Table 2.7 Apache Directory Authorization Modules

Module	Authorization Type
`mod_auth`	Basic authentication
`mod_auth_anon`	Anonymous authentication
`mod_auth_dbm`	Basic authentication using the DBM database
`mod_auth_db`	Basic authentication using the DB database
`mod_digest`	Digest authentication

To create the user `SecurityUser` password file in the example above and to add the `webmaster` user for the example, the following command would be issued.

```
htpasswd -c /security/SecurityUser webmaster
```

When executed, the command will prompt for the user password and repeat the password question to verify the password. The password entered is not echoed to the terminal window.

Once the file has been created, a user could be added using the following command:

```
htpasswd /security/SecurityUser art
```

Note that the system user id under which the Apache server is running must be able to read this file. If the server user id does not have permission to read the file, the server will still start and will merely report a failed authentication attempt to the browser each time authentication is requested for the location.

With basic authorization the user name and password are returned in a base 64–encoded string which, although not apparently a user name–password combination, could easily be decoded by a knowledgeable person. Digest is a more secure authentication method than basic authentication and is provided by the `mod_digest` (or `mod_auth_digest`) module. With digest authentication, passwords are transmitted using an MD5 encoding algorithm, which is more secure. But the digest authentication is not universally supported by browsers and so is not yet heavily used.

Even with proper user authentication, information transmitted over the Internet is not secure without encryption. The use of SSL encryption combined with a database to store user names and passwords for the login process is the preferred method of securing a site.

Security Information in the Directory: The .htaccess File

Alternatively, this security information can be placed in a file in the directory to be secured. The name of the security file is `.htaccess,` and the advantage of this approach is that to be recognized, changes in the security plan (as defined in the `.htaccess` file) do not require a server restart. Note that this does raise the possibility that a user other than the Web site administrator can manipulate security on the directory. This should be considered and managed before using this type of security definition (e.g., setting appropriate restrictive permissions on the directory and the `.htaccess` file itself).

Include Directive

The `Include` directive works in a manner similar to that of the C language `include` preprocessor directive: The text of the file referenced in the `Include` directive is included in the file. This allows configuration information to be organized in discrete units and then included in the final `httpd.conf` file for parsing and loading. The following is the syntax of the `Include` directive:

```
Include conf/addon-modules/mod_php3.conf
Include conf/tomcat-apache.conf
```

These entries would include both the `mod_php3.conf` and `tomacat-apache.conf` files into the current file. Since there is no leading "/" in the file path entry, the `conf` directory referenced is assumed to be `<SERVER-ROOT>/conf`.

Testing the Apache Environment

Once Apache has been installed and configured, it can be tested. To start Apache, simply run the command `apachectl`, passing it the appropriate argument as follows:

```
# apachectl start
```

The command should return a simple response indicating that the server has started:

```
# apachectl start
/usr/sbin/apachectl start: httpd started
#
```

To access the Apache server and verify its operation, the URL `//localhost:80` can be entered through a browser (the port number is optional). This should connect to the Apache server and display the default page as shown in Figure 2.5.

If the server status module has been loaded into the Apache configuration, entering the URL `//localhost:80/server-status` will display the page shown in Figure 2.6, providing further verification that the server is running correctly.

Figure 2.5 Apache Start Page

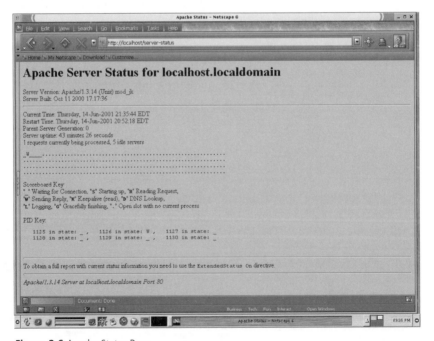

Figure 2.6 Apache Status Page

Summary

In this chapter we provided some useful information concerning the Apache server, the cornerstone of our Web site. A large number of the configuration directives available were explained, focusing on those that will be important to our site. Since we plan on using Java technologies to provide management of dynamic content, the Apache server will be used primarily to manage static content. With that goal in mind, we want the Apache server to manage document locations, log site access, manage virtual hosts, and perform other functions required by our site. After providing information on our database of choice and Java and JSP, we will return to Apache in Chapter 5 and provide suggestions and examples on how Apache can be used to develop a Web site where the dynamic content is composed of JSP.

Coming Up Next

In Chapter 3 we discuss the database we plan to use on our site: PostgreSQL. This database will provide storage for important data content of the site and allow dynamic Web site content to be created using these data. PostgreSQL supports SQL and is provided with JDBC drivers for access to the database using the Java programming language. Chapter 3 is an introduction to the database and explains the process of configuring and connecting to the database. The JDBC API is also discussed briefly.

3

CREATING THE WEB SERVER ENVIRONMENT:

Database in the Web Infrastructure

No truly dynamic Web environment would be complete without a database to store some portion of the dynamic, persistent content that will be an important part of the site. The examples in this chapter show use of the PostgreSQL database. This database sports a large number of very mature database features that make it a good choice for any number of applications.

In practice, however, the choice of the database could be driven by other factors, such as corporate standards, the need to store very large volumes of data, or the need to access a large amount of legacy data already stored in a relational database. Given the capabilities of the Java/JDBC API, the choice of database does not have a noticeable effect on development of the application. An application developed and tested with PostgreSQL could easily be shifted to Oracle or Informix for production-level testing and would involve little or no change in the code. Similarly, using remote database access, Oracle or Informix JDBC drivers could be used in testing to access a remote database, thus eliminating altogether the need to install and operate a database on the test platform. (Note that good database portability does imply the avoidance of vendor-specific SQL syntax in the application.)

There are, nevertheless, some good reasons why it may be easier to install and operate a test database on the development platform. In this chapter we explain what is needed to create a PostgreSQL database on the Linux platform.

Background

PostgreSQL has its roots in academia. It began as a project called Ingres at the University of California at Berkeley (UCB) in the period between 1977 and 1985. This code became the basis for one of the early relational databases, named Ingres. While the company Ingres attempted to make its way in the business world, work of a team led by Michael Stonebraker continued at UCB on a product called Postgres. The goal of this team was to create an object-relational database server. This code was later used by a company named Illustra and used to create a commercial product. Ultimately, Illustra was purchased by Informix Software, which combined their database product with their own existing database system to create an object-relational database product under the Informix name.

The PostgreSQL database represents a code stream that is distinct from that of the Illustra product (and the Informix product that was ultimately built from this code). PostgreSQL is a relational database with object-oriented extensions—what is sometimes referred to as an *object-relational database*. These object-relational features provide significant benefits for complex development efforts. These features are:

- Classes
- Inheritance
- Types
- Functions

Classes are represented in PostgreSQL as extensions of the concept of a table in a relational database. Classes contain attributes (columns) defined within a set (table). Classes can inherit from other classes, and thus a logical hierarchy can be developed, allowing for reuse and simplifying the development process. Custom data types can be defined that extend the conventional data types of relational databases. These types can then be used in the definition of classes (tables).

Behaviors can be defined in the database through functions. Functions can be defined with an internal language or using external languages such as C. This capability is important, since the standard language used for interaction with a relational database is SQL, which was never intended to be a programming language (and, in fact, lacks any significant procedural programming capability).

This inclusion of object-oriented features provides a powerful set of capabilities in the database, which include the ability to extend the database dynamically with modules created in other languages and the ability to treat relational tables as objects that can inherit the attributes of other tables. PostgreSQL adds to these object-oriented capabilities other mature relational database features, such as transactions and a solid ANSI SQL92 and SQL3 implementation.

PostgreSQL contains other features found in more popular (and expensive) proprietary relational databases:

- Constraints
- Triggers
- Rules
- Transaction integrity

Database constraints come in two forms: data integrity constraints and referential integrity constraints. PostgreSQL supports data integrity constraints in the form of *check constraints*, which apply limits to the data inserted into a column or columns (unlike many database vendors and the SQL92 specification, which limits check constraints to a single column).

PostgreSQL supports *primary key constraints,* which identify a column or concatenation of columns as a primary key and force the primary key to be a unique identifier. Alternatively, a *unique constraint* can be applied to a column or set of columns to force the columns to be unique. Support for referential integrity is currently (version 6.5) limited to primary key constraints; support for foreign key constraints is not explicitly available, although it is fairly simple to create one or more database triggers to provide the functionality of these constraints.

Triggers can be placed on a table to trap an event before, after, or during a database update operation (insert, update, or delete). Database triggers provide the ability to determine the integrity of a database update before it occurs and to stop the transaction and return an error if desired. Triggers can also be used to chain an update operation to insert or update other tables, as needed.

Transaction integrity allows a set of singleton database updates to be grouped together and treated as a single operation referred to as a *transaction*. Within a transaction, if one of the database updates fails, the entire transaction can be rolled back, leaving the database in the same consistent state it was in at the start of the transaction.

Running PostgreSQL

PostgreSQL uses a set of back-end application programs to manage database requests. The system architecture is that of a *two-tier architectural model,* with the client being the user's front-end program and the back end being the PostgreSQL applications (see Figure 3.1).

The client program will first initiate a request for a connection to the database. This connection request will be received by the postmaster daemon (or service) process running on the database machine. In most installations, this process runs in the background and listens to a TCP/IP port for connections (by default, it listens on port 5432).

Once the postmaster detects a connection on its listening port, it acts as a dispatcher for the connection (thus the name *postmaster,* since it is *dispatching* the request). The postmaster dispatches the request by starting a separate postgres process to perform the work required for the connection. From this point forward, the client process that requested the connection will communicate with the postgres process, submitting requests in the form of SQL statements and returning required results to the client.

Since PostgreSQL is a multiuser database, the problems of concurrent multiuser access to shared data must be managed. This means multiple server processes (postgres) working with clients must be able to communicate quickly and effectively. This is accomplished using semaphores (flags supported by the OS kernel) and shared memory. Multiple postgres back-end processes share information about their work in a common location. Before

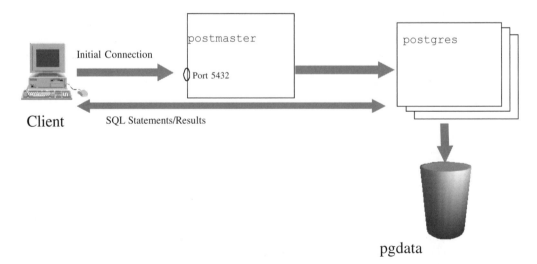

Figure 3.1 PostgreSQL Operational Components

any data are accessed in a database table, appropriate flags are tested and set to preserve data integrity in the database.

A directory referred to as the PGDATA *directory* (as determined by environment variables or runtime flags passed to the postmaster program) contains the configuration files for the database and, in subdirectories of the main PGDATA directory, the data for the database.

Installing PostgreSQL

The PostgreSQL database is included in most Linux distributions. It has also recently been ported to NT using the Cygwin library. It can be downloaded from the postgresql.org FTP site using the URL ftp://ftp.postgresql.org/pub. Installation on Linux using the Red Hat Package Manager (RPM) could be accomplished using the following command (for the Mandrake distribution):

```
rpm -i postgresql-6.5.3-1mdk.i586.rpm
```

Two directories are important to the operation of PostgreSQL: the PGLIB and PGDATA directories. The PGLIB directory contains the source and library files needed for the PostgreSQL applications to run. The PGDATA directory contains the database data files and configuration files for the installation. On Linux platforms under PostgreSQL version 7.0.2, the PGDATA directory is assigned to /var/lib/pgsql/data, and the PGLIB directory is set to /usr/lib/pgsql.

The defaults for these installation parameters can be changed by setting their values using environment variables as shown below. Additionally, it is a good idea to add the pgsql/bin directory to the PATH environment variable used on the installation machine. A ksh shell script to set these values is shown below.

```
PATH=$PATH:/usr/local/pgsql/bin
PGLIB=/usr/local/pgsql/lib
PGDATA=/usr/local/pgsql/data
export PATH PGLIB PGDATA
```

The JDBC driver should be included as part of the distribution. This driver is essentially a Java JAR file (a compressed set of Java class files) that provide the JDBC API with a means of accessing the database, a process that is necessary for the JSP examples in this book.

The installation process will place the necessary binaries and library files on the target system. A number of applications are contained in the PostgreSQL installation. Some of the more commonly used applications and their purpose are described in Table 3.1.

Table 3.1 PostgreSQL Applications

Application	Purpose
createdb	Creates a new database
createuser	Creates a new user account
destroydb	Destroys a database
destroyuser	Deletes a user account
initdb	Initializes a PostgreSQL database instance
initlocation	Initializes a location
pgaccess	Graphical PostgreSQL client (similar to psql but with a GUI interface)
pgadmin	Graphical PostgreSQL administrative client (requires installation of an additional RPM file)
pg_dump	Dumps a database into a file
pg_dumpall	Dumps all databases for this instance into a file
postgres	Runs a single-user back end (like postmaster, but for a single user)
postmaster	Runs a multiuser back end
psql	Interactive character-based client for database interaction
vacuumdb	Cleans the database by physically removing deleted records and performing other housekeeping functions

But the installation process alone is not enough to begin using PostgreSQL; before PostgreSQL can be started, a number of directories and files (loosely referred to as a *database* in the PostgreSQL installation documentation) must be created, as explained below. A database installation contains the data directories and configuration files that PostgreSQL requires to operate. These directories and files are located primarily under the PGDATA directory (which is specified via command line arguments to applications or through environment variables). The files under this directory are listed in Table 3.2.

Table 3.2 PGDATA Directory Files

File	Purpose
PG_VERSION	Version information for the installation
pg_database	Contains the database files
pg_hba.conf	Accesses permissions for database users
pg_pwd	PostgreSQL password file; used only if the PostgreSQL system has been configured to use its own passwords instead of the Unix password file
pg_variable	Used internally by PostgreSQL database; holds the next object id and the next transaction id
pg_group	Group permissions table
pg_shadow	Shadow password file; used only if shadow passwords have been configured for the system
pg_log	Used internally by the PostgreSQL database; stores the status of the transaction log

The database data files are contained in a subdirectory under the $PGDATA/base directory. Each database within the system is represented by a subdirectory under this directory. For instance, a database named user_preferences would create a directory $PGDATA/base/user_preferences.

The PostgreSQL installation requires a user named postgres to be present on the system. This user will be the default database administrator (the database *superuser*) for any database created in the instance and will be the user that will start the postmaster database process.

Creating the Database Files and Directories

Fortunately, the PostgreSQL distribution does not require the manual creation of all files and directories required. A utility named initdb is included in the distribution to create these files. Running this utility with the correct parameters will create the database. Once the database has been created, the postmaster SQL daemon can be started to provide access to the database. When the postmaster daemon is running, users can connect to the database using psql with a character front end or pgaccess with a GUI front end. The steps to creating and using the PostreSQL database are therefore as indicated in Table 3.3.

Table 3.3 PostreSQL Database Creation

Action	Command
Create `postgres` user	`adduser postgres`
Install binaries (RPM)	`rpm -i <distribution name>`
Initialize the database	`initdb <parameters>`
Start database daemon	`postmaster <parameters>`
Create a new database	`createdb <parameters>`
Connect to the database	`psql <parameters> | pgaccess` `<parameters>`

(*Note:* If installing from the RPM file, the `postgres` user may already have been created.)

Once the database has been built, the process for starting the database daemon can be placed in a startup script under Linux. When this has been done, the process of using the database will involve little more than executing `psql` or `pgaccess` to provide a client front end for the database.

Next, we describe the process of installation in more detail, including the execution of each command.

initdb Command

The `initdb` script is run with a series of command line arguments that create the appropriate files and directories for a PostgreSQL database instance. Note that a database instance can contain one or more databases. The syntax for this command is

```
initdb [ —pgdata=dbdir | -r dbdir ]
    [ —pglib=libdir | -l libdir ]
    [ —template=template | -t template ]
    [ —username=name | -u name ]
    [ —noclean | -n ] [ —debug | -d ]
```

The arguments passed to this command define how and where the files for the PostgreSQL installation will be installed. Environment variables can be substituted for most of the command line arguments. Generally, this command is just run with a few command line arguments to specify the directory where the data will be stored (`PGDATA`) and the user name for the superuser for the database (the user who will own the database tables or relations).

The two most important parameters are `PGLIB` and `PGDATA`. The `PGLIB` parameter defines where the library files for the database instance will belong. The `PGDATA` directory describes where the data directories for the database instance will belong. These and other parameters to the `initdb` command are described in more detail below.

Database Sizing

It is important to note that the expected size of the database and the behavior of the PostgreSQL `vacuum` command should be considered when deciding where to locate the database files. When the PostgreSQL `vacuum` command is used to clean a database, a copy is made of the original database, thus doubling the size of the database. So if the database is expected to grow to 300 megabytes in size, the location for the data directory for the database should have at least 600 megabytes (300 x 2) of available space.

PGLIB Parameter: —pglib=libdir, -l libdir, PGLIB

The `pglib` directory argument identifies the directory that contains the library files for the PostgreSQL installation. These files describe the distribution and also contain files used to execute the programs for the installation. This directory is identified when the software is compiled. For most installations, this directory is `/usr/lib/pgsql`.

PGDATA Parameter: —pgdata=dbdir, -r dbdir, PGDATA

The `pgdata` directory is the top-level directory for the database. Below this directory are the data files that comprise the PostgreSQL database.

PGUSER Parameter : —username=name, -u name, PGUSER

The `username` parameter identifies the user who will effectively be the database administrator for the database, the database superuser. This is usually the user `postgres`. Note that only the superuser (root) can create a database system for an owner other than the `postgres` superuser. (It is considered a security flaw to create a database owned by the user `root`.)

TEMPLATE Parameter: —template=template, -t template

The template parameter identifies the template that will be used to create the database. The template describes the basic configuration for creation of the database. Usually, the default template (template1) is adequate for this parameter, but in cases where the database is corrupted or the database needs to be upgraded, this parameter may be set to some other value.

NOCLEAN Parameter: —noclean, -n

By default, the initdb program will clean the database and remove any files that are not needed to complete the installation. This option tells the init-db program not to perform the cleaning operation. Unless there is a reason to perform debug operations after the database is created, it is best to let init-db clean up after creating the database.

DEBUG Parameter: —debug, -d

The debug option instructs the initdb program to print copious debug information during the installation process. This option also tells initdb not to perform the final PostgreSQL vacuum operation (to physically remove deleted records). Unless there are problems with the installation that could possibly be fixed using debug information, this parameter should not be used.

Creating the Database Instance

After running the initdb command, a database instance is created. The instance contains a file and data area but is not an actual database. A default database, the template1 database, is available but should not be used, since this database represents a template for other databases to be used.

An actual database in PostgreSQL represents the collection of tables that is relevant to the applications that will use the database. An application may use just one database or may use several databases, depending on the logical organization required. A great deal could be said about the process of data modeling, but that is beyond the scope of this book. Suffice it to say, data to be stored in the PostgreSQL database should be stored in one or more databases, as needed.

Databases can be created using either a client program such as psql or pgaccess or the createdb command and creating the database from the command line. A database is created internally by PostgreSQL by creating a physical directory under PGDATA/base directory with the same name as the database, and creating a number of database catalog tables to store information about the objects (classes, data types, tables, columns, views) in the database. The syntax for the createdb command is

```
createdb -a <authtype> -h  <server> -p <portnumber>
-D <location> [dbname]
```

The dbname parameter is the name of the database to create. If omitted, a database with the name of the user executing the command is created.

The authtype parameter indicates the authentication type to be used by the database. This is used only if security parameters have been established by using entries in the pg_hba.conf file. The server parameter is used to indicate the host name of the server to connect to for the database connection. The portnumber is the port number for the database connection. The location is the location of an alternative directory for the database. The default is the PGDATA directory of the current database instance. This parameter affects the location of all database tables, including the system catalog tables.

All parameters are optional. If run with no parameters, the createdb command will attempt to create a database with the name of the user executing the command. (For example, user "fred" running the createdb command with no parameters would create a database named fred in the default PGDATA directory, which may not necessarily be what the user intended.)

The createdb command creates a database to which the user executing the command is the superuser or database administrator. Alternatively, the database can be created by accessing the database instance through a client access tool (psql or pgaccess), attaching to the template1 database (the default database), and executing the SQL create database statement as follows:

```
create database testdb;
```

Executing this command will create the testdb database in the default PGDATA directory for the database instance.

Identifying Database Users: The pg_hba.conf File

Once the database has been created using the initdb command, the database permissions should be set in the pg_hba.conf file in the PGDATA directory. Two types of parameters are present in this file: *local* connection parameters for users connecting from the local host, and *host* parameters for users accessing the system from a remote location. The format of the host parameter within this file is as follows:

```
host <dbname> <ipaddress> <address_mask>
    <user_authorization> <authorization_argument>
```

Table 3.4 identifies the arguments to each parameter.

Table 3.4 Host Parameter Arguments

Parameter	Description
dbname	Database name for the user to connection
ipaddress	IP address from which the database connection will be made
address_mask	Address mask for the IP address parameter
user_authorization	Authorization allowed for this host
authorization_argument	Authorization argument for this host

A standard set of entries to allow local access to a database could be set as follows:

```
local   all                  trust
host    all   127.0.0.1      255.255.255.255   trust
```

For security reasons, the file system permissions on the pg_hba.conf file should be very restrictive, preferably set to read/write permissions for the database administrator user (usually, user postgres) and to no access for all other users.

Running the postmaster Process

The postmaster process is the back-end process that accepts connections to the PostgreSQL database and then spawns back-end server processes (instances of the postgres application) to manage these requests. It is effectively a broker between the front-end client requests and the back-end PostgreSQL process, which manages the front-end database request.

The postmaster process allocates shared memory buffers and initializes locking mechanisms to manage the front-end connection but does not interact with the front-end process; that is left to the back-end process, which `post-master` will spawn. Only one `postmaster` process should be started for a database directory (`PGDATA`). If additional database directories are being used, more than one `postmaster` process can be started.

The `postmaster` process is used for multiuser access to a single PostgreSQL database. This process is usually executed by the `postgres` system user, but this is not required. For security reasons it is important that the `postmaster` process not be started by the system user `root`. This process can be started from the command line and takes the following arguments:

```
postmaster [ -B nBuffers ] [ -D DataDir ] [ -i ]
postmaster [ -B nBuffers ] [ -D DataDir ] [ -N nBackends ] [ -S ]
   [ -d [ DebugLevel ] [ -i ] [ -o BackendOptions ] [ -p port ]
postmaster [ -n | -s ] ...
```

These command options are covered in detail in the following sections.

Buffers Option Parameter: -B <buffers>

This parameter specifies the number of shared-memory buffers that will be allocated to the database. Each buffer is sized to the `BLKSIZE` parameter in `config.h`, which usually represents 8K bytes of data.

Data Directory Parameter: -D <Data Directory>

This parameter specifies where the `postmaster` process will find the data directory containing the database instance to use. This directory must contain a valid PostgreSQL data directory (as created by `initdb`). If this parameter is not passed to the `postmaster` command, the value of the `PGDATA` environment variable will be used. If the `PGDATA` environment variable is not set, the value of the `POSTGRESHOME` environment variable will be used. If neither of these variables is set, the default directory set when the `postmaster` process was compiled will be used.

Number of Backends Parameter: -N nBackends

As `postmaster` accepts front-end connections, it allocates the connection to a back-end process. This parameter sets a limit on the number of back-end processes. The default is usually set to 32 but can be set as high as 1024. (Optionally, the `postmaster` build/compilation can set this number even higher.)

Silent Mode Operation Parameter: -S

This parameter indicates that `postmaster` will start in *silent* mode. The `postmaster` process will run in the background and create its own process group. Any output to standard error will be discarded.

Setting the Debug Level Parameter: -d <debug level>

This parameter sets the amount of debug information that will be output by the `postmaster` process. The debug output levels are given in Table 3.5.

Table 3.5 Debug Output Levels

Level	Output
1	Traces all connection traffic
2	Connection, back-end environment, and process traffic
3	Includes output of levels 1 and 2 plus additional information

Communication with postmaster Parameter: -i

This option allows `postmaster` to accept connections via TCP/IP sockets. If this option is not set, only local Unix domain sockets will be used.

Passing Options to the Backend Parameter: -o BackendOptions

This parameter is used to pass additional options to the back-end processes started by `postmaster`. These options are a subset of the `postgres` application options available and are generally used for debugging purposes.

Specifying a Connection Port Parameter: -p port

This parameter is used to specify the port to be used for connection to the `postmaster` process. The default port is 5432 and can be overridden by this parameter. Alternatively, this parameter can be set using the PGPORT environment variable. This is usually changed only if there is a contention for the default port or if there is a security reason to use a less common port number.

Starting the postmaster Process at System Boot Time

The `postmaster` process is usually started as a background process, not attached to a particular terminal, although this is not a requirement. This is a convenience issue, since it is usually best to run daemon/service processes as detached, background processes. The Unix `nohup` process, which allows a process to detach from a terminal without being killed (-SIGHUP) if the terminal closes, could be used as follows:

```
nohup postmaster -i
```

Note that the `postmaster` process should be run by the user `postgres`; running `postmaster` as the user `root` represents a serious security hole.

In a production environment, the `postmaster` process is usually started in a batch startup script during the system boot process. In Red Hat distributions, this directory is in the `/etc/rc.d/init.d` directory. In this directory a script file named `postgresql` will be launched by the boot process to start the `postmaster` process. (This script is installed automatically with the RPM file in the Red Hat distribution.) In this script file the `su` command is used to start `postmaster` as the user `postgres` as shown below.

```
su postgres -c "/usr/local/pgsql/bin/postmaster -S -D
/usr/local/pgsql/data"
```

Configuring PostgreSQL

PostgreSQL requires minimal configuration. What needs to be determined is how the database will be run. Optionally, connections to the database can use either a TCP/IP connection or can connect directly to the database. Security for database connections is defined by entries made in the `pg_hba.conf` file, as shown previously. Security once the user is connected to the database is controlled using a set of SQL statements. These statements are as follows:

```
GRANT <privilege1, privelege2, ... > ON <rel1, rel2, ...>   TO
{ PUBLIC | GROUP group | username }
```

Privileges can be assigned as noted in Table 3.6.

Table 3.6 PostgresSQL Security Privilege Names

Privilege Name	Description
ALL	All available permissions on the table are assigned to the user.
SELECT	User is assigned select permission for the table.
INSERT	User has permission to insert into the table.
UPDATE	User has permission to update the table.
DELETE	User has permission to delete rows from the table.
RULE	User has permission to create or delete a RULE for the table. (PostgreSQL RULEs are actions that can be assigned to certain operations on a relation or table; these are referred to as *triggers* by other database vendors.)

A Relation Is a Class Is a Table

The PostgreSQL database documentation refers to the sets of attributes in a database as *relations* (since they represent groupings or relations of attributes). Relations are effectively tables (or *classes* as PostgreSQL documentation refers to them). (Note that one of the more significant features of PostgreSQL is that these tables can form the basis for the creation of the other tables through *inheritance*.)

Table permissions can be related to users or to groups. The ability to relate permissions to groups allows certain permission roles to be grouped together. As users are added to the database, they are added to the permission groups. This could be a timesaver in a database where a large number of users may be added.

On a Web site it is possible that for convenience, access to the database may be distilled to a small number of user ids. Thus users who may be accessing a certain portion of a site could be designated as shopping users and will access the database by proxy as `shopping_user`. A user who will administer the site will be allowed to access the site as user `administrator`.

Using the JDBC Driver

Java provides the JDBC API for database connectivity. This API contains a number of classes and methods to access data stored in relational databases. JDBC is a vendor-neutral API that can communicate with any relational database for which there is a driver. JDBC is based on the X/Open CLI, the standard on which ODBC is based.

Before JDBC can communicate with a database, the *driver* for that database must be loaded. The job of the driver is to map the JDBC method calls for database access to the proprietary protocol used by the various database vendors. To this extent, the JDBC database driver is a middleman between the database application and the actual database. JDBC drivers have historically been classified as being type 1, 2, 3, or 4 (see Table 3.7).

Table 3.7 JDBC Driver Types

Driver Type	Description
1	JDBC–ODBC bridge; maps JDBC calls to ODBC calls, which are then mapped to the database vendor's native protocol; requires ODBC driver and probably, a driver from the database vendor
2	JDBC calls are mapped to native API calls; not a pure-Java solution; requires database vendor libraries
3	JDBC calls are mapped to a vendor-neutral protocol, which is then translated into the native protocol for the database vendor; requires vendor-neutral database driver (middleware)
4	JDBC calls are mapped to the native protocol for the database vendor using pure-Java code; requires vendor's JDBC driver

The quickest, most efficient solution is considered to be the Type 4 JDBC driver, since this driver, does not require a number of intermediary steps to execute database access. The Type 4 driver is also the easiest to deploy, since the driver itself is just another Java class to include in the Java compilation (in the CLASSPATH). Most database vendors will now provide a Type 4 JDBC driver free of charge. Included with this driver will be sample applications which demonstrate the URL and class name required to load and use the JDBC driver in Java applications.

Loading the DriverManager Class

Note that when the database driver is loaded, the Java code does not return an object reference for the driver loaded—it merely loads the class. Loading a class in Java is usually performed transparently when a program starts. When a Java program is compiled, the compiler identifies the classes that are used by the program and creates instructions for the JVM to load these classes when the program is executed.

Since JDBC allows a number of drivers to be loaded and since the choice of drivers may vary, the loading of the driver class is not known at compile time and must be identified at runtime using the steps described here. Note that a program is not limited to loading just one driver—multiple drivers may be loaded at runtime.

As part of the driver loading process, the driver must register itself with the driver manager. The driver manager in JDBC tracks all the drivers that have been loaded. When a connection is requested the driver manager must choose the correct driver. The driver can be loaded in a number of different ways. The major difference between the various approaches is whether or not to load the driver with parameters that are interpreted at runtime or to use a static string in the program (i.e., hardcode) driver parameters. The benefits of loading the driver parameters at runtime are obvious, and this is therefore the recommended method, but both approaches will be shown.

Getting the Driver Information at Runtime

Since JDBC is a vendor-neutral API, the application is not sensitive to the driver or database being used (this is in theory—see "Loading the Driver Manager Class"). This means that the driver which is performing the low-level protocol to communicate with the database can be changed without affecting the application; therefore, the name of the driver to load could change. This being the case, it would be wise to dynamically load the driver when the application starts. This can be accomplished in one of several ways, as discussed in the following sections.

Loading a JDBC driver essentially means loading the class. This involves a single Java API call using the `Class.forName` method of the redundantly named `Class` class:

```
...
Class.forName("xxxx.xxxx.com.JDBCDriver");
...
```

Note that this call does not capture a return parameter, since it is effectively not needed. What we need to do is load the class. We do not need a reference to any object; we only need access to `Class` and its methods.

To load a driver dynamically we need to receive a parameter on the command line. We can receive this parameter either as an argument to the program being run (one of the main `String[] args` parameters), or better yet, we can receive the parameter as a property that clearly identifies the purpose of the parameter, as shown below.

```
java myprog -Djdbc-driver=dbdriver.xx.com
```

This parameter or property, passed on the command line, is retrieved in the program using the following call:

```
String jdbcDriver = System.getProperty("jdbc-driver");
```

Once this property is retrieved into a string containing the driver name, we can then load the driver using the `Class.forName` method:

```
Class.forName( jdbcDriver );
```

Alternatively, in what may be the best approach, we can load the properties from a *properties file*. A properties file contains a series of name–value pairs with the format

```
jdbc-driver: postgresql.Driver
jdbc-url:
jdbc:postgresql://localhost/test1;user=puser;password=puser;
```

The properties file is read at runtime, and any property value needed is loaded into a string using the `getProperty` method of the `Properties` class, as shown in the following code fragment.

```
...

Properties p = new Properties();

// read the properties from the JDBC.prop file
p.load(new FileInputStream( "JDBC.prop") );

// get properties values for specific keys
String JDBCDriver  = p.getProperty("jdbc-driver");
String JDBCurl     = p.getProperty("JDBC-url");

// load the JDBC driver - throws Exceptions caught below
Class.forName( JDBCDriver );

// open a connection using the DriverManager
    Connection conn = DriverManager.getConnection( JDBCurl );

...
```

Note that the property name in the `getProperty` call is case-sensitive. Failure to find the property key requested returns a null object reference and does not throw an exception.

Once the property has been loaded into a `String` in this manner, the `Class.forName` method call can be used, as shown previously to load the driver class. Once the driver class has been loaded, we can begin using the JDBC driver. To access the database, we must first obtain a connection using the `getConnection` method of the `DriverManager` class, as shown below.

```
...
Connection conn = DriverManager.getConnection(JDBCurl);
...
```

The uniform resource locator (URL) is a string that provides information on connecting to the database. The format for this string is

```
...
String connURL =
"jdbc:postgresql://localhost/test1;user=puser;password=puser;";
...
```

If the JDBC driver name is being loaded dynamically at runtime, it makes good sense to load the connection URL in the same manner, since if the name of the driver has changed the contents of the connection URL may also have changed.

Together, these API calls allow a connection to the database. Once a connection is made, an SQL `Statement` object is instantiated and SQL statements can be executed. This process is fairly straightforward, as shown in the following complete code block.

```
public static void main( String[] args ) {
try {
        Properties p = new Properties();
        p.load(new FileInputStream( "JDBC.prop") );


        String JDBCDriver   = p.getProperty("jdbc-driver");
        String JDBCurl      = p.getProperty("JDBC-url");
        String javaVMVersion = System.getProperty("java.vm.version");

        Class.forName( JDBCDriver );
        Connection conn = DriverManager.getConnection( JDBCurl );
        Statement stmt = conn.createStatement();
```

```
        ResultSet rs = stmt.executeQuery( "select * from customer" );
        boolean more = rs.next();
        while ( more ) {
                System.out.println("last_name: " +
rs.getString("last_name") +
                                    " first_name: " + rs.getString(
"first_name" )                    more = rs.next();
        }

    conn.close();
}
catch (IOException e) {
 e.printStackTrace();
}
catch (ClassNotFoundException e) {
   System.out.println("Could not load class: " + e.getMessage());
}

catch (SQLException e) {
    System.out.println("JDBC error: " + e.getMessage() );
}
}
```

The first step in this example is to load the driver, which is accomplished with a call to the `Class.forName` method. If the driver load process were to fail, various exceptions would be thrown and program execution would stop. If the driver has loaded successfully, we can then call the `getConnection` method in the `DriverManager` to obtain a connection. Calling this method (as well as most other JDBC methods) throws an `SQLException` if it fails and requires that an `SQLException` be caught in the code block in which it is executed.

A connection represents a *handle* for database operations. Without a connection, no work can be performed in the database. This object will manage the input and output of database operations. In the course of the application, various objects will be created to interact with the database. The hierarchy of these objects is shown in Figure 3.2.

Virtually all relational databases are multiuser and can therefore manage multiple connections from multiple users. These connections need not be from different physical users or processes. Since Java is inherently multithreaded, it is possible for a single application to have multiple threads which need to interact with the database. The use of multiple connections within a single application must be considered carefully and managed appropriately.

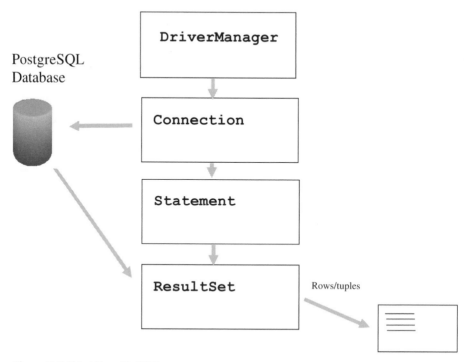

Figure 3.2 Object Use with JDBC

The issue of connections becomes even more important when performing database input/output on a Web site where a large number of users may be accessing the site performing relatively small database transactions. There is a certain amount of overhead associated with creating a database connection; the database must allocate internal memory and set locks. The consumption of this overhead can slow the performance of the client application and the database in general. It is best to avoid this overhead whenever possible by creating a connection and then reusing that connection for multiple database transactions.

Additionally, there is usually some limit to the number of user connections a database can support. Although this number is large and in some ways depends on the machine resources available on the server platform, it does exist and must be factored into the application design process. In the world of client–server applications, connections were generally not a problem. A client–server application could create a connection and keep the connection open for the duration of the application, however long that might be. The number of potential database connections would be roughly equal to the number of potential users who would have access to the system. For most client–server applications, this number was never very large.

But the World Wide Web is not client–server; Web sites are often visible to the Internet at large and have the potential for a large number of users to access the site. It is not uncommon for a relatively medium-sized site to support several thousand user connections within a day. Internet connections through a Web site have a different transactional footprint than that of client–server. Client–server applications had a small number of connections which performed a large amount of work. Conversely, Web applications have a large number of connections that generally perform a small amount of work. These transactions are small, short, and discrete and usually do not concern themselves with the work of other transactions that may be occurring on the system.

Since there may not be a real way to change the transaction profile of a Web user, the appropriate connection for a Web application should be lightweight, able to manage a large number of small, discrete transactions. These connections are often managed with a *connection pool*, a set of database connections that have been created and are available as needed to application threads. When a connection in the pool is closed, a lightweight close operation is performed that merely sets a flag in the pool and maintains the true database connection, thus avoiding the overhead of creating and breaking database connections multiple times for a large number of users.

`Statement` object is created from the connection. It is through the statement object that actual database work is performed using the `executeQuery` and `executeUpdate` methods and passing them various SQL statements to execute. After executing the SQL Query statement, these methods return `ResultSet` objects. By iterating through the `ResultSet` object, the results of the query can be discerned.

Information about the contents of a `ResultSet` can be gleaned using the `ResultSetMetaData` object. This object allows a `ResultSet` object to be examined to determine the number of columns in the `ResultSet`, the data types of those columns, and other useful information. This allows data queries to be dealt with in a general manner and allows flexible applications to be created where queries are constructed at runtime based on user input.

The `ResultSet` has a series of `getXX` methods to retrieve the column data in the `ResultSet`. These methods are overloaded to retrieve the data using the relative ordinal position of the column from left to right, or using the name of the column as shown below.

```
. . .
ResultSet rs = stmt.executeQuery(
"select first_name, last_name from customers");
String firstName1 = rs.getString(1);
String firstName2 = rs.getString("first_name");
. . .
```

In the example above, the `getString` method of `ResultSet` is first called using the position of the column as an argument to the method. The result of this call is the string representing the `first_name` column. The next call to the same method overloads the method to retrieve the column value using the column name as the argument. This call also returns the result of the call as a string. The `ResultSet` class includes other `getXX` methods that are available for the various primitive data types, as shown in Table 3.8.

Table 3.8 JDBC `getXX` Methods

Method	Description
getInt	Return `Int` data
getfloat	Return `Float` primitive data type
getString	Returns `String` data object reference
getLong	Returns `Long` primitive data type
getDouble	Returns `Double` primitive data type
getByte	Returns `Byte` primitive data type
getBoolean	Return `Boolean` primitive data type

Other `getXX` methods are available to retrieve many of the more common data types implemented by database vendors. For instance, `getBigDecimal` retrieves an object reference to a `BigDecimal` data type which supports the large decimal numbers that many database vendors provide as column data types.

SQL Results

It is often the case that execution of an SQL statement that can return rows does not. This is not an error per se; from the perspective of the database an SQL statement requested a set that is in fact the *empty set*. In JDBC this empty set is revealed with an initial call to `ResultSet.next` method, which would return a boolean false. It is a common programming error not to check for this condition.

The process of checking for the return of an empty set is fairly simple. Program logic must determine whether or not the first call to the `ResultSet.next` method has returned false. An example of this logic is shown in the following code fragment.

```
. . .
String  firstName = null;
String lastName = null;
. . .
boolean more = rs.next();
if ( more ) {
    while ( more ) {
        firstName = rs.getString("first_name");
        lastName  = rs.getString("last_name" );
        System.out.println("First Name: " + firstName +
                            "Last Name: " + lastName );
        . . .
                  more = rs.next();
    }
} else
{
System.out.println("No rows found.");
return;
}
. . .
```

The first call to the `rs.next` method positions the result set pointer at the first row and returns a boolean value indicating whether or not there is a row at the pointer. In this example, the results of the first call to `rs.next` are captured in a `boolean` variable. The value of this variable is used in the conditional statement to test for a "no rows found" condition. If the conditional statement determines that rows have been found (more = true), it branches to a section of code that iterates through the results. If it determines that no rows have been found, it branches to a section of code that prints an error message and returns.

Summary

This chapter covered the database portion of the Java Web site. Without the database, development of a dynamic site is virtually impossible. For our sample development environment, we have chosen the PostgreSQL database. This relational database contains a surprising number of features and is designed to scale up to a reasonable user load. As the name implies, the PostgreSQL database supports a very rich implementation of SQL as a query language (a superset of the SQL92 and SQL3 implementation of the language).

The installation of PostgreSQL is straightforward and is preinstalled with many Linux versions, thus precluding the installation step in its entirety. PostgreSQL can be configured by making entries in various configuration files in the directory defined by the `PGDATA` environment variable. Alternatively, some GUI tools are available to provide a simplified access to the database for querying and administration.

Since we will be accessing the database using the Java language, the JDBC API is a required component of our infrastructure. JDBC requires a database driver from the database vendor to be able to communicate with the database. Fortunately for us, the industrious development community that is our *vendor* has provided a database driver for JDBC. Although not always installed as part of the standard installation process, an installation package should be available either on a CD with the Linux distribution, or from one of the many open-source software sites on the Internet (see Appendix C).

Coming Up Next

In Chapter 4 we cover the final component of our infrastructure: the Tomcat JSP/servlet server. This final piece of our architecture will allow us to use the Java language to provide dynamic content for our site. We discuss the installation and configuration of the Tomcat server. In Chapter 4 we begin our discussion of the Java tools we will use to program the site—JSPs, JavaBeans, tag libraries, and servlets—and introduce the technologies. In the remainder of the book we provide a tutorial on these technologies using various examples.

BUILDING THE JAVA WEB SITE: THE TOMCAT SERVER

Introduction

In Chapter 2 we covered the installation and configuration of the Apache HTTP server. We plan to use the Apache server to serve relatively static HTML pages and potentially to provide user authentication for our site. In Chapter 3 we covered the installation and configuration of the PostgreSQL database server, which will be used to store and retrieve the data for our site.

We now have two pieces of our site architecture, the Web server and the database, but we do not have the ability to connect these two pieces. Although Apache can generate limited dynamic content using server-side includes (SSIs), it does not provide robust programming logic or the ability to retrieve data stored in a relational database. To build interesting, dynamic Web pages we need the ability to retrieve data from a database and apply appropriate business logic to the data before completing the presentation page. The capability to perform these functions will be provided by the middle tier (see Figure 4.1).

We need a server component for the middle tier: an application that can communicate with the Apache Web server, apply business logic as needed while dynamically building Web pages, and then return the results to the client browser. Since we have already established the benefits of using Java technologies, our basic requirement for this server is that it can manage the

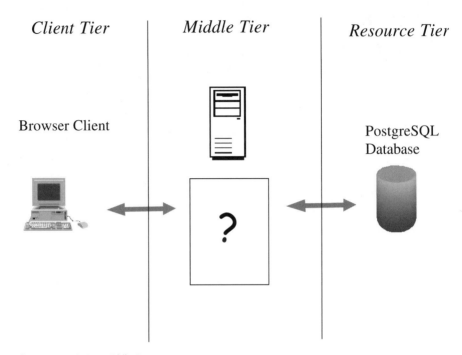

Figure 4.1 Missing Middle Tier

Java technologies we intend to use on the Web site: JSPs and servlets; it will be a *Java server*.

Because this tier lies in the middle between the client (the front end) and the data (the back end), it has sometimes been referred to as *middleware*, although in recent years that term has largely been replaced by the term *application server*, *Web infrastructure*, or a vast array of marketing terms that change daily. For our purposes in this book, we refer to the middle tier as a *Java server*.

In this chapter we cover the Tomcat server, detailing both the installation and configuration of the server. The basic operation of the Tomcat server, how its processes run, and how it is integrated with the Apache HTTP server are explained. The Tomcat server is a very flexible piece of software. This flexibility is reflected in its various configuration files and their numerous parameters. This configuration file (as of version 3.3 milestone 1) and its parameters, contexts, and containers are covered in some detail in this chapter.

Tomcat Server

The Tomcat server fulfills all our basic requirements for this tier and more, fits neatly into our site architecture (see Figure 4.2), and includes a number of production features (in versions 3.3 and 4.0) usually found only in high-end application servers, features such as load balancing (with mod_jk) and SSL encryption.

The Tomcat server provides what its developers refer to as a *JSP environment* and a *servlet container.* The JSP environment provides the preprocessor that is responsible for converting the JSP file to a servlet. The servlet container then provides the various services needed for executing servlets. The Tomcat server therefore provides the ability to execute Java code for the Web site, in the form of either a JSP or a servlet. This meets our requirement of being able to process business logic in our middle tier but does not directly address our requirement to access the data for the site.

Using the JDBC (Java Database Connectivity) API provided by Java, Java applications can access database content using a standard API. The API is essentially a set of interfaces defined by Sun that must be implemented by database vendors in their *JDBC driver*. Once the JDBC driver is loaded by the application, the application can access a database using the JDBC classes and methods.

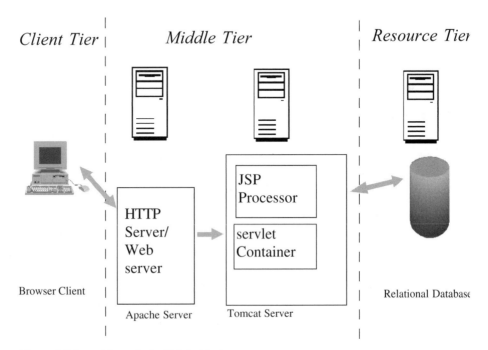

Figure 4.2 Tomcat Server in the Web Architecture

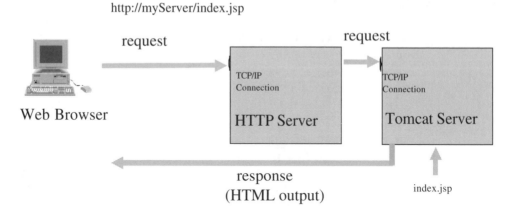

Figure 4.3 Apache and Tomcat Process a Request

Tomcat and Apache Together

The Tomcat server works with the Apache HTTP server to provide the capability to deliver dynamic Web site content. For our purposes, both Tomcat and the Apache server represent distinct applications (although it is possible to run Tomcat as *in-process* within Apache, we do not use this approach in this book), what would be distinct processes under Unix or distinct services under the Windows NT environment. These two applications communicate using TCP/IP sockets. This communication usually begins with the Apache server informing the Tomcat server that it has a request for it to process (probably a reference to a JSP or servlet). Part of the information provided by the HTTP server to the Tomcat server is *response* information for the request that informs the Tomcat server where to return the output for the request once it has completed processing it. Once Tomcat has completed processing the request, it returns its results to the client (probably a browser) in the form of a response (see Figure 4.3).

Processing Environment

The developers of Tomcat consider it to be a *servlet container* with a *JSP environment*. As such, it converts JSP into servlets and then executes the servlets within its servlet container. The servlet container provides the services for the servlet to execute at runtime. Servlet containers can be considered to be one of the three following types of containers.

Standalone Servlet Containers

A standalone servlet container is a container that is part of the Web server being used. This requires a Java-based Web server (such as JavaWebServer), and since there are not many Java-based Web servers, this is not the most common servlet container. The Tomcat container can optionally be used as a standalone server, in which case it will serve both static HTML (just like Apache) or will process and serve JSP and servlets.

But there are good reasons not to use Tomcat in standalone mode. Unlike Apache, Tomcat has not been optimized for serving HTML pages and will not scale as well as Apache. Additionally, Apache provides several useful facilities that can provide some dynamic content [e.g., server-side includes (SSIs)] and do not require the overhead of JSPs and servlets.

In-Process Servlet Containers

The in-process servlet container is a combination of a Web server executing a JVM through a Web server plug-in within its internal memory space. This JVM, in turn, executes the servlet by passing the servlet to the servlet container. This solution provides good performance at low loads but does not provide extensive scalability for busier sites.

Out-of-Process Servlet Containers

An out-of-process servlet container uses separate processes for the JVM container and the Web server. The JVM (and the servlet container) operate outside the address space of the Web server. The Web server communicates with the servlet container using some IPC facility (usually, TCP/IP sockets). If the browser requests a JSP or a servlet, the request is passed to the servlet container via the IPC connection, and it is then the responsibility of the servlet container to fulfill the request.

As mentioned previously, although there is some overhead to passing information back and forth between separate processes, this solution is more scalable, allowing heavier user loads. There is also added stability to running distinct processes; should one process fail for some reason, the other processes will probably continue to process, allowing some portion of the Web site to continue operating. This stability is not usually present in applications where multiple threads perform different functions and the failure of one thread runs the risk of causing the entire process to fail.

Tomcat Is Not Jserv

Tomcat was preceded by an Apache organization project known as Jserv, a servlet container. The Tomcat code is *not* Jserv. Tomcat represents a complete rewrite of the servlet container for Jserv. The Tomcat project also adds the JSP environment and the significant code that manages the operation of compiling and executing JSP in an efficient manner.

JSP Environment

A JSP environment involves the processing of the JSP file, essentially the conversion of the file into a servlet. Any set of HTML tags in the JSP file that are not Java code, which would be HTML tags, their attributes, and any related text, are converted into output statements which are then written to the output stream. The output stream is the response to the request that the client has presented to the server.

Any section of the JSP file that contains Java code is converted into a block of code within the resulting servlet, so that resulting output of this processing operation is a servlet that will produce an HTML page that will be the response to be sent to the client. (This process is described in more detail in Chapter 5.)

Installation of Tomcat

The Tomcat server requires that Java be installed on the machine where Tomcat is to be run. Specifically, a Java development environment must be installed, not just a runtime environment, since the JSP and servlets must be compiled into Java byte code. (As of this writing, the current Java development kit can be found at the URL `http://java.sun.com/j2se/1.3.`). The process of installing Tomcat is relatively simple. The appropriate file, whether a `zip` format or `tar format` or `gzip format` file, should be downloaded from the `jakarta.apache.org` Web site (current URL `http://jakarta.apache.org/tomcat/index.html`).

A directory should be created for installation of the Tomcat files and an environment variable set to the value of this directory. The directory below which the Tomcat server is installed is referred to as the `TOMCAT_HOME` directory. There is no specific requirement to set an environment variable named `TOMCAT_HOME`; the startup script for the container will set this variable automatically based on the its home directory (one directory up where the `startup.sh` script is invoked). If the `TOMCAT_HOME` directory has specifically been moved to another location (instead of the directory where the `startup.sh` script is installed), the `TOMCAT_HOME` environment variable should be set to the other directory.

Two scripts are provided to start and stop the Tomcat server: `startup.sh` to start the server and `shutdown.sh` to stop the server. These scripts are both located in the `TOMCAT_HOME/bin directory`. The Tomcat installation contains several other directories below the root directory, as shown in Table 4.1.

Table 4.1 Tomcat Installation Subdirectories

Directory	Description
bin	Contains the directories used to start up and shut down the server
conf	Contains the configuration files for the installation
doc	Contains the documentation for the installation, including a user guide, an FAQ, and information on application development with Tomcat
logs	Contains the various log files used by Tomcat to log system activity; can be configured with `Logger` element entries in the `server.xml` file
src	Java servlet API source files (not source files for the Tomcat server)
lib	Various JAR files used by Tomcat
webapps	Series of directories and subdirectories containing demonstration applications
work	Automatically generated by Tomcat; creates subdirectories to store Tomcat intermediate files such as compiled JSPs
classes	Location of additional class files used by Tomcat applications; Java class files in this directory will be added to Tomcat's class path.

The `conf` directory, in turn, has three subdirectories, as shown in Table 4.2.

Table 4.2 conf Subdirectories

Directory	Description
jk	Contains files relevant to the Apache `mod_jk` module, which allows Apache to work with the Tomcat server and provides some scalability and reliability features
jserv	Contains files relevant to the Apache `mod_jserv` module, which allows Apache to work with the Tomcat server
users	Contains user lists for use with servlet container managed security as implemented by Tomcat

Configuration Files

Tomcat (version 3.3) uses several different configuration files located in the `conf` directory. The `server.xml` contains the basic configuration for the site. The `apps-<host_name>.xml` (where `host_name` is the name of the Tomcat instance) contains information on the various *contexts* within the Web site. (Prior to version 3.3, all context information was contained in the `server.xml` file.)

Tomcat Configuration

Attempting to document Tomcat configuration files is, at best, like shooting at a moving target that at times is invisible. The configuration files differ notably from version 3.2x to 3.3x and 4.0x, and many configuration parameters and attributes are not documented. The material in this section is based primarily on version 3.3 milestone 1. Where I could not find clarification on a specific configuration parameter or attribute, it has been left out. Appendix A discusses the Tomcat 4.0 beta in some detail.

By default, Tomcat looks for the `server.xml` in the home directory for Tomcat, which is either defined by the `TOMCAT_HOME` environment variable or is determined by the `startup.sh` script based on the current working directory of the script. The `server.xml` script is then assumed to be in the directory `$TOMCAT_HOME/conf`. (This default can be overridden with a command line flag, as show later in this section.)

The `TOMCAT_HOME` directory is assumed to contain a series of subdirectories containing the applications or groups of applications for the installation. These applications are contained in what are referred to as *contexts*. Note that all contexts are assumed to be subdirectories of the home directory of the `Context Manager`; by default this home directory is assumed to be TOMCAT_HOME. The default directory can be changed when Tomcat is started as explained below.

Within the `Context Manager` (as subdirectories of the home directory of the `Context Manager` for the installation), there are four principal directories, used as described in Table 4.3.

These directories effectively provide a working instance of Tomcat and can be located somewhere other than the installation directory. The ability to identify different configurations of Tomcat is a requirement for sites working with multiple Web applications. At these sites, each different Web application can have a separate set of working directories under a separate `Context Manager` home directory.

Table 4.3 Context Manager Directories

Directory	Description
conf	Contains the configuration files for the installation
logs	Contains the log files used by the installation
webapps	Top-level directory for application files
work	Used for temporary work file creation

To get Tomcat to start using a configuration file other than the one located in the TOMCAT_HOME/conf directory, a command line argument needs to be passed to the Tomcat application. The syntax for this command line argument as passed to the startup.sh script (and then passed to the tomcat.sh script) is

```
startup.sh -f/lin/apps/tc321/conf/server.xml
```

Use of this command line argument will establish the full path to the server.xml file as /lin/apps/tc321/conf/server.xml. The contents of each configuration file are explained in the following sections.

server.xml File

The server.xml file contains the global configuration for the Tomcat server. The elements in this server configuration are identified by XML tags, with sections for debug level, home directory, log file output, and other server attributes. All entries relate to a single server, the server *instance* being run. This file contains a hierarchy of definitions that control the Tomcat server being started. It is possible (and not uncommon) to have more than one Tomcat server running on a single machine. For instance, in a development environment, each developer would run his or her own instance of Tomcat, each with its own application and logging directory. Or in a production environment, different servers could be started to manage processing for separate portions of the application.

The hierarchy of the definitions in the server.xml file ranges logically from the server to specific context entries for the server, as shown in Table 4.4.

Table 4.4 server.xml File Definitions

Definition	Attributes	Description
Server	\<none\>	Top-level definition of the server
Logger	name, path, customOutput, VerbosityLevel	Multiple loggers for each server; loggers defined for servlets, JSPs, and the Tomcat server in general
ContextManager	debug_level, home, workDir, debug	Defines the structure for the contexts that it will encapsulate; contains definitions for the working directory, the base directory for applications, and debug and logging output
ContextInterceptor/ RequestInterceptor		Contain definitions for events of the ContextManager; useful for Tomcat developers; should not be manipulated by users
Connector	className, handler, port	Defines a connection to a user, a consumer of Tomcat services; contains attributes for the class to load and manage connections, the name of the handler class, and the port to use for connections
Context	path, debug, reloadable, docBase	Represents the location for an application; contains attributes for the top-level directory, debug level, and a reload flag

Working from the top down in this table, for each definition in the table, the attributes of the previous definitions are inherited. Using this approach, the path defined in the Context definition is a subdirectory of the home directory defined in ContextManager (of which the Context is an attribute). The hierarchy tree for these definitions, shown as XML, would be as follows:

```
<server>
    <logger>
          < !- Define multiple loggers as needed ->
    </logger>
    <ContextManager>
          <ContextInterceptor>
                < !- Define multiple ContextInterceptors as needed ->
```

```
        </ContextInterceptor>
        <RequestInterceptor>
            < !- Define multiple RequestInterceptors as needed ->
        </RequestInterceptor>
        <Connector>
             < !- Define multiple Connectors as needed ->
        </Connector>
         <Context>
             < !- Define multiple Contexts as needed ->
         </Context>
    </ContextManager>
```

The `server.xml` is parsed using the Sax XML parser and code developed by the Tomcat development team. Should the Sax parser fail during parsing of the XML file (because of a malformed tag), the entire parsing operation will fail. Should there be an incorrectly formed tag in the `server.xml` file, the parser will complain with an error that clearly identifies the parsing process and the offending file name as the startup problem (see Figure 4.3).

```
[art@ataylor bin]$ ERROR reading /lin/local/jakarta/tomcat33/conf/server.xml
At Attribute names must not start with "-" characters.

FATAL: configuration error
org.xml.sax.SAXParseException: Attribute names must not start with "-" characters.
        at com.sun.xml.parser.Parser.fatal(Parser.java:2817)
        at com.sun.xml.parser.Parser.fatal(Parser.java:2811)
        at com.sun.xml.parser.Parser.maybeElement(Parser.java:1337)
```

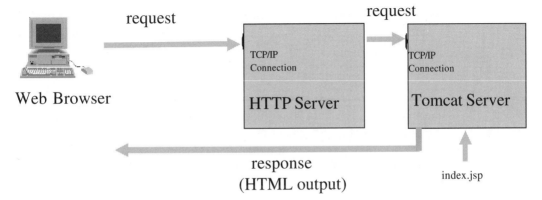

Figure 4.3 Parsing Error in the server.xml Configuration File

```
    at com.sun.xml.parser.Parser.content(Parser.java:1499)
    at com.sun.xml.parser.Parser.maybeElement(Parser.java:1400)
```
. . .

The attribute values within the elements provide the values for the configuration. Within the .xml file being read, the attribute values must be quoted
string values. They may, in fact, be values that will ultimately be interpreted as
numbers, but they must nevertheless be quoted.

If an attribute name is incorrect, it will silently be ignored by the parser and
the Tomcat sever. (For instance, if the attribute xyz="10" were to be placed in
a context, it would simply be ignored by the parser and by the Tomcat server
loading the configuration file.)

Tuning the Scalability and Reliability
of Tomcat with server.xml

By using Tomcat in conjunction with the Apache server, a production environment that provides scalability and reliability can be created. Using the
Apache server to provide the *front end* for the site, the Tomcat Web server
plug-in (mod_jk) can distribute the requests for the site to one or more
servers (see Figure 4.4).

Certain entries in the server.xml file and corresponding entries in the
workers.properties file (discussed later in this chapter) can be set to
support multiple Tomcat servers running on multiple machines, thus spreading the load for the site across multiple machines. The multiple instances of
the Tomcat server can be identical, in which case load balancing would be conducted through a *weighted round-robin* strategy. Since the Web server plug-
in is aware of sessions, load balancing will be conducted with what is known as
sticky load balancing, so that once a session is started, subsequent requests for
that session will be directed to the same server.

Alternatively, the application could be distributed across the multiple
instances of Tomcat based on the functions performed by the application; this
would entail a type of *functional application partitioning,* where long-running
accounting transactions could be directed to one machine and quick, simple
page requests for static HTML pages could be directed to another.

Application reliability, defined for our purposes as the ability of an application to withstand hardware failures, is an important factor in the development
of many applications. Given the inherently distributed nature of multitiered
Web applications, it is somewhat easier to provide some level of reliability. To
provide reliability for the application, multiple Java servers could be used to

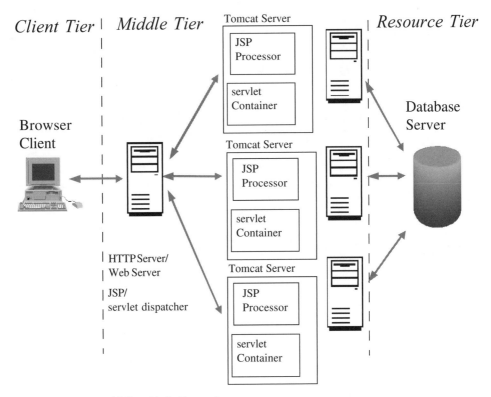

Figure 4.4 Scalability with the Tomcat Server

execute the business logic of the application; should one server fail, the other servers would continue to be available to execute the business logic for the application.

To perform load balancing and provide reliability, the configuration entries in the `server.xml` and the `workers.properties` file must be set correctly. In the following sections we explain the configuration file elements and attributes contained in these two files. Once these entries have been explained, the notion of load balancing and reliability will be revisited later in the chapter.

Scalability and Reliability Defined

The *scalability* of an application is the ability to begin with a given load on the system (e.g., a specific number of concurrent requests) and then as the load increases, easily be able to support a higher system load. For Web applications, system load is usually associated with the number of concurrent users or hits on the system or hits (requests) per some given time period. The metrics for this system load are usually in terms of the number of *hits per day* and the *number of concurrent users*. These two measures are not necessarily related, since Web site hits rarely are evenly distributed over the 24-hour day but are, instead, marked by periods of intense activity followed by periods of inactivity. A Web site must be prepared for periods of intense activity, spikes in usage. These periods are more closely measured by the number of concurrent users for the system at peak loads, and system stress testing should involve testing for peak concurrent user loads.

The *reliability* of a system can be measured by the *mean time to failure*, how often a system will fail within a given time period. For instance, 1 percent downtime for a system over an entire year would mean that the system could be down for three to four days annually ($3.65 = 365 \times 0.1$). For some sites this would be acceptable. For others, which depend on 24-hour uptime seven days a week, four days of downtime could be disastrous. Since some downtime is usually expected per machine, using multiple machines decreases downtime in a roughly linear fashion.

Addressing Scalability and Reliability

A Web site architecture that contains a single HTTP server and multiple back-end JSP/servlet servers running on multiple machines can address both reliability and scalability issues by intelligently distributing requests for the JSP/servlet servers across the multiple machines. To provide *scalability* given this architecture, the front-end Web server must distribute incoming requests across the multiple servers. This will distribute the application load over multiple machines, thus scaling the application in a roughly linear fashion across the available hardware. (This is *roughly* linear, in that using four machines instead of two would not be exactly twice as fast, but some number less than that, such as 1.8 times as fast, due to the overhead of request distribution and network i/o.)

To provide some degree of *reliability* with this architecture, the Web server dispatcher must have some knowledge of the state of the machines to which it is distributing requests. This knowledge can range from detailed information about the load and response time of the machine to simple knowledge that the machine is running and is available. With this knowledge, the request dispatcher can make decisions about which machine should receive the next request.

Should one of the machines in the distribution list become unavailable, the dispatcher would become aware of this and not send any more requests to the server running on that machine. Transactions running on the server when it failed would not be completed, but the Web site would continue to run, since incoming requests would be directed to the remaining machines. (More intelligent reliability is available through what is known as *failure recovery*, where sessions operating on multiple machines are aware of each other's state and can recover and continue processing should one of the machines fail. This requires more sophisticated application servers and intelligent components, such as Enterprise JavaBeans; the Tomcat server currently does not provide this capability.)

The Tomcat server following version 3.2x provides the ability to distribute incoming requests across multiple servers. This requires use of the `mod_jk` module (plug-in) in the Apache server and coordinating entries in the `server.xml` and `workers.properties` files. The `mod_jk` module is aware of session activity and provides both weighted load balancing and sticky load balancing. Weighted load balancing allows weights to be assigned to each of the servers in the module distribution list. Servers with the higher weights will receive more requests than the other servers in the list. Should one of the servers in the distribution list fail, the `mod_jk` module will become aware of that and direct system activity to the other servers in the list.

LogSetter Entry

Log files can be created for both the servlet and JSP using the `LogSetter` configuration element. The `Logger` definition includes attributes for `name`, `verbosityLevel`, `path`, a `customOutput` flag, a `timestamp` flag, and a `timestamp`. Following is a sample of the `LogSetter` element:

```
<LogSetter name="tc_log"
           path="logs/tomcat.log"
           customOutput="yes"
           timestamp="yes"
           timestampFormat="msec"
           verbosityLevel = "INFORMATION" />
```

This entry creates an internal reference to a log named `tc_log` with logging output to `TOMCAT_HOME/logs/tomcat.log`. The verbosity level for the log is set to `"INFORMATION"`.

Currently (as of version 3.3), there are three standard logs within Tomcat, shown in Table 4.5.

Table 4.5 Standard Tomcat Logs

Log Name	Description
tc_log	General logging for Tomcat
servlet_log	Logging for servlets; available through the ServletContext.log() method
JASPER_LOG	Logging for the JSP compiler (Jasper)

The internal names of these three log files are fixed in Tomcat (they are, in fact, *hardcoded* in the source code). Therefore, the name attribute in the configuration file for LogSetter should not be changed.

The verbosityLevel attribute specifies the amount of logging that will be performed. The various levels of verbosity supported are listed in Table 4.6.

Table 4.6 Tomcat Verbosity Levels

Verbosity Level	Description
FATAL	Logs only fatal errors
ERROR	Logs errors
WARNING	Logs warnings
INFORMATION	Provides informational output
DEBUG	Provides detailed debug information

The VerbosityLevel is a hierarchical value that when set for a Logger defines the logger as including the output of all other verbosity levels above that level (as shown in Table 4.6), so that by setting the Logger to a VerbosityLevel of WARNING, the output of WARNING, ERROR, and FATAL would be included in the log. (Note that for servlets, the VerbosityLevel should be set to **INFORMATION** to see normal servlet log messages.) The default VerbosityLevel is WARNING.

The value for the attribute path should be set to the path for the log file, including the file name for the log. If this attribute is omitted, the standard error (stderr) or standard output (stdout) will be used. The value for the path attribute can be either a full path name or a relative path name. If the value of the path attribute is a relative path name, it is considered relative to the value of the home attribute of the ContextManager.

By default, the Tomcat server will overwrite any existing log files on start-up. To override this behavior, the path can be set using special characters to create formatted data within a file name:

```
path="logs/tomcat-${yyyyMMdd}.log"
```

This will create a log file using the relative path of the logs directory and naming the file with a combination of the Tomcat name in a string `tomcat`-and the four-digit year, month, and day. The effect of this naming is that log files should be uniquely named log files. Although this will avoid the problem of overwriting, it can lead to an accumulation of log files in the log directory (one each new day the server is started) and therefore requires the administrator to purge old log files periodically. (Note that if Tomcat is restarted on the same day, the log file given the daily name as shown above would be overwritten.)

The `timestamp` attribute is used to indicate whether or not a time stamp (the date and time) will be attached to each line of the log file. This element takes two values: the string constants "yes" or "no." In conjunction with the `timestamp` element, the `timestampFormat` element is used to indicate the type of element that will be used to create the time stamp for the log record. Generating a long time stamp for a log record (to include year–month–day) can consume additional system resources, and therefore there are several options for creating the time stamp format. A custom format that uses the format of the `java.text.SimpleDateFormat` class can be used to place the year–month–day and hours and minutes on the time stamp, the common format for log records. If the format is set to the string `"msec"`, the milliseconds since the epoch will be used to generate the time stamp; this method is efficient but generally not as readable as using a formatted time stamp.

Alternatively, the time stamp can be turned off by setting the `time Stamp` attribute to the value "no." A `verbosityLevel` to a setting of INFORMATION can be used to produce less logging than a more verbose setting.

The `customOutput` attribute is used to control the output style of the log file. If the value of this attribute is set to `"yes"`, the log record is output without XML tags surrounding the record. If the value of this attribute is set to `"no"`, the log file output includes XML tags surrounding the log records.

ContextManager Entry

The `ContextManager` element defines the management of the contexts within an instance. The attributes defined within the `ContextManager` are inherited by the contexts within the instance as default values. These contexts can be defined within the `ContextManager` block in the `server.xml` file, or they can be defined in one or more separate files corresponding to separate sections of the site (the approach recommended). Only one `ContextManager` can be defined per Tomcat instance. The attributes defined in the `ContextManager` are listed in Table 4.7.

Table 4.7 ContextManager Attributes

Attribute	Value
debug	Debug setting; valid values are between 0 and 9
workDir	Working directory for servlets
home	Default home (`docBase`) directory; can be overridden by the individual contexts; default is `TOMCAT_HOME`
randomClass	Defines how the `ContextManager` will generate session ids
showDebugInfo	Flag indicating what debug information will be output by the `ContextManager`; default is "true"

The `debug` attribute is used to provide additional debug information for Tomcat processing and can be set to a value of between 0 and 9 inclusive, with more debug information output the higher the number is set. The `home` attribute defines where the home directory for this `ContextManager` will be located. The default value used (the value used if the home attribute is not defined) is the directory defined in the `TOMCAT_HOME` environment variable. All directory-related attributes within this context will be subdirectories of this directory. However, this behavior can be overridden by using a full path name for the directory attribute.

On a Web site, individual subdirectories are used to segregate the various portions of the site. It is a good development practice to place each application or a group of small applications in various directories which would be subdirectories of the directory defined to be the home directory for the `ContextManager`.

If more than one instance of Tomcat were running on a machine, each instance would be running in its own *home* directory. This directory would either be defined through the default entry, the `TOMCAT_HOME` directory, or explicitly through the definition of the home attribute in the `ContextManager` element. These multiple instances would have their own configuration and work directories as defined through the home directory (either the default or the one defined in the `ContextManager`) but would share the libraries and classes used to run the Tomcat server. Following is an example of setting the `ContextManager` element.

```
<ContextManager
        debug="0"
        home="/lin/local/JSPApps"
        workDir="work" />
```

This defines the home directory for the installation (not a particular context) to be in the directory `/lin/local/JSPApps`. The work directory defined in the same tag is a subdirectory of this directory (the home directory). The two other application-related directories, `conf` and `logs`, must be subdirectories of this home directory.

The `workDir` attribute defines what directory will be used as a work directory when the JSP documents are converted to servlets by the JSP processing environment of the Tomcat server. The `randomClass` attribute is used internally by the Tomcat server to generate session ids. These session ids are used to identify the session uniquely relative to other sessions the Tomcat server may be processing.

If session ids were known, they could be used by malicious hackers. For this reason, the Tomcat server starts by default using the `SecureRandom` class to generate session ids (`randomClass="java.lang.SecureRandom"`). Although this is secure, this does slow down the Tomcat server startup to some degree. To speed the startup process (e.g., in development), the class `SecureRandom` can be substituted with the `java.util.Random` class. This attribute could be set to the `java.security.SecureRandom` class in the production environment but set to the `java.util.Random` class in the development environment, where a fast restart time for the Java server would be useful.

The `showDebugInfo` attribute provides a flag to indicate whether or not `true` or `false` debug information should be output for the `Context`. This is information that is useful during the development process (e.g., stack traces for all exceptions) but that you may not want to transmit back to the user population in a production environment. For this reason, the attribute should be set to `true` in the development environment, but then set to `false` when the site is placed in production.

Connector Entry

The `Connector` entry is used to define the means by which Tomcat will communicate with the Web server. This defines the port and the class that will be loaded to perform this function. If there is contention for any of the default ports, the port number can be changed here. Note that if the port used to connect to the Web server is changed in this file, it must also be changed to an appropriate value in the Apache configuration file (httpd.conf), as explained later in this chapter.

The Connector represents a connection to the user. The Connector element for the HTTP connection defines the port where the HTTP connection will be made. The Tomcat connector is responsible for management of the Tomcat worker threads and for reading and writing data back to clients via the socket connection. The connector can be configured to identify a new handler class (to be used with caution), the TCP/IP port where the handler will listen and the TCP/IP port for the server socket.

The default connection port for the HTTP connector is port 8080, so the URL for connection to the Tomcat server on the host localhost would be http://localhost:8080/. To change the port for the HTTP connection for Apache, the value of the port parameter for the HTTPConnection could be changed as follows:

```
. . .
<Parameter name="handler"
value="org.apache.tomcat.service.http.HttpConnectionHandler"/>
          <Parameter name="port" value="9090"/>
. . .
```

This entry sets the port number for the HttpConnectionHandler to port 9090, making the URL for connection to the Tomcat server on the host localhost http://localhost:9090/.

The Connector entry provides an attribute for className, which is the fully qualified class name for the connector class, the class that will manage the connection. Additional parameters to define the *handler* for the connector and the *port* for the connector. These parameters are specified with two attributes: *name* and *value*. For the handler parameter, the name attribute specifies the name of the attribute and the value parameter is the fully qualified class name of the handler class. For the port parameter (for a particular connector), the name attribute specifies the name of the connector attribute we are setting, and the value is the port number. Following is an example of this entry.

```
<Connector className="org.apache.tomcat.service.SimpleTcpConnector">
     <Parameter name="handler"
 value="org.apache.tomcat.service.http.HttpConnectionHandler"/>
 <Parameter name="port"
             value="9020" />
     <Parameter name="max_threads"
               value="20"/>
```

```
      <Parameter name="max_spare_threads"
               value="20" />
      <Parameter name="min_spare_threads"
               value="5" />
</Connector>
```

This example establishes a connector for TCP/IP connections. The parameter for `className` is set to the fully qualified class name for the connector class and should not be changed. The parameter for handler is set to the class name for the HTTP connection handler and should also not be changed.

The value for port is set to the value 9020 and represents the port number where Tomcat will listen for HTTP connections. This can be changed to a setting appropriate for your site, but note that it is limited by the fact that by default, the Tomcat server running on Unix as a user other than user `root` does not have access to the lower 1024 ports, since only user `root` can access these ports. Tomcat running as a user other than `root` would need to choose a port above 1024; in this example it uses port 9020. The port number is a requirement in a development environment where more than one developer is using Tomcat. Each separate Tomcat user must use a separate configuration directory with a separate `server.xml` file to define its environment.

The connector is responsible for managing connections. When a connection is received, the connector needs to turn the processing of that connection over to a thread; the thread will then be responsible for the processing of connection. The `max_threads`, `max_spare_threads`, and `min_spare_threads` attributes are used to define how the connector will manage threads. These settings of these attributes are described in more detail later in the chapter.

Interceptor Definitions

Tomcat uses various *interceptors* to capture events that occur within the server. Interceptor elements contain attributes for the fully qualified Java class name of the interceptor and an optional debug flag to generate debug output. Other than possibly setting the debug flag for these connectors, most administrators will leave them as configured.

The `ContextInterceptor` listens for events that happen in the `ContextManager` such as the startup and shutdown events of the Tomcat server (as reported within the `ContextManager`). Following is an example of this entry.

```
...
    <ContextInterceptor
        className="org.apache.tomcat.context.DefaultCMSetter" />
<ContextInterceptor
        className="org.apache.tomcat.context.WorkDirInterceptor" />
...
```

The `RequestInterceptor` listens for various phases that the user request passes through during servicing of a request. A debug flag is available to provide debug output if needed.

```
    <Http10Interceptor
className="org.apache.tomcat.modules.server.Http10Interceptor"
        port="8080"
        secure="false"
        maxThreads="100"
        maxSpareThreads="50"
        minSpareThreads="10"
        />
```

Context Definition

The `Context` definition is used to define the attributes of a particular context within the Tomcat instance. This context generally relates to a specific application or set of applications managed by the Tomcat instance. The `Context` element supports several attributes: `path`, `docBase`, `debug`, and the `reloadable` flag.

The `path` attribute defines the path that this directory will reference. If a URL is presented with this path, the Tomcat server will be directed to the directory indicated by the `docBase` attribute for this `Context` and will search for the file in that directory (or under a subdirectory of that directory, depending on the URL).

The `docBase` attribute defines the document base for the application. This entry (similar to the `DocumentRoot` directory of Apache) is the root directory for all documents in this context. All documents in this context are expected to be under this directory.

More than one `Context` entry can exist within a `ContextManager` entry in the `server.xml` file. In fact, it is a good administration policy to have a separate context (and corresponding directory structure) for each separate application or group of applications being managed by the Tomcat server. The following provides an example of the `Context` element.

```
<Context path="/MyApplication"
         docBase="webapps/MyApplication"
         debug="0"
         reloadable="true" >
</Context>
```

In this example, a context is established for the "/MyApplication" directory. URLs that reference the "/MyApplication" directory (e.g., http://MyServer:8080/MyApplication) will cause the Tomcat server to look in the "./webapps/MyApplication" directory. If the ContextManager element in which this is contained has been defined with a home attribute of "/working/WebStuff", the full path name of the directory referenced by the "/MyApplication" directory would be "/working/WebStuff/webapps/MyApplication". Any additional paths referenced would be considered subordinate to this directory. The debug flag of zero indicates that no debugging output would be produced for this context. A nonzero setting would produce debug output. An application that was to be used only for the accounting department could use the following context entry:

```
<Context path="/Accounting"
         docBase="webapps/Accounting"
         debug="0"
         reloadable="true" >
</Context>
```

In this example, the path of "/Accounting" in a URL would reference a full path that would include the home attribute of the ContextManager ("/lin/working") plus the docBase attribute for the Context element ("webapps/Accounting") plus the path specified in the path attribute of the Context element. For this example, that would produce a full path name of "/lin/working/webapps/Accounting". To create a context for a URL with no subdirectory reference (e.g., http://MyServer:8080/) the following context would need to be created:

```
<Context path=""
         docBase="webapps/ROOT"
         debug="0"
         reloadable="true" >
</Context>
```

In this entry, the empty path references the "webapps/ROOT" directory relative to the home directory of the ContextManager. The most common approach to Web site development would place a default page in this directory (e.g., index.html) that would either direct the user to another page or contain some basic information and links that would carry the user into the site.

Logs and user validation methods can also be defined to be specific to a context. The LogSetter attribute can be used to define logs within the context, as shown below.

```
<webapps>

   <Context path="/myApp"
            docBase="webapps/myApp"
            debug="0"
            reloadable="true" >
             <SimpleRealm filename="conf/users/myApp-users.xml" />
                <LogSetter name="myApp_tc.log" path="logs/
myApp-${yyyyMMdd}..log" />
                   <LogSetter name="example_servlet_log"
                            path="logs/servlet_myApp-${yyyyMMdd}..log"
                              servletLogger="true"/>
   </Context>

</webapps>
```

Within this context, LogSetter elements are entered to define two logs for the context. These entries use the same LogSetter attributes explained in the preceding section.

The SimpleRealm tag is used to define a security realm for users attempting to access this context. Any user attempting to access this context will be validated against the user names and roles within the file referenced by the file attribute in the element.

Virtual Hosting with the Tomcat Server

Tomcat provides a type of virtual hosting using the Host element (as of Tomcat version 3.3). The Host element is a container within which distinct environments can be declared using the Context element. The following provides an example.

```
<Server>
      <Host name="myhost" >
         <Context path=""
                    docBase="webapps/myHost/ROOT" />

         <Context path="/Stuff"
```

```
                          docBase="webapps/myHost/Stuff" />
        </Host>
</Server>
```

These entries are located in an `.xml` file located in the `./conf` directory. The name of the file is arbitrary but is usually created to contain the host name or the IP address of the virtual host (as in `apps-<IP address>.xml`). When Tomcat starts, it attempts to read and parse the `.xml` files in the `./conf` directory. The IP address portion of the `.xml` file is the IP address of the virtual host.

The entries in this file begin with a `Server` element that defines a context for a server. Within this context, a `Host` tag is entered to create a context for a `Host`. This tag contains a single attribute that declares a name for the host, which in this case is the value `myHost`.

Within the `Host` container entries are made for the contexts that will be recognized within that virtual host. Each of these `Context` entries may contain the various attributes that are applicable to contexts. In this example, the `path` and `docBase` for the context are declared. In the first entry, the path is declared to be a blank, indicating that this will be the entry for the root directory of the context. Next, the `docBase` for the `Context` is declared to be `webapps/myHost/ROOT`, indicating that a URL of `http://myhost:8080/` would be directed to the directory `webapps/myHost/ROOT` (the `webapps` directory would be relative to the home directory declared for the `ContextManager`).

The next `Context` declared in this example declares a subdirectory of the virtual host named `Stuff`. This subdirectory is related to the directory `webapps/myHost/Stuff` using the `docBase` attribute of that `Context` element.

Note that while the addition of virtual hosts in Tomcat is an important feature, this capability is available in the Apache server and is much more mature and robust. As later examples will show, it is better to leverage the capabilities of the Apache server to provide virtual hosting capabilities and then to interface this capability with virtual hosting in Tomcat.

Configuring Thread Pooling through Connectors

Earlier releases of Tomcat created a new thread for each connection. Although this may seem like a logical approach, it creates problems at busier sites which could periodically receive a large number of concurrent connections. There is overhead to thread allocation especially in a Web environment where users often leave a site without a formal session end.

Tomcat manages this problem through *thread pools;* thread pools are pools of threads that are created and then allocated as Tomcat requires them. When Tomcat is finished with the thread, it is returned to the pool. When Tomcat requires another thread, it requests one from the thread pool, which returns a thread that has already been allocated, thus avoiding the overhead of allocating a new thread.

The threads used by a Tomcat server instance can be administered using the `Connector` definitions in the `server.xml` file (see previous sections). A variety of connectors can be defined in this file, but the two most commonly configured are for HTTP connections directly to the Tomcat server and for connections from the Apache Web server to the Tomcat server. The configuration for the HTTP connection is as follows:

```
<!- Normal HTTP ->
     <Connector className="org.apache.tomcat.service.PoolTcpConnector">
         <Parameter name="handler"

value="org.apache.tomcat.service.http.HttpConnectionHandler"/>
         <Parameter name="port"
             value="8080"/>
         <Parameter name="max_threads"
                   value="20"/>
         <Parameter name="max_spare_threads"
                   value="20" />
         <Parameter name="min_spare_threads"
                   value="5" />
     </Connector>
```

By defining the `className` for the connector to be `PoolTcpConnector`, we have identified this as a *thread pool* resource. This is a Java class within Tomcat that will provide the thread management resources for connections being made over the port identified. Parameters can optionally be defined for `max_threads`, `max_spare_threads`, and `min_spare_threads`. These parameters and their defaults are identified in Table 4.8.

The same set of definitions can be established for a specific protocol. For instance, the `ajp13` protocol provides a new protocol for Tomcat with, among other things, provisions for the handling of SSL connections from Apache. A thread pool can be established for this resource using the following definition:

```
<Connector className="org.apache.tomcat.service.PoolTcpConnector">
     <Parameter
         name="handler"
```

Table 4.8 Thread Management Parameters

Parameter	Default	Description
max_threads	50	Upper limit on the number of threads that can be allocated
max_spare_threads	25	Maximum number of threads that will be kept idle; if the number of idle threads is above this number, idle threads will be killed until this number is reached
min_spare_threads	10	Minimum number of idle threads that will be kept; if fewer than this number of threads are available, the pool will allocate new threads until this number is reached

```
        value=
"org.apache.tomcat.service.connector.Ajp13ConnectionHandler"/>
            <Parameter
                name="port"
                value="8007"/>
            <Parameter
                name="max_threads"
                value="30"/>
            <Parameter
                name="max_spare_threads"
                value="20"/>
            <Parameter
                name="min_spare_threads"
                value="5" />
</Connector>
```

According to the configuration shown above, the ajp13 connector will listen on port 8007 for connections coming from the Apache server as defined using the port parameter (attribute name is set to "port" and the value attribute is set to "8007"). Since the PoolTcpConnector is being defined for the className attribute for the Connector element, thread pooling will be used to manage the connections coming from this port.

Based on the definitions for the other parameters, a maximum of 30 threads will be created for the pool. This means that at any given point in time, the connection will allow only 30 threads to be operational. Should the number of active threads exceed 30 threads, no more connections will be allowed on this connector; this behavior effectively limits runaway session behavior that could crash the server.

The connector keeps a number of spare threads available to distribute to incoming connections (which means that the connection will not need to wait for creation of a thread). Based on the definition for max_spare_threads, the connection pool will limit the number of spare threads to maintain to a maximum of 20 threads. Based on the definition of minimum spare threads, the connection pool will not let the number of spare threads drop below 5.

This means that, initially, between 5 and 30 threads will be created for the thread pool. Once the connector begins processing connections, a maximum of 20 spare connections, connections available for distribution to incoming connections, will be maintained. Should fewer than 5 spare threads be left in the pool at any time, the connector would begin to create new spare threads until at least 5 were available.

Note that request processing for a Web application is not the same as for two-tier, PC-based client–server applications. A client does not open a connection to a resource and then maintain that connection. By definition, an HTTP transaction is stateless, meaning that a connection is received by the Web server and processed and then formulated as a response which is sent back to the client that sent the request. Once the response has been sent, the connection to the client is terminated and the connection within the server is freed. This same approach is used with the Tomcat Java server. A connection is received, processed, the response is returned to the client, and the connection is then terminated. Thus 30 session users would not necessarily use 30 connections, since some connections would have completed processing, returned their response, and then terminated.

Also note that 30 concurrent requests are requests that have been sent to the Web site. A site could have 100 users on the site, but only a very small subset have sent a request at the same time to the Web server managing the site; the remaining users are either reading a page they have received or have moved on to perform some other processing on their local machine. (This is one of the attractive aspects of Web applications—that for a large part of the client processing performed, they require very little work of the server managing their requests.)

As shown above, the default values for the PoolTcpConnector are considered adequate for a 10 to 30 concurrent requests. If a site has fewer concurrent requests, the same parameters should be adjusted downward (e.g., the max_threads parameter). If a site has more concurrent requests, the values could be adjusted upward, depending on the machine resource available.

Summary

We began the chapter by explaining the requirements for a middle tier to provide dynamic Web page generation and the ability to interact with a data resource. We had previously described a multitier design that includes a client tier, a middle tier or business tier, and a resource tier. We have now identified specific technologies for each of these tiers, with a Web browser (Netscape, Internet Explorer, Mozilla), the business tier with the Apache HTTP server to provide static HTML and the Tomcat server to provide a JSP engine and servlet container, and the resource tier with the PostgreSQL database server. Although we provide specific solutions for these technologies in this book, using server-side Java by no means requires these specific technologies. The IPlanet and the BEA WebLogic server both provide a JSP engine and servlet container. Oracle and SQL servers both represent database engines that can be used for the resource tier.

Coming Up Next

Our proposed environment involves use of the Apache Web server to provide static HTML to the client and possibly perform some authentication services and the Tomcat server to provide dynamic page presentation. To use both the Apache server and the Tomcat server requires some integration of the two components. This integration is important because using a configuration that included distribution of requests to multiple Tomcat servers, it provides not only some scalability features but also allows for a certain degree of failover. The next chapter covers integration of these components, and the Tomcat and Apache configuration files that define this integration.

## CHAPTER 5

MAKING THE PIECES WORK: INTEGRATING THE TOMCAT SERVER WITH APACHE

Introduction

In Chapter 4 we detailed the installation and configuration of the Tomcat server. In this chapter we discuss how to get the Tomcat server to recognize an application. Unlike client–server applications, we can't simply create a single monolithic piece of code, point it at a database, and run the application. Web applications are comprised of numerous static HTML pages, page content, and in our case, dynamic pages that use application-specific class files and library class files.

Placement of our application and its components is important. We want to do this in such a way that the application is both portable across multiple server environments and is consistent and easy to understand. Fortunately, there is a specification from Sun that describes this process. In this chapter we cover the deployment of applications in the Tomcat environment per the Sun servlet specification that details this process.

Additionally, we want to integrate the Tomcat server with the Apache HTTP server. This can be accomplished using an Apache module and an appropriate configuration file. This integration will allow us to have the Apache server do what the Apache server does well (serve static HTML, provide authentication services) and have the Tomcat server do what it does well (serve JSPs and servlets). In this chapter we cover the configuration files and modules that provide this integration.

Web Application

The goal of our efforts is to deploy a Web application. But unlike other development environments, the Web application is not one or two components, but a collection of numerous elements that must be combined properly for the application to work as shown in Figure 5.1.

To deploy a Web application to a particular Java server, these components must be properly combined when requests are received against the Web application. There is no specific intrinsic organization that is required for a Web application; configuring Tomcat and Apache to locate static HTML and JSP files and their elements correctly will allow the application to run. But this lack of a consistent organization has made application maintenance difficult, limits portability, and makes integration of applications difficult.

The servlet 2.2 specification has addressed these shortcomings with a specification for a directory structure for locating components and an archive file

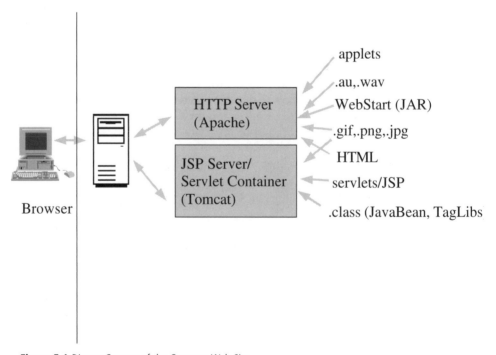

Figure 5.1 Diverse Content of the Common Web Site

that can compress and encapsulate these same components. An archive file known as a `.war` file (despite the peaceful intentions of most developers) can be used to encapsulate these components in an archived format. (WAR is an acronym for Web ARchive file.)

A specific directory structure is used within a WAR file. Although not required by Tomcat, it makes sense to use this directory structure for consistency. This structure includes the directories listed in Table 5.1.

Table 5.1 WAR Files Directories

Directory	Purpose
`<document root>`	Arbitrary name for the root directory of the application context (e.g., `accounting`); static HTML, JSP, and any content required by those pages should be in this directory or possibly a subdirectory of this directory
`WEB-INF`	Should contain the `web.xml` file, which contains information about the application and its components; this directory should also contain the `./classes` and `./lib` subdirectories
`WEB-INF/classes/`	Class files that comprise the application, including servlets, JavaBeans, and any helper classes; any Java package hierarchy should be represented below this directory
`WEB-INF/lib/`	Any JAR files that contain classes required by the application (e.g., JDBC driver classes)

Configuring Apache to Communicate with Tomcat/Jakarta

In our architecture, the Apache server provides a number of services concerning the site content that does not require Java processing. But when Java processing is required, the server must recognize the Java content and pass the request to the Tomcat Java server. This recognition and subsequent processing are performed using an Apache module (sometimes referred to as a *plug-in*).

There are currently two Apache modules available for Apache-to-Tomcat communication: `mod_jserv` and `mod_jk`. The `mod_jserv` module is the original module used with the `Jserv` servlet container. Although effective, the design of this module and the protocol used were not going to provide the functionality needed to manage the additional features that Tomcat needed to support. So the mod_jk module was developed.

The mod_jk module supports many advanced features, including SSL, distribution of requests to multiple servers, sticky load balancing, and recognition of failed servers. The benefits of using these features are significant, so in this chapter we cover only the mod_jk module.

The mod_jk module communicates with the Tomcat server using *workers* (see Figure 5.2). The job of these worker threads is to catch any request that needs to be processed by the Tomcat server and dispatch the request to that server (see Figure 5.2). Therefore, various configuration parameters must be set for the workers to identify how many workers need to be created and what operations the workers will perform.

Workers are defined in a configuration file that identifies various configuration parameters (or properties) for the workers. This file is usually named workers.properties and is usually located in the Apache configuration directory (although the name and location of the file could be any valid operating system path/file name). Entries in the mod_jk configuration in Apache provide the name and location of this configuration file. Note that by default, the location of this file is in the Tomcat configuration directory, not the Apache configuration directory.

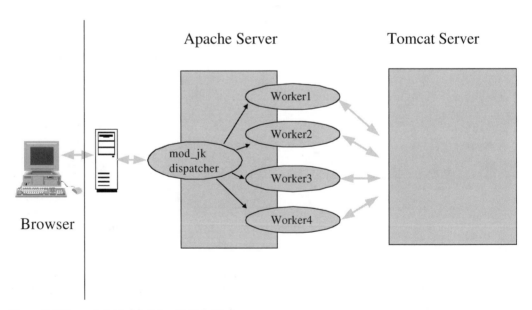

Figure 5.2 The mod_jk Module Using Multiple Workers

Autoconfigure Feature of Tomcat

The Tomcat server provides an autoconfigure feature that can optionally be run when the server is started (as of version 3.3; autoconfigure was automatic prior to this version). This feature will have the Apache server read the configuration files for the Tomcat instance and produce an Apache configuration file for the `mod_jk` module with the appropriate Apache directives for the various contexts within the Apache site. The configuration file will be located in a subdirectory of the Tomcat configuration directory named `jk` (`./conf/jk`). The file is named `mod_jk.conf-auto`. A generic `workers.properties` file is also located in the `jk` subdirectory. The contents of this file should form the basis for the worker's configuration file to be used for the Apache module. The Tomcat server will generate these files (as of version 3.3) only if the `ApacheConfig` directive appears in the `server.xml` file as `<ApacheConfig />`.

In the following section we detail the configuration of the `mod_jk` module, first identifying the configuration entries that the Apache server will use and then detailing the entries of the `workers.properties` file. (Note that in Tomcat versions prior to 3.3, the autoconfigure option was automatic and wrote the configuration files to the `TOMCAT_HOME/conf` directory.)

Configuring the Apache mod_jk Module

For the Apache Web server to communicate with Tomcat, several configuration parameters need to be set in the Apache configuration file (`httpd.conf`). These parameters instruct Apache to load the communications module to provide communication between the Apache server and the Tomcat server and contain information on when and how to trigger the communication process. Rather than clutter the already cluttered Apache `httpd.conf` file with these entries, they are usually placed in a separate file named `mod_jk.conf` (although this name is not required), placed in the Apache configuration file directory (`conf`), and then *included* in the Apache `httpd.conf` file using the `Include` directive:

```
Include conf/mod_jk.conf
```

This will insert the contents of the `mod_jk.conf` file into the Apache configuration file. (Note that if Apache cannot make sense of the entries in the `mod_jk.conf` file, the Apache server will not start.)

The first section of the `mod_jk.conf` configuration file instructs Apache to load the `mod_jk` module and sets several global configuration settings for the module, as shown below.

```
LoadModule jk_module libexec/mod_jk_apache_1.3_stdapi.so
JkWorkersFile /usr/local/apache/conf/workers.properties
JkLogFile /lin/local/jakarta/tomcat33/logs/mod_jk.log
JkLogLevel error
```

In this example, the `LoadModule` directive instructs Apache to load the `mod_jk` module. The module loaded is the specific module needed for the Apache distribution. (In this case, the standard Apache module API is loaded; alternatively, some Apache distributions use a different module architecture and require the loading of an Extended Apache API version of the module. Currently, both are available at the Jakarta download site for Tomcat.)

The `JkWorkers` directive identifies the file that contains the property definitions for workers that will perform the work of the `mod_jk` module. This example identifies the full path name for the file.

The `JkLogFile` configuration directive defines where the log file will be located. In this example, the `JkLogLevel` entry sets the logging level to "error." Possible settings for `JkLogLevel` are "debug," "warn," "error," and "emerg." The default setting is "warn." Unfortunately, these settings are not consistent with the settings for `VerbosityLevel` of logging in Tomcat. Nevertheless, the debug setting produces extremely good debugging output if there are problems with Apache-to-Tomcat communication. Note that logging from the `mod_jk` module is written by Apache to the log file defined by the previously identified `JkLogFile` directive.

The next set of entries in the `mod_jk` configuration file are used to identify which URL entries will map to which workers. These are the entries that require coordination between the `mod_jk` and `workers.properties` files. The `JkMount` directive takes two arguments: the URL to map and the worker to map it to. In this example, the URL `/examples/servlet` is mapped to the `ajp13` worker, and the contents of the URL `/examples` with the `.jsp` entry is also mapped to the `ajp13` worker.

```
JkMount /examples/servlet/* ajp13
JkMount /examples/*.jsp ajp13
```

Note that the name of the worker is arbitrary. This example and the default entries with the Tomcat server use workers with the names `ajp12` and `ajp13`. But the workers could just as well be provided with more meaningful names, as shown in the following example.

```
JkMount /Accounting/*.jsp    AcctgWorker  # send to accounting server
JkMount /HR/*.jsp            HRWorker     # send output to HR server
JkMount /Shopping            SSLWorker    # secure server
```

In this example, specific workers are used to redirect output to specific servers. The URL `Accounting`, which we will assume contains an accounting application, is directed to the `AcctgWorker` worker. The URL HR is directed to a worker named `HRWorker`. The URL `/Shopping`, which requires special treatment for security, is directed to a worker named `SSLWorker`, which we can assume will provide an SSL connection to the Tomcat server. (Corresponding entries in the `workers.properties` file, shown in the next section, will direct requests for these workers to specific servers.)

The next set of entries establishes a layer of security for the `WEB-INF` and `META-INF` directories. These are directories that contain internal information for the Web application and should not be accessible to the user.

```
<Location "/examples/WEB-INF/">
    AllowOverride None
    deny from all
</Location>

<Location "/examples/META-INF/">
    AllowOverride None
    deny from all
</Location>
```

The following set of entries creates *contexts,* entries that provide information about applications or groups of applications that exist within the container. Although Tomcat does not require any specific organization, it does make sense to provide some consistency to the JSP or servlet environment being developed. The first entry in the context is the declaration of an Apache alias. This is done for convenience, to avoid having to reference the full path name for the `/lin/local/jakarta/webapps/examples` directory, and for security reasons to help disguise the true (operating system) directory from the user.

```
# first, create an Apache alias for our directory
Alias /examples /lin/local/jakarta/webapps/examples
```

The next entry in this set is an Apache `directory` element that identifies configuration entries for the directory being configured. In this example, only two `options` entries are configured for the directory.

```
<Directory "/lin/local/jakarta/webapps/examples">
    Options Indexes FollowSymLinks
</Directory>
```

More generalized mapping could also be done. With these examples, any file with a `.jsp` extension will be directed to the Tomcat server for processing through the `ajp13` worker. Additionally, any reference in the `/servlet` URL will be directed to the `ajp13` worker.

```
JkMount /*.jsp ajp13
JkMount /servlet/* ajp13
```

workers.properties File

The `mod_jk` module works within the Apache server to listen for URLs presented to the server. These URLs are matched against the list of URLs it has developed (through `JkMount` directives at Apache startup). If it finds a match, the request is delivered to the worker specified in the `JkMount` directive.

Load balancing in Tomcat is accomplished using the worker threads of the `mod_jk` module that runs in Apache. The worker threads in Apache are made aware of an outstanding request that must be handled by them (based on a match to the pattern defined in the `JkMount` directive).

The behavior of the worker thread is dictated by the configuration entries in the `workers.properties`. The file contains entries that represent property value pairs using the syntax

```
<property name> = <property value>
```

The property name is a series of strings separated by a period (.). Tomcat requires specific naming for some portions of a property and allows arbitrary naming of other portions. Comments are supported using the # character at the start of the line. White space (blanks) preceding any character on a line is ignored. Each worker defined in the file is a specific worker type, as detailed in Table 5.2.

Note that by default, the worker threads will only use the `ajp12` protocol worker. To change this behavior, the `JkMount` directive in the Apache configuration file (`mod_jk.conf` in our example) must instruct workers to deliver requests to other connector workers, as shown in previous examples. Additionally, the `workers.list` property, which carries the list of active workers, must be changed to identify any new workers to work with.

The `workers.properties` file allows for the configuration of workers to distribute requests to the Tomcat Java server. One or more workers can be

Table 5.2 workers.properties File Worker Types

Worker Type	Description
`ajp12`	Connects to a port identified on the specified host (default is `localhost` port 8007) using the `ajp12` communication protocol
`ajp13`	Connects to a port identified on the specified host (default is `localhost` port 8009) using the `ajp13` communication protocol
`jni`	Uses Java JNI to allow Tomcat to run in-process within the Web server
`loadbalancer`	Worker responsible for load balancing among target servers

defined. The file also allows definition of an internal Tomcat server (thus providing the *in-process server* described in Chapter 1). The in-process server is also referred to as an *in-process worker* and is defined in this configuration file.

To provide an in-process worker (Tomcat server), the `mod_jk` module must be aware of the location of both the Tomcat server and the Java runtime environment. The `workers.tomcat_home` property should be set to the installation directory for the Tomcat server. The `workers.java_home` property should be set to the directory of the Java installation on the local machine.

```
workers.tomcat_home=/lin/home/jakarta/tomcat33
workers.java_home=/lin/local/jdk/jdk1.2.2
```

Note that these entries need to be set only if the JNI in-process worker is going to be used by `mod_jk`. If that is not the case (a JNI worker thread is not being created), these entries can be commented out using a leading # on the line. (If you are using the Tomcat server as an external server, the JNI worker thread is not needed.)

The `mod_jk` properties file allows macros to be used in the file. The use of macros allows complicated declarations to be encapsulated and generally makes the process of defining the worker properties easier. The following example defines the character string `ps` to be set equal to the forward slash character. The `ps` string is then used as a macro to create a path name for access to a specific file.

```
ps=/
...
worker.inprocess.class_path=$(workers.tomcat_home)$(ps)lib$(ps)jaxp.jar
```

The ps entry identifies the path separator for files. The following entry sets the path separator to a forward slash character:

```
ps=/
```

Defining the Worker

The next portion of this file contains a set of entries for the workers to be defined. The syntax for these entries is

```
worker.<worker name>.<property> =   <property value>
```

The value of the worker name is arbitrary and can be any valid Java string. The workers running in the Apache mod_jk module communicate with the Tomcat server via the port and host name defined later in this file.

The Tomcat server listens on the port defined using an *interceptor*. There must be a correspondence between the worker/port/worker protocol type and the Tomcat interceptor and protocol type (see Figure 5.3). This means that if a mod_jk worker wishes to communicate with a Tomcat server on local-host at port 8009 using the ajp13 protocol, the Tomcat server should have defined in the server.xml file a connector listening on that port ready to communicate using the ajp13 protocol.

The worker.list identifies the workers that will be created at runtime:

```
worker.list=ajp12_server, ajp13_server1, ajp13_server2
```

The lbfactor property is used to define the *load-balancing factor* for the worker thread. A low factor indicates that this worker (on this host and port) will receive a lower priority for work than will workers with a higher priority. This load-balancing factor is directly related to the Tomcat server represented by the worker—the Tomcat server to which it will connect at the host name:port name. If the server represented by the connector is more powerful than the other servers in use, the lbfactor for the worker serving that Tomcat server should be higher than for the other servers. Similarly, if the server is not as powerful, the lbfactor should be lower. The lbfactor must be greater than zero (0). Following is an example of a worker definition for a worker named AcctgWorker.

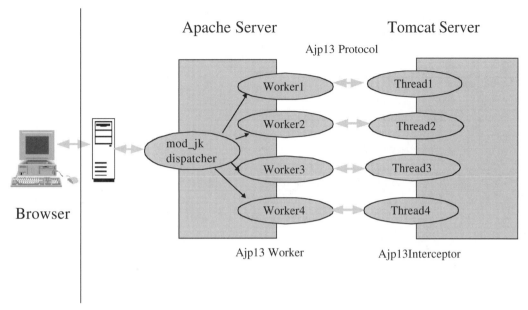

Figure 5.3 Worker and Thread Communication

```
worker.AcctgWorker.port=8007
worker.AcctgWorker.host=AcctgServer
worker.AcctgWorker.type=ajp13
worker.AcctgWorker.lbfactor=1
```

The next set of entries defines properties for the `AcctgWorker`, setting the port to 8009 and the host name to `HRServer`. Note that the `ajp13` protocol allows the definition of a `cachesize` property. Cache size refers to the number of open socket connections that will be cached by the worker. Web servers that support this feature (Apache 2.xx, IIS, and IPlanet) can improve performance by eliminating the overhead of constantly opening and closing TCP/IP socket connections. Its value should be set close to the number of estimated concurrent users for the site. If this entry is commented out (put a # at the start of the line), a socket cache will not be used.

```
worker.HRWorker.port=8009
worker.HRWorker.host=HRServer
worker.HRWorker.type=ajp13
worker.HRWorker.lbfactor=1
worker.HRWorker.cachesize=30
```

The next set of entries defines a load balancer thread to be used to distribute work among the various workers that have been defined.

Load Balancing with Tomcat

The Tomcat server provides load balancing through a worker specifically designed to manage the task of load balancing. This worker is responsible for creating workers in the Web server and then using the load-balancing factor (lbfactor) of each of those workers to distribute requests to the workers in a round-robin fashion (see Figure 5.4). Tomcat uses a *sticky* load-balancing routine where requests that belong to the same session will be directed to the same worker, and it is the responsibility of the load balancer to see that successive requests for a session go to the same server.

In the event that one of the workers fails (possibly due to a failed server that is assigned to the worker), the load balancer will recognize this situation and suspend requests to that worker, effectively *falling back* to the other servers it has available (see Figure 5.4). (Note that this is not a robust fail-over implementation

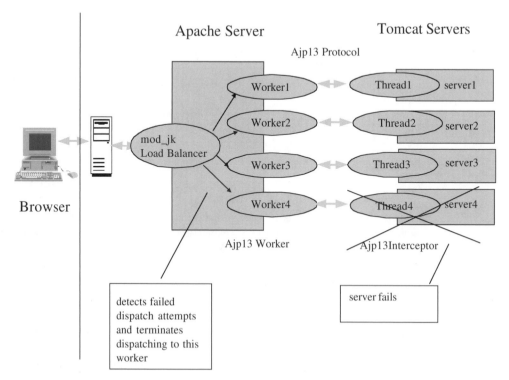

Figure 5.4 Load Balancing with the Tomcat Server

where session information is retained and recovered; session information on the failed machine that has not been written to a database is lost.)

The following entries define a worker, appropriately named `loadbalancer`, of type `lb` (for load balancer). The load balancer is assigned the task of balancing the workload for the list of workers assigned to the `balanced_workers` property.

```
worker.loadbalancer.type=lb
worker.loadbalancer.balanced_workers=server1, server2, server3
```

In this example, the load balancer assigned will balance the workload among three servers: `server1`, `server2`, and `server3`.

If both the Tomcat server and the Web server reside on the same machine, this approach requires additional overhead for communication with the standalone server. If the Web server supports multithreading, allowing the Tomcat server to run as a separate thread within Web server could improve performance.

The Tomcat server provides the ability to run the Tomcat server in-process within the Web server. This should be used only with Web servers that use internal multithreading (e.g., IPlanet, Apache 2.0, IIS).

Running the JNI Thread in Apache

As discussed previously, the Java Native Interface (JNI) worker operates the Tomcat server internally within the Apache server, thus reducing the overhead of communicating with the Tomcat server using the network interface. To provide the ability to run Tomcat within the Web server, the JNI is used. Thus, the worker type for this worker is `jni`, and the first entry shown below defines the worker named `inprocess` as a worker type `jni`.

Since the Tomcat server is a Java application and uses Java development tools and compile and load classes, a number of Java resources need to be identified. (This also requires that a valid Java runtime environment be installed on the machine where Tomcat will run as a `jni` worker within the Web server.)

The entries below identify the cLASS pATH for the Java environment and identify specific library files (`.jar`) for the environment. The "`$(workers.tomcat_home)`" entry is a macro defined at the top of the `workers.properties` file, which resolves to the home directory for the Tomcat installation. Note that for `.jar` files, the CLASSPATH includes the full path name to the file, including the name of the file. Not all properties need to be set for all installations; some properties only apply to older revisions of the Java Development Kit.

```
worker.inprocess.type=jni
worker.inprocess.class_path=$(workers.tomcat_home)$(ps)classes

worker.inprocess.class_path=$(workers.tomcat_home)$(ps)lib$(ps)jaxp.jar
worker.inprocess.class_path=$(workers.tomcat_home)$(ps)lib$(ps)parser.jar
worker.inprocess.class_path=$(workers.tomcat_home)$(ps)lib$(ps)jasper.jar
worker.inprocess.class_path=$(workers.tomcat_home)$(ps)lib$(ps)servlet.jar
worker.inprocess.class_path=$(workers.tomcat_home)$(ps)lib$(ps)webserver.jar
worker.inprocess.class_path=$(workers.java_home)$(ps)lib$(ps)tools.jar
```

Additional properties are then set to configure the command line that will be used to start the `jni` worker.

```
worker.inprocess.cmd_line=-config
worker.inprocess.cmd_line=$(workers.tomcat_home)/conf/jni_server.xml
worker.inprocess.cmd_line=-home
worker.inprocess.cmd_line=$(workers.tomcat_home)
worker.inprocess.jvm_lib=$(workers.java_home)$(ps)jre$(ps)bin$(ps)classic$
    (ps)jvm.dll
#worker.inprocess.jvm_lib=$(workers.java_home)$(ps)bin$(ps)javai.dll
```

The "standard in" and "standard out" for the inprocess server are identified below. These are standard file handles in Unix which are often used for debugging output. They can be mapped directly to files as done in this example. The home directory for the Tomcat server instance to use is identified. In this case it is set to the TOMCAT_HOME directory we have established as a macro for this configuration. But this setting could have been used to set TOMCAT_HOME to some other directory specific to the Web application being supported by the in-process Tomcat server. (This property setting is similar to using the -f option when Tomcat is being started from the command line.)

```
worker.inprocess.stdout=$(workers.tomcat_home)$(ps)inprocess.stdout
worker.inprocess.stderr=$(workers.tomcat_home)$(ps)inprocess.stderr
worker.inprocess.sysprops=tomcat.home=$(workers.tomcat_home)
```

Pulling It All Together

Now that the configuration is in place, it is possible to run Tomcat and verify its operation. If Tomcat is installed as a standalone server, it will listen on port 8080 of the local host (usually, this is IP address 127.0.0.1). (This is defined by the HTTP Connector entry in the `server.xml` file.)

Before starting the Tomcat server, you may want to check to see that environment variables important in Tomcat are set correctly. The TOMCAT_HOME environment variable should be set to the root-level installation directory (the top) for the Tomcat server installation. Additionally, the JAVA_HOME environment variable should be set to the root-level directory for the Java JDK that will be used by the Tomcat installation.

Note that it is also important that the permissions for the work directory be set in such a way that the directories and their contents are accessible to the user that will be running the Tomcat server. If the permissions in these directories are not set correctly, Tomcat may return a 404 error. (Changing the ownership of all files in these directories to the user running Tomcat will fix this problem.)

The Tomcat server can be started by running the `startup.sh` command in the `TOMCAT_HOME/bin` directory. This should display a series of messages to the console window that should resemble the output shown below.

```
[tomcat@ataylor bin]$ ./startup.sh
Using classpath: /lin/local/jakarta/tomcat33/lib/tomcat.jar
Using JAVA_HOME: /lin/local/jdk/jdk1.2.2
Using TOMCAT_HOME: /lin/local/jakarta/tomcat33
[tomcat@ataylor bin]$
```

The logging output generated by the Tomcat server is dependent on the definition of the `LogSetter` element in the `server.xml` file. The Tomcat server does not provide output for the startup operation unless the `LogSetter` for the log `tc_log` (with the path `tomcat.log`) is set to a `verbosityLevel` of DEBUG. This log setting provides useful debugging information on the configuration files Tomcat is using, the contexts being established, where the interceptors are listening, and other copious debug output, as shown in the log file fragment below.

```
001-02-27 09:47:42 - ContextManager: set work dir /lin/local/jakarta/
    tomcat33/work
2001-02-27 09:47:42 - PathSetter: home=/lin/local/jakarta/tomcat33
2001-02-27 09:47:42 - LogEvents: engineInit
2001-02-27 09:47:44 - ContextXmlReader: Context config=$TOMCAT_HOME/conf/
    apps-admin.xml
2001-02-27 09:47:45 - ContextXmlReader: Context config=$TOMCAT_HOME/conf/
apps-127.0.0.1.xm2001-02-27 09:47:45 - ContextXmlReader: Context config=
$TOMCAT_HOME/conf/apps-examples.xml2001-02-27 09:47:45 - ContextXmlReader:
Context config=$TOMCAT_HOME/conf/apps-127.0.0.2.xm2001-02-27 09:47:45 -
AutoWebApp: Auto-Adding localhost:/examples
2001-02-27 09:47:45 - AutoWebApp: Auto-Adding localhost:/admin
```

```
2001-02-27 09:47:45 - AutoWebApp: Auto-Adding localhost:/
2001-02-27 09:47:45 - LogEvents: engineState 1
....
2001-02-27 09:47:46 - LogEvents: addContext localhost:/examples
2001-02-27 09:47:46 - ContextManager: Adding  localhost:/examples
2001-02-27 09:47:46 - LogEvents: addContext localhost:/admin
2001-02-27 09:47:46 - ContextManager: Adding  localhost:/admin
2001-02-27 09:47:46 - LogEvents: addContext localhost:/ROOT
2001-02-27 09:47:46 - ContextManager: Adding  localhost:/ROOT
2001-02-27 09:47:46 - LogEvents: contextInit DEFAULT:/admin
2001-02-27 09:47:47 - LogEvents: contextInit DEFAULT:/examples
2001-02-27 09:47:48 - LogEvents: contextInit 127.0.0.2:/lin/Website
2001-02-27 09:47:48 - LogEvents: contextInit localhost:/examples
2001-02-27 09:47:48 - LogEvents: contextInit localhost:/admin
2001-02-27 09:47:49 - LogEvents: contextInit localhost:/ROOT
2001-02-27 09:47:51 - LogEvents: engineState 2
2001-02-27 09:47:51 - LogEvents: engineStart
2001-02-27 09:47:51 - Http10Interceptor: Starting on 8080
2001-02-27 09:47:52 - Ajp12Interceptor: Starting on 8007
2001-02-27 09:47:52 - Ajp13Interceptor: Starting on 8009
2001-02-27 09:47:52 - LogEvents: engineState 3
```

Once the server is started, it can be tested by starting a browser on the local machine and directing it to this URL: `http://localhost:8080/examples`. If the Tomcat server is up and running and listening on port 8080, the page shown in Figure 5.5 should be displayed.

There will be links on this page to servlet and JSP examples. Choosing these links will bring you to pages that provide sample applications of both server-side programming facilities (see Figure 5.6).

Running both the servlet and JSP samples will verify that the Tomcat server is working. Be sure to test both the servlets and the JSP, since they use different portions of the server and you could have a problem with installation—one facility may work but not the other. Executing the "Date" sample will generate a page similar to that shown in Figure 5.7.

To shut down the server, execute the `shutdown.sh` script in the TOMCAT_HOME/bin directory. This script will shut down the Tomcat server and display a series of messages to the Tomcat log in the `TOMCAT_HOME/logs` directory indicating that the contexts are being removed. These messages will be similar to those shown below.

```
001-02-27 09:47:52 - LogEvents: engineState 3
2001-02-27 09:48:41 - LogEvents: engineState 2
2001-02-27 09:48:41 - ContextManager: Removing context DEFAULT:/admin
2001-02-27 09:48:41 - LogEvents: contextShutdown DEFAULT:/admin
```

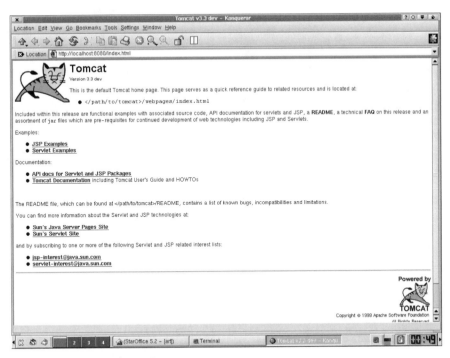

Figure 5.5 Tomcat Introductory Page

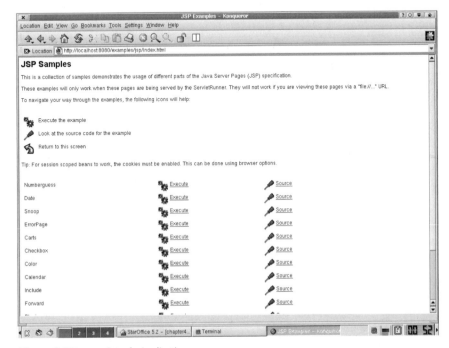

Figure 5.6 Tomcat Sample Applications

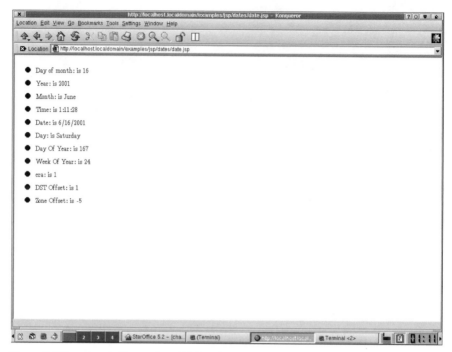

Figure 5.7 Executing the Tomcat Date JSP Sample

```
2001-02-27 09:48:41 - LogEvents: removeContextDEFAULT:/admin
2001-02-27 09:48:41 - ContextManager: Removing context DEFAULT:/examples
2001-02-27 09:48:41 - LogEvents: contextShutdown DEFAULT:/examples
2001-02-27 09:48:41 - LogEvents: removeContextDEFAULT:/examples
2001-02-27 09:48:41 - ContextManager: Removing context localhost:/examples
2001-02-27 09:48:41 - LogEvents: contextShutdown localhost:/examples
2001-02-27 09:48:41 - LogEvents: removeContextlocalhost:/examples
2001-02-27 09:48:41 - ContextManager: Removing context localhost:/admin
2001-02-27 09:48:41 - LogEvents: contextShutdown localhost:/admin
2001-02-27 09:48:41 - LogEvents: removeContextlocalhost:/admin
2001-02-27 09:48:41 - ContextManager: Removing context localhost:/ROOT
2001-02-27 09:48:41 - LogEvents: contextShutdown localhost:/ROOT
2001-02-27 09:48:41 - LogEvents: removeContextlocalhost:/ROOT
```

Testing the Link of Apache to Tomcat

The communication from the Apache server to the Tomcat server should also
be tested. The Apache server should be configured appropriately, with the
parameter values that make sense for your installation. In earlier sections of

this chapter we detailed the `mod_jk.conf` parameters and the workers.properties file settings that must be made for each installation. The Tomcat server will generate copies of these files on startup (and will place them in the `$TOM-CAT_HOME/conf/jk` directory), and it is these default files that should be used for initial testing.

After starting the Tomcat server, start the Apache server using the `apachectl` command as follows:

```
apachectl start
```

This should generate the following output:

```
# ./apachectl start
./apachectl start: httpd started
#
```

This is an indication that at least initially, there were no problems with the configuration of your system. Next, test to see that the Apache server is running correctly by using the localhost:80 URL (by default the Apache server should listen on port 80 of the local machine). That should generate the Apache default welcome page, a page similar to the image shown in Figure 5.8.

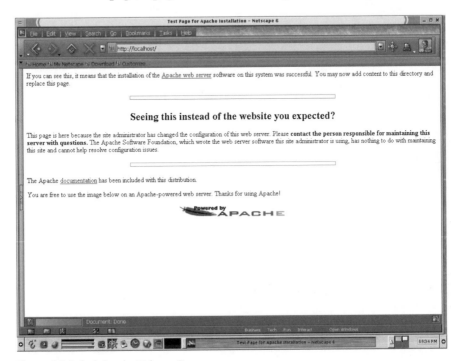

Figure 5.8 Default Apache Welcome Page

If you've created the examples location in the `mod_jk.conf` file as shown in the preceding section, the Apache server is aware of an aliased location of `/examples`, so that entering the URL `localhost:80  examples` should provide the directory listing shown in Figure 5.9.

Choosing the JSP directory link will cause the JSP samples page (the `index.html` page in that directory) to be displayed as shown in Figure 5.6. Choosing the execute link for the Date JSP page should produce the output shown in Figure 5.10.

This page appears to be almost the same as Figure 5.7, but note that the URL is different. Where Figure 5.7 showed `localhost:8080` as the server and port, this URL shows `localhost:80` as the server and port used to serve the request: the host and port for the Apache server, not the Tomcat server (the server that must ultimately have serviced the request).

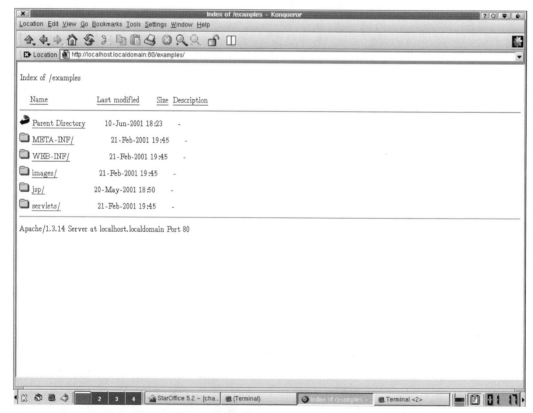

Figure 5.9 Directory Listing for Tomcat Examples Directory

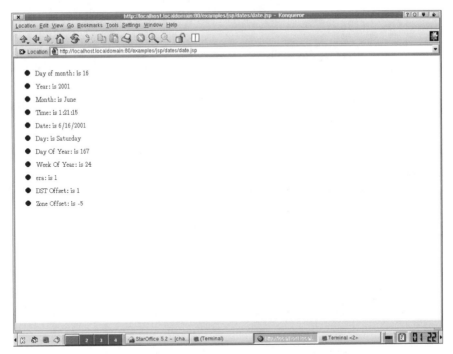

Figure 5.10 Tomcat JSP Page Executed through Apache Server

Recommendations

A number of recommendations can be made for the final installation. In general, the production installation should include both a Web server and the Tomcat server. This has the benefit of distributing the workload and eliminating a single point of failure for the site. Should the Tomcat server fail, the static pages on the site (and there should be more than a few of these) could continue to be served. Similarly, if the Apache server were to fail, the dynamic content from the Tomcat server could continue to be served. The default port number for the Tomcat server is 8080, which is a fairly common port number. On sites that are exposed to the Internet, you may want to change these port numbers to something less well known.

Locating Class Files for Resources

The JDBC driver is a resource used by the application. This resource is a set of class files packaged in a JAR file. These files must be placed in a directory that will include its contents (not just the directory) in the Java class path.

These files can either be placed in the $JAVA_HOME/lib/jre/lib/ext directory, or in the $TOMCAT_HOME/webapps/MyApp/WEB-INF/lib directory for each application that will use the resource. Since a database driver is probably going to be deployed and used by multiple applications, it is easier to share the drives among those multiple applications by placing it in the CLASSPATH for the Java runtime environment, as shown in the first example above.

Summary

Web applications have various components that must be located when the application is executed. As detailed in this chapter, these components could be static HTML, graphic images, sound files, and JSP and servlets. Placing the various components in consistent directories for the Tomcat server is important. Using the directories specified in the Java servlet 2.2 specification provides the ability to port the application easily to any servlet 2.2–compliant server.

It is important for our Web site to use the Apache server in combination with the Tomcat server. This requires the Apache server to communicate or integrate with the Tomcat server. This capability is provided by the mod_jk Apache module. By configuring this module through Apache configuration files and properties files, the Apache server can submit requests to the Tomcat server. With proper configuration, multiple workers can be configured within the mod_jk module. A load balancer within the mod_jk module will distribute the requests received to multiple Tomcat servers in a round-robin fashion. This distributor or dispatcher is aware of sessions and can notice and react when one of the servers in the list has stopped processing requests. This provides scalability and fail-over features for the Tomcat server.

Coming Up Next

Now that we have our infrastructure in place, it is time to take a look at our server-side programming language of choice: Java and JSPs. In the next chapter we cover the basics of JSPs, the syntax, and their background. Some small program fragments are shown and explained. In later chapters we describe and demonstrate more complex examples.

## CHAPTER 6

JAVA SERVER PAGES

Introduction

The use of dynamic Web pages on a site requires some sort of server-side scripting or programming to be done. As we have stated in previous chapters, Java is the preferred language to use for server-side development. But there are primarily two approaches to using Java on the Web: Java servlets and Java Server Pages (JSP). In this chapter we discuss the benefits of both approaches.

The focus of this book is on JSP. In this chapter we provide an introduction to JSP, explaining how it is used in conjunction with HTML to create dynamic Web pages. Understanding the reasoning behind JSP, the drivers for creating this technology, and the basic architecture of JSPs is an important start in understanding how to develop Web sites with this tool.

In this chapter we first explain the reasoning for JSP and the basic architecture of this technology. JSP is built on servlet technology; the specifics of how this is implemented is explained in this chapter. The basic syntax, the elements used (tags and directives), and the implicit objects of JSP are also covered in some detail.

Reason for Java Server Pages

A large portion of the development of Web pages is now performed by people who know nothing of procedural programming languages. They often know more about the artistic placement of graphics and text on a page than they do about programming control loops. For these Web page developers, a Web page involves some knowledge of HyperText Markup Language (HTML) and the use of GUI development tools to manipulate graphics and text to create an interesting Web page.

It is easier and less expensive to build a site using Web page developers than to find and pay a staff of Java developers to write Java servlet code to drive a Web site (and to maintain the site once it's complete), making it very attractive from an IT management perspective. But the tools do not currently exist to allow Web page developers to develop a truly dynamic site. To create dynamic Web content, some server-side coding is required.

Java servlets provide one method of creating dynamic Web content. With servlets, Java code is created and executed by the Web server in a *servlet container*. When a client (usually, a Web browser) references a servlet as a Web page, the servlet container executes the Java code, and the output of the code is the response that will be sent to the client.

Java servlets do a fine job of creating dynamic content, but unfortunately, there is no simple solution that allows a Java servlet developer to share work with a Web page developer who has no knowledge of Java. Using servlets to develop dynamic content for a site requires Java developers to essentially *own* the development of the dynamic pages they create. Once the servlet is created, making any changes to the page require a Java developer.

A more flexible and less expensive development paradigm would have the Java developer write the code (using the required business logic) to create the dynamic content for the site. All other Web page development that concerned presentation of the content would be the responsibility of the Web page developer. More important, once this dynamic page is completed, the Web page developer could perform the bulk of the maintenance on the page.

Using this approach to Web site development, the Web page developer is responsible for *presentation* of the Web site, and the Java developer is responsible for the application of *business logic* and data access. This provides for an attractive *separation of roles*, specifically the role of the *Java programmer* and the role of the *Web page developer*.

For this approach to work, the Web page developer must be able to execute business logic and access data using a tool or language that he or she understands. What most Web page developers understand are HTML tags. Java developers must therefore be able to hide the details of their work behind special HTML tags.

Java Server Pages Development

JSP provides the ability to implement the separation of roles in a development effort in using an simple, flexible approach. The Java developer can create a large body of code that is easily accessible through the Web page using special HTML-like tags. The process for creating access to Java code from within a Web page is simple and straightforward. What is significant is that virtually the complete Java language and the vast majority of the APIs available are accessible through JSP.

If developed correctly, the JSP page would contain minimal Java code and would perform most of the work with Java code off the page (in JavaBeans or through tag libraries). Since the developmental goal is to divide the visual presentation and business logic of the application, the JSP page should be composed primarily of visual aspects of the page: the graphics, fonts, and layout of the page as expressed in HTML. The business logic should reside largely outside the page, in JavaBeans or some other external component. The actual Java code (referred to as *scriplets*) on the page should be kept to a minimum.

This is not to say that servlets do not have their place; they certainly do. When the depth and complexity of the application logic exceed the description of the visual portion of the page, execution of a servlet may be preferable: for instance, a dynamic page that creates a report where the dynamic content would control the layout and flow of the page, or where the inclusion and placement of a large number of fields on the page would require the execution of extensive business logic. Any page where over 60 percent of the page would be the execution of logic would be better represented with a servlet or, more appropriately, a servlet and JavaBeans to encapsulate some portion of the business logic. For instance, a page that performs authentication and then makes a decision concerning which view the authenticated user should see should be implemented as a servlet.

How JSP Works

JSP is implemented *on top of* servlet technology. JSPs are compiled or converted into servlets, which are then run within a servlet *container* (see Figure 6.1. The container is an abstraction which provides various services, usually related to the operating infrastructure, for the components running within the container. In the case of the Tomcat server, both the JSP engine and the servlet container are contained within the same server environment. The JSP 1.1 specification requires a servlet container that implements the Java servlets 2.2 specification; the Tomcat server provides both of these (and is, in fact, the reference implementation for servlets and JSPs for the Java2 Enterprise Edition, J2EE).

Client

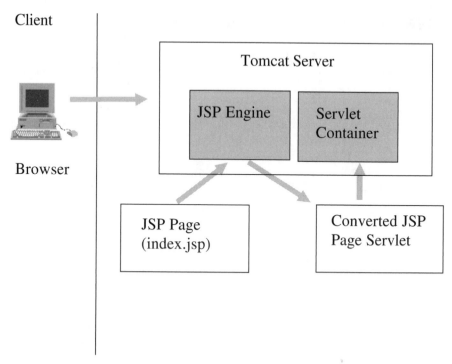

Browser

Figure 6.1 Java Server Pages and Servlet Technology

This logically simple approach takes the JSP and converts non-Java statements (statements outside the special JSP tags) into servlet output statements
as shown below.

```
...
<h2> Why JSP is Good </h2>
<p> Of all the important strides made in Web development ...
<h2> Why servlets are Great</h2>
<%
if ( x == 10 ) {
 %>
<p> This is displayed only if x == 10
<% } %>
...
```

These statements would be converted into the following:

```
...
PrintWriter out = response.getWriter();
```

```
out.println("<h2>Why JSP is Good</h2>");
out.println("<p> Off all the important strides made in Web
development ...");
out.println("<h2> Why servlets are Great</h2>");
if ( x == 10 ) {
    out.println("<p> This is displayed only if x == 10");
}
```

The *JSP environment* (as distinguished from the servlet *container* within which the JSP will ultimately run) manages all aspects of processing the JSP. The Web server handles the initial request for the page, recognizes that the page is a JSP, and passes the page to the JSP environment for processing. The JSP environment must then process the page and return the results of the page processing to the browser that requested the page.

The initial request for the JSP, as initiated by the Web browser or from some other source, is known as the *request*. The results of processing the page that was requested is known as the *response*. Output from the response is eventually sent back to the browser that initiated the request (or in some cases, to another destination specified in the initial request).

The JSP are converted into servlets, which are then compiled to Java class files (if necessary) and executed. This process of JSP translation to Java code and subsequent compilation is performed only when needed. If the source JSP has not been modified since the last time the related servlet class file was compiled, the compiled class file will be executed to satisfy the request.

Both JSP and servlets are referred to as *Web components*. Conceptually, JSPs are delivered to a *server environment* that provides the necessary processing to convert the page into a valid HTTP response which will then be sent to the browser that requested the page. This server environment will provide both the JSP processing and the servlet container. The environment may be a separate thread within the Web server or a complete separate process that communicates with the Web server through a network connection.

Component-Oriented Architecture

Multitiered architectures are conceptually composed of *components*, portions of software that reside on the multiple tiers. On the Web tier, Java servlets, JSP, and JavaBeans represent components. Enterprise JavaBeans (EJBs) also represent components. They are considered components that reside on the business tier. EJBs provide a more robust environment for components, but to deliver this extended functionality, they require a more complex development and runtime environment. (See Appendix B for a discussion of EJBs.)

The JSP is effectively converted into a servlet class through a translation phase. The translation phase converts the page first to Java code that supports the servlet API, then compiles the page to a Java class file. This class file represents a servlet that is created at runtime when the page is requested (the resulting servlet will manage the request).

This translation process can be completed before the page is requested when the application is deployed, or at runtime when the page is requested. Because of the overhead involved in the translation process, the recommendation is that a page be compiled before runtime. The Tomcat server supports both approaches, allowing pages to be compiled before they are deployed or on-demand when the pages are requested. When the Tomcat server receives a request for a JSP it makes an effort to determine if the source for the page has been *touched* (modified) since the last translation and compile of the page, and if the source has been touched since the last time the page was compiled, the page will be recompiled before the request is processed.

The JSP will be used to formulate a response that is ultimately converted into a Java object of type `HTTPServletResponse`. The JSP itself is a `HttpJspPage` and will receive and process a parameter of type `HttpServletRequest` from the client. The responsibility of the JSP container during the translation phase is to create a Java class that represents the JSP, the page that must be used to formulate the response. According to the JSP specification, the container has some freedom in the specifics of this class creation. The translation phase is for the most part transparent to the developer, although the developer does need to be aware of the nature of the process. Specifically, the developer needs to be aware that all Java code in the JSP will be represented in a single class file and that any scripting variable declared in one section of the page will have scope (be visible) in other sections of the page.

JSP Syntax and Usage

JSPs are conceptually divided into *elements* and *template data*. Elements are data in a JSP that are with the JSP processing environment. Conversely, template data are any portion of a JSP that is not important to the system. For example, standard HTML tags that concern headers, footers, or links would be considered template data within a JSP.

JSP elements are the tools used to express JSPs within the Web page. These elements are either *scripting* elements, *directive* elements, or *action* elements. JSP elements may use attributes and corresponding values to express information about that element. Attribute values must be quoted. These elements are described in more detail below.

Scripting elements, actions and JavaBeans components are used to describe the dynamic content of a JSP. The prevailing recommendation for development of JSP is that scripting elements be kept to a minimum and wherever possible, custom tags and references to JavaBeans components be used to manage the dynamic content. Using such a design strategy would result in a JSP that concentrates on presentation while business logic is managed *off-the-page* using other facilities.

Web Application and the Session

As explained previously, the Web application is a combination of *components*, from static HTML, graphic images, and text to the dynamic content provided by JSP and servlets. When users accesses a site using their browser, they are accessing any number of these components. Each user access is represented by a request to the Web server. This request is directed to a *location*, which results in a response being generated by an HTML page, a JSP, or a servlet. Over the course of a visit to a site, a user may access more than one of these locations over a period of time. This association between the HTTP client (the user's browser) and the HTTP server (the Apache or Tomcat server) is considered a *session*. Although the HTTP protocol does not provide a session (it is, in fact, a *stateless* protocol, and without state you cannot preserve session information), the servers that use this protocol usually provide mechanisms to create a *logical session*.

Capturing Session Information

Session-capturing mechanisms usually require a cookie, a state object, to be stored on the client's machine through the browser, implying that the client must support and allow cookies for a session to be maintained with a Web server using the HTTP protocol. Using this approach a session ID is placed in a cookie in the client's browser and is then sent to the server with each HTTP request. (All active cookies are sent with each request.) The server uses this session id to access the internal session information that corresponds to the session. This internal session information is then made available to the page being accessed by the request, thus making maintenance of the session transparent to the page. Alternatives to the use of cookies (e.g., URL rewriting) to maintain sessions are available but have associated problems. The most common approach is to use cookies.

The servlet can maintain a logical session through the `HttpSession`, and since a JSP is based on the Java servlet, it can participate in sessions using the

`HttpSession` interface and its representation in the JSP, the `session` object. In the following sections we explain the use of this object in more detail.

Concept of Scope

The term *scope* applies to the visibility of the programming elements within a program. This term is usually applied to the variables within the program. For Java, variables either represent primitive data types or object references. Java provides eight primitive data types: `byte`, `char`, `short`, `int`, `long`, `float`, `double`, and `boolean`. Everything else in the Java language is an object reference. Since object references can represent any valid Java class, there is a great deal of flexibility and extensibility in this process. Since for all effective purposes, a Java class is a data type, the Java language is type extensible—whatever data type is needed can be created as a class.

All Java references have some form of scope. For Java programs, this scope centers on the notion of the Java *class*. But the JSP is not a Java program; in fact, the JSP specification refers to the Java code in the JSP as *a page* that contains objects and *scriplets*.

Additionally, the JSP is not executed as a Java application might be. A JSP is executed as some component of a Web application and would represent only a portion of the application, not the complete application. As such, it must participate with the other components in the application as part of the session or part of the application as a whole.

The JSP will be translated into a class and the Java code within this page will become part of that class. Any variables declared outside a block become class variables of the JSP class. All of the code and HTML within the page are converted into code within a single method, the `_jspService` method.

For these reasons, JSP has scope attributes that extend those of the Java language. JSP objects can be have a scope attribute of *page, request, session,* or *application*. An object with *page* scope is visible only on the page. Once the page has been processed and the request sent back, the object is no longer in scope (i.e., no longer available). References to objects with page scope are stored in the `pageContext` object.

A page declared with *request* scope is visible throughout the life of the request. In most cases, the request lives for the same duration as the page. But in cases where the request is forwarded to another page, the request object will be sent along with the request. The reference to the request scope object is stored in the `request` object. The object reference is released when the request is completed.

A page declared with *session* scope survives for the duration of the session. A session is considered a succession of request–response operations from the same client, and all pages that are in the same session have access to the same session objects. References to these objects are stored in the `session` object that is created during page activation and is available implicitly to the JSP. (Note that pages using page scope have access to the `session` object.)

An object that is declared with *application* scope is available to all pages that are part of a given application. Application objects in another application are not visible to other applications. If a page has chosen not to participate in a session (the session attribute of the page directive is set to `false`), the application object is still available. These references are stored in the `application` object created during page activation (as obtained from the servlet configuration object). This object reference is released when the runtime environment reclaims the `ServletContext` object.

Directive Elements

Directives are elements that are interpreted by the preprocessing of the page; they are processed before the JSP (or resulting servlet page) is executed at runtime. Associated with a directive can be a number of attribute–value pairs. The syntax for directives is

```
<%@ directive_name attribute_1 = "value" attribute_2="value" %>
```

A *directive element* is used by the JSP preprocessor as part of the page preprocessing effort. It is used to provide information to the preprocessor about other elements and scriplets contained within the page. This element is described in more detail later.

Scripting Elements

Scripting elements are the syntactical mechanism that allows Java code to be placed in a JSP. Three types of scripting elements are allowed: *declarations*, *scriptlets*, and *expressions*. JSP declarations are used to declare elements of the script. The syntax for this element is

```
<%! declaration
%>
```

This construct can be used to declare both variables and methods, as follows:

```
<%!
    int counter = 0;
    public int mkInt(String s) {
        String s1 = s.substring(4, s.length());
        return Integer.parseInt(s1);
    }
%>
```

The first statement in the example declares an integer variable named counter and initializes it to the value of 0. The next declaration declares a method mkInt to perform a simple string parsing operation. Note that both of these declarations are members of the class that will be created to implement the JSP. This has implications for variables declared in these blocks. A JSP server may potentially share instances of the JSP class among multiple requests. Since member variables will retain their value between references (as opposed to local member variables, which will be recreated and must be initialized explicitly before each use), member variables could develop unexpected values in this type of environment.

Unless there is a compelling reason to create member variables using the declaration element in JSP, it is best to declare variables needed on the page in scriplets where they are local to the _jspService method created for execution of the page. Since variables declared within the _jspService method are local variables, they are destroyed and recreated on each invocation of the page and are thus more inclined to contain expected values. In keeping with the advice "declare variables as close as possible to where they are used," declaring variables within the scriplet close to their usage is recommended.

Scriplet blocks provide for Java code within the page. The syntax for these elements is

```
<%
for (int n=0;n< 10;n++) {
%>
<p> This, that and the other
<% } %>
```

A programming expression is a programmatic expression that is any legal statement in the Java language that returns a value that is a valid Java data type. Expressions can be equality statements or method calls. An expression in JSP is more specifically defined to be an expression in scriplet code directed to the output stream (JspWriter). This is denoted by the syntax

```
<%= myVar %>
```

This expression is effectively a shorthand for the statement

```
...
out.println( myVar );
...
```

What appears as a variable in this expression can be any Java data type that can be freely converted to a `String`. This includes all of the primitive Java data types as well as Java object references that have a sensible `toString` method implementation.

Scriplets must start and end in the same JSP; they cannot span pages. Scriplet variables have scope within a page, so that a variable declared in one scriplet is visible in another scriplet. But variables have scope only within that page. To store values that will be visible on other pages, the value must be stored as an attribute of the `session` or `application` object shown below, or the value must be passed as a parameter to a new page.

Each JSP is compiled into an class where the declarations section of the class is a concatenation of all declaration blocks with the JSP, and the body of the `_jspService` method in the class is a concatenation of all scriplets within the page. Concatenation is performed in the order in which the declarations or scriplets appear in the page.

Element Syntax

JSP *elements* use XML syntax. They have a start tag, an optional list of attributes and values, an optional body, and either an end tag or a closing tag. An example of this syntax is

```
<specTag attribute1="10" attribute2="20" >
    This is the body of the action element
</specTag>
```

The element name in this example is `specTag`; note that the name is case-sensitive. Attributes are set in the start tag and are assigned values that must be quoted. An optional format for an element with an empty body is

```
<specTag attribute1="20" attribute2="myValue" />
```

In this example, the closing tag is a `/>` set of characters that indicates the end of the element. Note that JSP tags are case-sensitive.

Comments in JSP

Comments can be placed in a JSP either in the HTML portion using an HTML comment or in a JSP element. The syntax for an HTML comment is

```
<!- this is a comment ->
```

JSP elements can be placed in an HTML comment using the following syntax:

```
<!- this is a comment with <%= jspVal %> some JSP data ->
```

Note that since the JSP compiler will read the entire JSP file (including the HTML comments), this JSP element will be parsed, compiled, and executed. The ultimate output to the client will contain the HTML comment with the runtime value of the JSP expression. The browser will receive the comment but will not display it unless the user chooses to display the page source at the browser. (In a practical sense, this would only be useful for debugging request output from the JSP.)

To place a comment within a JSP element, use the syntax

```
<%!- this is a JSP comment  -%>
```

Within a scriplet, the syntax for Java language comments is also valid.

```
...
<%
// build HTML list from contents of collection
// peopleList is Iterator for list of participating staff
while (myBean.peopleList.hasNext() ){
%>
<li><%= myBean.i.next() %>

<%
}
%>
...
```

Scripting elements can be quoted with a backward slash (\) character as follows:

```
<% String s = "this is a quoted quote character (\") "; %>
```

If the backward slash character were eliminated as shown in the following example, an error would be returned by the JSP preprocessor.

```
<!- this is bad syntax - don't try this at home ... ->
<% String s = "this is a quoted quote character (") "; %>
```

This would result in the following error:

```
Error: 500

Location: /examples/jsp/art/t.jspInternal Servlet Error:

org.apache.jasper.JasperException: Unable to compile
/lin/local/jakarta/tomcat33/work/DEFAULT/examples/jsp/art/t_1.java
:62: ';' expected.
                String s = "this is a quoted quote character
(") ";

^
/lin/local/jakarta/tomcat33/work/DEFAULT/examples/jsp/art/t_1.java
:62: String not terminated at end of line.
                String s = "this is a quoted quote character
(") ";

^
2 errors
^
...
```

Implicit JSP Objects

A number of useful objects are available implicitly in JSP scriplet code. The types (Java classes) for these variables are detailed in Table 6.1.

request Object

The request object represents the HTTP request which accessed the JSP page and contains information about the request. This object is generally used to access the parameters passed to the request (as part of the query string). Many HTTP requests use these parameters to detail the specifics of the request. For instance, a form that has been filled in on the browser will paste the values of the fields in the request. Following is an example of using a request object to retrieve parameter values.

Table 6.1 JSP Variable Types

Object	Class	Description	Scope
request	javax.servlet.ServletRequest	Represents the request from the client	Request
response	javax.servlet.ServletResponse	Response to be formulated for the request	Page
page	java.lang.Object	Instance of this page's class	Page
exception	java.lang.Throwable	Exception object available only on an error page	Page
out	javax.servlet.jsp.JspWriter	Provides access to the response output stream	Page
config	javax.servlet.ServletConfig	Servlet configuration for this JSP	Page
page	javax.lang.Object	Instance of this page's class	Page
exception	javax.lang.Throwable	Exception object available only on an error page	Page

```
String custName = request.getParameter("custname");
String custID   = request.getParameter("custid");
```

The string value passed into the getParameter method is the name of the parameter. A string value for the parameter (all parameters must be strings) is returned as a Java String.

For convenience, parameter names can also be retrieved as an enumeration, as shown in the example.

```
...
Enumeration e = request.getParameterNames();
while ( e.hasMoreElements() ) {
        String s = e.nextElement();
    // process parameters
...
```

Additionally, the corresponding values can be retrieved in a `String` array using the `getParameterValues` method.

```
String[] s  = request.getParameterValues("CheckBox1");
```

The `request` object can also be used to retrieve information on the HTTP header for the request, such as the content type, length, and character encoding. Additionally, a method is available to determine whether or not the request was made on a secure channel such as HTTPS.

```
if ( request.isSecure() ) {
   // perform secure processing
   ...
```

response Object

The `response` object represents the output to the client. It is, in fact, the job of the JSP to produce this output stream; this happens implicitly in the processing of the JSP and its constituent `scriplets` and tags. Although this object is used in servlet development to provide output, with JSP, output processing is performed differently. JSP uses the `out` object, an instance of the `jspWriter` class, to provide direct access to output.

With servlets, the `response` object is generally used to obtain the output stream for the response. This output stream can be used for binary or character output. A binary data output stream could be obtained from the response object using the following call:

```
ServletOutputStream so = response.getOutputStream();
```

To obtain an output stream for character output, the `PrintWriter` would be obtained using the `getWriter` method.

```
PrintWriter pw = response.getWriter();
```

The `response` object is also useful for setting the various headers being returned to the client and thus providing some degree of control of client-side forwarding, cache control, content expiration, and content type.

page Object

The `page` object represents an instance of the current page. It is therefore a self-referencing object to the currently processing page. Within the body of the page, the `page` object reference is similar to the `this` reference within a Java program.

out Object

The `out` object represents the character response output stream for the current page. The `out` object is an implementation of the `javax.servlet.jsp.JspWriter` interface that is provided by the JSP server (and managed by the corresponding servlet container environment). This object provides the functionality of a `java.io.PrintWriter` or `java.io.BufferedWriter` object in that I/O is buffered and filtered.

Since the JSP scriplet syntax provides a convenient means of producing output without using a method call (the `<%=` syntax), use of the `out` object is usually just reserved for certain sections of code where it is simply more convenient to express output using a method call, as shown in the following code.

```
...
<%
    for (n = 1, Iterator i = c.iterator();
        i.hasNext(); n++ )   {
        if ( n < 20 )
            out.println("row: " + n " - output: " + i.next() );
...
```

Within the body of a programmatic `for` loop, it is more convenient to insert a method call than it is to close the scriplet block, perform output using a JSP expression, and start another scriplet block.

Note that although it is possible to perform response I/O processing with the `out` object, it is not recommended. Java scriplet code within the JSP should be kept to a minimum, and alternatives to method calls should be used whenever possible. Therefore, use of the JSP expression for output (`<%= MyVar %>`) is preferable to an `out.println()` method call because it is more understandable to a page developer who knows nothing about Java programming.

config Object

The `config` implicit object represents the `ServletConfig` (`javax.servlet.ServletConfig`) for the current JSP page. This object can be used to provide information on the underlying servlet, such as the servlet name and the servlet context.

The `ServletContext` is available from the implicit `config` object using the `getContext` method. This method returns a `ServletContext` object which contains useful information on the parameters, attributes, and MIME type for the servlet. It can also be used to access the log for the servlet using the `log` method (which actually writes a string to the servlet log).

pageContext Object

The `pageContext` implicit object contains a reference to the page context (`javax.servlet.jsp.PageContext`) for the JSP being processed. This object can be used explicitly to request references to a number of the implicit objects as detailed in the abbreviated list in Table 6.2.

Table 6.2 pageContext References Request Methods

Method	Returns	Type
`getOut`	Reference to implicit out object	`JspWriter`
`getPage`	Reference to the current page	`Object`
`getRequest`	Reference to the current HTTP request	`ServletRequest`
`getResponse`	Reference to the response for the current request	`ServletResponse`
`getServletConfig`	Reference to the configuration object for the current servlet (converted JSP)	`ServletConfig`
`getServletContext`	Reference to the servlet context	`ServletContext`

This object reference also provides methods to forward to another page and to include another page into the response output stream for the current page. Since these methods all involve manipulation of the presentation logic, it is best to perform this work in the JSP using JSP tags whenever possible.

session Object

The `session` implicit object contains a reference to the currently active session (`javax.servlet.http.HttpSession`). The session object is generally used to represent a user session across multiple requests. Attributes and corresponding values can be stored within the session object during one request and then retrieved during successive requests. These attributes can be set with calls to the `setAttribute` and `getAttribute` methods, as shown below.

```
1.    ...
2.    <% session.setAttribute("custName",
3.
request.getParameter("custName")); %>
4.    <% session.setAttribute("custID",
5.                            request.getParameter("custID"));
%>
6.    ...
7.    <!- retrieve the customer name and ID from the session
object ->
8.
9.        <p> Customer Name:  <%= (String)
session.getAttribute("custName") %>
10.        <p> Customer ID: <%= (String)
session.getAttribute("custID") %>
11.    ....
```

These methods accept and return an object reference, so that the `getAttribute` call generally requires a Java cast, as shown on lines 9 and 10 in the example above.

application Object

The `application` implicit object represents the `ServletContext` (`javax.servlet.ServletContext`) for the current servlet/JSP. This object can be used to gather information about the servlet container and includes methods to set and retrieve attributes for the current servlet and their values, to remove attributes, and to write to a log file for the servlet container. This object can also be used to get the MIME type of file, to access the request dispatcher (to forward a request to another JSP, servlet, or HTML page), or to get a list of all attribute names for the servlet.

The exception Object

The `exception` object is only available on an error page, a special JSP that can optionally be called when an exception is thrown. The `exception` object is used like an exception object in a Java program, an argument to a `catch` block. It is an instance of `Java.lang.Throwable` and thus has a getMessage method available that can be used to display an error message for the exception that was thrown and the printStackTrace method that will output the stack trace for the current execution point with the Java program (the JSP./servlet execution).

Directives

Directives are elements that are interpreted by the preprocessing of the page; they are processed before the JSP (or resulting servlet page) is executed at runtime. Associated with a directive can be a number of attribute–value pairs. The syntax for directives is as follows:

```
<%@ directive_name attr1="value" attr2="value" ... %>
```

Table 6.3 lists the directives available in JSP version 1.1.

Table 6.3 JSP Version 1.1 Directives

Directive	Description
page	Information about the JSP that is visible to the user; can provide basic information about the page, the error page to use, whether or not the page is thread safe, and other information
include	Incorporates text (not necessarily a JSP) into the current page; in JSP 1.2, two mechanisms are provided, one to provide includes that will be parsed by the JSP preprocessor, and the other to provide runtime includes that will not be parsed
taglib	Indicates that the page uses a tag library and contains attributes to locate the tag library and to reference the tag library within the page

page Directive

A page directive is used to perform certain actions before a page is loaded. This directive can have one of the attributes listed in Table 6.4.

Table 6.4 page Directive Attributes

Attribute	Descriptive
import	Java language import directive
errorPage	URL of the error page for this page; if an exception is thrown on this page or in one its helper classes, this page will be the loaded and returned to the client
extends	The Java class name this JSP will extend (note that this use of this feature must be carefully considered)
session	Set to either true or false, depending on whether or not this page must participate in a session
language	Scripting language to be used (currently, only Java is supported as the scripting language, but vendors could potentially implement other scripting languages)
buffer	Set to either none or an integer value indicating the size of the output buffer (where appending "kb" is mandatory to indicate the buffer size in kilobytes)
autoFlush	Set to either true or false, depending on whether or not the buffer will be flushed automatically (note that this requires that the buffer attribute be set to some valid value)
isThreadSafe	Set to true or false, depending on the level of thread safety in the page
info	String entry that can be set to any arbitrary text value and can then be retrieved using the servlet method servlet.getServletInfo.
contentType	Defines the character encoding for a JSP and the MIME type for the response of a JSP
pageEncoding	Defines the character encoding for a JSP
isErrorPage	true if this is the error page, false if this is not the error page

Using the extends Attribute of the page Directive

The JSP container converts each JSP to a Java class that is a superclass specified by the JSP container (implementing either the JspPage or HttpJspPage interface). The extends attribute of the page directive allows the superclass of the page to be identified. This is not a capability that can be taken lightly, since the JSP container depends on appropriate implementation of the `JspPage` or `HttpJspPage` inter-faces. The expectation is that the developer of a JSP container would develop certain classes that could be used to provide additional capabilities within the page and that these classes would be used as arguments to these attributes. The `taglib` facility and the `jsp:useBean` tag can be used to provide additional functionality within a JSP and for the average developer provide a much safer alternative than extending the base class for the JSP page.

More than one page attribute can be included with the page directive, as shown in the following example.

```
<%@ page errorPage="/share/ErrorPage.jsp" info="Standard Customer
login page." isThreadSafe="false" %>
```

include Directive

The `include` directive (see Figure 6.2) provides the capability to include arbitrary text within a JSP. This seemingly benign capability provides significant advantages for the developer. The common syntax for this directive is

```
<%@ include file="file_name" %>
```

This directive inserts the file specified in the file attribute at the location in the JSP where the directive was inserted. This form of the `include` directive inserts the file *after* running the file through the preprocessor and is processed (parsed and converted) when the page is translated. The content of the file is **not** loaded when the page is executed or requested.

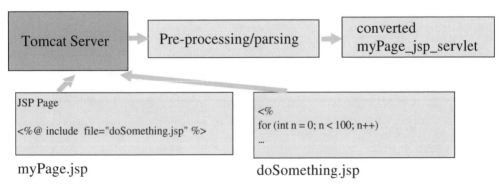

Figure 6.2 include Directive

Alternatively, there is a form of includes that does **not** translate or pre-process the contents of the included file and performs its operation at the time when the JSP is requested. Using this form of the include operation, the contents of the target page are simply placed on the output stream at the point where the tag is encountered in the page (see Figure 6.3). The syntax for this statement is

```
<jsp:include page="footer.html" />
```

The difference between the implementation of these two versions of includes is the difference between static and dynamic content. If the contents to be included in the page are static, they will not change from the point where the page has been created to the point at which the page is requested. Then the first form of the statement is recommended (and will perform better, since it will require less work of the container at request time).

Alternatively, if the contents to be included change constantly, the second form of the directive is recommended. This form of the directive will read the contents of the file when the request is made so that the page will always access the most current version of the file. This would be useful for a daily message or a list of currently relevant news stories and links that should be included in a JSP.

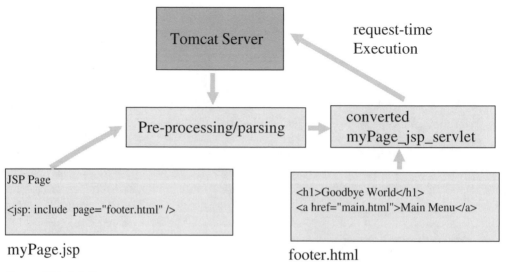

Figure 6.3 include Tag

taglib Directive

The `taglib` directive is used to create custom tags that can be used within a Web page. The use of tags is more intuitive for Web page developers not familiar with Java, those commonly responsible for a significant part of Web site development and maintenance. A number of tag libraries are available both commercially and as open-source code. To use these libraries with JSP, Java code needs to be called using custom tags created using a special API. The syntax for the use of this directive is as follows:

```
<%@ taglib uri="libraryURI" prefix="tagPrefix" %>
```

The `taglib` directive uses two attributes: `uri` and `prefix`. The `uri` attribute identifies the location of the XML file that describes the properties of the tag library, including the location of the class file which implements the library. The `prefix` attribute will be used to distinguish a custom action.

Once a tag library has been identified, the tags contained in the library can be used within the JSP. The tags can accept arguments from the page and dynamically produce page content by executing the Java code contained in the tag library. (Several JSP that use `taglibs` are shown in Chapter 8.)

JSP Tags

The JSP container provides a number of useful tags that can be used in a JSP page. These tags are given in Table 6.5.

jsp:useBean Tag

The `jsp:useBean` tag is used to identify the JavaBean to be used in the JSP. The attributes of this tag identify the name of the Java class file that contains the JavaBean and the id or name that will be used to identify this bean in the page. Once a JavaBean has been *included* with the page, all the members of the object that comprise the JavaBean are available within the Java code used on that JSP. The `useBean` tag must specify a value for either the type or class attribute. (Java needs this before it can create the corresponding object to represent the bean.) The `useBean` tag has a number of attributes associated with it, shown in Table 6.6

Table 6.5 JSP Tags

Tag	Purpose
`jsp:useBean`	To identify a JavaBean to use
`jsp:setProperty`	To set a property value for a JavaBean
`jsp:getProperty`	To retrieve a property value from a JavaBean
`jsp:include`	To include a text file in a JSP page; the contents will not be preprocessed and will be retrieved at request time
`jsp:forward`	To forward a request to another page; the current request will stop processing
`jsp:param`	Pass parameters via a key–value pair; used with the `jsp:include`, `jsp:forward`, or `jsp:plug-in` tag
`jsp:plugin`	To allow a browser `plugin` to be invoked from the server in order to manage some part of the page to be rendered by the browser

Table 6.6 jsp:useBean Tag Attributes

Attribute	Description
`type`	Type of the scripting variable to be created; if this is not the class specified in the class attribute, it must be a superclass of the class specified
`class`	Name of the class for the JavaBean
`beanName`	Name of the bean as used by the `java.beans.Beans.instantiate()` method
`scope`	Scope of the bean: one of either page, request, session, or application
`id`	Name for the resulting object; also the name of the scripting variable

If the class and the `beanName` attribute are not specified, the object referenced must be visible within the current scope (as specified in the attributes list).

In this example, the bean named myBean is loaded using this directive.

```
<jsp:useBean id="myBean" class="tools.myBean">
      <jsp:setProperty name="myBean" property="beanMember"
value="Freddy">
  </jsp:useBean>
```

In this example, the myBean property beanMember is set to the value "Freddy". The setting of bean properties based on the context of the application (effectively *initializing* the properties) is a common reason for using a body with the useBean tag. Also note that in this example the body of the useBean tag is terminated on the final line of the example.

jsp:setProperty Tag

The setProperty tag allows a bean property to be set via the value attribute in the tag. The following example demonstrates.

```
<jsp:setProperty name="myBean" property="userName" value="Fred" />
```

In this example, the property userName in the JavaBean myBean is set to the value specified by the value attribute, which in this case is the string value "Fred." Alternatively, the property value can be set using a request parameter as shown in the following example.

```
<jsp:useBean id="myBean" class="examples.myBean" />
...
<jsp:setProperty name="myBean" property="userName" param="user" />
```

In this example, the bean named myBean will have the property userName set to the value of the request parameter "user" (request.getParameter("user")). (The request parameter is usually passed from an HTML form.) If the attribute param is not supplied to the setProperty tag and no value parameter is supplied, the JSP container will assume that the param name is the same as the property name, and it should find a method named set<param name> or get<param name>. Since most commonly the name of the getXXX and setXXX methods is the same as the property name, there is no need to use the param attribute, and it is not used.

Note that the param and value attributes cannot appear in the same tag. The reason for this is obvious: These are mutually exclusive attributes and values can only be retrieved from one or the other, not both. Conversion of the value attribute will take place as needed. Since the value attribute will initially be passed as a Java String, if it is being placed into a String in the JavaBean, no conversion needs to take place. If it is not being placed into a String, conversion must take place using the valueOf method of the Java language primitive data type of the wrapper class, as indicated in Table 6.7.

Table 6.7 JAVA Primitive Data Type Wrapper Classes

Data Type	Class
boolean	java.lang.Boolean
byte	java.lang.Byte
char	java.lang.Character
int	java.lang.Integer
long	java.lang.Long
float	java.lang.Float
double	java.lang.Double

The setProperty tag is converted (during the JSP pre-processor stage) into a call that converts the String value into the primitive data type (the data type that is a parameter to the setXXXX method in the JavaBean). The String value is passed to the valueOf method as follows:

```
...
String s;
...
int i = Java.lang.Integer.parseInt( s );
...
```

The valueOf method will return the primitive data type of the wrapper class being used. In this example, the valueOf method will return a Java int data type for the value of String s.

jsp:getProperty Tag

The getProperty tag retrieves the value of a bean property and returns it to the output stream of the JSP. The bean value is first converted to a type String and is then placed on the output stream. Conversion is performed using the Java language classes that correspond to the primitive Java data types (integer, float, double, short). The format for the getProperty tag is

```
<jsp:useBean id="myBean" class="examples.myBean" />
...
User Name:   <jsp:getProperty name="myBean" property="userName" />
```

In this example the getProperty tag is used to retrieve the userName property and return the output into the JSP. Note that the userName will appear on the page as part of the HTML generated and will appear appropriately enough directly next to the User Name: string that appears in the page.

jsp:include Tag

The include tag performs a function similar to that of the include directive. This tag will retrieve the text in the file referenced in the attribute of the tag, but unlike the include directive, it will not run the file contents through the preprocessor but will instead place the contents directly on the output stream when the JSP is requested. The content included will not be parsed. The page attribute of the include tag specifies the page to be included. Its argument must be a value that evaluates to a URL string:

```
<jsp:include page="/headerPages/header1.html" />
```

In this example, the page header1.html is included in the output stream of the current page.

jsp:forward Tag

The forward tag is used to *forward* processing to a specified page. This means that the container running the page (servlet) will terminate processing of the current page and then retrieve the contents of the forward page into the current ContextManager. At that point, processing of the forward page will begin. The syntax for this tag is as follows:

```
...
<jsp:forward page="/jumpPages/jump1.html" />
...
```

The forward tag can also include parameters to be passed to the forwarding page by using a tag body containing param tags, as shown in the following example.

```
. . .
<jsp:forward page="/jumpPages/jump1.jsp" >
   <jsp:param name="jumpCount" value=" <%= jumpsCount %>" />
   <jsp:param name="jumpApplication" value=" <%= appName %>" />
</jsp:forward>
. . .
```

In this example, two parameters are passed to the page jump1.JSP: the jumpCount and jumpApplication parameters. These two parameters will be received by the jump1.JSP page as request parameters. Note that the parameters are set using dynamic values (local script variables) in the JSP.

jsp:param Tag

The param tag is used to set request parameters for an HTTP request to be generated. This element is used in the body of jsp:include, jsp:forward, and jsp:plugin tags and the request parameter sets only have scope within that call. Parameter sets augment or are appended to any existing parameter list. If there is a conflict with parameters, the values set by the param tag take precedence. The syntax for this tag is

```
. . .
<jsp:forward page="/errorPages/error1.JSP" >
   <jsp:param name="jumpCount" value=" <%= jumpsCount %>" />
   <jsp:param name="applicationName" value=" <%= appName %>" />
</jsp:forward>
. . .
```

In this example, page execution is being forwarded to an error page named error1.JSP and is being passed parameter values for jumpCount and applicationName, which are set from the values of script variables.

jsp:plugin Tag

The plugin tag allows a browser plugin to be invoked (from the server side) to manage some part of the page to be rendered by the browser. The use of tag attributes allows parameters to be passed to the plugin. This is commonly used to invoke an applet or a JavaBeans component. A `<jsp:fallback>` tag can be used to indicate an action to be taken if the plug-in cannot be loaded. The syntax for this tag is

```
. . .
<jsp:plugin type="applet" code="clientCustMaint.class" code-
base="/classes">
    <jsp:param name="userName" value="<%= userName1 %>"
    <jsp:fallback>
                <b> Unable to start plugin. </b>
    </jsp:fallback>
</jsp:plugin>
. . .
```

In this example, the `plugin` tag designates the plug-in type to be an applet through the type attribute. The code to be run by the plug-in (the applet) is identified as `clientCustMaint.class` using the code attribute. The directory where the class will be found is identified as `"/classes"` using the `codebase` attribute.

Within the `plugin` tag block, a single parameter is passed using the `param` tag. This element is used to set the `userName` parameter to the value of the `userName1` variable. Also within the `plugin` tag, a fallback tag designates a block of JSP that will be rendered if the `plugin` cannot be loaded; in this example, a single line of HTML is displayed to indicate that the plug-in cannot be loaded. As of this writing, only arbitrary text can appear in this block.

Summary

In this chapter we provided an overview of the JSP architecture and described how JSP implementations are built on the technology of servlets. JSP are converted into servlets and then run in a servlet container. Using existing technology infrastructure in this way has provided a smooth development path for software vendors who already had a servlet container in place. This approach also has the added advantage of now having software products that provide two server-side solutions: JSPs and servlets.

The JSP syntax includes the entire Java language (a powerful feature in itself) and a number of tags and directives that were detailed in this chapter. Using these tags, JSPs can integrate Java code into a JSP with minimal Java code (scriplets) in the JSP.

Coming Up Next

Now that we understand the JSP architecture and are familiar with the syntax of JSP, we can begin to pursue the actual building and execution of a dynamic Web page. But avoiding the "write it and then see" approach to development, we apply some common *design patterns*, proven solutions to repeatable problems: solutions not only to this problem but to other problems that could be solved using JSP.

After reviewing some common design patterns, in Chapter 7 we examine the process of writing a JSP that uses some Java classes within the page. We do not focus on the functional aspects of the application, but instead, focus on the deployment of application within the Tomcat directory hierarchy. In later chapters we focus on lengthier, more complex applications and provide detailed descriptions of the code.

DESIGNING JSP APPLICATIONS

Introduction

Designing and running Web applications, applications comprised of distributed components, require us to use different design strategies from those for other applications. Design strategies must not only choose what components to create and how to model the components, but how to model the classes that will help the components perform their work. The multitiered J2EE application model has been identified in previous chapters and will be applied here to identify roles and responsibilities to assign to the components and classes used to create the application.

Design patterns identify proven solutions to recurring problems, problems that have been encountered over and over in the application development process and for us specifically with the development of Java Web applications. In this chapter we focus on several useful design patterns that will be used to develop the sample application shown in Chapter 9. The logical distinction of multiple tiers is used to determine the responsibilities and location of the distributed components we develop.

Application Components

Our Web application is comprised of *components*, deployable portions of our software application. These components could be HTML pages, JSP, servlets, JavaBeans, or Enterprise JavaBeans.

The development of Web applications represents a *multitiered* approach to application development. Unlike the *fat-client* approach, where a single application included presentation logic, business logic, and data access (resources) logic, the Web application takes this functionality and places it in various components across multiple tiers. The use of multiple tiers requires a different development approach, one that takes into account the capabilities of the components that will reside on each tier and the developers who will create the components. This is referred to as providing a *division of responsibilities* for the components (services) of the application (see Figure 7.1).

As discussed previously, the distributed tiers of a Web application are *logical* divisions and do not necessarily relate to physically separate divisions.

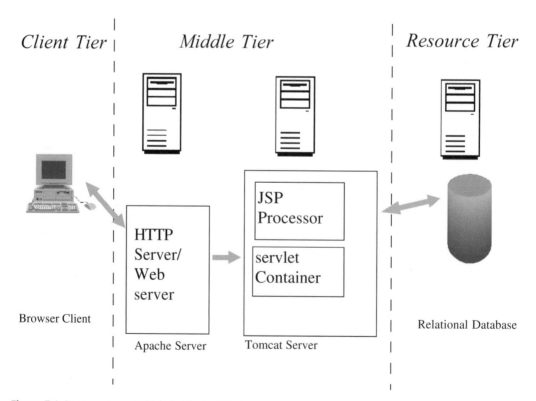

Figure 7.1 Components on Multiple Architectural Tiers

Components that are distributed across two or three tiers could reside on a single server. The multiple tiers of our Web application are listed in Table 7.1.

Table 7.1 JSP Web Application Tiers

Tier	Description
Client	The client side of the application. This should be a thin client with the responsibility to render the application's visual components, accept user interaction, and relay the results of any interaction to the presentation tier. In our examples, this tier will be represented by a Web browser.
Presentation	The responsibility of this tier is to control the presentation of the application and to relay user interactions to the business tier. For our examples, this tier is synonymous with the Web tier, comprising HTTP servers, JSP environments, and servlet containers.
Business	Components in this tier encapsulate the business logic of the application. Development in this tier will primarily be in Java using JavaBeans, although other components could be used (e.g., Enterprise JavaBeans).
Integration	The responsibility of components in this tier is to provide access to the resource tier. This access usually requires integration with some data resource. This data source is usually a relational database but could also be a legacy data source such as a mainframe database.
Resource	The resource tier represents the persistent data store for the site most commonly a relational database. Integration tier components communicate with this tier.

Client Tier

The client tier logically enough represents the client application. The purpose of this tier is to render the presentation prepared by the presentation tier and to react to input from the user. The client tier must also communicate with the presentation tier and relay the user's input to that tier. The client tier is usually a Web browser but could be any application that can perform the functions required of the client tier.

Using a thin-client architecture, this tier should have a minimal footprint. The goal is to avoid the problems of fat-client architectures, where deploying to the client tier was difficult and expensive. By using a Web browser on this tier, the goal of the thin-client architecture is met. Web browsers provide the client portion of the application by displaying small packets of information—

HTML pages. These pages are generated dynamically via a remote connection. There is no need to deploy anything to the client in order to deliver an application (other than an HTML-capable Web browser).

To keep this client a thin client, the responsibilities of this tier must be minimized. By minimizing and focusing the responsibilities of this tier, the amount of information that must be sent to the tier will be minimized. If we determine that this tier should only render the display and respond to the user's input, decisions on what to display and how to display it should be left to another tier.

This approach to the client tier has proved effective, allowing the Web browser to do what it does best, display Web pages and collect input. Although it is possible to perform more complex presentation and business logic at the client tier, this work is usually left to other tiers in our architecture.

Presentation Tier

The presentation tier is responsible for preparation of the output to the client tier. This tier encapsulates the logic required to create the presentation. Since we are usually preparing these pages dynamically, this tier must be able to store and retain information between calls, either in memory or in a data store.

If we are using a Web browser as our client, the protocol between the client tier and the presentation tier is HTTP. The most logical server for the presentation tier is a server that can perform the HTTP protocol. A server such as Apache can perform this function. Additionally, we would like the server to be able to manage dynamic content using a robust language such as Java. The Tomcat server provides this capability using servlets and JSP.

The components used on this tier are either Java servlets, JSP, JavaBeans, or tag libraries. The question we need to answer at the design stage is which type of component should be used. If we want to create components on this tier that require minimal support from Java developers, JSPs should be used to provide the bulk of the presentation logic. JavaBeans and tag libraries could be used to isolate more complex logic, leaving a JSP that would be familiar and maintainable by most Web page developers.

By maintaining this separation of roles, staff with more specialized skill sets can maintain the presentation tier components. If these components are primarily HTML, developers familiar with HTML can be used to maintain these pages. Java provides a number of tools that make this approach even more attractive: tag libraries and JavaBean integration into the JSP. Using these tools, presentation tier logic can be isolated in a JSP, and any additional logic can be moved to back-end components such as JavaBeans and tag libraries.

Business Tier

The business tier isolates and encapsulates business logic for the application. Logic that could have resided in the presentation tier in Web components such as JSP pages or servlets is effectively pushed off and encapsulated in this tier. The components on this tier can be created using a variety of Java tools: JavaBeans, tag libraries, and Enterprise JavaBeans. (Although Java scriplets in Web pages could be used to manage business logic, this is generally not recommended.)

The business tier should be used to isolate business logic—the business rules of the organization. These are rules such as how to select sales regions for the sales reports, including the usual list of exceptions that always seem to exist for many business rules. As disclosed previously, the selection of business tier components should be based on a number of factors, such as performance, availability requirements, and the scalability required for the application. Only when the application requires it based on these needs should Enterprise JavaBeans be used.

Business tier components should provide for the retrieval of data from the data store and the application of business rules against these data. This data retrieval is accomplished by communicating with integration tier components that will provide the data retrieval. The business tier components can, and for our purposes will, operate within the same container as the presentation tier components. The Tomcat server will provide execution of the JSP and the resulting servlet, and will also execute Java Beans or tag libraries that will contain the business logic of the organization.

Integration Tier

The components on the integration tier are tasked with the retrieval of data from the data store. These components will communicate with the business tier to provide the data requested. The purpose of this tier is to encapsulate the data access of the application and to effectively shield the business tier and other tiers from the details of this access.

These components must have knowledge of the location of the data store and the protocol required to retrieve the data. The most common data store in use today is the relational database, and the Java JDBC API provides the means of communicating with this database. But access to other legacy data stores may be required. The Java `Connector` API will ultimately provide a common, standard method of connecting with these data stores when it becomes available. Both APIs would be used on this tier. The components of this tier will operate in the same container as the presentation tier and business tier components within the Tomcat server. The separation of this tier from the other tiers is a logical one.

Resource Tier

The resource tier is represented by the data store, most commonly the relational database to be used. For our purposes the resource tier is represented by the PostgreSQL database. The resource tier is responsible for storing the persistent data and maintaining the consistency of the data. Communication with the resource tier is accomplished with a standard API such as JDBC for relational databases.

Design Patterns

A *design pattern* is a proven solution to a recurring problem in the software development process. Originally, design patterns were applied to physical building architecture, but several prescient individuals felt that these same principles could be applied to the design of object-oriented software.

Design patterns can be used to promote consistency in the software development process. They provide a common means of communicating tried and proven solutions to frequently encountered problems. Although design patterns have been applied to object-oriented software development for a number of years, including the development of Java applications, in recent years Sun Microsystems has increased the emphasis on design patterns with Java applications, more specifically on J2EE design patterns. Sun has identified a number of design patterns to be used with J2EE for three tiers: the presentation tier, business tier, and integration tier.

Design patterns are applied to the design of the software components. For the presentation tier the components would be either JSP or servlets. For the business and integration tiers, the components would be either JavaBeans, tag libraries, or Enterprise JavaBeans. Several of the more important patterns for these tiers are identified in the sections below.

Presentation Tier Patterns

Presentation tier patterns provide a means of applying order to the complexities of managing the presentation of the application. These patterns do not provide a means of applying business logic in the presentation tier, since that logic should be applied on the business tier. These patterns are for applications with complexity in the presentation tier, where security or the complexity of the presentation is important. If an application does not have a complex presentation, application of this design may not be needed.

DispatcherView Pattern

The DispatcherView pattern is applied to applications that require some degree of logic to be applied to client requests to determine how the client should proceed (see Figure 7.2). With this pattern, a client request is received and is examined by a FrontComponent, and decision logic is applied to determine which View should be used to manage the request. Once the View has been chosen, the client request is forwarded to an appropriate View. The View, working with a ViewHelper, is then responsible for generating dynamic content and producing a response to the client request.

Using the Web as our presentation tier, our request is an HTTP request. This request will be received and evaluated by the FrontComponent before being forwarded. Since this evaluation process does not involve any presentation to the client (even though it exists on the presentation tier), a servlet is appropriate for this component, although a JSP could also be used.

Once the FrontComponent has evaluated the request, it will forward the request to an appropriate View. The View has the responsibility of generating the display for the client. It is assumed that this will involve the generation

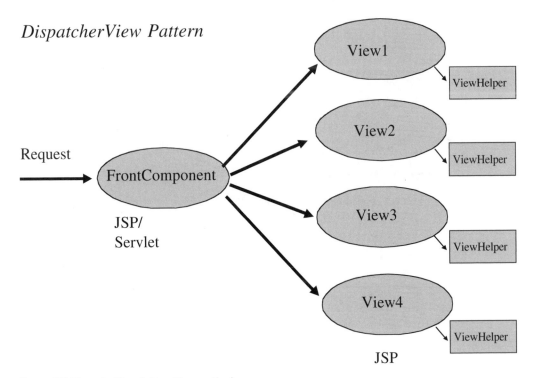

Figure 7.2 DispatcherView Pattern (Process Flow)

of dynamic content, and therefore the `View` will require a helper in the form of a component known as a `ViewHelper`. The `ViewHelper` will perform whatever Integration Tier or Resource Tier communication is necessary to formulate the response for the client request. In simpler terms, this means that the `View` will produce the dynamic Web page by using session or application variables and performing database interaction as needed. This will no doubt involve working with other components, which may logically be denoted as belonging to the Integration Tier or Resource Tier in our architecture.

ServicetoWorker Pattern

The `ServicetoWorker` pattern is used to manage applications which must apply a large amount of logic to incoming requests to determine how to process those requests. This pattern is similar to the `DispatcherView` pattern but differs in the approach to managing the logic (see Figure 7.3). With the `ServicetoWorker` pattern, the logic is processed by the `FrontController` rather than passing off that responsibility to the `View` to make decisions.

Service-to-Worker Pattern

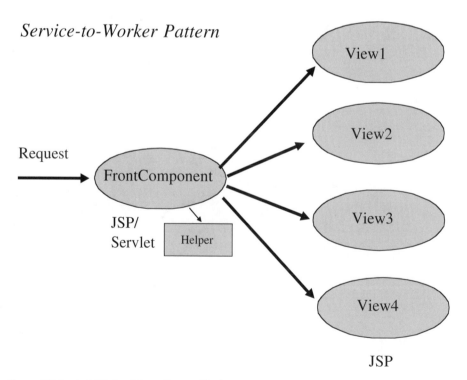

Figure 7.3 ServicetoWorker Pattern (Process Flow)

With this design pattern, the request from the client is managed by a `FrontComponent`. The `FrontComponent` evaluates the request and determines which security requirements must be met to handle the request. If business decisions need to be made to manage the request, the `FrontComponent` will communicate with a `Helper` (playing the same role as a `ViewHelper` in the `DispatcherView` pattern), which may in turn interact with a `BusinessDelegate` to accomplish its work. (The Business Delegate pattern is discussed later in this chapter.)

Once the `FrontComponent` has completed evaluating the logic necessary to make its decision, it will forward the request to the appropriate `View`. The `View` may then refer to a `ViewHelper` to create its dynamic content and build the response for the client.

Business Tier Patterns

A number of Business Tier patterns are available to apply order to the construction of business logic components. The main purpose of these patterns is to reduce the interaction or coupling between Presentation Tier components and Business Tier components. The benefit of this approach is that changes in the Business Tier components (which are common) should not affect the Presentation Tier components, thus creating a more flexible (and less *brittle*) application.

SessionFacade Pattern

The `SessionFacade` pattern works primarily to reduce coupling between the Presentation Tier component making the request and the Business Tier component responsible for managing the request. The component on the Presentation Tier may need to perform a number of business functions in order to complete the request (a dynamic Web page) that must be sent back to the client (see Figure 7.4). These functions may involve detailed calls to retrieve data from the Integration Tier and to apply business logic to the results before producing the response for the client. To maintain our division of responsibilities, we would like to encapsulate all of our business logic on the Business Tier and to shield the Presentation Tier from these details.

Using this pattern, the presentation tier component must execute business logic and possibly retrieve data on behalf of the client. These requests are forwarded to a `SessionFacade` component that will manage the work flow for the request. The process of managing this request may involve making several additional calls to other components in order to process the request. These other objects could be `BusinessObjects` (which manage the details of

Session Facade Pattern

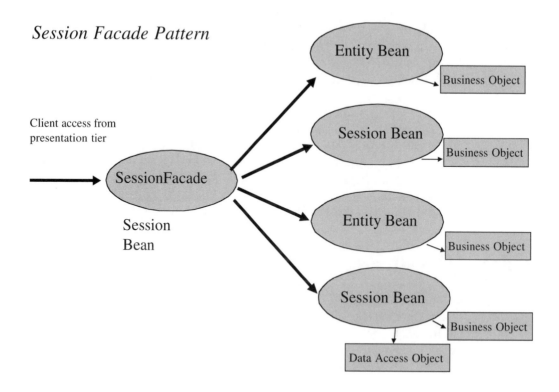

Figure 7.4 SessionFacade Pattern (Process Flow)

access to the Integration Tier) or `DataAccessObjects` (which are Integration Tier components that manage the details of access to the persistent data store). (The `SessionFacade` object shields the client from these details.) When it has completed its processing, the `SessionFacade` component will return results to the Presentation Tier component.

BusinessDelegate Pattern

The `BusinessDelegate` pattern is used on the Business Tier to provide access to Business Tier components using a *client-side* (presentation tier) object (see Figure 7.5). The `BusinessDelegate` encapsulates any business logic that must be used by the Presentation Tier component to complete its work. The purpose of this component is to hide the complexity of Business Tier components from Presentation Tier, thus reducing the coupling between these two tiers and minimizing the effect of Business Tier changes on Presentation Tier components.

This component may be implemented on the Web tier; that is, it may be implemented as a JavaBean or tag library rather than as an Enterprise JavaBean. The reason for this is that the `BusinessDelegate` is intended to protect the Presentation Tier component from the Business Tier components and may do this by caching data and encapsulating Business Tier logic on the client side (where the Presentation Tier is a client for Business Tier services).

This also has the effect of reducing the communication traffic between the Presentation Tier and Business Tier components. Although this may not seem significant for components that are operating in the same JVM (which would be the case with servlets/JSP pages, JavaBeans, and tag libraries), this does become a consideration when using Enterprise JavaBeans that may be spread over one or more servers in a clustered network configuration.

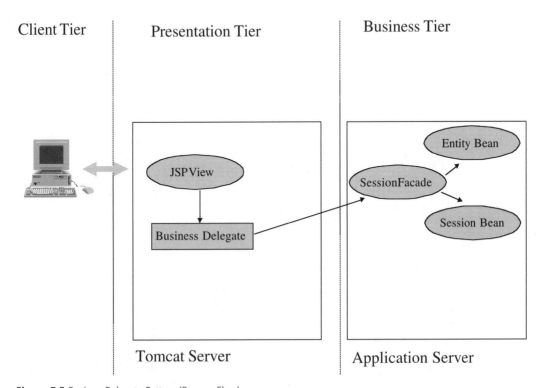

Figure 7.5 BusinessDelegate Pattern (Process Flow)

Value Object Pattern

The ValueObject pattern encapsulates the data elements of a business domain object and provides a means of transporting that information from the Business Tier to the Presentation Tier, where it can be cached (see Figure 7.6). The ValueObject contains members that represent the elements of the business domain object and methods to retrieve those members.

The ValueObject is generally intended to be immutable, meaning that it is a *read-only object* and the members should not be changed. A ValueObject may contain setXX methods that allow members to be changed, but calling these methods alone will not change the persistent data behind the ValueObject; instead, they will only change the ValueObject on the Presentation Tier. It is the responsibility of the BusinessObject to manage the persistent data store, and it is therefore the BusinessObject that must be called to update the persistent data store by exposing an update method to the Presentation Tier client.

Use of this pattern has the practical benefit of reducing the amount of communication between the Presentation Tier and the Business Tier, since only one method call must be made to retrieve all the data required, as opposed to making numerous method calls to the Business Tier to populate an object on the Presentation Tier. (Note that the performance benefits of this approach are more significant when using Enterprise JavaBeans than when using JavaBean components, but the practical benefits derived during the development process from the reduced coupling and exposure of the Presentation Tier to the Business Tier still apply.)

Value Object Pattern

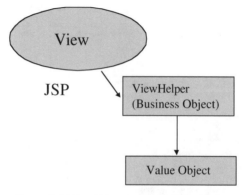

Figure 7.6 Value Object Pattern (Process Flow)

The `ValueObject` is created and loaded via a `BusinessObject` component. The responsibility of this `BusinessObject` component is to instantiate the `ValueObject` and then load the attributes of the `ValueObject` with the correct values. This is performed using a create method that the `BusinessObject` component exposes to the Presentation Tier.

Integration Tier Patterns

It is the responsibility of the Integration Tier to provide access to the persistent data store. The responsibility of components on this tier is to abstract the specifics of data access away from the Business Tier components. This allows developers knowledgeable in the specifics of data access to work on these components and developers who may have little knowledge of the data access operation to work on Business Tier components and access the Integration Tier data via a well-defined API.

Data Access Object Pattern

The `DataAccessObject` pattern provides encapsulation of the data access process (see Figure 7.7). The `DataAccessObject` details the specifics of data access and exposes a simplified API to allow Business Tier components to access Integration Tier data.

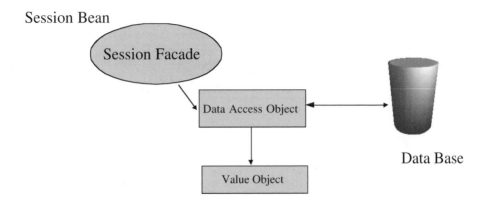

Data Access Object Pattern

Figure 7.7 DataAccessObject Pattern (Process Flow)

The component created by this pattern will be accessed from the Business Tier by the Business Object. The component will request data in the data store using an API method call which will conceal the details of the request. The `DataAccessObject` will execute the details of the data access operation, which may involve requesting access to the data source as a specific user, connecting to the data source, performing transactional logic, preparing and executing a query, and retrieving data.

Summary

Developing Web applications with Java requires the developer or system architect to choose from among a number of choices for components and design strategies. In this chapter we reviewed those choices and provided some guidance on which choices are best under which circumstances.

The most significant part of design for a Java Web application is identifying components and then determining what technology will be used to create those components and where those components will run. These decisions can be aided by using a design strategy that identifies roles and responsibilities based on logical tiers. The tiers identified and explained in this chapter were the client tier, presentation tier, business tier, integration tier, and resource tier. Our focus in this book is on the presentation, business, and integration tiers.

This chapter also covered a basic set of design patterns that have proven useful with Java applications, J2EE applications in particular. These design patterns will help with the development process by implementing a consistent design structure throughout the application and by facilitating code reuse with many of the business objects. These design patterns can be used on the presentation tier, business tier, or integration tier.

Coming Up Next

In Chapter 8 we continue our discussion of JSP by providing several examples of its use. We present some simple examples demonstrating basic concepts and then provide a more complex example with a JSP calendar display application.

JSP PROGRAMMING:
A BASIC EXAMPLE

Introduction

In earlier chapters we introduced many of the basics of building an application with JSP. The syntax of the JSP language and the tag directives and scriplets that make up the language were explained. In this chapter we build on the work of Chapter 7 by using a series of examples to explain how to develop Web applications using JSP with JavaBeans and custom tag libraries.

Since it is not uncommon for Web applications to require the display of a one-month calendar on a Web page, in this chapter we provide an example of a JavaBean that can provide this functionality. This example provides a useful demonstration of JSP/scriplet development as well as the use of custom tags. The conversion of the JavaBean into the custom tag will highlight the differences of tag libraries from JavaBeans and demonstrate the relative ease of performing this conversion.

Some JSP Examples

As discussed in Chapter 7, the JSP includes HTML tags interspersed with special tags that are interpreted by the JSP compiler. (These are, in fact, XML tags that are parsed with an XML parser.) These tags can contain attributes or a body that is interpreted by the compiler. The "<%" tag is used to indicate that Java code follows. The Java code that is contained within a block of these tags is not a formal Java class declaration with data members and method declarations; instead, it is a fragment of Java code that will be executed when the page is accessed. For this reason, this Java inserted is considered to be a *script* and often referred to as a *scriplet* and is not considered to be a complete Java program. The following fragment contains an example of a JSP script.

```
1.        <HTML>
2.        <BODY bgcolor="#FFFFFF">
3.
4.        <%@ page errorPage="ErrorPage.jsp" %>
5.
6.        <% for (int n = 0; n < 10; n++ ) { %>
7.
8.        <p> This text will be displayed 10 times.
9.
10.       <% } %>
11.
12.       </BODY>
13.       </HTML>
14
```

In this example, a directive is used at line 4 to identify an error page to be used in the event an error is triggered within the page. At line 6 a Java for loop is started and will run for 10 iterations. An opening brace appears on the same line. Note that the entire line 6, the declaration of the for loop and a starting brace, are enclosed in a single scriplet block which is terminated at the end of line 6.

On line 8, HTML paragraph text appears. On line 10, a scriplet block is used to provide a closing brace which is matched with the opening brace on line 6, and for that reason, all HTML text that appears between lines 8 and 10 is subject to the control of the for loop. With this technique, HTML in a JSP can enjoy the benefits of Java flow-of-control loops. The output of this page is shown in Figure 8.1.

Using JavaBeans

JSP also provides convenient access to Java code (or classes) external to the page. This is provided through either an import directive that works like the Java language import statement or the useBean tag. The useBean tag includes JavaBeans in a JSP and provides a mechanism for associating the JavaBean with a tag within the JSP. The syntax for the useBean tag is

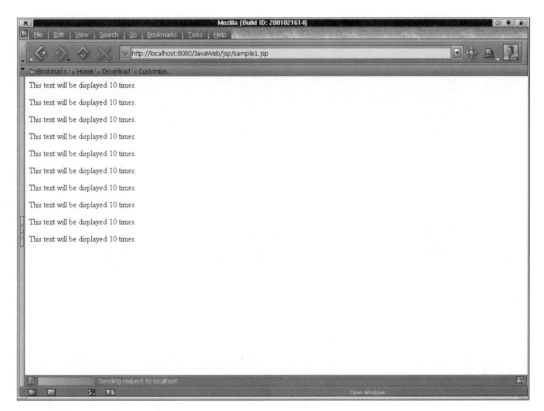

Figure 8.1 JSP sample1.jsp Output

```
...
<jsp:useBean id="dbutil" class="db.dbUtil" scope="ses-
sion" />
<jsp:useBean id="kbutil" class="knowledgebase.kbUtil"
scope="session" /> ...
```
These tags provide for the inclusion of JavaBeans modules into a JSP, pro-
viding for modularized code and code reuse throughout the JSP application.
Specifically, these tags include modules that will be referenced on the JSP
using the names dbutil and kbutil. The class files for the modules are also
specified without the .class extension.

Displaying Query Results

The following example processes the results of a database query and uses a
control loop to create an HTML table for the results.

```
...
<!- table for ResultSet output ->
<table border=0 cellpadding=2 bgcolor="white">

<tr>
<td bgcolor="#C0D9D9"><b>Problem Description<b></td>
<td bgcolor="#C0D9D9"><b>Message<b></td>
<td bgcolor="#C0D9D9"><b>Category<b></td>
<td bgcolor="#C0D9D9"><b>Action<b></td>
</tr>

<!-     // print each column ->
<%
     while ( more ) {
%>

<tr>
<td bgcolor="#E0E0E0"> <%= rs.getString( "doc_name" ) %> </td>
<td bgcolor="#E0E0E0"> <%= rs.getstring( "message_txt" ) %> </td>
<td bgcolor="#E0E0E0"> <%= rs.getString( "category" ) %> </td>

<td bgcolor="#C0C0C0"> <a href="viewKB.jsp?pdoc_key=<%= doc_key
%>" >View Entry</a> </td>

<% if ( !request.getParameter( "action" ).equals( "showthread" )
) { %>
<td bgcolor="#C0C0C0"> <a href="listKB.jsp?pdoc_key=<%= doc_key
%>&action=showthread" >Show Thread</a> </td>
<% } %>

</tr>

<%
     more = rs.next();
     } // end while
%>
</table>
```

In this example, an HTML table is created to display the output of a database query, which is returned in a JDBC ResultSet object (name rs). To place the contents of the ResultSet object into the HTML table, a Java while loop is executed for each row returned in the ResultSet object.

Note that the while loop is not completed in the first Java code block in the HTML page. Instead, a great deal of HTML is inserted between the sections of the `while` loop. This is allowed in JSP scriplets. At the end of the while loop, a call is made to the `ResultSet next` method to retrieve the next row in the `ResultSet`. If this call succeeds, the script variable `more` is set to the `boolean` value of `true`. If the call fails, the script variable is set to the `boolean` value of `false`. The `boolean` value of the script variable `more` is tested at the start of the `while` loop, and if it tests `false`, the `while` loop will not be executed.

Note that this code demonstrates a direct approach to JSP script programming. In this example, a portion of the underlying business logic is exposed to a JSP. Since it is exposed, it is visible and can be changed by the same developer who will develop the HTML code within the page. Using the *separation of roles* concept, this HTML page developer will most likely know nothing of JSP and could easily become confused, and worse yet, may change some of the Java code.

The preferred development model for JSP is to make every effort to limit the amount of Java code that appears on a JSP. Although it may be necessary to have some Java code on the page (e.g., to perform decision logic or to execute a loop), this code should be limited and the majority of the business logic should be handled within the Java code behind the page, not in the scriplet code on the page. JavaBeans and tag libraries are two techniques for limiting scriptlet code and will be discussed in the following sections.

Java Software Components: JavaBeans and Enterprise JavaBeans

To hide the business logic of the application and thus reduce the complexity of the Java code on a JSP page, we need a facility to encapsulate the business logic of the application. This business logic should be encapsulated in the form of software components. Use of these software components fits into what is known as a *software component architecture* and Java provides two forms of software components: *JavaBeans* and *Enterprise JavaBeans* (see Figure 8.2).

JavaBeans are a coding facility in Java that allows for the creation of a local component that provides some degree of encapsulation. These components are not as complex as Enterprise JavaBeans (EJBs), and for applications that do not need the features of Enterprise JavaBeans, they are more than suitable. Most notably, they do not explicitly support a distributed environment, an environment where the location of the component is not defined (i.e., the component could be on the local machine, or the component could be on a machine elsewhere on the network).

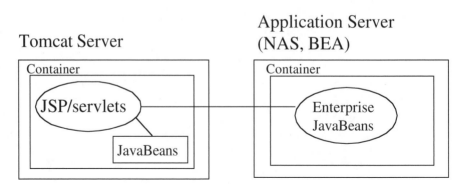

Figure 8.2 Tomcat Server: Application Server Comparison

Enterprise JavaBeans provide a number of features that are suitable for a more intensive, robust production environment. Java EJBs are designed with a notion of *containership*. Just as servlets and JSPs have containers that implicitly provide many of the services needed by those components, an EJB has a container that provides a number of services. EJB containers and their servers provide persistence, location transparency, transactions, failure fall-back capabilities, and scalability features that heavily used, business-critical applications require.

But this robust feature set comes with a price. Enterprise JavaBeans can be difficult to develop and even more difficult to deploy. The servers they use are complex, can be expensive (although some interesting open-source EJB servers are available), and can require some level of system maintenance. This is not to say that EJBs should not be used; they have significant value with the right application. But there are simpler, more direct approaches to development that are appropriate for a large number of small to medium-sized applications.

Enterprise JavaBeans are generally used on applications that will have either a heavy user load, require integration with legacy applications on disparate systems (e.g., a Unix-based system must use mainframe data), or require high availability. For these applications, EJBs provide significant value and are easier to use and more flexible than many of the alternatives available on the market today. (See Appendix B for a discussion of Enterprise JavaBeans.)

Using JavaBeans with Java Server Pages

JavaBeans as used with JSPs are Java classes coded using a set of methods with a standard naming. With these classes it is assumed that class data members (or attributes) will be declared with `private` accessibility and will only be manipulated using *get* and *set* methods, named with the naming standard get<attribute_name> and set<attribute_name>, where the attribute name is the name of the attribute or private data member that is to be set. These getXX and setXX methods are sometimes referred to as *accessor* and *mutator* methods of the class. JavaBeans do not require the implementation of a Java interface and do not need to be a subclass of any particular class; they are just another Java class with appropriate methods written to manage its attributes. Following is an example.

```
1.      package samples;
2.
3.      public class myBean {
4.      private int counter;
5.      private String name = "MyBean"; // default name
6.
7.      public void setCounter( int count ) {
8.      this.counter = count;
9.      }
10.     public void setName( String name ) {
11.     this.name = name;
12.     }
13.
14.     public String getName() {
15.         return name;
16.     }
17.
18.     public int getCounter() {
19.         return counter;
20.     }
21.
22.     public void incrementCounter() {
23.         counter++;
24.     }
25.     }
```

In this example, a JavaBean named myBean is created as a Java class. The JavaBean class has two private data members (or properties): counter and name, as declared on lines 4 and 5. The four public methods used to access these private members are declared on lines 7 through 20. The set methods are used to set the values of these members, and the get methods are used to access the value of the member. The setCounter method on line 7 is written to set the value of the counter member, and the setName method on line 10 is used to set the value of the name member. Similarly, the getName method on line 14 is available to retrieve the value of the name member. The getCounter method on line 18 is available to retrieve the value of the counter member.

The incrementCounter method on line 22 is an example of how a simple method could be part of a JavaBean. This method increments a counter variable and then returns. The following JSP demonstrates the use of this JavaBean in a JSP.

```
1.   <HTML>
2.   <BODY>
3.   <jsp:useBean id="myBean" class="samples.myBean" scope="page" />
4.   <jsp:setProperty name="myBean" property="counter" value="1" />
5.
6.   <H1>JSP Samples<H1>
7.   <p>
8.
9.   <% myBean.incrementCounter(); %>
10.
11.  <p>Name: <jsp:getProperty name="myBean" property="name" />
12.
13.  <p>Counter: <jsp:getProperty name="myBean" property="counter" />
14.
15.  </BODY>
16.  </HTML>
```

In this sample page, the useBean tag on line 3 is used to identify the bean to be used, to associate the bean with an id name in the page. The useBean tag uses the id attribute to identify the name of the class to load for the bean, and the scope attribute to identify the scope of the JavaBean within the JSP.

The scriplet on line 9 is used to invoke a method within one of the JavaBeans loaded on the current page, or potentially one of the classes available to the servlet built from the page. This scriplet invokes the incrementCounter method to increment the internal counter variable for the JavaBean.

The getProperty tags on lines 11 and 13 retrieve the value of the members of the JavaBean class (counter and name). The value of these members is retrieved and inserted into the HTML page at line 11 after the "Name:" string and at line 13 after the "Counter:" string.

Note that it is not required to write public get and set methods for all members. Should you wish to hide certain details of the JavaBean, the get and set methods could either be eliminated or could be declared private methods, thus restricting access to the instance members.

The process of *introspection* is the capability of a Java application to examine the members of a class dynamically and then access the members of that class. This is the facility used by runtime JavaBeans activation and by the JSP container when it implements the `getProperty` or `setProperty` tags on the JSP.

When a JavaBean is used in a JSP, the `useBean` tag is used to identify the JavaBean class to load for the bean. The JSP container will then find and load the class. When a `getProperty` tag is encountered for the JavaBean, the container will use *introspection* to determine whether an appropriate `get<PropertyName>` method is available to call, and if it is available, will make the method call and return the value. If a `setProperty` tag is encountered, introspection is once again used to determine whether or not an appropriate `set<PropertyName>` method is available to call. If an appropriate `set<PropertyName>` method is found, it is called and passed the correct value for the call. Note that the property name in the `set<PropertyName>` method must match the `property` attribute of the `jsp:getProperty` tag or the call will fail.

A JSP/JavaBeans Example

A common problem that must be tackled when developing a Web site is to create Web pages dynamically based on the contents of some subset of database tables. Since it is safe to assume that we will be retrieving multiples rows of data from the database, we must be able to iterate through these rows.

The JDBC API provides methods that, among other things, execute a query and return an object representing the set of results (a `ResultSet` object). Methods within the `ResultSet` class can then be used to iterate through the results. Although we could place this code directly into the JSP page, it would involve placing some portion of business logic into the page where it would be visible (and subject to change) for anyone with access to the page.

It is preferable to encapsulate as much business logic for the application into JavaBeans. To accomplish this hiding with JDBC operations, principal JDBC methods must be wrapped with Java code and combined into a small, manageable set of methods. We will create a `CustBean` class to perform this wrapping. The process of iterating through the `ResultSet` must include the populating of private members of the `CustBean` class with internal calls to its `set` methods. The `next()` method of the class will provide this functionality. Once this method has been called in the JSP script, the properties of `CustBean` will contain the appropriate value and can be retrieved on the page using the `getProperty` tag. Following is an example of this approach.

```
1.  <HTML>
2.  <BODY>
3.
4.  <jsp:useBean id="custBean" class="/classes/custBean"
scope="page" />
5.  <jsp:setProperty name="custBean" property="userID" value="<%
request.getParameter("userID") %>" />
6.  <jsp:setProperty name="pageID" property="pageID"
value="P2023" />
7.  ...
8.  <%
9.  while ( custBean.getNext() ) {
10. %>
11.
12. <tr>
13. <td bgcolor="#E0E0E0"> <jsp:getProperty name="custBean"
property="doc_name" /> </td>
14. <td bgcolor="#E0E0E0"> <jsp:getProperty name="custBean"
property="message_text" /> </td>
<td bgcolor="#E0E0E0"> <jsp:getProperty name="custBean"
property="category" /> </td>
15. <td bgcolor="#C0C0C0"> <a
href="viewKB.jsp?pdoc_key=<jsp:getProperty name="custBean"
property="doc_key" />" >View Entry</a> </td>
16.
17. <% if ( !request.getParameter( "action" ).equals(
"showthread" ) ) { %>
18. <td bgcolor="#C0C0C0"> <a
href="listKB.jsp?pdoc_key=<jsp:getProperty name="custBean"
property="doc_key" />&action=showthread" >Show Thread</a> </td>
19. <% } %>
20. </tr>
21. <%    } // end while %>
22. </BODY>
23. </HTML>
```

In this example, the JSP needs to read the contents of a database table, the customer table, and then, based on the results of this iterative read operation, create an HTML table using the contents. Our goal is to limit the amount of Java code that we must expose in the JSP and to use HTML/JSP tags as much as possible.

On line 4 of this example, the JavaBean that is to be used for this page is identified in a JSP useBean tag. This tag directs the JSP container to load the bean. On lines 5 and 6, parameters required to perform the retrieval of customer records from the database are set. By the time the getNext method is called on line 9, the information needed to retrieve the data has been loaded into the JavaBean. The call to the `getNext` method will position the data retrieval to the first row of the data set returned and set the properties of the `custBean` object internally to the appropriate values for the first row retrieved.

Within the `<td>` tags in the table on lines 13 through 15, a series of `<jsp:getProperty/>` tags are then used to retrieve the data and insert them into the output stream for the HTML table that will be created from this JSP page. The terminating tag for the `while` loop on line 19 forces execution to branch back to line 9, where the `while` loop will call the `CustBean.next` method again. If no rows are available, the method will return false and the `while` loop will terminate. If rows are available, the method will once again load the properties internally (set the local data members) for the object.

JSP Example: The Calendar JavaBean

Many business applications work with calendars, requiring a presentation that both displays a calendar and displays the current date. Although many GUI APIs provide controls (or widgets) to display this information, basic HTML does not provide this. Since static HTML cannot provide this capability, JSP/Java is uniquely suited to this task, providing a calendar API that can retrieve the current date and time for the time zone of the computer and return information about specific dates that can be used to create a calendar display.

The JavaBean shown in Figure 8.3 provides several methods to display a calendar for either the current month (the default) or a specific month. Since the purpose of this JavaBean is to provide a display *widget*, producing the calendar output at a specified point on the page, it should be invoked with a small number of JSP tags and produce the output necessary.

The Java code that generates the output for these tags will be required to send output to the response stream `JspWriter`. Although on the surface this may appear to break our rule of having separation of presentation logic appearing only on the JSP and not in the Java code, given our requirements for this widget this development approach makes sense. A JSP that uses the calendar JavaBean is shown below.

```
1.    <HTML>
2.    <HEAD><TITLE>
3.    Calendar
4.    </TITLE></HEAD>
5.
```

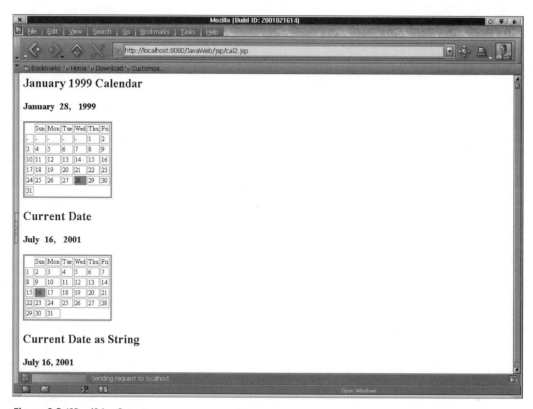

Figure 8.3 JSP cal2.jsp Output

```
6.      <%@ page errorPage="ErrorPage.jsp" %>
7.      <BODY BGCOLOR="white">
8.
9.      <h1> JSP Calendar  </h1>
10.     <jsp:useBean id="Cal" scope="page" class="JSPCal.Cal" />
11.     <b>Current Date:</b> <jsp:getProperty name="Cal"
12.                          property="currentDate" />
13.     <%
14.     Cal.printCal( out );
15.     %>
16.
17.     </BODY>
18.     </HTML>
19.
```

In this example, jsp:useBean tag on line 10 locates and loads the JSPCal.Cal class and associates the class with the name Cal to be used within this JSP. The bean is given `page` scope, since it will only be used for the current page.

Once the bean is loaded, the `getProperty` tag on line 11 is used to request the `currentDate` from the bean. As shown in the code, the `currentDate` property will have the JSP/servlet engine call the `getCurrentDate` method which will retrieve the current date from the calendar and display the date in a text string.

Finally, the `printCal` method is called on line 14 and is passed the `out` object, which in a JSP relates to the `JspWriter` for the output stream (the response) for the page. The results of this operation is a page the appears as shown in Figure 8.4.

Alternatively, custom tags could be used to display the calendar. Although very similar to the JavaBean approach, the JSP custom tag library provides a cleaner, simpler set of tags to be used in the JSP.

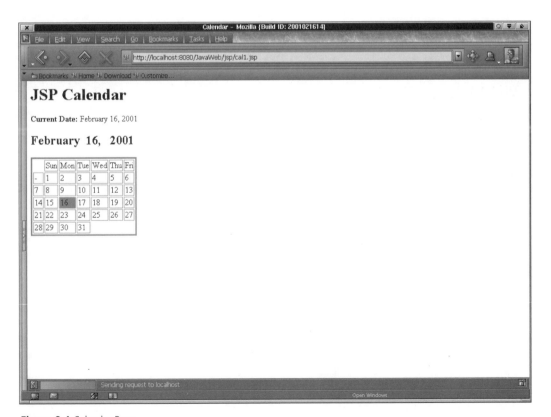

Figure 8.4 Calendar Page

```
1.
2.    <html>
3.    <body>
4.    <%@ taglib uri="/jsp/TagCal.tld" prefix="tagcal" %>
5.    <H1>January 1999 Calendar</H1>
6.    <tagcal:Calendar year="1999" month="1" day="28"   />
7.
8.    <H1>Current Date </H1>
9.    <tagcal:Calendar  />
10.   <H1>Current Date as String</H2>
11.   <H2><tagcal:Calendar dateString="true" /></H2>
12.
13.   </body>
14.   </html>
```

This page loads the tag library using the `taglib` directive, which instructs the JSP/servlet engine to read the `TagCal.tld` to obtain information about

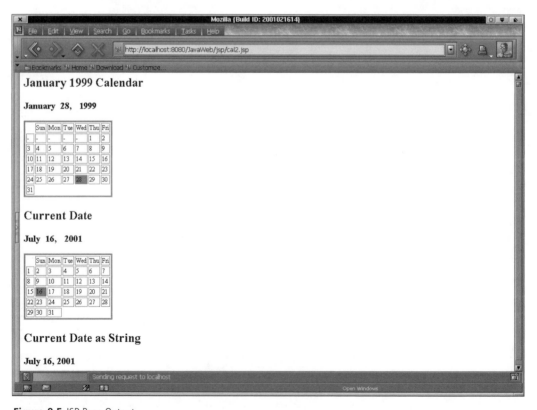

Figure 8.5 JSP Page Output

how to load the custom tag library class and identify the tags. The `prefix` attribute identifies the prefix to be used to identify the tags on the JSP.

This tag library contains one tag, the `Calendar` tag, but allows the tag to be called with different attributes. The first set of attributes used on lines creates the calendar in HTML table format for the specific date passed to the `Calendar` tag. The next use of the `Calendar` tag online sets the `dateString` flag to true and does not specify the date for the calendar. The result of using these attributes to invoke the `Calendar` tag is that the current date will be output in text string format. This page produces output as shown in Figure 8.5.

JavaBeans versus Custom Tag Libraries

As we can see from these examples, two different approaches are available for placing content on a JSP: using JSP scriplets and tags (`getProperty`, `setProperty`) or using custom tags. The differences between the implementation of these two approaches will become more apparent as we examine the code behind these JSP in more detail. Although the two approaches share many similarities, there are distinct differences between the structure of the Java code required for each, and later in this chapter we discuss both solutions and provide recommendations on where each is considered appropriate.

In the following sections we present these approaches using both the calendar JavaBean and the calendar custom tag library. The first code example uses the JavaBean solution to provide the calendar, and the following example modifies this JavaBean code to create a custom tag to provide the same calendar output.

JSP Calendar: JavaBean Code

The Java code for the calendar bean defines a class named `Cal`, which contains data members and methods to implement the calendar. A series of `getXX` and `setXX` methods within the class are used to access the class methods from JSP `getProperty` and `setProperty` flags. The `Cal` class uses the `GregorianCalendar` class to create the calendar requested. The `GregorianCalendar` class contains a number of convenience methods to create calendars, including a number of methods to perform date arithmetic and determine the day of the month and day of the week, essential information needed to display a calendar.

The code begins by first importing packages as shown below.

```
1.          package JSPCal;
2.          import java.text.*;
3.          import java.util.*;
4.          import java.io.*;
5.          import javax.servlet.*;
6.          import javax.servlet.jsp.*;
```

Within the body of the Cal class, Java final static members are created to store the names of the months and the names of the days of the week as well as the abbreviations for the days of the week.

```
...
1.          public class Cal {
2.
// array for months
3.          private static final String[] months = new
DateFormatSymbols().getMonths();
4.
// array for days of week in string format
5.          private static String days[] = new
DateFormatSymbols().getWeekDays();
6.
7.          // array for day abbreviations
private static String daysAbbrev[] =
  new DateFormatSymbols().getShortWeekdays();
8.          ...
```

Locale and Dates

As most Java developers are aware, the display of dates differs depending on the country. Various locales identify a specific country and Java provides a rich API to support locale-specific formatting. If applications are coded correctly, they can let Java manage this locale-specific formatting for them.

The Cal class makes some use of locale by using java.text.DateFormat Symbols to generate the array of weekday names. But note that the syntax used here loads these names when the class is loaded (since they are static final variables and thus belong to the class), not at runtime. Since the syntax for the DateFormatSymbol constructor does not specify a locale, the locale of the Java runtime environment will be used, **not** the locale of the user accessing the page.

A more robust implementation that needed to support multiple locales based on user logins would need to move the generation of these headings into the constructor for the `Cal` class and then set them based on the known locale of the user as shown in the code fragment below.

```
1.
2. ...
3. private static final String[] months;
4. ...
5. // constructor
6. public Cal( Locale loc) {
7. DateFormatSymbols(loc)
8.     months = new DateFormatSymbols(loc).getMonths();
9. }
```

In this code fragment, the months array is declared `static` and `final` (a *blank final variable*) and must be initialized in the constructor (or all constructors if the constructor is overridden). The constructor on line 6 is then called with a parameter of type `java.util.Locale`, which is used to set the values of the months array. This code assumes that the application has determined the correct locale of the user and passed this information to the constructor.

Internal members are also used to store the month, day, and year of the calendar to be created. A highlight color is defined for the color to use to highlight the current day (and a `setXX` method is available to change this property as needed).

```
1. // internal date
2. private int month;
3. private int day;
4. private int year;
5. private  String printHighLightColor = "grey";
6. private Calendar  mCalendar = null;   // internal calendar
7. private JspWriter mOut = null;          // response output stream
8. private boolean dateStringOnly = false;
9.
```

The next block of code defines the bean methods to be used by the bean. A number of set methods are defined that can be used via `setProperty` tags in the JSP. These methods allow the month, day, and year for the calendar to be defined.

```
<jsp:setProperty name="Month" value="6" />
<jsp:setProperty name="Day" value="6" />
<jsp:setProperty name="Year" value="91" />
```

The responsibility of the setXX methods is to take arguments passed and to apply the value of those arguments to specific local data members (instance members).

```
1.  // Bean methods
2.  public void setMonth( int month ) {
3.     this.month = month;
4.  }
5.  public void setYear( int year ) {
6.     this.year = year;
7.  }
8.
9.  public void setDay( int day ) {
10.     this.day = day;
11. }
12. public void setHighLightColor ( String color ) {
13.     this.printHighLightColor = color;
14.
15. }
16.
17. public void setDateString( boolean flag ) {
18.   this.dateStringOnly = flag;
19.
20. }
21.
22. public void setCalDate( int month, int day, int year )
23. {
24.     mCalendar = new GregorianCalendar( year,  month, day );
25. }
26. public void setOut( JspWriter out ) {
27.
28.     mOut = out;
29. }
30.
31.
```

The set method for the current date (setCalCurrentDate) as shown below performs some additional work. The purpose of this method is to get the current date for the system and set the instance of the calendar class to that date. (Note that for a Web-based application, this will be the date of the server where the JSPs are running, not the date of the browser that invoked the HTTP request.)

The body of this method begins by creating an instance of GregorianCalendar and assigning that to the calendar for the instance. The methods setDay, setMonth, and setYear are then called to set the internal members to these values. Since the Calendar.month is zero-based, it is incremented to reflect use of the month within this class (which is not zero-based but, instead, starts at the value 1).

```
public void setCalCurrentDate()
{

    mCalendar = new GregorianCalendar();

    setDay(   mCalendar.get( Calendar.DAY_OF_MONTH ));
    setYear(  mCalendar.get( Calendar.YEAR) );
    setMonth( mCalendar.get( Calendar.MONTH )+ 1 );


}
```

The getXX methods are used to wrap the private elements of the calendar, and in the case of the getCurrentDate method, provide a convenient access to a date string within a JSP.

```
// return the Current date (month day, year) as a string
public String getCurrentDate() {

if ( mCalendar == null )
    setCalCurrentDate();

return months[ this.month ] +
                    "   " +
                this.day +
                "," +
                "   " +

        this.year;
}
```

The output of this class would be a text string with the current date. This could be used in a JSP as follows. [It should be noted that the output of the Cal.getCurrentDate method is functionally equivalent to DateFormat.get DateInstance(DateFormat.MEDIUM).format(mCalendar.getTime()), which has the advantage of being non–locale specific. The approach shown here, however, is intended to take advantage of the internal members of the Cal class.]

```
. . .
<b>Today's Date:</b>    <jsp:getProperty
name="myCal" property="CurrentDate" />
. . .
```

The printCal method provides the output to produce calendar output in HTML format. This method takes as an argument the output stream for the response, which with JSP is the JspWriter. (This is actually an instance of a class that provides functionality similar to that of the PrintWriter class and is not a subclass of PrintWriter.) The printCal method uses the JspWriter output handle to output the resulting calendar. The calendar is produced based on the values of the internal members for the Cal class instance.

A local reference is used throughout the method; this is done for convenience and to allow for easy substitution of a calendar object as a parameter in later revisions of this method. This local reference is first assigned to the internal calendar on the first line of this method.

Since the calendar to be output will print all the days of the month, the printCal method starts by setting the internal calendar to the first day of the month using the set method of the GregorianCalendar class.

```
public void printCal( JspWriter out ) throws
ServletException {

Calendar cal = mCalendar;
String printAttr;

// set to the first day of the month
cal.set( Calendar.DAY_OF_MONTH, 1 );
. . .
```

A try/catch block is used to catch i/o exceptions for any of the statements that provide output to the JspWriter output stream. The output for the calendar is produced within this block.

The first output statement in this block is used to print a header for the calendar. This header displays the date in string format using the months array (which contains the months of the calendar in string format), the day member (member variable of the Cal instance), and the year of the calendar.

```
. . .
try {

// print the header
out.println("<H2> " +
            months[ this.month ] +
            "  " +
            this.day +   // day of month
            "," +
            "   " +
            this.year +
        "</H2>" );
. . .
```

The next section of the method begins production of an HTML table for
the calendar. This section of code currently hardcodes table attributes but
could be expanded to add additional attributes for the table display.

A table row tag is used to denote the start of a week in the calendar output.
Since a table header is needed for the calendar to display the days of the week,
a `for` loop is used to loop for 7 days (0 through 6 inclusive) and display the
days of the week. The days of the week are displayed in text format using
abbreviations stored in the `daysAbbrev` member variable.

```
. . .
out.println("<table border=3>");

// print the days of the week
out.print("<tr>");
for ( int n = 0; n <= 6; n++ )
    out.print("<td>" + daysAbbrev[n] + "</td>");

out.println("</tr>");
. . .
```

The next few sections of code are used to display the days of the week in
rows of seven cells (one for each day). Since the first and last rows of output
require cells to be produced which may not include a numerical day (i.e., days
from the preceding month and days from the next month), there is a block of
logic that must determine whether or not a numerical day needs to be output.
This is the block of code shown below. If a numerical day is not displayed, a
dash ("—") is output. Additionally, if the day of the week being output is the
current day for the calendar (`this.Day`), the day is output using the highlight color attribute. Since Sunday represents the end of the week (in the for-

mat used on this calendar), this represents the end of the row and must be output using the table row terminator tag ("</tr>"). Days of the week are represented as integer numbers ranging from 0 through 6.

```
. . .
// print blanks up to the start day
out.print("<tr>");

// if this is the day of the month highlight the table cell
// using the highlight display attribute
if (  Day == 1 )
    printAttr = "<td bgcolor=" + '"' + printHighLightColor + '"'
+ ">";
else
    printAttr = "<td>";

if ( cal.get( Calendar.DAY_OF_WEEK) > 1 ) {

    for ( int x = 0; x <= ( cal.get( Calendar.DAY_OF_WEEK) - 1);
x++ ) {

        if ( x < ( cal.get(Calendar.DAY_OF_WEEK )-1) )
            out.print( "<td>" + "-" + "</td>" );
        else
            out.print( printAttr + "1" + "</td>" );

        if ( x == 6 ) {
            out.println("</tr>");
            out.print("<tr>");
        }
    }
}
else // day_of_week == 1 == 'Sunday'
    out.print( printAttr + "1" + "</td>" );
. . .
```

The next section of code stores the print attribute for the highlight block for the current day of the month in a string for convenience. A loop is then executed starting from the second day because at least one day of the month (the first day) has been printed in the control previous loop. This control loop will continue to process until the value of the loop control variable is greater than the maximum number of days in the month, at which time the loop will terminate.

As in the previous block of code, if the day of the week is the end of the week as determined by the value of the call to `get( Calendar.DAY_OF_WEEK)]`, the table row terminator will be printed.

```
. . .
printAttr = "<td bgcolor=" + '"' + printHighLightColor + '"' + ">";

for ( int n = 2; n <= cal.getActualMaximum( Calendar.DAY_OF_MONTH
); n++ ) {

    if ( n == Day ) // this is the day selected. let's highlight
it
        out.print( printAttr + n + "</td>" );
    else
        out.print( "<td>" + n + "</td>" );

    // print <tr> at end of week
    cal.set( Calendar.DAY_OF_MONTH, n );
    if ( cal.get( Calendar.DAY_OF_WEEK) == 7) {
      out.println( "</tr>" );
      out.print( "<tr>" );
    }
}
. . .
```

At the end of the processing loop, two tags are output: the table row terminator and the table terminator. An `IOException` catch statement is required for the i/o performed by the `JspWriter` statement.

```
. . .
out.println( "</tr>" );
out.println("</table>");
}

catch (IOException e) {

    throw new ServletException("I/O Exception in Cal.printCal() " );
}

}

}
```

The complete code for the `Cal.java` class without breaks is shown in Appendix D.

Using Custom Tags in JSP

With JSP version 1.1, *custom tag libraries* were introduced. These tag libraries provide a facility for creating custom JSP page tags. They provide a capability in which a common, well-understood approach to page programming, the page tag, can be used to access custom behaviors programmed in Java.

Tags provide a great deal of flexibility and are very effective in hiding the specifics of the operation from the user. For this reason, tags are an excellent mechanism for providing access to business logic to the HTML developer. These tags resemble HTML tags in the use of a tag name, tag attributes, and a tag body using the following syntax:

```
<myTag:tagName attribute1="value" attribute2="value">
optional tag body
</myTag:tagName>
```

A tag can be created and inserted into a JSP. When the JSP container encounters this tag as it preprocesses the page, the underlying code behind the tag will be invoked. Custom tags provide additional value with the ability to perform programming flow-of-control functions within the JSP. These are operations such as loops or iterations, and execution of conditional statements. Unlike HTML tags, which are just translated into a form which is then rendered on the browser, JSP tags can produce output based on input parameters and can iterate over output producing lists and tables in the resulting JSP.

Coding Tags: Custom Tags and Business Logic

The creation of custom tags is more involved than creating a JavaBean and implies some code restrictions. JSP custom tag libraries must implement an interface defined in the `javax.servlet.jsp.tagext` package. Although tags offer many significant capabilities to the JSP, they still do not eliminate the need for scripting. HTML was designed to provide for static page content; it does not provide programmatic flow-of-control statements that are required to perform robust rendering of dynamic content. For this reason, there are many valid reasons for placing scripting elements in a JSP.

However, the developer must be careful not to confuse the coding of appropriate conditional logic to provide for the creation of the JSP with the insertion of business logic into the JSP. Business logic, logic that involves decisions concerning business rules (e.g., a rule that indicates that sales region 1 should be excluded from district 4 totals if this report is for the first quarter), should be placed in *helper classes*, which should, if necessary, be called from within tag code. Decisions that involve the presentation of the page (e.g., what color should region 1 text be, what color should region 2 text be) can be included in the page and may require some decision logic. But wherever possible, this logic should be placed in helper classes, thus providing a clear separation of roles and a much more manageable JSP.

Using a Custom Tag Library: The JSP Calendar Utility

The following section of code uses the calendar creation code shown in the first JSP/JavaBean example to create a custom tag library to display calendar information in a JSP.

```
<?xml version="1.0" encoding="ISO-8859-1" ?>
<!DOCTYPE taglib
 PUBLIC "-//Sun Microsystems, Inc.//DTD JSP Tag Library 1.1//EN"
 "http://java.sun.com/j2ee/dtds/web-jsptaglibrary_1_1.dtd">

<!- a tag library descriptor ->

<taglib>
...
```

Using a JSP tag library requires the implementation of an interface (e.g., TagSupport) and the preparation of an XML descriptor file that provides information on the tag library (a .tld file). The XML descriptor file is referenced on the JSP using the taglib directive:

```
...
<%@ taglib uri="/jsp/TagCal.tld" prefix="tagcal" %>
...
```

This tag indicates that in the TOMCAT_HOME/webapps/jsp directory, a .tld file named TagCal.tld is stored. This directs the Tomcat server to read the file and determine how to access the custom tag library that will be referenced on that page using the tagcal prefix.

The Tag Library Descriptor (TLD) file describes the JSP custom tag library to be used by the JSP. The JSP is made aware of the TLD by the taglib descriptor. Since the TLD is an XML document, there is a corresponding Document Type Description (DTD) for the document. The first few tags in the document identify this DTD.

Additional tags are used to indicate the JSP version of tag library being used. The short name for the tag library is identified followed by an alternative URI to which this tag library may be mapped. An informational tag is used to provide an entry that describes the tag library. These tags do not change from library to library and can generally be copied into the TLD.

```
<tlibversion>1.0</tlibversion>
<jspversion>1.1</jspversion>
<shortname>TagCal</shortname>
<uri></uri>
<info>
Tag library for display of a calendar widget
</info>
```

The next block in the file is used to describe the tag library.

```
1.
2.          <tag>
3.              <name>Calendar</name>
4.              <tagclass>JSPCal.TagCal</tagclass>
5.              <info> Display calendar</info>
6.
7.              <attribute>
8.                  <name>month</name>
9.                  <required>false</required>
10.             </attribute>
11.             <attribute>
12.                 <name>day</name>
13.                 <required>false</required>
14.             </attribute>
15.             <attribute>
16.                 <name>year</name>
17.                 <required>false</required>
18.             </attribute>
19.
20.          <attribute>
21.                 <name>out</name>
22.                 <required>false</required>
23.             </attribute>
24.
25.             <attribute>
26.                 <name>dateString</name>
27.                 <required>false</required>
28.             </attribute>
29.
30.          <bodycontent>EMPTY</bodycontent>
31.
32.          </tag>
33.      </taglib>
```

This block is identified as the tag block and contains the information most commonly provided by the developer. The tag block contains entries for the name of the tag, the `class` that will be loaded to implement the tag, and some general information about the tag. These entries are made on lines 3, 4, and 5 of the listing.

The `class` entry identifies which Java class will be loaded to execute the tag. This class must provide an implementation of `BodyTag` or some other interface in the `javax.servlet.jsp.tagext` package. The `name` entry identifies the name that will be used to reference the tag. A large portion of the remaining tag block on lines 7 through 28 is devoted to the various attributes that may be passed to the tag. The attribute is identified followed by a "required" tag, which indicates whether or not the attribute is required for the tag. The example below show the tags for each attribute passed to the `TagCal` calendar example, with tags for the optional attributes of `month`, `day`, `year`, `out` (output), and `dateString` (which sets the boolean `dateString` flag); each of these tags sets the `required` attribute to false, since the attribute is optional.

The `bodycontent` tag is used to indicate whether or not the body of the tag will have content. In this example, it is empty.

The code for the tag library begins with a number of import statements identical to the JavaBean code for the calendar with the exception of the statement to import the `javax.servlet.jsp.tagext` package, which is used to specifically retrieve the tag library interfaces into the class name space for the program.

```
package JSPCal;

import java.text.*;
import java.util.*;
import java.io.*;

import javax.servlet.*;
import javax.servlet.jsp.tagext.*;
import javax.servlet.jsp.*;
. . .
```

The major difference between this example and the JavaBean example is in the class definition. A JSP custom tag library must implement one of the interfaces in the `javax.servlet.jsp.tagext` package or extend one of the convenience classes in that package. In this example, the `TagSupport` class is extended, which provides empty body implementations for the methods in the `javax.servlet.jsp.tagext.Tag` interface (many of which won't be used here) and thus reduces the amount of work required to create the tag library.

```
public class TagCal extends TagSupport {

// array for months
private static final String months[] = new
DateFormatSymbols().getMonths();

// array for days of week in string format
private static final String days[] = new
DateFormatSymbols().getWeekdays();

// array for day abbreviations
private static final String daysAbbrev[] = new
DateFormatSymbols().getShortWeekdays();

// internal date
private int month;
private int day;
private int year;

private  String printHighLightColor = "grey";
private Calendar  mCalendar = null;  // internal calendar
private JspWriter mOut = null;       // response output stream
...
```

Using Static Variables in JSP Pages

Since many JSP/servlet implementations allow servlet classes to be shared among sessions, the use of `static` variables could potentially create problems, since in Java `static` variables belong to the class, which would in turn be shared among multiple sessions. But the use of `static` variables in the calendar JavaBean and tag library would not create a sharing conflict, since the variables declared `static` are also declared `final` (which indicates that they cannot be changed once they are initialized). They are effectively constants that contain the calendar column headers—the names of the days of the week. As such, they can be shared among multiple objects or multiple JSP/servlet sessions without a problem.

The tag library implementation also adds a boolean flag to the calendar JavaBean code to indicate the behavior required of the `doStartTag` method. Specifically, this boolean variable is used to indicate that the tag is being used to print the date as a character string and should not print the entire calendar.

```
...
        private boolean dateStringOnly = false;
...
```

The doStartTag method is executed when the tag is encountered in a JSP. The body of this tag is executed *after* the corresponding setXX method have been called for the attributes in tag.

```
...

public int doStartTag() {

// use the current day as the default date
if ( ( mCalendar == null ) && ( this.month == 0 ) && ( this.day
== 0 ) && ( this.year == 0 ) )
    setCalCurrentDate();

if ( ( this.month != 0 ) && ( this.day != 0 ) && ( this.year !=
0 ) ) {
    this.month-; // GregorianCalendar expects 0 - based month
    setCalDate( this.month, this.day, this.year );
}

// set the default output stream to the JspWriter in the
pageContext
if ( mOut == null )
    setOut( pageContext.getOut() );
...
```

The body of the doStartTag method acts as both a virtual constructor and a main program block for the tag. The first few lines of the method check the local members of the tag class to determine whether or not they have been set by the setXX methods of the tag (attributes that are not required to be set as indicated in the TLD). These attributes indicate the date for the calendar to use. If the attributes have not been set, the tag body assumes that the current date should be used and the setCalCurrentDate method is called. If the attribute values for the date have been set, the setCalDate method is called to set the date for the calendar to the date specified in the attributes. Additionally, if the JspWriter output stream has not been specified in an attribute, the output stream is set to the output stream in the page context (as returned by pageContext.getOut).

Once all initialization has been done, a simple if/else block is used to determine the action to be performed by the tag.

```
. . .
try {

// print the calendar
if ( !dateStringOnly )
    printCal();
else // print the current date as a string
    mOut.println( getCurrentDate() );

}

catch (ServletException e) {

  System.out.println("TagCal error: " + e.getMessage() );

}
catch (IOException e) {
      System.out.println( "IOException in TagCal: " +
e.getMessage() );
}
. . .
```

If the dateStringOnly flag has *not* been set, the printCal method is
called to output the HTML calendar for the date specified in the member
variables of the calendar. If the dateStringOnly flag has been set, the current date for the calendar (either the current date or the date specified in the
attributes) is output as a text string. All of this work is performed in a
try/catch block which catches a ServletException.

When work is complete, the doStartTag method returns a SKIP_BODY
flag indicating that processing is complete (there are no additional iterations)
and there is, in fact, no body to process for this tag.

```
. . .

// the tag shouldn't have a body to process
return (SKIP_BODY);
}
. . .
```

The class used to turn the calendar JavaBean into a custom tag has an additional method used to set a dateStringOnly flag, indicating that the tag
should only display the date as a string (and not display the full HTML formatted calendar). This instance member requires a setXX method to set the

value of this flag. With the exception of this method, the body of the two classes for the JavaBean and the tag library is virtually the same.

```
. . .
public void setDateString( boolean flag ) {

    this.dateStringOnly = flag;

}
. . .
```

JavaBeans or Custom Tag Libraries: Tips on Use

JavaBeans and custom tag libraries are two different approaches to the same problem: how to extend the Java code on a JSP. Since we would like to keep the use of scriplets on the JSP to a minimum, we need some mechanism to make use of Java helper classes on the JSP. JavaBeans provides this capability in such a way that almost any valid Java class could be made into a JavaBean. The only requirement is that any properties accessed using the JSP `getProperty` or `setProperty` tag would require the coding of `get` and `set` methods in the class using a specific naming convention; but this is not required.

The use of tag libraries with JSP is more restrictive in terms of the coding effort but in many ways is more powerful and provides easier access to the library methods on the JSP. As we have seen here, JSP custom tag libraries require specific Java interfaces to be implemented, and various methods in these interfaces must be coded for the tag to be executed properly from the JSP. The integration of existing classes into custom tag libraries would therefore be more difficult than converting the same code into JavaBeans.

One approach to converting existing Java class libraries into custom tag libraries is through the creation of *wrapper classes*, classes that extend the class being converted using methods that consolidate and simplify one or more method calls in the class being converted. Wrapper classes can make the conversion process simpler and can make the process of creating a custom tag library easier.

Where a custom tag library makes sense is when there is a requirement to perform an operation repeatedly within an application. This operation could be a general-purpose operation (e.g., a calendar) that could be required across multiple applications, or it could be a business-specific operation such as retrieving customer or account information.

Creating a simple custom tag to perform an operation that must be executed repeatedly provides a better solution relative to performing the same operation with several lines of Java code (calling JavaBeans methods) in a scriplet. Essentially, the custom tag approach will reduce the lines of Java code (in a scriplet) that would be required with the JavaBeans approach, and reducing the amount of Java code on a JSP improves the maintainability of the page and enhances the *separation of roles* between presentation and business logic.

The conclusion then is that JavaBeans work best with class libraries that map neatly into a `get`/`set` access approach: for instance, providing access to a database record or building a dynamic Web page based on a set of records. Custom tag libraries work best when an operation must be performed repeatedly (as opposed to only once) across many Web pages and the operation does not map easily into a simple `get`/`set` access approach.

Summary

In this chapter we covered using JSP to create dynamic Web content. Since we know that we don't want to place too much Java code on the JSP in scriplets, we need to have a facility for moving Java code off the page. We have two basic approaches to doing this: using JSP with JavaBeans and using custom tag libraries.

Both approaches to using Java classes on JSP pages were covered in this chapter using an example that created a set of calendar utilities. The first example used JavaBeans to display an HTML-formatted monthly calendar. Then, to demonstrate the same approach using a custom tag library, the code required to implement the calendar utility as a custom tag library was shown. Finally, we discussed the benefits and drawbacks of each approach and established some guidelines for the use of these two techniques.

Coming Up Next

In Chapter 9 we provide a more detailed example of JSP use with the development of a threaded message list. This example shows the development of more complex Web pages using database access. Using the example of a discussion group system, Chapter 9 will cover the creation of pages that are created dynamically based on the contents of various database tables. Included is coverage of dynamic input forms, use of session variables, forwarding of requests, and using exceptions with JSP.

JSP IN PRACTICE: A DISCUSSION GROUP SYSTEM

Introduction

There is no better way to learn the use of a technology than through example. Whereas in Chapter 8 we showed several simple examples to demonstrate some basic concepts, in this chapter we detail the use of Java and JSP in a more complex example. The system developed in this chapter is a discussion group system designed to maintain a database of messages stored by topic. The system tracks message threads, and users of the system can start a message thread or add to existing message threads. The code behind this system is used to demonstrate login security, the creation of dynamic HTML tables, storing data in session variables, passing request parameters, and other important concepts.

As detailed in Chapter 7, a basic design strategy of separating presentation logic from business logic is used. To maintain this separation of business logic from presentation logic, use of Java scriplets on a JSP will be kept to a minimum, and Java *design patterns* introduced in Chapter 7 will be applied whenever possible.

These design patterns will also be used heavily in the development of the classes for data access and workflow control. *Data Access Objects* are used to model and encapsulate database operations, and Value Objects are used to encapsulate and model the logical data records used throughout the application. *Facade patterns* are used to manage the workflow control and marshal the resources of the DAO to facilitate the creation of the dynamic Web pages.

Discussion Group System: Application Description

The application shown here is designed to allow users to enter messages. The messages can be part of a thread, so that a user can enter an initial *message* and users can add to the message by providing either additional information relative to the message or a reply to the message. These additional messages added to the initial message are referred to as *message threads*. This type of application, often referred to as a discussion group, *threaded message list* or *knowledge base*.

The Message

The focus of the discussion group application is the manipulation of messages posted to various discussion groups. These messages are tracked in the system using information on the user that entered the message, the date the message was entered, and the type and category of the message. This information about the message is used to store, manipulate, and sort the message when it is output on the message review pages.

Each message has a *message type* and *message category*. The valid message types and categories can be defined for a particular installation of the discussion group application, so that different installations of the message system could be used to track different types of messages. (This adds flexibility to the system, but for us, the developers, implies additional work since these dynamic values for the message types and message categories must be managed by the discussion group application.)

An example of the use of the flexibility of dynamic message types and message categories would be to use the discussion group application to create a common *problem tracking system*. This system would store information on problems as messages, and potential solutions to those problems could be posted as responses to the initial "problem" message. The initial problem message would be created with a message type of "problem," and the message response, a message that is posted as a threaded message to the initial message, would be created with a message type of "resolution."

Another use of the system would be as a system to store online discussions. A message could be created with a message type of "post" for initial posted messages. Responses to the initial message, added as threaded messages, would be created with a message type of "reply" for replies to those messages.

Message Threads

A message that has been entered into the message system is either an initial message posting (or *base message* of a message thread) or a response posting to an initial thread, also referred to as a *threaded message*. Using the example for a problem tracking system, a user may enter an initial message, perhaps identifying and explaining a particular problem identified. Another user of the message system may then read that initial message and add to the identification of the problem by adding to that message. At this point two messages would be considered part of that message thread: the initial message or the base message entered by the user who identified the problem and the message that was added by the second user, a threaded message. Both of these messages could be entered with a message type of "problem," indicating that they identified a problem (see Figure 9.1).

Finally, a message system user may read both messages and provide a resolution to the problem identified. This message would also be added as a

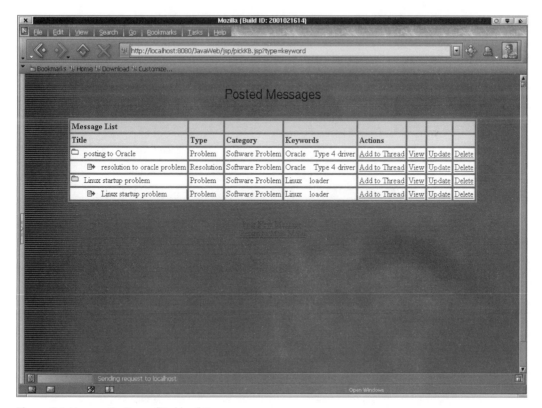

Figure 9.1 Message Posting as "Problem" Type

thread of the initial message but would be added with a message type of "resolution," indicating that it provided a resolution to the problem identified by the other users (see Figure 9.2).

Message Categories

Each message is associated with a message *category*. This association is maintained in the database through a field in the message header that contains the category for that message. For a problem tracking system for example, these categories could be "hardware" for hardware problems, or "software" for software problems. Messages could be posted to either category and dynamic JSP pages that searched or listed the message database could use these categories to restrict listings to either hardware or software problems.

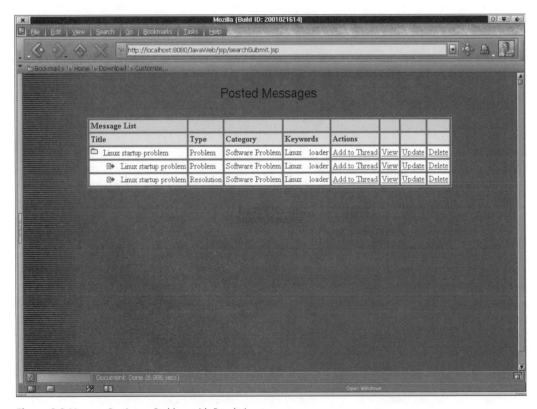

Figure 9.2 Message Posting as Problem with Resolution

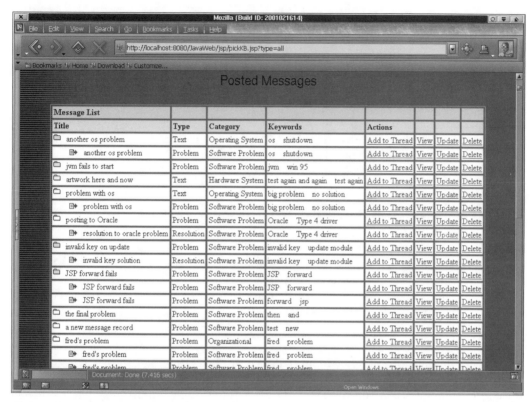

Figure 9.3 Complete Message List

Alternatively, the message system could be used for a discussion group, and these categories could be used as topics for discussions. Users could be allowed to add categories for different discussion topics. Other users could read these user postings and add additional postings. In essence, the message system application could provide a forum for the user community (see Figure 9.3).

Database Structure

The message system uses a relational database to store configuration information for the system (message types, message categories), user login ids and related security information, and messages and related information. Each message entered in the message system has a primary key, known as a *document key* (`doc_key`). This primary key is maintained automatically by the database as a unique integer number. Maintaining the list of messages involves tracking the *base* key for the initial message in each of the threaded messages for that initial message.

Stored with the message is the date the message was entered and the last date the message was modified. When the message list is displayed, it is sorted by the base document key and the date the message was entered, so that the initial message is at the top of the sorted list followed by the messages that have been posted to the initial message. The posted messages are displayed in the order in which they have been entered, based on the date they were entered and the last date they were modified.

Application Flow for the Message System

Any Web application is constructed using a certain procedural flow, which assumes that the user of the application is going to move through the application in a certain fashion. With larger Web sites a great deal of consideration is applied to this process, creating large wire-frame diagrams that detail the flow of the system. The message system, although not as complex as some Web sites, does contain a number of pages that you would expect on a Web site: a login page, a main menu, a search page, a message listing page, a message view page, and a message input/update page. Taken together, these pages comprise the message system Web site.

But our Web site is not just static HTML pages; it includes JavaBean code that supports these pages and a database and corresponding database schema. The JavaBean code for this application comprises both business objects, control objects and database access objects. Keeping the flow of the application in mind, our discussion of the message system will begin with a discussion of the pages of the message system in the order in which those pages would probably be accessed. Following this discussion, the database schema for the message system is discussed. This discussion provides the framework for a discussion of the code behind the message system in Chapter 10.

Login Page

A login page on a Web site is used to perform several different functions. First, it should authenticate each user and verify that the user is who he or she claims to be. This will usually involve checking a user id and password entered by the user against a user id and password stored on the system.

Next, a login page (or the processing behind the page) will retrieve some information about the user and retain this information for the user session. For many sites this information would include the user name and user preference information. The message system performs these operations, although it does not collect the user preference and history information that many commercial sites may collect. The login page initially asks the user to enter a user id and password (see Figure 9.4).

Once the user has entered the user id and password on the login page (login.jsp), the form is posted to another page, which will process the information (loginSubmit.jsp). If the user login is successful (the user is known to the system and the password is valid), the successful login page is as shown in Figure 9.5. If the user login is not successful, a Java exception is thrown and the error page (ErrorPage.jsp) shown in Figure 9.6 appears.

The message system does not require every user to log into the system. A user who is not logged in is allowed to review the messages on the message board but is not allowed to post a message until they have completed the login process. The login page retrieves user information (user name, location, last login date) from a database table and ultimately stores this information in a JSP session object, an object available in all the pages in the user session (defined as pages called as part of a list of pages starting with the first page accessed). Other pages in the session will use the user information in the session object. Some pages will use the information to determine whether

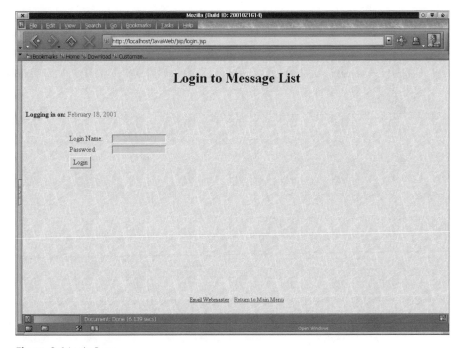

Figure 9.4 Login Page

Figure 9.5 Successful Login Page

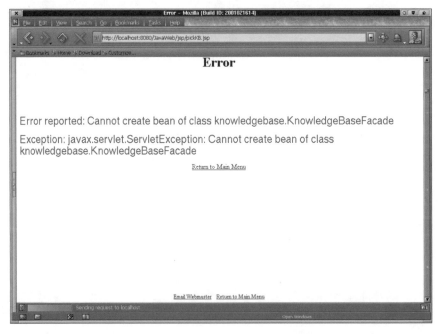

Figure 9.6. Error Page

or not the user has logged in and whether or not the user is valid. The message input/update page will use the user information to populate part of the input form for the user, information that will become part of the message record to be inserted or updated into the database.

(An alternative to using an HTML input form for user authentication and login is shown in Chapter 12. This version of user authentication allows Apache to authenticate the user using basic authentication. Apache will perform the authentication and if the login and authentication are successful, will pass the authentication information on to Tomcat, where it is then used by the JSP to populate the `session` object with the user information.)

The Main Menu

The main menu for the application is a simple static HTML page. This page will be accessed by the user using the Apache Web server using server-side includes to display information on the current date and to retrieve the header and elements to be used throughout the application (see Figure 9.7). Since the page is static HTML and can be served by the Apache server, it has the benefit of reducing some of the workload for the Tomcat server.

Figure 9.7 Main Menu

The options to search the message base, to list all messages, and (later) to view the contents of the message base do not require a valid login. The option to post a new message does, however, require a valid login. These options and their associated pages are explained in more detail in the following sections.

Post New Message

The post new message process allows the user to create a new message in the message database. This option will execute the inputKB.jsp page, which will require the user to have valid login entries in the JSP session object. If the user does not have a valid login, the user will be redirected (using a JSP forward) to an error page, indicating that the user needs to log in before posting a message (see Figure 9.8).

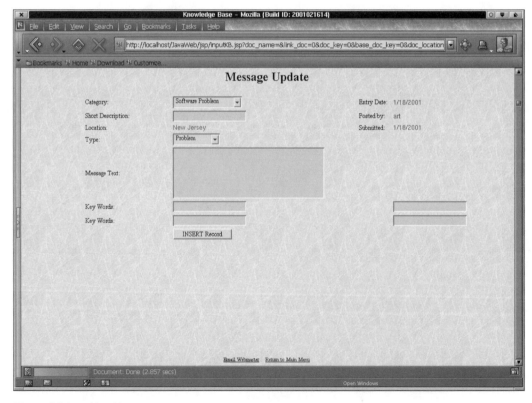

Figure 9.8 Input New Message

Note that some fields are displayed but cannot be changed by the user; these fields are either generated programmatically or obtained from the session object as part of the login record.

Search Existing Messages

The message search page allows messages to be searched using the keywords assigned to the messages. The page provides fields to input up to four keywords to be used to perform the search (see Figure 9.9).

Once the keywords have been entered, the "submit query" button on the page would be pushed by the user. This will send a request to the message listing page (pickKB.jsp), passing parameters which indicate that the user has requested a filtered list. The filter operation will select not only the messages that match the search criteria, but also the messages that are part of the message thread for those messages.

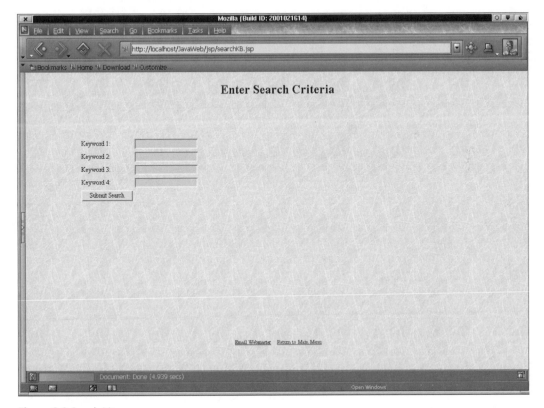

Figure 9.9 Search Messages

Message List: All Messages

The message list page provides a listing of all messages currently in the message database (see Figure 9.10). (The current implementation of this feature displays all messages in the database. A more refined production version should limit the number of rows returned for efficiency purposes.)

Message List: Filtered

The message listing for a filtered set of rows uses the same display as the listing for all rows, but applies the filter before producing the page output (see Figure 9.11).

Update Message

The update message page is called with parameters that indicate the message document that should be displayed. The message document is then retrieved and its contents are displayed in a form that allows the user to modify components of the record (see Figure 9.12). Note that some fields are displayed but

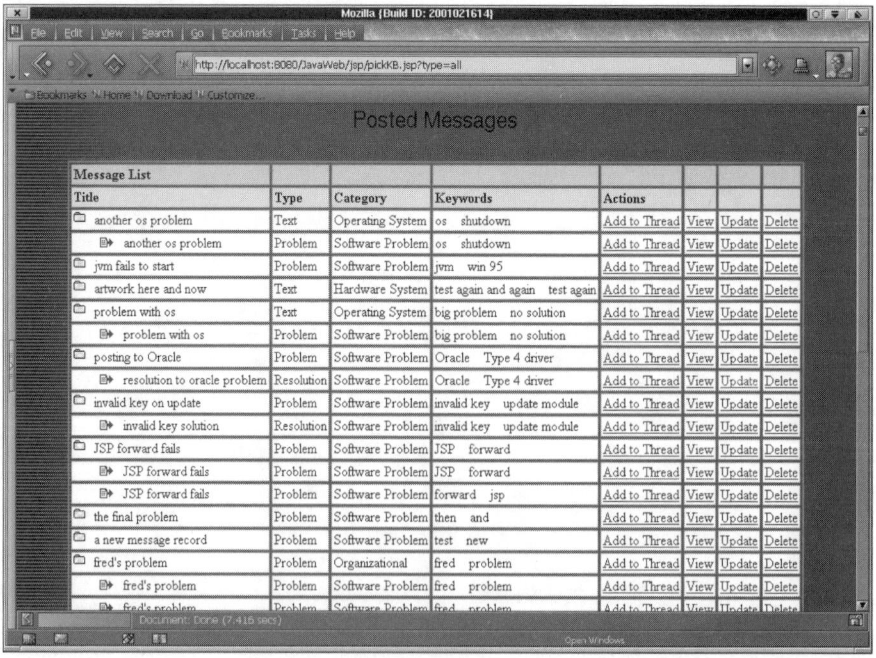

Figure 9.10 List All Messages

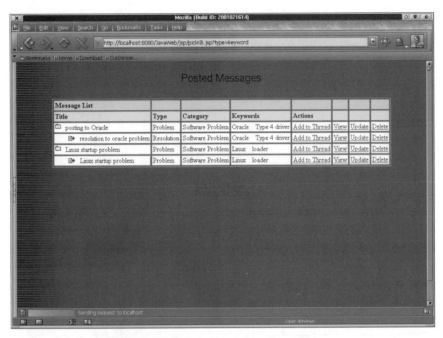

Figure 9.11 Filtered Message Listing

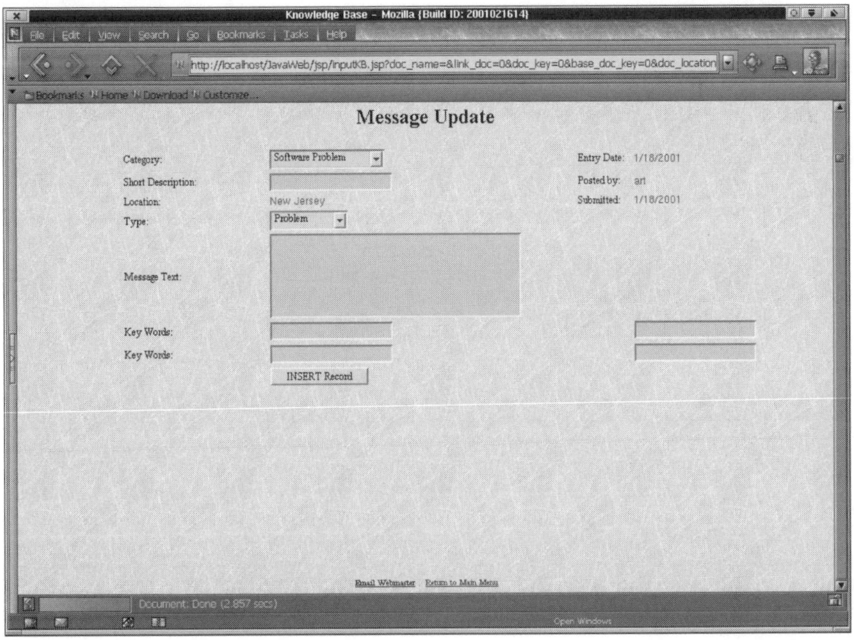

Figure 9.12 Update Existing Message

cannot be changed by the user; these fields are either generated programmatically or obtained from the `session` object as part of the login information.

Delete Message

The delete message operation allows the user to delete a message but checks to determine that the user attempting to delete the message is actually the user who entered the message or is a user with permissions to delete the messages entered by another user (e.g., a system administration user or a message group moderator). Messages are deleted using a link on the message listing page to the message view page. This process allows the user to view the message before it is deleted.

If the message delete operation is successful, a page is displayed indicating that the delete operation was successful; if the delete operation has failed, an exception is thrown which displays the error page with a message about the failed delete operation (see Figure 9.13).

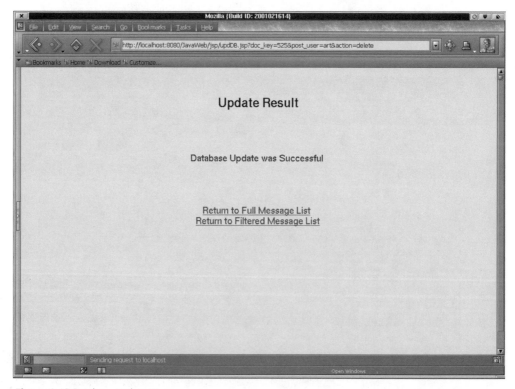

Figure 9.13 Database Update Message

Technical Description of the Message System

In Chapter 7 we provided a number of recommendations on the design of Java applications, specifically Java Web applications with JSP pages. This discussion included the concept of architectural tiers and design patterns applied to those architectural tiers. To "practice what we preach" effectively, the message system was designed using these architectural tiers and applies several of the design patterns discussed in that chapter.

The logical tiers described in Chapter 7 are used to dictate the responsibilities of the components of the system. This applies structure to the design process and allows certain components to be used for what they do best. The tiers described in Chapter 7 and the components used for those tiers are as follows.

- Client
- Presentation
- Business
- Integration
- Resource

For our purposes, the client tier is represented by a user with a Web browser, and the resource tier is represented by the PostgreSQL relational database (or any relational database that supports SQL and JDBC). Three of these tiers are the focus of the next few chapters:

- *Presentation:* creates the output for the page (JSP)
- *Business:* manages the business logic and application workflow (JavaBeans)
- *Integration:* manages database access, encapsulates database components (JavaBeans)

Message System Component Design

The *logical tiers* identify the responsibilities of the components (the JavaBeans and JSP pages) in the application. These responsibilities dictate the functions the components will perform within the application and are then used to dictate the lower-level design details of these components.

The login process has the responsibility of authenticating the user and then directing the user to a particular view. This management of view is primarily a presentation issue and will therefore dictate that this component, the login component, is a Presentation Tier component. Some of the work of this component will involve database and workflow activity; this work will be managed by Business Tier components which will be responsible for building the views to which the login component will direct the user.

The message application uses a number of *facade* classes on the Business Tier. The purpose of these classes is to manage the dynamic output of the pages. Their job is to marshal resources of the data access objects (DAOs), send the Value Objects back and forth to the DAO, and provide wrapper methods for the Value Objects. They are essentially the interface between one or more of the JSP and the database resources they access. They encapsulate the business logic of the application and control the flow of work being performed.

(Although this use of facade classes allowed the DAOs and Value Objects to remain focused on their tasks, it did create what was ultimately a very large and complex facade class for a number of the pages. A design revision would probably include the use of multiple business objects by the facade classes to reduce the exposure of the facade class.)

These Business Tier objects are used by the JSP to build the pages and perform the processing required. They are effectively helper classes for the JSP. To simplify the operations performed on the JSP, a single Session Facade object, an instance of the `KnowledgeBaseFacade` class, is used by the various JSP in the application.

Two Integration Tier patterns are applied to the database operations. Data Access Objects are used to provide access to the database, and Value Objects to encapsulate database objects in a form that can be conveniently passed from method to method in the application (these Value Objects are also used on the Business Tier). The use of these design patterns allowed database operations to be isolated, tested, validated, and then easily shared by other objects. This allowed the database resource to be protected and controlled in the application and provided a means of reducing the amount of work required to access the database. Code for database access is shared among the multiple business objects that access the database, and should the database vendor change (an all too common occurrence), the code change is isolated to a small set of classes.

The database operations are further abstracted in this application. A database utility class (`dbUtil`) is used to to provide low-level access to the database. This database utility class is accessed by the DAOs and contains virtually all JDBC database calls (with the exception of some `ResultSet` manipulation that appears elsewhere). This abstraction of database operations from the business classes of the application is used to encapsulate low-level database operations and provide some flexibility in how they are managed. For instance, while the code used in this sample application does not use database connection pooling, it could easily be inserted into the database utility class in a manner that would be transparent to the rest of the application.

Database Design of the Message System

The message system makes use of a number of relational tables to store pertinent information for the system. This includes information about the messages that have been posted, the text of the messages, any keywords applied to the message, security information for the system, and message categories and message types. The design of the database is a relatively normalized relational structure with tables and descriptions as detailed in Table 9.1.

Table 9.1 Message System Database Tables

Table	Description
`knowledge_base`	Contains the *header* information for messages entered into the system
`knowledge_messages`	Contains the message text for the message; this is a child table of the `knowledge_base` table, meaning that every record in this table must have a corresponding entry in this table
`message_user`	Contains information on the users of the system, including user names and their passwords
`base_keys`	Contains the keywords associated with the messages in the system; currently, messages can have up to four entries in this table; optionally, the message can have zero entries in this table (which is true for many threaded responses to existing message entries)
`categories`	Contains the categories of messages that exist on the system
`message_types`	Contains the types of messages that can be entered in the message system
`message_security`	Security information for users of the message system, including the security role of the user

These tables and their contents are explained in more detail in the following sections.

knowledge_base Table

The `knowledge_base` table stores the base information for the message, message header, or parent in the parent–child relationship for the message database. This table uses a document key (`doc_key`) column as the primary key for the table—the column that uniquely identifies the row in the table. This column is an integer value that is incremented and maintained automatically by the database. (For the PostgreSQL database, this is managed using a `sequence` in the database; the Oracle database uses a similar approach, while the Informix database would use a `serial` column and SQL Server, and mySQL would use an `AutoNumber` column.)

The date the message was first entered is stored in the `date_submitted` field. This field indicates the date the message was submitted to the system. Like the `entry_date` field, this field is stored in the database as a `date` type but is managed by the JSP pages and Java code as a string.

The `knowledge_base` table stores the category of the message, the date the message was submitted, and the last date the message was updated (`entry_date`). The date columns are stored as `date` data types in the database, although for convenience and a certain amount of portability they are treated as strings by the JSP/Java code, which uses the database to perform the conversion on inserts and updates. The `knowledge_base` table also stores the location (`doc_location`) where the message document was entered and the user name of the user (`post_user`) who entered the message. This information appears in the `knowledge_base` record but is not entered by the user. Instead, it is retrieved from the `session` object, where it has been populated based on the entries in the `message_user` table for the current user.

A short description of the document is contained in the `doc_name` field. This provides a description or *name* for the message. The `level` field is intended to store the level of the message within the message threads for the initial posting. This field is currently not used. (Messages are displayed in the date order, based on the date the message was first submitted or entered in the system.)

The `post_user` field is used to store the name of the user who first entered the message. This field is inserted automatically based on the user login information stored in the `session` object (which is stored in the `message_user` table). The user entering the message is not allowed to change this information.

The `link_doc` field is used to store the document to which this document is linked. (This field is not currently used.) The `base_doc_key` field is used to store the base document key (`doc_key`) for the message thread to which this document belongs. This key is used to select and display message documents for a particular thread. The complete schema for this table is shown in Table 9.2.

Table 9.2 knowledge_base Table Schema

Column Name	Data Type	Description
doc_key	integer	Primary key for the messsage document
doc_name	varchar(50)	Short name/short description for the message
doc_location	varchar(50)	Location where the document was entered
level	integer	Level of the message in the message thread list
category	varchar(50)	Category for the message
post_user	varchar(50)	User name for the user who posted the message
date_submitted	date	Date the message was submitted (last changed)
link_doc	integer	Link document for this message; the message for which this document represents a response
base_doc_key	integer	Document key for the base document in this message thread
entry_date	date	Date this message document was entered

knowledge_messages Table

The knowledge_messages table stores the actual message text for the message. The message is stored using the doc_key as the primary key and foreign key for the corresponding header record in the knowledge_base table. This message system stores the message as a variable-length character data type with a limit of 500 characters [a varchar(500)]. (The database enforces the limit on the size of the message, not the application, so the size of the column could be increased at the database and the application would support the larger size.)

The message_type field is used to capture additional information about the message being stored. While the message category groups the message based on a category name, the message type indicates the general nature of the message. For example, the message type could be a "post" message or a "response" message for a message system that was providing a forum for discussion groups. Or the message type could be used to store a "problem" message to identify and describe a problem and a "resolution" message to describe a possible resolution for a problem. These message types are configurable and are contained in the `message_types` table in the database. The contents of this table are used to produce a list box for the message input page. The schema for the `knowledge_messages` table is shown in Table 9.3.

Table 9.3 knowledge_messages Table Schema

Column Name	Data Type	Description
doc_key	integer	Primary key for this message document
message_txt	varchar(500)	Text of the message
message_type	varchar(10)	Type of the message

message_user Table

The `message_user` table is used to store information on users for the message system. This table stores the user's first name and last name, the location of the user, and the user password. Information is also stored on the location of the user, the date the user login record was submitted, and the date of the last login for the user. The complete schema for this table is shown in Table 9.4.

Table 9.4 message_user Table Schema

Column Name	Data Type	Description
login	varchar(20)	Login name for the user
first_name	varchar(30)	First name for the user (given name)
last_name	varchar(30)	Last name for the user (surname)
location	varchar(50)	Location of the user
date_submitted	date	Date login record was submitted by the user
last_login	date	Last login date for the user
pwd	varchar(15)	Password for the user

base_keys Table

The `base_keys` table is used to store the lookup keywords for the messages stored in the database. Currently, the system allows four keywords to be stored for each message (although there is nothing in the schema for this table that enforces a limit). The keywords are referenced using the `doc_key` column and there can be zero, one, or many entries in this table for a given message document key.

If a user enters no keywords for a message (this is common with threaded responses to an initial posting), no entries would be stored in this table. The schema for this table is shown in Table 9.5.

Table 9.5 base_keys Table Schema

Column Name	Data Type	Description
doc_key	integer	Primary key for the message document
keyword	varchar(50)	Keyword to be associated with the message document

categories Table

The `categories` table stores the various categories of messages that can be stored in the system. This provides some flexibility for the system, allowing categories to be customized for the particular installation. This table contains a column for the category name and a column for a description of the category. The schema for this table is shown in Table 9.6.

Table 9.6 categories Table Schema

Column Name	Data Type	Description
category	varchar(20)	Category name
description	varchar(30)	Description of the category

message_types Table

The `message_types` table stores additional information on the type of message being stored in the system. For instance, for a problem tracking system, the message type could be a "problem" message for a message that identifies a problem, and a "resolution" message for a message in the same thread that provides resolution to the problem identified in the thread. The complete schema for this table is shown in Table 9.7.

Table 9.7 message_types Table Schema

Column Name	Data Type	Description
message_type	varchar(20)	Message type
description	varchar(50)	Description of message type

The message_security Table

The message_security table is used to store security information for users of the discussion group system. This table relates user (through the login id) to security roles. A user (as indicated by the login field, the link to the message_user table) can be assigned to more than one role. The role contains the arbitrary name assigned to the security role. The upd_date field stores a date that indicates the date the role record was last updated.

Table 9.8 message_security Table Schema

Column Name	Data Type	Description
login	varchar (20)	The login id of the user
role	varchar (20)	The role assigned to the user
upd_date	date	The last date the record was updated

Additional Database Components

The logical concept of a message document has no natural primary key, a field that uniquely identifies the row in the table. For this reason, a generated primary key was needed. This required a counter within the database that could be used to generate unique integer id numbers. The PostgreSQL database (and other databases) provides this feature in the form of a sequence.

The sequence is created in the database and then accessed using certain database functions. The statement to create a sequence named doc_key with a starting number of 500 is

```
create sequence doc_key start 500;
```

To access the next value of a sequence, the nextval ('<sequence_name>') function can be used. In the message system, the insert statement used to insert the message into the database makes use of this function. The value generated by the `nextval('doc_key')` function call is used as the primary key for the record being inserted.

Since the other records related to the message header must use the doc_key generated by the database insert operation, the insert function for the message header record (`knowledge_base`) must return the `doc_key` generated during the insert operation. This `doc_key` will then be passed to other methods to perform their respective insert operations.

Additionally, the system is designed to use a single database user id to provide access to the data. For the message system shown in this example, the user id is `"puser"`. This user is added to the PostgreSQL system with the command

```
create user puser;
```

This would create the `user` `"puser"` in the database. To allow the `user` `"puser"` to access specific tables in the database and perform specific database operations, the `grant` statement would be used:

```
grant select on knowledge_base to puser;
grant update on knowledge_base to puser;
```

The complete process of creating the message_user database and granting permissions is covered in Chapter 12.

Summary

This chapter laid the foundation for our discussion of a sample JSP application: the discussion group system. It detailed the design and page flow and also provided details on the database structure of this application.

Coming Up Next

In Chapter 10 we provide the details behind the JSP pages shown in Chapter 9. The code behind the JSP pages in the discussion group is shown and discussed, and the details of the Java code used to support the pages (in the form of JavaBeans and additional utility classes) are also shown, so that the discussion of the pages traces execution of the page from the JSP into the classes that support the page.

CHAPTER **10**

JSP Development: JavaBeans Programming

Introduction

In Chapter 9 we introduced a sample JSP application, the discussion group system, and provided details on the design of the system. Now we let the "rubber hit the road" and discuss the various components of the discussion group system: the JSP pages, the design of the database tables, and the classes that will perform the bulk of the work necessary to produce the dynamic pages of the discussion group system. The majority of this chapter is devoted to the JSP and the business tier JavaBeans classes that support those pages.

Organization of the Discussion Group System

The code for the message system is divided into three distinct Java packages based on the functional responsibility of the code in those packages. These three packages are as shown in Table 10.1.

Within the application there is quite a bit of interaction between the classes in the `db` package and the `knowledgebase` package. The classes in the `JSPCal` package are used as needed throughout the system. In the following sections we explain these packages and their classes in more detail.

Table 10.1 Message System Packages

Package Name	Description
JSPCal	General-purpose calendar classes
db	Database utility access routines; class used to wrap the JDBC calls to the database
knowledgebase	Classes used to manage the access to the message system, including the Value Object classes, the Database Access Object classes, and the Session Facade classes.

JSPCal Package

The JSPCal class contains a number of utility methods to provide access to the current date and to display a calendar in HTML format. The two classes contained in this package are Cal and TagCal. The Cal class contains the methods listed in Table 10.2.

The TagCal class uses the same methods as the JSPCal class but wraps the calls to those methods using the methods that it must implement to be used as a custom tag library. The TagCal class extends the TagSupport class, which in turn implements the Tag interface and provides implementations for the various methods in that interface. The TagCal class as implemented here only provides an implementation for the doStartTag method, which is executed when the custom tag is encountered. (Custom tag processing will also make use of the set methods in the TagCal class, but these methods also existed in the Cal class and were explained in Table 10.1.

db Utility Package

The db utility package is used to abstract the details of low-level database access from the DAO classes. Whereas the DAO are still used to manage the database access operations and return results in the form of Value Objects, the db utility class methods are used to load the database driver, open and close connections to the database, create prepared statements, and execute queries against the database.

These methods are fairly flexible in dealing with database connections; if a connection has not currently been made to the database, a connection is made. Similarly, if the database driver has not been loaded, the driver is loaded before an attempt is made to create a connection. This removes the responsi-

Table 10.2 JSPCal Class Methods

Method	Description
`setMonth( int month )`	Sets the month for the calendar
`public void setYear ( int year )`	Sets the year for the calendar
`public void setDay ( int day )`	Sets the day for the calendar
`public void setHighLightColor ( String color )`	Sets the highlight color to be used for the calendar
`public void setDateString ( boolean flag )`	Flag indicating whether or not to print a date string for the date (used with the calendar tag)
`public void setCalDate ( int month, int day, int year )`	Sets the day, month, and year for the calendar with a single method call
`public void setOut ( JspWriter out )`	Sets the output stream for the calendar
`public void setCalCurrentDate()`	Sets the calendar to the current date on the server (the machine where the JSP page is executed)
`public String getCurrentDate()`	Retrieves the current date for the calendar (not necessarily the current date for the machine) as a string
`public String getCurrentDate ( String format )`	Retrieves the current date for the calendar as a formatted string (the only format currently supported is "mm/dd/yy")
`public void printCal ( JspWriter out ) throws Servlet Exception`	Prints the current calendar, sending output to the `JSPWriter` passed to the method

bility of managing these low-level database details from the DAO. All methods share the same active connection for the instance, thus avoiding the overhead of creating additional connections for each query. This class contains the methods listed in Table 10.3.

Table 10.3 db Utility Class Methods

Method	Description
`public void getConnected() throws Exception`	Obtains a connection to the database if one has not currently been obtained
`public void createDBStatement() throws Exception`	Creates a database statement from the current connection; obtains a connection if one has not currently been made
`public PreparedStatement createPreparedStatement ( String stmt ) throws Exception`	Creates a prepared statement from the query string passed to the method; obtains a connection if one has not already been made
`public ResultSet executePreparedStatement ( PreparedStatement pstmt ) throws Exception`	Executes a prepared statement passed to the method; obtains a connection if one is not currently active; returns a JDBC `ResultSet`
`public int executePreparedStmtUpd ( PreparedStatement pstmt ) throws Exception`	Executes a prepared update statement and returns an integer indicating the number of database rows touched by the update; obtains a connection if one is not currently active
`public ResultSet executeDBQuery ( String query ) throws Exception`	Executes a database query contained in the string passed into the method; obtains a connection if one is not currently active; returns a `ResultSet` of rows returned by the query
`public int executeUpdDBQuery ( String query ) throws Exception`	Executes a database update query for the string passed into the method; obtains a connection if one is not currently active; returns an integer indicating the number of rows updated
`public ResultSet getdbResultSet()`	Returns the current `ResultSet` used by the utility class
`public String getdbDriverName()`	Returns the name of the database driver currently being used
`public Connection getdbConnection()`	Returns the JDBC connection being used by the utility class
`public String getDbURL()`	Returns the URL of the database currently being used
`public Statement getdbStatement()`	Returns the database statement currently being used

Table 10.3 db Utility Class Methods (cont.)

Method	Description
`public void setdbDriverName ( String dbDN )`	Sets the driver to be used by the db utility class
`public void setdbURL ( String dbURL )`	Sets the URL to be used by the db utility class

knowledgebase Package

The `knowledgebase` package contains the bulk of the code used by the message application. This package contains the facade classes, the Value Objects and the DAOs as shown in Table 10.4.

The Value Objects in this package contain internal data members that mirror the attributes or columns of the database tables that they represent and `get` and `set` methods that are the accessor and mutator methods, respectively, for each of these class members. Each value object will not be covered in detail since the description of each method in these classes would quickly become redundant.

Table 10.4 knowledgebase Package Classes

Class Name	Description
`Base_keysDAO`	DAO for the `base_keys` table
`Base_keysVO`	Value Object for the `base_keys` table
`CategoriesDAO`	DAO for the `categories` table
`CategoriesVO`	Value Object for the `categories` table
`Knowledge_baseDAO`	DAO for the `knowledge_base` table
`KnowledgeBaseFacade`	Facade class for the `knowledge_base` system as a whole; this class controls the access to all DAOs and provides an interface for the presentation layer (the JSP) to the DAO
`Knowledge_baseVO`	Value Object for the `knowledge_base` table
`Knowledge_messagesDAO`	DAO for the `knowledge_messages` table

Table 10.4 knowledgebase Package Classes (cont.)

Class Name	Description
Knowledge_messagesVO	Value Object for the knowledge_messages table
loginFacade	Facade class for the login process; provides access to the DAOs used in the login process; provides an interface for the presentation layer, the JSPs.
Message_securityDAO	DAO for the message_security table
Message_securityVO	Value Object for the message_security table
Message_typesDAO	DAO for the message_types table
Message_typesVO	Value Object for the message_types table
Message_userDAO	Data Access Object for the message_user table
Message_userVO	Value Object for the message_user table
searchFacade	Facade class for the search page; encapsulates the search operation; provides an interface for the search process and the database operations required for the search process

The methods listed in Table 10.5 are common to the DAOs used in this example.

A DAO may also contain getXX and setXX methods for retrieving and setting local members, although these are generally not used. The preferable method for setting or retrieving the values of the DAO is to pass a Value Object to set the values of the DAO and retrieve a Value Object reference from the DAO to get the values of the DAO. This is done using the loadVO and setVO methods.

KnowledgeBaseFacade Class

The KnowledgeBaseFacade class provides an *interface* between the JSP used to provide the visual access to the message system and the logic and workflow required of the application. The division of responsibilities is that the JSP will manage the display, the facade class will manage business logic and

Table 10.5 Common Methods for Data Access Objects

Name	Description
`public int insertDAO( )` `throws SQLException, Exception`	Inserts the current contents of the DAO into the data base
`public void updateDAO( )` `throws SQLException`	Updates the current contents of the DAO into the database
`public void deleteDAO( )` `throws SQLException`	Deletes the current DAO from the database

`public void loadDAO`
`( int doc_key )`
`throws Exception`
	Loads the DAO from the database using the key passed as a parameter

`public void loadDAO`
`( Knowledge_baseVO`
`knowledge_base )`
	Loads the values of the DAO from the Value Object passed as a parameter.

`public void setVO`
`( Knowledge_baseVO vo )`
`throws Exception`
	Sets the Value Object to the current contents of the DAO

`public void`
`createPreparedStatements( )`
`throws Exception`
	Creates the prepared statements used by the DAO to
	
	perform database access

workflow, and the DAOs and value objects will manage access to the resources of the system. The `KnowledgeBaseFacade` class includes the methods listed in Table 10.6.

Table 10.6. KnowledgeBaseFacade Class Methods

Method	Description
`public void setRowsUpdated` `( int rows )`	Sets an internal member to the number of rows updated
`public void setAction` `( String action ) throws Exception`	Used to define the action (add,update, insert) for the `inputKB.jsp` page
`public void setSubmitTitle` `( String submitTitle )`	Used to set the title for the submit button on the `inputKB.jsp` page

Table 10.6. KnowledgeBaseFacade Class Methods (cont.)

Method	Description
`public void setNextKBVO ( boolean val ) throws Exception`	Used to move to the next Value Object in the list of value objects retrieved to populate the `pickKB.jsp` page
`public Iterator getCategoryList()`	Used to retrieve a list of categories used to populate an HTML select list on the `inputKB.jsp` page
`public Iterator getMessageTypesList()`	Used to retrieve a list of message types and to populate an HTML select list on the `inputKB.jsp` page
`public String makeCategoryString( Object obj )`	Used to convert an Object parameter into a character string representing a category (essentially wraps a Java cast operation and avoids having to place this code into a JSP)
`public String makeMessageTypesString ( Object obj )`	Used to convert an Object parameter into a character string representing a message type (essentially wraps a Java cast operation and avoids having to place this code into a JSP)
`public boolean isDefaultCategory ( String category )`	Returns a boolean value indicating whether a category passed in is the default category
`public boolean kbRecsHasMore()`	Returns a boolean value indicating whether or not there are more `knowledge_base` records to be retrieved
`public void setFilterKBRecs ( ServletRequest request, HttpSession session )`	Used by the `filterKB.jsp` page to pass the filter criteria for the JSP page
`public void setFilterSelection ( ServletRequest request, HttpSession session )`	Used to set the filter selection for the `pickKB.jsp` page; reads the "type" parameter of the request and processes two selections: "all" for viewing all records, or "keyword" for a keyword filter
`public void setAllKBRecs ( boolean val ) throws Exception`	Retrieves all message system records from the database (the boolean parameter is currently not used)

Table 10.6. KnowledgeBaseFacade Class Methods (cont.)

Method	Description
`public void insertKBRecs ( ServletRequest request, HttpSession session )`	Used to insert message system records into the database; data for the operation are contained in both the request object and session object which are passed as parameters
`public void deleteKBRecs ( ServletRequest request, HttpSession session )`	Used to delete message system records from the database; data for the operation are contained in both the request object and the session object
`public void processParameters ( ServletRequest request, HttpSession session ) throws Exception`	Used to process parameters for the operation
`public void updateKBRecs ( ServletRequest request, HttpSession session )`	Used to update message system records; data for the operation are contained in both the request object and the session object
`public void doUpdate ( ServletRequest request, HttpSession session )`	Called by the `updDB.jsp` page to perform database update operations
`public void loadKnowledgeBase ( int doc_key ) throws Exception`	Loads a message system (`knowledge_base`) record for the doc_key passed

Message System Application Flow

It is difficult, if not impossible, to understand the operation of a Web application without understanding the process flow of the system. With Web applications this flow is indicated by the pages which are loaded as the user progresses through the application. Therefore, to understand the message system application, in the following sections we detail the page flow through this system. For starters, Table 10.7 lists the pages used in the system.

Table 10.7 JSP Pages in the Message System

Page	Description
`pickKB.jsp`	Lists the existing messages in the system; provides menu options for viewing, updating, and deleting any of the messages listed; must choose a type of listing as either "all" to list all messages within the system, or "keyword" to filter on a set of keywords (as contained in a Collection in the `session` object)
`viewKB.jsp`	Views all elements as a single message, including the message header (`knowledge_base`), message text (`knowledge_messages`), and keywords (`base_keys`); provides menu options to delete the message (if allowed) and to return to the main menu
`inputKB.jsp`	Provides data entry form for a new message or to update a current message
`menu.html`	Main menu for the message system
`login.jsp`	Provides a form to execute the login for the message system
`loginSubmit.jsp`	Posted to by `login.jsp`; page used to process the login information and forward to an error page if the login failed
`ErrorPage.jsp`	Error page for the message system
`updDB.jsp`	Updates the database and forwards to the error page if there is an error during the update
`searchKB.jsp`	Provides a search page using a form that allows searching the message system database based on four keywords; links to the `pickKB.jsp` page with submission of the search criteria form

The flow into the system begins with a user login. If the user logs into the system successfully, the user can proceed to the main menu, which provides the user with a number of choices:

- Login
- Search Messages

- List All Messages
- Post New Message

The most common course of action will be to proceed to the search page (searchKB.jsp). This page will allow the user to enter search criteria to allow them to narrow their search to a set of keywords. This page displays an input form that will post to the pickKB.jsp page when the submit button is pressed (see Figure 10.1).

After entering search criteria, the user would then be displayed the message list page (pickKB.jsp) with a filtered list of messages. The pickKB.jsp page provides menu options with each message listed. These menu options allow the user to display the contents of the message (viewKB.jsp) optionally, or to update or delete the message (updDB.jsp) (see Figure 10.2).

If the user chooses to display the contents of the message, the message view page is displayed (viewKB.jsp; see Figure 10.3). This page allows the user to view the complete contents of the message, including the message header, the text of the message, the message type, the message category, and the keywords for the message.

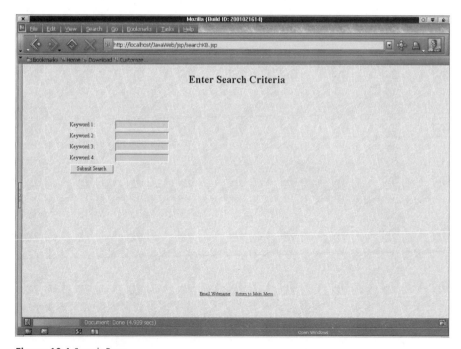

Figure 10.1 Search Page

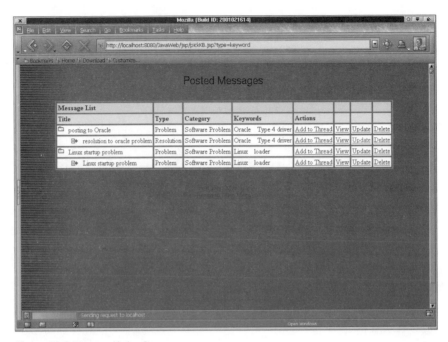

Figure 10.2 Message Listing Page

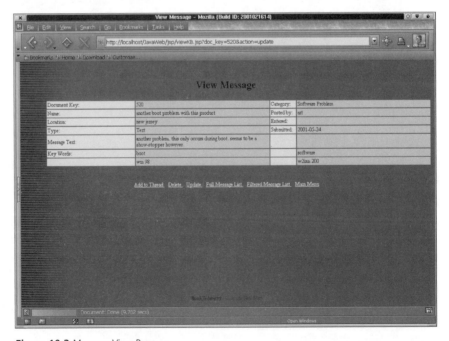

Figure 10.3 Message View Page

The user has menu options on this page that allow the user to add a message to the message thread, delete the message, update the message, return to the message list, or return to the main menu. If the user chooses to update the message, the message update page is displayed (see Figure 10.4).

The message update page displays an input form that allows the user to make changes to certain fields and then submit the form. The form provides a drop-down list box for the message category and message type. The user is allowed to change any field on the page. Once submitted, this form will post to the update page (updDB.jsp), which will perform the work necessary to update the changes to the database. If there is no error, the updDB.jsp page will display a "rows updated" message, indicating that the change was updated to the database (see Figure 10.5).

If the user chooses to input a new message, the message input (inputKB.jsp) page is displayed with a blank form. (This is the same page as that used for the message update operation.) Once the user completes input for this form and chooses to submit, it is posted to the database update page (updDB.jsp) to send the changes to the database.

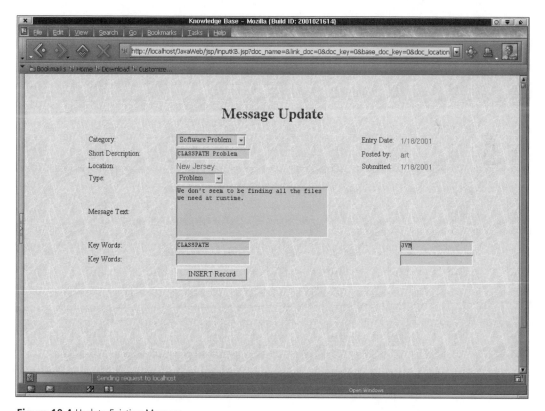

Figure 10.4 Update Existing Message

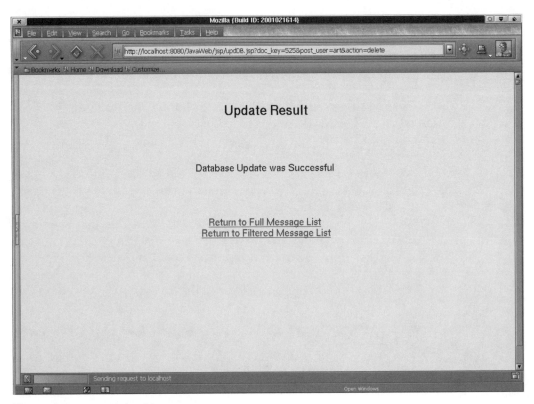

Figure 10.5 Message Updated Page

If the user chooses to delete an existing message, the view message page is displayed, forcing the user first to view the contents of the page. At this point, the user must select the message delete link to delete the message from the database. The delete message link on this page will submit a request to the `updDB.jsp` page to delete the message. If the message deletion is successful, the message update page will output a success message.

If an exception is thrown in any of these pages, the `ErrorPage.jsp` is invoked with the Exception that has been thrown. This page outputs the exception that was thrown and provides a menu option to allow the user to return to the main menu page (see Figure 10.6).

This page displays the contents of the exception that triggered the message and provides links to allow the user to move back to the main menu.

In the preceding section we explained the page execution that the user would use to move through the message system. This explanation provides a good basis for understanding how this system was developed. But now we need to examine these JSP in detail as well as the code behind the JSP, the code that is executed when the JSP is accessed.

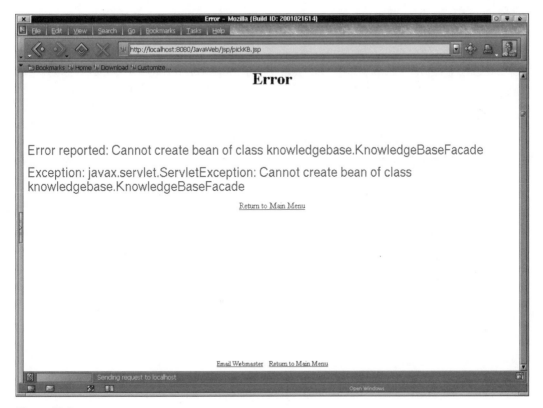

Figure 10.6

Since we have kept close to the separation-of-roles concept in developing this application, the majority of the processing for a JSP is performed by JavaBeans classes that are accessed by making a small number of method calls in the scriplets on the JSP. In the following section we show both the JSP and the Java code behind the page and provide a detailed explanation of both.

The Rest of the Story:
JSP and JavaBeans Code Explained

The page flow gives us half the story. At this point, we need to see the contents of the JSP and understand the interaction of the page with the Java code behind the page, the JavaBeans. To understand the actions performed by the page and to understand the process for programming a JSP application, the code behind each page will be explained *in-line* with the JSP. This means that if a JSP calls a method, which in turn calls another method (as many of the facade class methods will do), all of those methods will be examined at that point in the text. This means that some of the more complex JSP pages will be examined in fragments while the code behind them is examined in detail. This will lead to a better understanding of the procedural flow of the application and of the reasoning behind the approach to coding the application.

JSP and the Multithreaded Issues

For performance reasons, a JSP (servlet) container may create an instance of a JSP that is shared among multiple JSP page requests. This allows the server to avoid the overhead of object instantiation (an expensive process) for each request that must be handled by the server. Although this provides obvious performance improvements, it introduces problems for the developer. This implies that JSP should not contain member objects that depend on values that were set on previous invocations. Since local member variables do not retain their values between invocations, problems arise with the use of variables declared as part of the class: either *instance members* or `static` *class members*.

The sharing of JSP instances does not imply that a class member, whether instance members or static members, cannot be used, just that they must be used correctly. Consider the scenario where a page is invoked by a user, "Fred," and some instance members are set with information specific to that user. Now Fred moves on to another page and user "Jim" accesses that page. The JSP container decides to give Jim access to the page previously accessed by Fred. Since Fred has already used that page, some of the class members have been set for Fred and will reflect the work he was doing on the site. If the application does not reset the values of those instance members to values appropriate for Jim, Jim will be seeing Fred's information. This means that each JSP should set all members of the page, whether they are variables declared within the scriplet declaration block, or JavaBeans, to values that are appropriate for that page invocation. This does not mean that all objects used on the page must be instantiated each time the page is accessed (although that would work), but that members of the object should be set to appropriate values either through a succession of `set` method calls, or by invoking one or two methods that set all instance members to values appropriate for the current page invocation.

The problem arises in the use of the declaration operator ('<%!') in JSP. The members declared using this operator become instance members of the page class and are thus shared among invocations of the page. The '<%!' operator should be used with caution, primarily for the declaration of discrete methods for use on the page.

Alternatively, any JavaBeans declared with 'session' scope are stored as references of the session object and are thus part of the user session. When the page is loaded and executed, the appropriate session object for the user session is loaded and used as the JavaBean reference on the page. For this reason, the instance members of JavaBeans declared with 'session' scope on the page will not have problems with multithreaded pages (since they are part of a reference to the distinct user session).

Managing the Login Process: login.jsp and loginSubmit.jsp

login.jsp Page

The login page provides a simple input form for the user to enter the login name and corresponding password. The bulk of this form is HTML, with the exception of the output of the current date on the top of the form (see Figure 10.7).

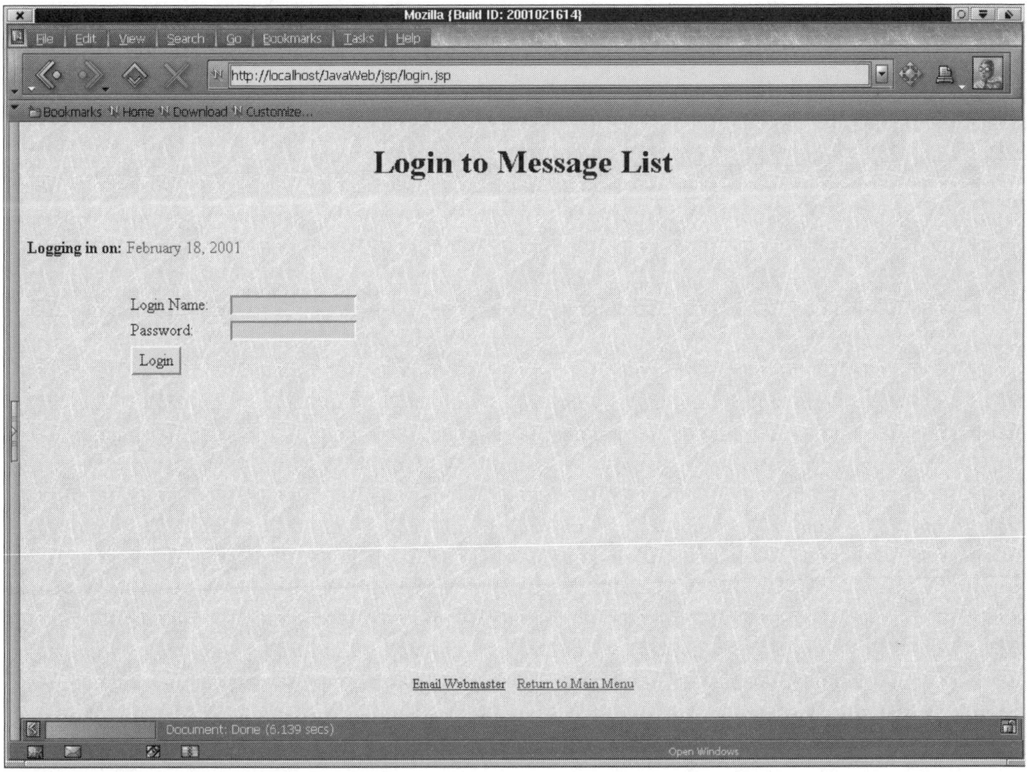

Figure 10.7 Login Page

This date is output with the use of the `loginFacade` class, using the `currentDate` property, shown below. This is used to output the current date in a string format using green text to indicate that the user does not need to enter this information.

```
<html>
<!- <body bgcolor="#FFFFFF"
background="/JavaWeb/img/bggradient.gif">  ->
<body bgcolor="#FFFFFF" background="/JavaWeb/img/bg2_grey.jpg">

<jsp:useBean id="loginFacade" class="knowledgebase.loginFacade"
scope="page" />
<center>
<h1>Login to Message List</h1>
</center>

<br>
<br>
<b>Logging in on:</b> <font color="green"><jsp:getProperty
name="loginFacade" property="currentDate" /></font>
<br>
<br>
<br>

<center>
<table border=0 width=100% >
<form method="post" action="loginSubmit.jsp">

<tr>
<td width=10%>   </td>
<td width=10%>Login Name: </td><td><input name="login"
type="text" value=""></td>
</tr>

<tr>
<td width=10%>   </td>
<td width=10%>Password: </td><td><input name="pwd" type="pass-
word" value=""></td>
</tr>

<tr>
<td width=10%>   </td>
<td width=10%> <input name="submit" type="submit" value="Login" >
</td>
```

```
</tr>

</form>
</table>
</center>
</body>
</html>
```

This page submits its contents to the loginSubmit.jsp page, which is responsible for processing the login information passed to it. If the login is successful, a message is displayed indicating that the login succeeded. If an error occurs, the page forwards processing to an error page which will indicate that the login failed and allow the user to return to the main menu, where they can choose the login option and try the login again. (Alternatively, they can press the browser "back" button and move directly to the login page.)

loginSubmit.jsp Page

The login page (login.jsp) will post the input from the form to the loginSubmit.jsp page, which will use the loginFacade class to process the information input on that page. The handleSubmit method is passed both the request object and session object as parameters. The information entered in the input form is available as request parameters, and the session object is used to store session parameters to be used elsewhere in the application. If the handleSubmit determines that there is a problem with the login, for example the login name is not found in the database or the password entered is incorrect, it will throw an exception and will forward processing to the error page for the loginSubmit.jsp page, the errorPage.jsp page. The JSP code for this page follows.

```
<html>
<body bgcolor="#FFFFFF" background="/JavaWeb/img/bg2_grey.jpg">

<%@ page errorPage="ErrorPage.jsp" %>

<jsp:useBean id="loginFacade" class="knowledgebase.loginFacade"
scope="page" />
<center>
<h1>Login to Message List</h1>
</center>


<% loginFacade.handleSubmit( request, session ); %>
```

```
<br>
<br>
<b>Login Completed for user: </b> <jsp:getProperty
name="loginFacade" property="first_name" />   
<jsp:getProperty name="loginFacade" property="last_name" />
<br>
<b>Last logged in: </b> <jsp:getProperty name="loginFacade" prop-
erty="session_last_login" />
<br>
<br>
<br>.
<a href="menu.html">Back to Menu</a>

</body>
</html>
```

The handleSubmit method performs the bulk of the processing for the login process. This method is part of the loginFacade class, which acts as a facade for the login process. This class creates a message_user Value Object named message_userVO and a message_user DAO named message_userDAO; both of these relate to the message_user table in the database. The calendar utility class JSPCal is imported and a local HttpSession object reference is added as a local member of the class.

```
package knowledgebase;

import javax.servlet.*;
import javax.servlet.http.*;
import java.util.*;
import java.sql.*;

import db.*;
import JSPCal.*;

public class loginFacade {

Message_userVO      message_userVO;
Message_userDAO     message_userDAO;
Cal cal;
HttpSession localSession;

. . .
```

The `handleSubmit` method receives `ServletRequest` and `HttpSession` arguments. The local `HttpSession` reference is assigned to that of the `HttpSession` parameter. The login name has been passed as a parameter to the request, so this parameter is retrieved and then passed to the `message_userDAO.loadDAO` method as a parameter. This method will use the login passed (which is the primary key for the `message_user` table) and will load the DAO with the `message_user` table values for that login. The code for this section follows.

```
. . .
public void handleSubmit( ServletRequest request, HttpSession
session) throws Exception {

try {

localSession = session;

// load the user information
message_userDAO.loadDAO( request.getParameter( "login" ) );
message_userVO = message_userDAO.getVO();

// load the role for this user
// current implementation allows a single role
message_securityDAO.loadDAO( request.getParameter( "login" ) );
message_securityVO = message_securityDAO.getVO();
. . .
```

Once the login record has been retrieved, the password is checked to determine whether the password entered matches the password in the `mes-sage_user` table. If the password does not match, an error message is written to the log file and an exception is thrown.

```
. . .
//
if
(!(message_userVO.getPwd().trim()).equals(request.getParameter(
"pwd" ).trim())) { // an invalid login

   System.out.println("Login error: " +
message_userVO.getFirst_name() + " - " +
message_userVO.getLast_name() );
   throw new Exception( "Login error." );

}
```

. . .

As shown in the code below if the login authentication is successful, a series of `message_user` table attributes are stored in the `session` object, including the user name, the location, login name, and date of the last login. Once the session attributes have been set, the database is immediately updated with the *new* user "last login" date (which would be the current date). Errors are caught in the `try/catch` block, where they are logged and then thrown to the calling method.

. . .

```
else {  // a valid login

    // store session information about the user
    session.setAttribute( "first_name",
message_userVO.getFirst_name() );
    session.setAttribute( "last_name",
message_userVO.getLast_name() );
    session.setAttribute( "last_login",
message_userVO.getLast_login() );
    session.setAttribute( "location", message_userVO.getLocation()
);
    session.setAttribute( "login", message_userVO.getLogin() );
    session.setAttribute( "role", message_securityVO.getRole() );

    // immediately update the database with the new last login
date
    message_userVO.setLast_login ( getCurrentDate( "mm/dd/yy" ) );
// the new last_login date
    message_userDAO.setVO( message_userVO );
// update the database
    message_userDAO.updateDAO();
}
```

. . .

This current implementation of the login page does not forward the user to a menu, which could easily be done using the JSP forward tag. Instead, it merely displays a message confirming that the login was successful, displays the last login date for the user, and provides a link that allows the user to proceed to the main menu.

. . .
```
<br>
```

```
<br>
<b>Login Completed for user: </b> <jsp:getProperty
name="loginFacade" property="first_name" />   
<jsp:getProperty name="loginFacade" property="last_name" />
<br>
<b>Last logged in: </b> <jsp:getProperty name="loginFacade" prop-
erty="session_last_login" />
<br>
<br>
<br>
<a href="menu.shtml">Back to Menu</a>
...
```

Storing Information in the session Object

Following the login operation, the message system now has a `session` object populated with separate attributes for the user first name, last name, location, login (name), and security role. These `session.setAttribute` calls are a good example of how to add objects to the session object. The syntax for the `HttpSession.setAttribute` method is

```
setAttribute( String name, Object obj);
```

In this example the `name` parameter is a string name that will be associated with the object to be stored; this name will be used to retrieve the attribute. The obj parameter is an `Object` reference that contains the *value* to store for the attribute. Since an `Object` reference is being stored, and any Java object can upcast to an `Object` reference, this allows any Java object to be stored in the `session` object. Once this information is stored in the `session` object it becomes global (visible) to the entire user session. Note that although it would be easy to store a large amount of information in the `session` object, this should be avoided. It is a better, more modular and flexible solution to pass information via the `request` object as parameters than to use the `session` object.

Sessions and JSP

JSP pages ultimately use the HTTP protocol to communicate with the client. The HTTP protocol is *stateless*, meaning that connections to the client do not persist. But a session implies a persistent connection, a client state that persists and is maintained over multiple requests. The servlet container within which the JSP runs (once converted into a servlet and loaded by the server) must mimic a session by tracking requests that are made against the server. Each request is assigned a *session id* and must communicate that session id to the server through some mechanism. The default behavior is to have the client browser store a cookie on the browser and then send that cookie (along with others) to the server on each request. The servlet specification requires this cookie to be named JSESSIONID.

If for some reason the client does not allow a cookie to be added, a URL rewriting mechanism will be used that adds the session id to the URL so that it will appear as a request parameter each time the client browser sends a request to the server. The required name of the session id request parameter is `jsessionid`. (Be sure to use the `HttpServletResponse.encodeURL` method to encode any forwarded URLs with the `jsessionid` if you think you may be using URL rewriting.)

Using Static HTML and Server-Side Includes for the Main Menu

Once the login process is completed, the user must choose a link that leads to the main menu. The main menu is an HTML page that displays the various menu options available to the user.

```
1.     <html>
2.     <body bgcolor="#FFFFFF"
background="/JavaWeb/img/bg2_grey.jpg">
3.     <!--#config timefmt="%A %B %d" -->
4.     <br>
5.     <br>
6.     <center>
7.     <h1>Welcome to the Message System</h1>
8.     </center>
9.     <br>
10.    <h3>Date: <font color="blue"> <!--#echo var="DATE_LOCAL" -->
</font>
11.    <br>
12.    <center>
13.    <table width=100% border=0>

14.    <tr>
15.    <td width=20%>
16.    </td>
17.    <br>
18.    <br>
```

```
19.    <td width=30%>
20.    <font size=+2>
21.    <br><a href="login.jsp">Login</a>
22.    <br><a href="searchKB.jsp">Search Messages</a>
23.    <br><a href="pickKB.jsp?type=all">List All Messages</a>
24.    <br><a
href="inputKB.jsp?doc_name=&link_doc=0&doc_key=0&base_doc_key=0&doc
_location=&action=insert">Post New Message</a>

25.    </font>
26.    </td>
27.    </table>
28.    </center>
29.    <br>
30.    <br>
31.    <br>
32.    <br>
33.    <!--#include file="footer.txt" -->
34.    </html>
35.    </body>
```

The menu.shtml page uses *server-side includes* (SSIs) to retrieve the current date for display on the main menu and to retrieve the footer for the page. (The footer.txt file is the same file included by the JSP pages for the footer.) The highlighted tag on line 3 is an SSI directive used to set the format for the time to be displayed using the DATE_LOCAL variable. This is the format used in the highlighted statement on line 10 to display the date. (This will be the date the page was served by the Apache server to the client browser, not the date on the browser's computer.)

On lines 21 through 24 in the listing, various menu options are displayed as links on the Web page. On line 33, an SSI directive is used to include the footer for the site into the page.

Alternative Menu Implementations

An alternative menu, and one very common with Web applications, would have the menu displayed on the left-hand side of the page in a frame or table cell and put some content on the right-hand side of the page. As the user moves through the site, the menu would remain displayed on the left-hand side of the page either by being included in the page or by remaining in an unchanging frame (see Figure 10.8).

This approach to managing the menu has the benefit of allowing the user continually to see the menu options available to them and to select from those options.

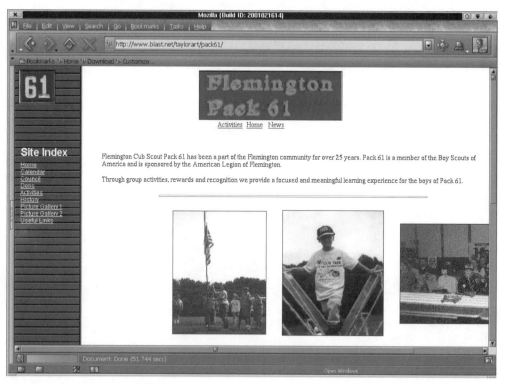

Figure 10.8 Left-Hand Side Menu

Implementing this different menu option would not require much work: changing the `menu.shtml` file to incorporate frames and then changing the links on the menu to work within the context of those frames.

The discussion group menu provides the option of displaying a list of messages in the message database (see Figure 10.9). They can optionally list all messages or filter the message list for a listing of messages that contain a specific keyword.

The user can optionally select one of the options from the menu page. The most common path would be to search the discussion group database based on search criteria. These search options will provide a listing that will be displayed and then, based on what the user views in the listing, the user can choose to add to a thread or post a new message. The following discussion will proceed with the assumption that a user has chosen to search the discussion group database for a particular set of topics and then review the listing that search returns.

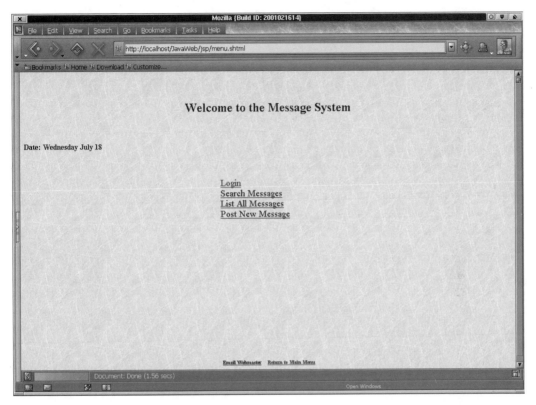

Figure 10.9 Discussion Group Main Menu

Collecting and Passing Search Criteria: The searchKB.jsp Page

If the user has selected the search option from the main menu, they will be allowed to search the message system database based on keyword entries. The searchKB.jsp page displays an HTML input form that allows the user to enter up to four search criteria (see Figure 10.10).

The page itself is a standard HTML input form with the exception of the one JSP directive, the JSP include directive highlighted at the bottom of the page. (This page could easily have been implemented in HTML by changing the JSP include directive at the bottom of the page to an SSI include directive and renaming the page with a .shtml extension.)

```
<html>
<body bgcolor="#FFFFFF" background="/JavaWeb/img/bg2_grey.jpg">
```

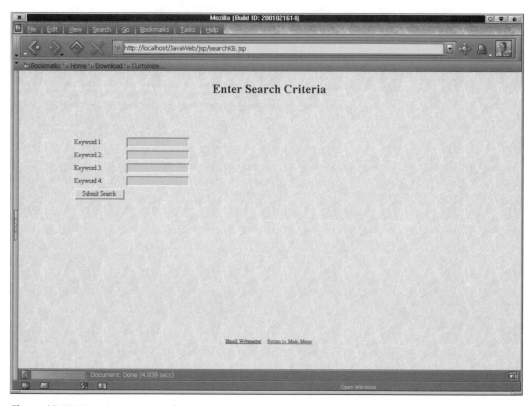

Figure 10.10 Discussion Group Search Page

```
<center>
<h1>Enter Search Criteria</h1>
</center>

<br>
<br>
<br>
<br>

<table border=0 width=100% >
<form method="post" action="searchSubmit.jsp">

<tr>
<td width=10%>   </td>
<td width=10%>Keyword 1: </td><td><input name="keyword1"
type="text" value=""></td>
</tr>
```

```
<tr>
<td width=10%>   </td>
<td width=10%>Keyword 2: </td><td><input name="keyword2"
type="text" value=""></td>
</tr>

<tr>
<td width=10%>   </td>
<td width=10%>Keyword 3: </td><td><input name="keyword3"
type="text" value=""></td>
</tr>

<tr>
<td width=10%>   </td>
<td width=10%>Keyword 4: </td><td><input name="keyword4"
type="text" value=""></td>
</tr>

<tr>
<td width=10%>   </td>
<td width=10%>              <input name="submit" type="submit" submit
value="Submit Search" > </td>
</tr>

</form>
</table>

<br>
<br>
<br>
<br>
<br>

<%@ include file="footer.txt" %>
</body>
</html>
```

Loading Request Parameters into a Collection

The search criteria that have been entered on the `searchKB.jsp` page are needed to execute the database query, so these parameters must have a way of making it to the Database Access Objects that will ultimately interact with the database. Although the parameters could have been forwarded as a request and then retrieved by the DAOs, we would prefer to shield the database access code completely (on the integration tier) from the details of the presentation, which certainly include the request object (an instance of ServletRequest). For this reason we place the contents of our filter criteria into a Collection object that will be added to the session object. Since we would like to be able to allow the user to move back to the filtered selection page and redisplay it using the same filter criteria (as when a user adds to an existing message thread and then wishes to continue examining the same filtered list for additional messages to read or respond to), we would store these filter criteria in the session object. With the criteria stored in the session object, when the user is linked to the posted messages page and the "type" parameter is set to "keyword," the session object will be examined to determine if there is a Collection of keywords, and if there is, we execute the query again with those keywords. If the query criteria were not stored in the session object, it would be difficult to implement this functionality.

Aggregating and Forwarding Request Parameters

The searchSubmit.jsp page is responsible for aggregating or collecting the search criteria entered on the searchKB.jsp page and then forwarding processing to another page. This page demonstrates both the use of the session object for storing session-specific information and the use of the JSP forward directive to forward request processing to another page. The request parameters from the searchKB.jsp page are loaded into a Collection object and processing is forwarded to the pickKB.jsp page to execute and display the results of the query. The code for this page follows.

```
1.    <html>
2.    <!- <body bgcolor="#FFFFFF" background="/JavaWeb/img/bggra-
dient.gif">  ->
3.    <body bgcolor="#FFFFFF"
background="/JavaWeb/img/bg2_grey.jpg">
4.
5.    <%@ page errorPage="ErrorPage.jsp" %>
6.    <jsp:useBean id="searchFacade"
class="knowledgebase.searchFacade" scope="page" />
7.    <center>
8.
<h1>Login to Message List</h1>
```

```
9.
</center>
10.
11.    <!— load the search criteria into a collection which is
stored in the session object —>
12.    <% searchFacade.handleSubmit( request, session ); %>
13.
14.    <!— forward to pickKB.jsp which will execute the query and
display the results —>
15.
16.    <jsp:forward page="/jsp/pickKB.jsp?type=keyword"/>
17.
18.    <br>
19.    <br>
20.    <br>
21.
22.    </body>
23.    </html>
24.
```

This page uses the searchFacade class as a JavaBean; this is loaded using the jsp:usebean tag on line 6. Only one method in this class is called on line 12, and on line 16 processing is forwarded using the jsp:forward tag. If an error occurs in the searchFacade handleSubmit method, an exception will be thrown and the error page declared for the page (ErrorPage.jsp declared at line 5) will be invoked. If no exception is thrown, the jsp:forward statement at line 16 is called. This is passed a single request parameter, the "type" which is set to the "keyword" indicating that a keyword search should be conducted based on search parameters that have been stored.

Storing Search Parameters: The searchFacade.handleSubmit Class

The searchFacade class is used by the searchSubmit.jsp page to manage the details of storing the search criteria collected on the searchKB.jsp page. This class contains a single method, the handleSubmit method, which is called on the searchSubmit.jsp page.

```
package knowledgebase;

import java.util.*;
import javax.servlet.*;
import javax.servlet.http.*;


public class searchFacade {

public void handleSubmit( ServletRequest request, HttpSession
session ) {

Vector v = new Vector();

v.add( request.getParameter("keyword1"));
v.add( request.getParameter("keyword2"));
v.add( request.getParameter("keyword3""));
v.add( request.getParameter("keyword4"));

session.setAttribute( "filter_criteria", v );

}


}
```

This method is called with two parameters: the request parameter and the session parameter. The method merely creates a new `Vector` (which implements the `Collection` interface) and then adds the values of the four keyword parameters to the `Vector`.

We then want to add the `Vector` object into the `session` object for our session. This can be accomplished using the `setAttribute` method of the `HttpSession` class. This method takes two parameters: a `String` name and a corresponding `Object` reference. Once an object has been added using this method, calls to the `HttpSession.getAttribute` method can then be used to retrieve the attribute value using the corresponding name, which was used when it was added. In this example, the `Vector` object that has been loaded with the filter criteria is added to the `session` object and assigned the name `filter_criteria`. At this point, the `session` object has been populated with the filter criteria for our session and we are ready to execute the JSP that will ultimately execute the database query using these parameters and display the results.

Building Dynamic HTML Tables with JSP: The Posted Messages Page

Because of the nature of page formatting with HTML, tables are often used to format and present content. So it is not uncommon when dealing with dynamic content to need to create an HTML page based on some combination of request parameters and the results of a database query. The creation of the posted message list page is an example of just such a page. To understand this page, portions of the JSP code are examined and then the portions of the JavaBeans code that support the page are shown, effectively tracing the program execution from the JSP page to the JavaBeans code and then back to the JSP.

The posted message page (`pickKB.jsp`) provides a listing of a set of message from the discussion group database. As explained previously, this listing can be either a listing of all messages in the database or a filtered listing based on filter criteria that has been made available to this page. This listing is an HTML table that is dynamically created with columns for the topic of the message, the keywords entered for the message, and links to pages that allow the user to view the message in full, to update the message or to delete the message (see Figure 10.11). This page will show links for update and delete even

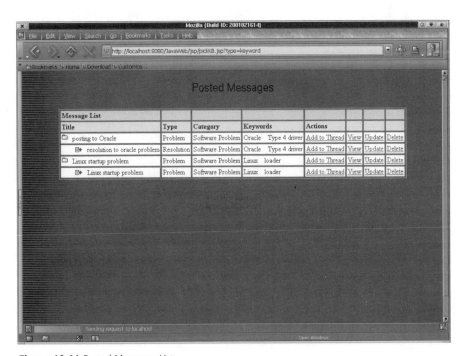

Figure 10.11 Posted Messages List

though the user may not have permission to perform these operations on the message. (Permissions are checked before the operation is attempted, and if the user does not have the appropriate permissions, they are not permitted to perform the operation.)

This page provides a good example of techniques for building dynamic table output using JSP. The listing is sorted based on the primary key of the message document and the date the message was submitted and the last date the message was changed. The message listing includes not only the messages selected but threaded messages that were posted to the message selected (i.e., a *base message* or a *threaded message*). Any messages that are part of the message thread are indented from the left margin so that the base message appears flush with the left margin, and all messages posted to the base message appear below the base message and are indented from the base message. A different .gif image is also placed each line of output, depending on whether the line being output is a base message or a threaded message.

Although this approach to creating the table with indented entries improves the readability of the table content, the code required to perform this indentation adds to the complexity of the control loop used to produce this table. The JSP code for this page (`pickKB.jsp`) follows.

```
1.     <HTML>
2.     <body bgcolor="#FFFFFF"
background="/JavaWeb/img/bg0020.gif">
3.     <%@ page errorPage="ErrorPage.jsp" %>
4.     <jsp:useBean id="KBFacade"
class="knowledgebase.KnowledgeBaseFacade" scope="page" />
5.     <br>
6.     <font face="Helvetica, Sans-serif" size=+2 >
7.     <center>
8.     Messages
9.     </center>
10.    </font>
11.    <br>
12.    <br>
13.    <center>
14.    <font face="Helvetica, Sans-serif" size=+2 color="blue">
15.
16.    <% KBFacade.setFilterSelection( request, session ); %>
...
```

The `pickKB.jsp` page performs its work using the `KnowledgeBaseFacade` class. The `KnowledgeBaseFace` class is a JavaBean and is identified on the page (and assigned a reference id) using the

JSP:useBean tag on line 4. Through this tag, the KBFacade name is associated with the knowledgebase.KnowledgeBaseFacade class and is given the id of KBFacade. Other HTML content is used to display the header and set the suggested font for some of the text on the page. On line 16, the controlling method for the page is called: setFilterSelection. This method is passed the reference for the request object for the page and the reference for the session object.

setFilterSelection Method

The setFilterSelection method shown below is called from the pickKB.jsp page.

```
. . .
public void setFilterSelection( ServletRequest request,
HttpSession session ) {

try {
    if ( request.getParameter("type").equals("all") )
        setAllKBRecs( true );

    if  ( request.getParameter("type").equals("keyword") )
        setFilterKBRecs( request, session );
    }
    catch ( Exception e) {
        System.out.println("Exception in
KnowledgeBaseFacade.setFilterSelection() : " + e );
    }
}
. . .
```

This method is part of a facade class (KnowledgeBaseFacade) and as such is designed to reduce the coupling (the calls) between the JSP and the business classes and data access objects that retrieve the data for the page. This method will perform a simple test of the requests passed into the pickKB.jsp page and determine what type of filter is to be used. This method acts as a "traffic cop" of sorts, examining one of the request parameters passed to it and determining which action to perform (which method to call). If the "type" parameter is set to the value "all," all entries in the discussion group database are listed. This is achieved by calling the setAllKBRecs method with a boolean value of true.

If the request parameter is set to "keyword," a keyword filter will be applied to the database lookup operation using the setFilterKBRecs method and passing both the request and session. Since exceptions may be thrown up the call stack to this method, a catch block is used to trap and report messages. (The setAllKBRecs and setFilterKBRecs methods will in turn call methods in the Knowledge_baseDAO class to perform the low-level database operations required to retrieve the data; the code for these methods is shown in Chapter 11.)

setAllKBRecs and setFilterKBRecs Methods

The setAllKBRecs method takes a boolean argument and simply wraps a DAO method to retrieve the records necessary for the message listing of all message records. The method calls the knowledge_baseDAO.getAll method to retrieve all message records currently in the discussion group database and returns an Iterator object reference named iterateKBList, which is an instance member of the KnowledgeBaseFacade class.

```
...
public void setAllKBRecs( boolean val ) throws Exception {

iterateKBList = knowledge_baseDAO.getAll(); // get a collection
of ValueObjects for all knowledge_base records

}
...
```

The setFilterKBRecs method shown below is used to obtain a filtered list of messages based on the filter criteria contained in the session object. (In code explained previously, the filter criteria are assembled as part of the processing for the searchKB.jsp and searchSubmit.jsp pages.) This method wraps the Knowledge_baseDAO.getFilteredList method (shown in Chapter 11), which returns an Iterator reference, that is assigned to the iterateKBList reference which is part of the KnowledgeBaseFacade class.

```
1.    ...
2.    // use a filter to retrieve the list of knowledge base
records
3.    public void setFilterKBRecs( ServletRequest request,
HttpSession session ) {

4.    try {
```

```
5.          // filter criteria passed as a Collection in the ses-
sion object
6.
7.          Collection filterCriteria
8.            = (Collection) session.getAttribute( "filter_crite-
ria" );

9.          iterateKBList  = knowledge_baseDAO.getFilteredList(
10.               filterCriteria );
11.    }
12.    catch (Exception e)
13.       System.out.println("Exception in
14.    KnowledgeBaseFacade.setFilterKBRecs(): " + e );
15.
16.    }
17.
18.    }
19.    ...
```

Before the `getFilteredList` method is called, the `Collection` object stored in the `session` object must be retrieved since this object stores filter criteria for the database query. This is performed on lines 7 and 8, where the `HttpSession.getAttribute` method is called.

As explained in the preceding section, the session attribute `filter_criteria` stores an object of type `Collection` that contains the filter criteria for the page to use (see the description of the `searchSubmit.jsp` page processing which populates this collection). The `session.getAttribute` method is used to retrieve the filter criteria on line 8. This method returns an `Object` reference which is cast to a `Collection` reference and stored in an object named `filterCriteria`.

This object is passed to the `getFilteredList` method of the `Knowledge_baseDAO` class object on line 9. This method will access the database, retrieve the records that match the filter criteria, and place those records (in the form of Value Objects) into a Java `Collection` (a `Vector`). The `Vector` object is then converted to an `Iterator` and the reference to the `Iterator` object is returned and stored in the `iterateKBList` reference of the `KnowledgeBaseFacade` class. (The inner workings of the DAOs are explained in detail in Chapter 11.)

Once the DAO `getFilteredList` method has returned the list of records (value objects) from the database, the `KnowledgeBaseFacade` object will see to it that the `Iterator` that has been returned (from the DAO) is kept internally. This `Iterator` is later used by the JSP page to loop through the Value Object records stored in the `Collection` and create the dynamic table output for the posted messages table.

Back to the pickKB.jsp Page

At this point we have established the filter criteria for the page and have populated the `Iterator iterateKBList`, an instance variable of the `KnowledgeBaseFacade` class, with the results of the query operation. We now need to take the results in the `Iterator` and use them to create those results shown in Figure 10.12.

The approach shown in this example will minimize the use of scriplet code and maximize the use of JSP tags and directives. Since the `jsp:getProperty` tag can be used to retrieve values from a JavaBean using a HTML-like tag, we use an approach that uses an instance member of the `KnowledgeBaseFacade` class to maintain a collection of records that have been returned from the database for display on the page. The `get` and `set` methods called by the `jsp:getProperty` tags return values or references to instance members of the `KnowledgeBaseFacade` class. We must set these instance members with the correct values from our collection of rows returned by the query. Since this collection is stored in an `Iterator`, we use a loop increment method to move through the `Iterator`, and for each new row, we set the instance members of the `KnowledgeBaseFacade` class to the same values as those in the `Iterator` row. The code sample below uses a `setNextKBVO` method to perform this operation.

```
1.     ...
2.     / increment the iterator and make the next knowledge_baseVO
our current VO
3.     public void setNextKBVO( boolean val ) throws Exception {

4.     try {

5.     if ( iterateKBList.hasNext() ) {
6.         knowledge_baseVO = (Knowledge_baseVO)
iterateKBList.next();
7.         loadKnowledgeBase( knowledge_baseVO.getDoc_key() );
8.       }
9.     }
10.    catch (Exception e) {
11.        System.out.println("Exception in
12.    knowledgeBaseFacade.setNextKBVO(): " + e );
13.        throw new Exception("Exception in
14.     knowledgeBaseFacade.setNextKBVO(): " + e );
15.    }
16.    }
...
```

As shown on line 5, the `hasNext` method is called to determine if there are more elements to the `Iterator`. If there are, the `next` method is called to retrieve the Value Object from the `Iterator` and assign it to the instance member, `knowledge_baseVO`.

A call to the `NextKBVO` method of the `KnowledgeBaseFacade` class moves to the next element of the `Iterator` and sets the internal reference for the Value Object representing the current message (`knowledge_baseVO`) to the next Value Object within list stored in the `iterateKBList Iterator` as shown in the code below. A `catch` block is used to catch any exceptions that may be thrown by any of the methods called in this block.

Building the Dynamic Table

The next task in creating the output for this listing is to create a HTML table to hold the listing. This table is created on line 2 in the JSP fragment shown below. On line 3 in this listing a row is created to hold a header describing the table and on lines 4 through 11, empty cells are added to the table to provide a consistent, spreadsheetlike appearance to the table. On lines 13 through 24 another header row is created to output the columns headers for the table.

```
. . .
1.     <!—build table for output of selected messages —>
2.     <table border=2 cellpadding=2 bgcolor="white">

3.     <tr>
4.     <td bgcolor="#C0D9D9"><b>Message List<b></td>

5.     <td bgcolor="#C0D9D9" >     </td>
6.     <td bgcolor="#C0D9D9" >     </td>
7.     <td bgcolor="#C0D9D9" >     </td>
8.     <td bgcolor="#C0D9D9" >     </td>
9.     <td bgcolor="#C0D9D9" >     </td>
10.    <td bgcolor="#C0D9D9" >     </td>
11.    <td bgcolor="#C0D9D9" >     </td>
12.    </tr>

13.    <!— header row —>
14.    <tr>
15.    <td bgcolor="#E0E0E0" > <b>Title     </b> </td>
16.
```

```
17.    <td bgcolor="#E0E0E0" > <b>Type      </b> </td>
18.    <td bgcolor="#E0E0E0" > <b>Category </b> </td>
19.    <td bgcolor="#E0E0E0" > <b>Keywords </b> </td>
20.    <td bgcolor="#E0E0E0" > <b>Actions  </b> </td>
21.    <td bgcolor="#E0E0E0" > <b>     </b> </td>
22.    <td bgcolor="#E0E0E0" > <b>     </b> </td>
23.    <td bgcolor="#E0E0E0" > <b>     </b> </td>
24.    </tr>
25.    ...
```

The next portion of the JSP shown below is responsible for taking the rows that met the filter criteria and producing table rows that contain that output. A Java while loop begins at line 6. The loop iterates based on the results KnowledgeBaseFacade.kbRecsHasMore method, which returns a boolean value indicating whether or not there are records remaining in the Iterator. The kbRecsHasMore method does little more than wrap the Iterator.hasNext method.

```
...
public boolean kbRecsHasMore() {
    return iterateKBList.hasNext();
}
...
```

Creating the Table Rows

The table is now ready to be constructed. Since there are multiple records to use, it makes sense to perform this operation within a loop. At the start of the loop on lines 4 and 5 in the listing, two control variables are set. These variables are used later in the loop to make decisions about whether or not to indent records based on their settings.

```
1.    <!- columns ->
<!- use program logic to indent threaded messages ->
<%
2.
3.        // start of loop
4.        int currBase_doc_key = 0;
5.        boolean firstLoop = true;

6.    while ( KBFacade.kbRecsHasMore() )   {
7.
```

```
8.     %>
9.
10.
11.    <jsp:setProperty name="KBFacade" property="nextKBVO"
value="true" />
12.    <tr>
13.    <td> <% if ( !firstLoop && (currBase_doc_key ==
KBFacade.getBase_doc_key()) ) { %>
14.
15.      <!- indent if this is a thread off the base message ->

16.                  
17.    <img src="/JavaWeb/img/quote.gif">  

18.         <% } else { %>  <!- not a thread - the base message -
display a closed folder ->
19.               <img src="/JavaWeb/img/folder_closed.gif"
name="Base Folder" align=left >  
20.
21.       <% } %>


22.       <jsp:getProperty name="KBFacade" property="doc_name" />
</td>
23.    <td> <jsp:getProperty name="KBFacade"
property="message_type" />
24.    </td>
25.    <td> <jsp:getProperty name="KBFacade" property="category"
/> </td>

26.    <td> <jsp:getProperty name="KBFacade" property="keyword1"
/>
27.               <jsp:getProperty name="KBFacade" prop-
erty="keyword2" />
28.         <jsp:getProperty name="KBFacade"
property="keyword3" />
29.    </td>
```

Within this loop, a jsp:setProperty tag is used to make a call to the nextKBVO method. This jsp:setProperty tag ultimately executes the nextKBVO method and moves to the next record in the internal list (iterateKBList). This process of moving the pointer in the list will set the internal knowledge_base Value Object to the next Value Object in the internal list of Value Objects, so that once this call has been made, all calls to the `get` methods of the `KnowledgeBaseFacade` class will return the values of the current `knowledge_base` value object.

The contents of each `<td>` tag within the message listing table represent a column on that row. The contents of the columns for this table are now stored in instance members of the class and will be retrieved using `jsp:getProperty` tags (which will in turn call the `get` methods of the `KnowledgeBaseFacade` class). These tags are used on lines 22 through 28 and are used to retrieve the short description of the message document (`doc_name`), the message type of the message (`message_type`), and two of the keywords associated with the document (`keyword1` and `keyword2`).

The output of the columns is fairly straightforward, but the code on lines 13 through 21 requires more explanation. The purpose of this code is to provide indentation of the output lines. This indentation is based on whether or not the line is a base message or a threaded message. If the message is a base message, the short message description will not be indented and an image of a closed folder will be output on that line. If the message is a threaded message, the short message description will be indented and a different image will be output on that line.

The determination of whether or not a message is a threaded message requires examination of the based document key (`base_doc_key`). A variable is used to track the current base document key and is set equal to the base document key of the current record at the end of each loop iteration. At the beginning of each loop iteration, the value of this current base document key is checked against the base document key of the record currently being output. If the base document key of the current record is the same as the current base document key, this record is assumed to be a *threaded* message (since some previous record must have been used to set the current base document key to its value).

The first pass through the loop represents an exception to this rule. Since the value of the current base document key is not set until the end of the loop, on the first iteration of the loop this value will not have been set. For our purposes, we assert that the first message in the loop is a base message and we ignore the setting of the current base document key.

Next to the output of the message header are table cells that contain the actions that can be executed for the message document in the row. The JSP code that produces these actions is shown below. The cells in this output contain anchor references that reference other JSP in the application. Parameter values for these references are set according to the current message document key. These settings are made by using `jsp:getProperty` tags, which will retrieve appropriate values for the current message document being processed.

```
...
1.      <!- actions ->
2.      <td> <a
href="inputKB.jsp?doc_key=0&action=insert&base_doc_key=<jsp:getPro
perty name="KBFacade" property="base_doc_key"
/>&link_doc=<jsp:getProperty name="KBFacade"
property="doc_key"/>">Add to Thread</a> </td>
3.      <td> <a href="viewKB.jsp?doc_key=<jsp:getProperty
name="KBFacade" property="doc_key" />&action=update" >View</a>
</td>
4.      <td> <a href="inputKB.jsp?doc_key=<jsp:getProperty
name="KBFacade"
property="doc_key"/>&link_doc=0&base_doc_key=<jsp:getProperty
name="KBFacade" property="base_doc_key"
/>&action=update">Update</a> </td>
5.      <td> <a href="viewKB.jsp?doc_key=<jsp:getProperty
name="KBFacade"
property="doc_key"/>&base_doc_key=0&link_doc=0&action=delete">Dele
te</a> </td>
6.      </tr>


7.      <%
8.       firstLoop = false;
9.       if ( KBFacade.getBase_doc_key() > 0 )
10.         currBase_doc_key = KBFacade.getBase_doc_key();
11.      else
12.         currBase_doc_key = KBFacade.getDoc_key(); // this IS
the base
13.      } %>
14.      </table>


15.      <br>
16.      <br><a
href="inputKB.jsp?doc_key=0&link_doc=0&base_doc_key=0&action=insert">
Post New Message</a>
17.      <br><a href="menu.html">Main Menu</a>

18.      </font>
19.      </center>
20.      </BODY>
21.      </HTML>
```

Note that the `jsp:getProperty` tag can appear within the double quotes of the anchor `href` attribute:

```
<a href="viewKB.jsp?doc_key=<jsp:getProperty name="KBFacade"
property="doc_key" />&action=update" >View</a>
```

The final section of this listing contains the termination of the loop that produces this table. On line 8 of the listing, the `firstLoop` flag is set to false and on lines 10 through 13 a conditional statement is used to determine how to set the base document key. If the base document key is nonzero, the base document key for the current record is used to set the current base document key variable on line 10. Alternatively, if the base document key is 0, this code asserts that the document is in fact the base document and sets the base document key to the value of the document key for the current document (which is the base document for this thread).

On line 16 of the listing, two links are provided to allow the user to return to the main menu or to post a new message.

The user of this page will have options to view the current document, add to the message thread, update the current document or, delete the document. The code for these pages is shown in the following sections.

Creating Read-only Output: The View Message Page

If the user chooses to view an existing message, the `viewKB.jsp` page will be displayed. Each message is composed of messages from a number of different tables. This page retrieves all related message records for a single message and displays them in a table. The page does not allow the user to update any of the information on the page. Menu options, however, are provided to allow the user to add to the message thread, update the message, delete the message, or return to the main menu.

The coding of this page is fairly straightforward. The page merely needs to load the document key passed as the request parameters for the page and then use the `jsp:getProperty` tag on a JavaBean that contains all the appropriate values. Fortunately, the `KnowledgeBaseFacade` class contains all the necessary `get` and `set` properties to create the view page. Since only one message will be displayed, it isn't necessary to create a loop and iterate through multiple records as with the posted messages page (`pickKB.jsp`). This page begins by using JSP directives and tags to set the error page for this JSP and to load the `KnowledgeBaseFacade` class and assign the class to a JavaBean named `KBFacade`. The document key for the message document to view is passed as part of the request parameter.

The contents of this page require data from a number of different tables in the message database. For this reason, the method that retrieves the data for this page must load the appropriate data access objects and value objects from not only the `knowledge_base` table but also the `knowledge_messages` for the `message text` and `base_keys` for the message keywords tables.

```
<title>Message</title>

<center>

<%@ page import="java.util.*" %>
<%@ page errorPage="ErrorPage.jsp" %>

<jsp:useBean id="KBFacade"
class="knowledgebase.KnowledgeBaseFacade" scope="page" />

<!— set the doc_key first, before setting 'action' —>
<% KBFacade.setDoc_key( Integer.parseInt(
request.getParameter("doc_key").trim() )); %>
<% KBFacade.setAction( request.getParameter("action")); %>

<br>
<br>
<H1>Message Display</H1>

</center>
```

Once the current message document has been loaded, it is then just a matter of describing the output of an HTML table where the `<td>` tags will contain bodies that will use `jsp:getProperty` tags to retrieve the appropriate values for the document being viewed.

Continuing with this example below, a table definition is made on line 2 and a blank cell entered on line 4. On line 5 the document key for the document is entered using a `jsp:getProperty` tag for the output. (A space is added after every output on the page because some browsers will not render the cell color correctly if it does not interpret output for the table cell.) On lines 6 through 11, additional table rows and cells are created and output is generated using `jsp:getProperty` calls.

```
1.     ...
2.     <table border=0 cellpadding=2 >

3.     <tr>
4.     <td width=5%><br></td>
```

```
5.    <td width=5% bgcolor="#E0E0E0"> Document Key: </td> <td
width=30%
bgcolor="#C0C0C0"> <jsp:getProperty name="KBFacade"
property="doc_key" />   </td>


6.    <td width=5% bgcolor="#E0E0E0"> Category:        </td> <td
width=30% bgcolor="#C0C0C0" > <jsp:getProperty name="KBFacade"
property="category" />   </td>
7.    </tr>

8.    <tr>
9.    <td width=5%><br></td>
10.   <td width=5% bgcolor="#E0E0E0"> Name:           </td> <td
width=30% bgcolor="#C0C0C0" > <jsp:getProperty name="KBFacade"
property="doc_name" />   </td>
11.   <td width=5% bgcolor="#E0E0E0"> Posted by:    </td> <td
width=30% bgcolor="#C0C0C0" > <jsp:getProperty name="KBFacade"
property="post_user" />   </td>
12.

13.   </tr>
14.   ...
```

The remainder of the table uses additional jsp:getProperty calls to retrieve data for the creation of the table.

```
1.    <font color="white" family="times roman">
2.    <p><a
href="inputKB.jsp?doc_key=0&action=insert&base_doc_key=<jsp:
getProperty name="KBFacade" property="base_doc_key"
/>&link_doc=<jsp:getProperty name="KBFacade"
property="doc_key"/>">Add to Thread</a>   
3.    <a href="updDB.jsp?doc_key=<jsp:getProperty name="KBFacade"
property="doc_key" />&action=delete">Delete</a>   
4.    <a href="inputKB.jsp?doc_key=<jsp:getProperty
name="KBFacade" property="doc_key"
/>&base_doc_key=<jsp:getProperty name="KBFacade"
property="base_doc_key" />&link_doc=0&action=update">Update</a>
  
5.    <a href="pickKB.jsp?type=all">Message List</a>   
6.    <a href="menu.html">Main Menu</a> </p>
7.    </font>
8.    </center>
```

At the end of the table, a menu is created to allow the user to perform certain actions on the current message. The user can add to the current thread, delete the current record, update the current record, see a full listing of messages, or return to the main menu page. The references on lines 2, 3, and 4 use the `jsp:getProperty` tag to retrieve the document key for the current message document.

Note that these options are output for this page regardless of whether or not the user has the appropriate permissions to perform these operations. The user permissions are checked but not until they attempt to load the page to perform that operation; at that time permissions are checked, and if the user does not have permission to perform that operation, an exception is thrown and the page is not loaded.

Performing Input with JSP: The Message Update Page

From the posted message list, users who have requested the message list have various options available to them. If a user is the one who entered the message, he or she will be allowed to change the text of the message, the category, or the type of message, or to delete the message. Or the user may choose to add to the message thread: that is, to add a new message under a specific base message. The `inputKB.jsp` page is used for all message updates, either to an existing message or to enter a new message as either a base message or as an addition to a message thread (see Figure 10.12).

The `inputKB.jsp` page uses an input form to insert a new message or update an existing message. The page uses the same HTML input form for insert or update, the difference being in how the existing field values are populated. If the page is being used for update, the document that is being updated is loaded into the internal Value Objects.

If a new message document is being input, default values are loaded into certain fields and the remaining fields are initialized to default Java values for the data types (this is done by nature of the fact that the JavaBean carrying these Value Objects is of page scope and is therefore created new each time the page is loaded). If an existing message document is being input, the document key for the message document is passed into the page. The `KnowledgeBaseFacade` JavaBean will then load the corresponding document for the document key. If the page is threaded message, the message description will default to that of the base for the message thread, but users are allowed to override this text if they wish.

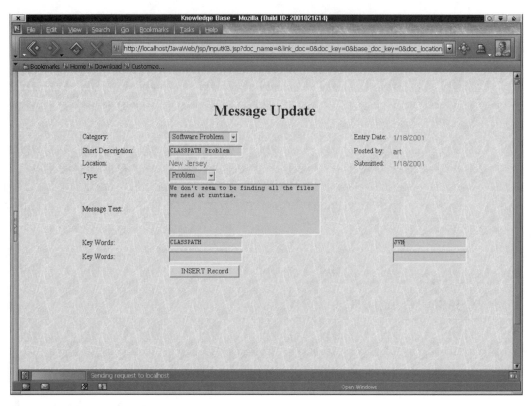

Figure 10.12 Message Input Form

The inputKB.jsp JSP page begins by importing the java.util package (which contains Collections interface used in scriplets on the page) and identifying ErrorPage.jsp as the error page to be used if an exception is caught in the code generated for the page on lines 4 and 5. A jsp:useBean tag loads the KnowledgeBaseFacade JavaBean class and associates it with the KBFacade name for the page on line 6 of the listing. On line 8 the KnowledgeBaseFacade.processParameters method is called to perform the work necessary for the page to be output with the HTML form. This method is passed the request and session object for the page.

```
1.    <html>
2.
3.    <body bgcolor="#FFFFFF"
background="/JavaWeb/img/bg2_grey.jpg">
```

```
4.    <%@ page import="java.util.*" %>
5.    <%@ page errorPage="ErrorPage.jsp" %>

6.    <jsp:useBean id="KBFacade"
class="knowledgebase.KnowledgeBaseFacade" scope="page" />

7.    <!— the 'action' parameter indicates whether or not this is
an insert,update or delete operation —>
8.    <% KBFacade.processParameters( request, session );   %>
```

. . .

Prepare Input Form: the KnowledgeBaseFacade. processParameters Method

The processParameters method of the KnowledgeBaseFacade performs the work necessary to prepare the inputKB.jsp page for processing. For that reason it is useful to look at the code for this method at this point to understand what is required to get this page (or any input page) ready for user input. This method is called at the start of the inputKB.jsp page and is passed the HttpRequest object for the page (request) and the HttpSession object (session) for the page (and for the session).

. . .

```
1.    // called by inputKB.jsp at the start of the input page

2.    public void processParameters( ServletRequest request,
HttpSession session ) throws Exception {

3.    Cal cal = new Cal();
4.    int doc_key = 0;

5.     // assert these parameters are always passed to
inputKB.jsp which will call this method
6.        if ( request.getParameter("doc_key") != null )
7.            setDoc_key( Integer.parseInt(
request.getParameter("doc_key").trim() ));

8.     // set action will load the DAOs and the value objects for
the knowledge_base (in loadKnowledgebase() )
9.        if ( request.getParameter("action") != null )
```

```
10.            setAction( request.getParameter("action"));

11.    if ( request.getParameter( "link_doc" ) != null )
12.        setLink_doc( Integer.parseInt(
request.getParameter("link_doc").trim() ));


13.     // add some of these to our session object, since they
may not be passed via the input form
14.     session.setAttribute( "doc_key", new Integer(
request.getParameter("doc_key")));
15.     session.setAttribute( "link_doc", new Integer(
request.getParameter("link_doc")) );
16.     session.setAttribute( "base_doc_key",
17.                           new
Integer(request.getParameter("base_doc_key")));

18.   // store the dates as String ... let the database perform
conversion
19.     if ( request.getParameter("action").equals("insert") ||
20.          request.getParameter("action").equals("update")  )
{
21.        session.setAttribute( "entry_date",
cal.getCurrentDate( "mm/dd/yy" )); // date last changed
22.         knowledge_baseVO.setEntry_date( cal.getCurrentDate(
"mm/dd/yy" ));
23.     }
```

. . .

The method begins by creating a new `Calendar` object using the `Cal` convenience class shown in Chapter 8. The parameters passed into the method are checked at line 6, specifically the parameter `doc_key`, which should always be passed to the method.

The document key (`doc_key`) value is an integer but is sent in the request parameter as a `String` data type. It must therefore be converted using the `Integer.parseInt` method as shown on line 7. The results of this conversion are passed immediately to the `setDoc_key` method of the `KnowledgeBaseFacade` class. This will set the document key for the local Value Object to the converted value of the request parameter.

At line 11, the same test is performed for the request parameter for the `link_doc` (the document key for the document to which this document is linked). This converted value is passed to the `setLink_doc` method of the `KnowledgeBaseFacade` class. (Although this is stored in the Value Object and in the `knowledge_base` database table, the value of this column is currently not used.)

Beginning on line 13, a number of the values are stored in the `session` object to be passed to the `updDB` page, which will perform the database update for the values entered on this page. The document key (`doc_key`), the link document key (`link_doc`), and the base document key (`base_doc_key`) are stored as `Integer` object values in the `session` object. (Alternatively, these values could have been entered as hidden form fields and passed as request parameters.)

The next block of code on lines 18 through 23 is used to set the default date for the `entry_date` field on the form (and ultimately in the database record). The definition of the entry date field is the date when the record was last updated, so logically, this field should be set to the current date. On lines 19 and 20, a conditional statement evaluates the "action" parameter to determine if an "insert" or "update" is being performed. (Currently, these are the only two valid actions for the page, but this conditional testing allows different actions to be added   later.) If the conditional statement tests true, an `entry_date` attribute is set using the current date as returned by the `Cal` class `getCurrentDate` method. The `setEntry_date` method for the internal knowledge base Value Object is also called to set this date to the current date. The remainder of the method is used to set default values for the form fields depending on the action being performed.

The next block of code is executed only for an insert operation [action..equals("insert")] and is used to set a number of default values for the insert operation.

. . .

```
1.       if ( request.getParameter("action").equals("insert") ) {

         // date first entered (submitted)
2.           session.setAttribute( "date_submitted",
cal.getCurrentDate( "mm/dd/yy" ));
3.           knowledge_baseVO.setDate_submitted( cal.getCurrentDate(
"mm/dd/yy" ));

         // get the user name and location from the login information
stored in the session object
4.           knowledge_baseVO.setPost_user( (String)
session.getAttribute( "login") );
5.           knowledge_baseVO.setDoc_location( (String)
session.getAttribute( "location" ) );
```

```
// if this is a threaded message, get the doc_name from the
base_doc_key record
// since this is an insert, knowledge_baseVO has not been
loaded, so need to create a DAO to
        // get the base_doc_key

        // no base_doc_key value passed
6.          if (
Integer.parseInt(request.getParameter("base_doc_key").trim()) ==
0   )
            // then use the link_doc
7.              doc_key = Integer.parseInt(
request.getParameter("link_doc"));
8.          else
9.              doc_key = Integer.parseInt(
request.getParameter("base_doc_key"));

10.         Knowledge_baseDAO baseDAO = new Knowledge_baseDAO( );
11.         baseDAO.loadDAO( doc_key );
12.         knowledge_baseVO.setDoc_name( baseDAO.getDoc_name() );

13.     }


   // if this is an update or delete, does the user have permis-
sion to do this
14.    if ( request.getParameter("action").equals("update") ) {

 // if this isn't the user that posted the message
15.    if ( (!((String) session.getAttribute("login")).equals(
                        knowledge_baseVO.getPost_user()
)) ||
16.        (!((String) session.getAttribute("role")).equals(
"admin" ) ) ) {  // this is the sysadmin

17.             throw new Exception("You do not have permission to
perform this function.");


18.        }
19.      }
20.    }
```

A number of these fields are set in the internal Value Object and in the `session` object to be sent to the `updDB.jsp` page for the database update operation. On line 3, for example, the `date_submitted` field of the `knowledge_base` Value Object is set to the current date. The same value is placed in the `date_submitted` attribute at line 2.

At lines 4 and 5 the user name (`login`) and user location (`location`) are retrieved from the `session` object where they were placed by the login process. They are placed in the appropriate fields in the current `knowledge_base` Value Object (`post_user` and `doc_location`, respectively).

The next block of code deals with the contingency that the message being inserted is a threaded message. Since this is a threaded message, the short description of the message will probably be the same as the short description for the base message for the thread. In this application, then, the default short description for a threaded message should be the short description for the base message, but this is not a requirement. This block of code will get the short description from the base message and then use that description for the current message. (This description will be placed in the input field and the user will have the option of changing the description.)

On line 6, the contents of the document key for the base message for the thread (`base_doc_key`) are examined. If this is currently set to 0, the value of the link document is used and is retrieved on line 7. Otherwise, the value of the base message document key (`base_doc_key`) is retrieved on line 9. A local `Knowledge_baseDAO` object is created on line 10 and uses the document key (`doc_key`) populated on previous lines to load the DAO with database values for that document key, which will be the base document for this message thread. The short name for the local message document is then set to the short name from the base message `knowledge_base` DAO on line 12.

On line 14 a series of security checks are performed to determine whether or not the user has permission to perform the operation they have requested. This block of code checks to determine if the user is performing an update operation (action = `"update"`) and if so, is this the user who created the document or the system administrator (currently *hardcoded* as a user role of `"admin"`)? Lines 15 and 16 perform these validations, examining the `session` object attributes of `"login"` and `"role"`. If the user does not have correct permissions, an exception is thrown at line 17.

inputKB.jsp Page

The next section of the `inputKB.jsp` page outputs a header and then starts the HTML table that will house the input form. The table is created at line 7 and a form tag is created at line 10, which directs the output of the form as a POST operation to the `updDB.jsp` page.

```
1.    <title>Knowledge Base</title>
2.    <center>
3.    <br>
4.    <br>
5.    <H1>Message Update</H1>
6.    </center>
7.    <table border=0 width=100% >
8.    <tr>
9.       <td width=10%><br></td>
10.   <form method="post" action="updDB.jsp">
11.   <input name="action"   type="hidden"
value="<jsp:getProperty name="KBFacade" property="action"/>" >
12.   <input name="link_doc" type="hidden"
value="<jsp:getProperty name="KBFacade" property="link_doc"/>" >

13.   <td width=10%> Category: </td> <td width=20%>

. . .
```

On lines 11 and 12, hidden fields are created to store the "action" and the "link" document as request parameters. (Although still included on a number of these pages, the link_doc field is not currently used by the discussion group application.)

The next section of the page displays a list box of categories which must be created dynamically. To format the form fields, including the list box, the list box is placed in table cell using the <td> tag on line 1.

```
. . .
1.    <td width=10%> Category: </td> <td width=20%>
2.    <!- create category list box ->
3.    <select name="category"
4.    <%
5.    String category = null;

// iterate through category list to create a listbox of cate-
gories

6.    Iterator i = KBFacade.getCategoryList();
7.    while ( i.hasNext() )   {
8.     category = KBFacade.makeCategoryString( i.next() );
9.     if ( KBFacade.isDefaultCategory( category ) ) { %>
10.      <option selected> <%= category %>
11.   <% } else { %>
```

```
12.          <option> <%= category %>
13.      <%
14.          }
15.        }
16.      %>
17.      </select>
18.      </td>
...
```

To dynamically create the list box based on the current contents of the database table containing the categories, the `getCategoryList` method retrieves the contents of the `message_categories` table (by calling a method in the `message_categoriesDAO`) and returns the results as an `Iterator` on line 6. The `while` loop starting on line 7 loops through this `Iterator` and converts the members to a `String` data type on line 8.

A conditional test is performed on line 9 to determine if the category is the default category. If this conditional test is true, the category will be displayed as the list box item selected, as shown in the output on line 10. If the category is not the default category, the output on line 12 is produced.

Following the creation of the category list box, a series of input fields are produced by the JSP code on the page. In order to format the fields of the form, each form field is enclosed in a table cell. Since the `"entry_date"` field being output on line 1 is not an input field, it is output in a different color than the fields which allow input. A `jsp:getProperty` tag is used to retrieve the contents of the `entry_date` field in the current knowledge_base Value Object in the `KnowledgeBaseFacade` JavaBean.

```
...
1.      <td width=5%> Entry Date: </td> <td width=20%><font
face="helvetica, sans-serif" color="green">
2.      <jsp:getProperty name="KBFacade" property="entry_date" />
3.      </font></td>
4.      </tr>

5.      <tr>
6.      <td width=10%><br></td>
7.      <td width=15%> Short Description: </td> <td width=20%>
8.      <input name="doc_name" type="text" value="<jsp:getProperty
name="KBFacade" property="doc_name" />"> </td>
9.      <td width=5%> Posted by:    </td> <td width=20%> <input
name="post_user" type="text" value="<jsp:getProperty
name="KBFacade" property="post_user" />"> </td>
10.     </tr>
```

```
11.    <tr>
12.    <td width=10%><br></td>
13.    <td width=15%> Location:        </td>
14.    <td width=20%> <input name="doc_location" type="text"
value="<jsp:getProperty name="KBFacade" property="doc_location"
/>"> </td>

15.    <td width=5%> Submitted: </td> <td width=20%> <font
face="helvetica, sans-serif" color="green"> <jsp:getProperty
name="KBFacade" property="date_submitted" />
16.    </font>
17.    </td>
18.    </tr>
...
```

Lines 5 to 10 provide an example of an HTML form input field defined using a jsp:getProperty tag to provide a value for the field. On line 8, the value of the doc_name field is used to provide a value for the short description field. Using this JSP tag, the contents of the doc_name field in the current knowledge_base value object is output as part of the value attribute for this field.

On line 14, the same syntax is used to retrieve the contents of the doc_location field. On line 15, the date_submitted field does not allow user input, so the contents of the date submitted field are output without an input field. To clarify that this field is not like the other fields on the form and does not allow input, the contents of the field (as returned by the jsp:getProperty tag) is output in a different font color.

The message type field also requires the user to choose from multiple selections. This is accomplished using the list box created on line 2 in the following code listing. As done in previous list box examples, a call is made to the getMessageTypesList method on line 5 to retrieve the values needed to populate the list box. This call returns an Iterator that is used to iterate through the contents of the message_types table.

```
...
1.    <td>
2.    <select name="message_type">

3.    <%
// iterate through message types list to create a listbox of
message types
4.    String message_type=null;
```

```
5.      i = KBFacade.getMessageTypesList();
6.      while ( i.hasNext() )   {
7.           message_type = KBFacade.makeMessageTypesString(
                                  i.next());
8.      if ( (KBFacade.getMessage_type() != null ) && (
     KBFacade.getMessage_type().equals(message_type) ) ) {
%>
9.         <option selected><%= message_type %>
10.     <% } else { %>
11.         <option><%= message_type %>
12.     <% }
13.       }
14.     %>
15.     </select>
. . .
```

The while loop initiated on line 6 is used to iterate through the contents of the message_types table. As stored in the Iterator i. A conditional statement on line 8 is used to select the message type of the current record in the select list. This is done by comparing the contents of the message type Value Object contained in the KnowledgeBaseFacade class with the contents of the message_types list being used. If the message type of the current record is found, it is output as the selected item on line 9. If the message type of the current record is not the message being iterated in the list, the output on line 11 is output.

The remainder of the inputKB.jsp page contains a series of form fields for the input or update of the message.

```
1.      <tr>
2.      <td width=10%><br></td>
3.      <td width=15%> Message Text: </td> <td width=20%> <textarea
name="message_txt" cols=40 rows=5 wrap><jsp:getProperty
name="KBFacade" property="message_txt" /></textarea> </td>
4.      </tr>

5.      <tr>

6.      <td width=5%> <br>
7.      <td width=2%> Key Words: </td> <td width=2%> <input
name="keyword1" type="text" value="<jsp:getProperty
name="KBFacade" property="keyword1" />"> </td>
8.      <td width=5% align="left"> </td> <td width=5%> <input
name="keyword2" type="text" value="<jsp:getProperty
```

```
name="KBFacade" property="keyword2" />"> </td>
9.     </tr>

10.    <tr>
11.    <td width=5%> <br>
12.    <td width=2%> Key Words: </td> <td width=2%> <input
name="keyword3" type="text" value="<jsp:getProperty
name="KBFacade" property="keyword3" />"> </td>
13.    <td width=5% align="left"> </td> <td width=5%> <input
name="keyword4" type="text" value="<jsp:getProperty
name="KBFacade" property="keyword4" />"> </td>
14.    </tr>

15.    <tr>
16.    <td width=10%><br></td>
17.    <td width=10%><br></td>

18.    <td width=5%> <input name="submit" type="submit"
value="<jsp:getProperty name="KBFacade" property="submitTitle"
/>" >
19.    </td>
20.    </tr>

21.    </form>
22.    </table>

23.    </body>
24.    </html>
25.    </tr>

26.    </form>
27.    </table>

28.    </body>
29.    </html>
```

The form fields are wrapped in table cells and contain values retrieved using jsp:getProperty tags, as shown on lines 3 through 13 in the listing. The tag on line 18 creates the submit button for the page. Since the page is used for both inserts and updates, the button title is generated based on the action for which the page is being used. This button title is generated using the submitTitle method as accessed through the jsp:getProperty tag on that line.

Performing Database Updates

The updDB.jsp page is posted to by the inputKB.jsp page and is responsible for performing the database update operations required by any input done on that page. The page contains very little presentation output and the bulk of the work performed is done by the KnowledgeBaseFacade.doUpdate method. If the update succeeds, the page produces output indicating the number of rows updated. If some part of the update operation throws an exception, the error page is displayed with information about the error. If the update fails to update any rows (which usually indicates a problem since at least one row should have been updated), the current implementation of this page will simply indicate that '0 rows' have been updated.

```
1.    <html>
2.    <body bgcolor="#FFFFFF" background="/JavaWeb/img/bkg.gif">
3.    <%@ page errorPage="ErrorPage.jsp" %>
4.    <jsp:useBean id="KBFacade"
class="knowledgebase.KnowledgeBaseFacade" scope="page" />
5.    <br>
6.    <font face="Helvetica, Sans-serif" size=+2 >
7.    <center>
8.    <h1>Update Completed</h1>
9.    </center>
10.   </font>
11.   <br>
12.   <br>
13.   <% KBFacade.doUpdate( request, session ); %>
14.   <center>
15.   <font face="Helvetica, Sans-serif" size=+2 color="blue">

16.   <br>Updated <jsp:getProperty name="KBFacade"
property="rowsUpdated" /> Rows.
17.   <br>
18.   <br>
19.   <br><a href="pickKB.jsp?type=all">Return to Message
List</a>
20.   <br><a href="menu.html">Return to Main Menu</a>
21.   </font>
22.   </center>
23.   </body>
24.   </html>
```

The errorPage directive is used at line 3 to indicate that the error page will be ErrorPage.jsp. On line 4 the jsp:useBean tag is used to indicate that the bean to be used for this page will be the knowledgebase.KnowledgeBaseFacade class and will be identified on the page using the KBFacade.

A header is output on lines 6 through 10 and then on line 13, the doUpdate method of the KnowledgeBaseFacade class is called to perform the database update operations required for this method. This method is the workhorse of this page, performing the relatively complex processing required to update the message database with form input it has received. (The processing performed by this method is discussed in the next section.)

Following the call to the doUpdate method, a value is placed in the rowsUpdated member of the KnowledgeBaseFacade bean. This value indicates how many rows have been updated by the page. The current implementation merely reports this number using a jsp:getProperty tag without comment on line 16. (An alternative implementation would be to interpret a "no rows updated" condition as an error condition and forward control to an error page.) On lines 19 and 20, links are provided to allow navigation back to the main menu page or to return to a full listing of all messages.

The full processing of this page is performed off the page, in the doUpdate method. You can't really understand the processing being performed without examining the code behind this method. In the next section we provide the details of this method.

Updating the Database:
The KnowledgeBaseFacade.doUpdate Method

The doUpdate method shown below is responsible for updating the database with the input from the HTML form generated by the inputKB.jsp page. This method receives two parameters: the request object (HttpRequest) and the session object (HttpSession). This method is responsible for marshaling the resources of other methods within the KnowledgeBaseFacade class to execute the update and for enforcing security. A great deal of code within the method is spent validating that the user has permission to perform the update operation he or she is requesting.

```
1.     ...
2.
3.     public void doUpdate( ServletRequest request, HttpSession
session ) throws Exception {
4.     int doc_key=0;
```

```
5.
6.      try {
7.
8.      // let's make sure we have a doc_key
9.      if ( request.getParameter("doc_key") != null )
10.         doc_key = Integer.parseInt(
request.getParameter("doc_key").trim() );
11.     else
12.       if ( session.getAttribute("doc_key") != null )
13.           doc_key = ((Integer)
session.getAttribute("doc_key")).intValue();
14.
15.     // if our doc_key is still 0 and this isn't an insert,
throw an exception
16.     if (( doc_key == 0 ) && (
request.getParameter("action").equals("update")) )
17.         throw new Exception ("Invalid document key.");
18.
19.     // update can be an insert,update or delete operation
20.     // check security before allowing an update
21.     // user must be logged in to perform an insert
22.     if ( request.getParameter("action").equals("insert") ) {
23.       if ( session.getAttribute("login") == null ) // the
user has not logged in
24.         throw new Exception("User must log in to add a mes-
sage.");
25.     }
26.     // if user is performing an update or delete, then
27.     // this must be the user that posted the message
28.     if ( session.getAttribute("login") == null ) // user has
not logged in
29.         throw new Exception("User must login to perform this
operation." );
30.
31.     if ( request.getParameter("action").equals("update") ||
32.         request.getParameter("action").equals("delete") ) {
33.       if ( (!((String) session.getAttribute("login")).equals(
request.getParameter("post_user") )) ||
34.           (!((String) session.getAttribute("role")).equals(
"admin" ) ) ) {  // this is the sysadmin
35.           throw new Exception("User does not have permission
to perform this function.");
36.       }
37.     }
```

```
38.
39.    // security is ok, so perform the update
40.    if ( request.getParameter("action").equals("insert") ) {
41.        insertKBRecs( request, session );
42.        return;
43.    }
44.
45.    if ( request.getParameter("action").equals("update") ) {
46.        session.setAttribute("doc_key", new Integer( doc_key )
);
47.        updateKBRecs( request, session );
48.        return;
49.    }
50.
51.    if ( request.getParameter("action").equals("delete") ) {
52.        session.setAttribute("doc_key", new Integer( doc_key )
);
53.        deleteKBRecs( request, session );
54.        return;
55.    }
56.
57.    // if at this point, then we have not been passed a valid
action
58.    // log an error and throw an exception
59.    System.out.println("knowledge_baseFacade.doUpdate() called
with invalid action: " +
60.                            request.getParameter("action"));
61.    throw new Exception( "KnowledgeBaseFacade.doUpdate called
with an invalid action " +
62.                            request.getParameter("action"));
63.
64.    }
65.    catch (Exception e) {
66.      System.out.println("Exception in
KnowledgeBase.doUpdate(): " + e );
67.      throw new Exception ("Exception in
KnowledgeBase.doUpdate(): " + e );
68.    }
69.
70.
71.
72.    }
73.    ...
74.
```

On lines 9 through 13, the document key is examined to determine whether or not it has been set correctly. Since the document key is the primary key for any messages, we must have a document key to be able to perform any update operations. If the doc_key is found, it will be converted into an integer and stored in a local variable where it can be used later without having to perform an integer conversion.

On line 16 the method checks to see if the doc_key is 0 and the action is "update". If this condition is true, an exception is thrown since we cannot perform an update without a doc_key. On lines 22 and 23, we check to see if an insert operation is being performed. If an insert is being performed, the user must be logged into the system. If the user is not logged in and they are attempting an insert, an exception will be thrown.

On line 26, the method checks again to determine whether or not the user is logged in, and on lines 31 through 34 the method checks to determine whether or not the logged-in user is allowed to perform the operation they've requested. If the user is not a system administration user and the user is not the user who entered the message, the user is not allowed to perform the operation and an exception is thrown.

If we have arrived at line 41, we are allowed to perform the update operation. The request getParameter method is used to retrieve the "action" parameter. The content of this parameter will indicate which update action the user wishes to use. On line 41, if the user has permissions to perform the operation, the insertKBRecs method is called and is passed both the request and session objects. The method will return immediately once the insert operations have been performed.

On lines 45 through 49, the update option is handled. A session object attribute is assigned for the doc_key and the updateKBRecs method is called with both the request and session objects. On lines 51 through 54, the delete option is managed. A session object attribute is assigned for the doc_key and the deleteKBRecs method is called passed both the request and session objects. If the method arrives at line 58, it has not received appropriate parameters. It will log an error and then thrown an exception, thus returning control to the calling method.

All the update methods in the message system facade class use the data access objects for the various tables involved in the update operation. These objects encapsulate the insert, update, and delete operations for the database tables they represent and are explained in Chapter 11. (Note that DAOs do not need to wrap a single relation but can, in fact, map to multiple relations, although that is not done in this example.)

Since the doUpdate method can optionally call either the insertKBRecs, updateKBRecs, or deleteKBRecs methods, this would be a good point to discuss the code behind these methods. Each of these methods uses one or more DAO to manipulate the database. So that we can focus on the business logic of the facade class, detailed operation of these DAOs is not covered in this chapter (but is covered in Chapter 11). In the following sections we discuss each of the `insertKBRecs`, `updateKBRecs`, and `deleteKBRecs` methods in turn.

Inserting Records: The insertKBRecs Method

The `insertKBRecs` method in the `KnowledgeBaseFacade` class is used to insert records into the database. Since discussion group messages are stored in multiple tables, this method is responsible for managing these multiple inserts into several tables using DAOs for each of the tables.

The `insertKBRecs` method is passed the `request` (`HttpRequest`) object and the `session` (`HttpSession`) object from the JSP.

```
1.    public void insertKBRecs( ServletRequest request,
HttpSession session ) {
2.
3.    int doc_key;
4.
5.    try {
6.
7.    // use the request to get the values for our DAO members
8.    knowledge_baseDAO.setDoc_location( request.getParameter(
"doc_location" ) );
9.    knowledge_baseDAO.setDoc_name( request.getParameter(
"doc_name" ) );
10.   knowledge_baseDAO.setCategory( request.getParameter( "cate-
gory" ) );
11.
12.   knowledge_baseDAO.setPost_user( request.getParameter(
"post_user" ) );
13.
14.
15.   // these parameters aren't in the form, they're stored in
the session object
16.   knowledge_baseDAO.setLink_doc( ((Integer)
session.getAttribute( "link_doc" )).intValue() );
17.   knowledge_baseDAO.setBase_doc_key( ((Integer)
session.getAttribute( "base_doc_key" )).intValue() );
18.
19.
```

```
20.    if ( knowledge_baseDAO.getBase_doc_key() == 0 )
21.       if ( knowledge_baseDAO.getLink_doc() > 0  )
22.          knowledge_baseDAO.setBase_doc_key(
knowledge_baseDAO.getLink_doc() ) ;
23.
24.    knowledge_baseDAO.setDate_submitted( (String)
session.getAttribute( "date_submitted") );  // only set on ini-
tial insert
25.    knowledge_baseDAO.setEntry_date( (String)
session.getAttribute( "entry_date" ) );
26.
27.    doc_key = knowledge_baseDAO.insertDAO();
28.
29.    // should throw an execption if we get a 0 back from
knowledge_baseDAO.insertDAO
30.
31.    // knowledge_messages
32.    knowledge_messagesDAO.setDoc_key( doc_key );
33.    knowledge_messagesDAO.setMessage_txt( request.getParameter(
"message_txt" ) );
34.    knowledge_messagesDAO.setMessage_type(
request.getParameter( "message_type" ) );
35.    knowledge_messagesDAO.insertDAO();
...
```

The first order of business is to set the DAO members with the values from the input form. This is done on lines 8 through 25. Data values are retrieved from the request object on lines 8 through 12. Lines 16 and 17 retrieve values from the session object, data values that are not entered in the input form that provides the data for this method. Lines 20 through 22 provide some conditional logic to set the base document key (the base message document for a threaded message) if it has not yet been set. The result of this logic is that if the base document key is not set and the link document key is set, the link document key is used as the base document key for this message. Lines 24 and 25 are used to retrieve the date submitted and the entry date for the message from the session object.

Note that up to this point the document key (doc_key) for the message document has not been set. The reason for this is that the document key for the discussion group database is a database-generated unique key. Its value is set by the DAO (ultimately by the database) as part of the insert operation into the knowledge_base table. But since there are a number of related tables that must be updated as part of the message insert operation, this unique key generated by the database must be returned to this method to be used in insert operations for the related tables. This is done on line 27, where the `Knowledge_baseDAO.insertDAO` method is called. This method returns an integer corresponding to the document key (`doc_key`) of the `knowledge_base` record just inserted.

The remainder of the method is devoted to updating the multiple tables related to the `knowledge_base` table. On lines 32 through 35 the `knowledge_messages` table is updated. On line 32 the document key (`doc_key`) from the `knowledge_base` update operation is used to set the document key for the `knowledge_messages` table. The data for the `knowledge_messages` fields is retrieved from request parameters and on line 35 the `insertDAO` method of the `Knowledge_messagesDAO` class is called to perform the database insert.

The next set of statements performs the insert operation for the `base_keys` table.

```
...
1.      // base_keys - the keywords for our message
2.      base_keysDAO.setDoc_key( doc_key );
3.      base_keysDAO.setKeyword( request.getParameter( "keyword1" )
);
4.      base_keysDAO.insertDAO();
5.
6.      base_keysDAO.setDoc_key( doc_key );
7.      base_keysDAO.setKeyword( request.getParameter( "keyword2" )
);
8.      base_keysDAO.insertDAO();
9.
10.     base_keysDAO.setDoc_key( doc_key );
11.     base_keysDAO.setKeyword( request.getParameter( "keyword3" )
);
12.     base_keysDAO.insertDAO();
13.
14.     base_keysDAO.setDoc_key( doc_key );
15.     base_keysDAO.setKeyword( request.getParameter( "keyword4" )
);
16.     base_keysDAO.insertDAO();
17.     }
18.     catch (SQLException e) {
19.         System.out.println( "SQLException caught in
KnowledgeBaseFacade.insertKBRecs(): " + e.getMessage() );
20.
21.     }
22.     catch (Exception e) {
23.         System.out.println( "Exception in
```

```
KnowledgeBaseFacade.insertKBRecs(): " + e.getMessage() );
24.    }
25.
26.    }
```

In the current implementation, four keywords are stored in this table. These keywords are each inserted into the table in separate insert operations on lines 2 through 16. The document key from the `knowledge_base` insert operation is used for the document key for these records and is set in the DAO on lines 2, 6, 10, and 14. Each insert operation on lines 4, 8, 12, and 16 inserts a separate row into the database using the values from the keyword parameter values retrieved on lines 3, 7, 11, and 15. Lines 18 through 25 catch various exceptions that may be thrown.

No specific success or failure flags are returned by this method; if any of the database update methods fails, an exception would be thrown by the `insertKBRecs` method, which would be caught and then thrown to the `doUpdate` method, which will in turn throw an exception to the JSP that called it. (Note that the current implementation does not use a transaction for these multiple updates, an so it could leave the database in an inconsistent state.)

updateKBRecs Method

The `updateKBRecs` method is responsible for updating the records updated on the `inputKB.jsp` page. Like the other update methods, this method receives the `request` object and the `session` object as parameters.

```
1.     public void updateKBRecs( ServletRequest request,
HttpSession session ) {
2.     int doc_key = 0;
3.
4.
5.
6.     try {
7.
8.     doc_key = ((Integer)
session.getAttribute("doc_key")).intValue();
9.
10.    // use the request to get the values for update
11.    knowledge_baseDAO.setDoc_key( doc_key );
12.    knowledge_baseDAO.setDoc_name( request.getParameter(
"doc_name" ) );
```

```
13.    knowledge_baseDAO.setPost_user( request.getParameter(
"post_user") );
14.    knowledge_baseDAO.setDoc_location( request.getParameter(
"doc_location") );
15.    knowledge_baseDAO.setLink_doc( Integer.parseInt(
request.getParameter( "link_doc" )) );
16.    knowledge_baseDAO.setCategory( request.getParameter( "cate-
gory" ) );

17.    knowledge_baseDAO.setEntry_date((String)
session.getAttribute( "entry_date")); // date last changed
18.
19.    // knowledge_messages
20.    knowledge_messagesDAO.setDoc_key( doc_key );
21.    knowledge_messagesDAO.setMessage_txt( request.getParameter(
"message_txt" ) );
22.    knowledge_messagesDAO.setMessage_type(
request.getParameter( "message_type" ) );
23.    knowledge_messagesDAO.updateDAO();
24.
25.    // base_keys - the keywords for our message
26.    // no true primary key in this table - it's just a list
27.    // so delete all existing recs and then insert them again
28.    base_keysDAO.setDoc_key( doc_key );
29.    base_keysDAO.deleteDAO();
30.
31.    base_keysDAO.setDoc_key( doc_key );
32.    base_keysDAO.setKeyword( request.getParameter( "keyword1" )
);
33.    base_keysDAO.insertDAO();
34.
35.    base_keysDAO.setDoc_key( doc_key );
36.    base_keysDAO.setKeyword( request.getParameter( "keyword2" )
);
37.    base_keysDAO.insertDAO();
38.
39.    base_keysDAO.setDoc_key( doc_key );
40.    base_keysDAO.setKeyword( request.getParameter( "keyword3" )
);
41.    base_keysDAO.insertDAO();
42.
43.    base_keysDAO.setDoc_key( doc_key );
44.    base_keysDAO.setKeyword( request.getParameter( "keyword4" )
);
```

```
45.     base_keysDAO.insertDAO();
46.
47.     }
48.     catch (SQLException e) {
49.         System.out.println( "SQLException caught in
KnowledgeBaseFacade.updateKBRecs(): " + e + " - " + e );
50.         throw new Exception( "Database exception in
updateKBRecs." + e.getMessage() );
51.
52.     }
53.     catch (Exception e) {
54.         System.out.println( "Exception in
KnowledgeBaseFacade.updateKBRecs(): " + e );
55.         throw new Exception( "Database exception in
updateKBRecs." + e.getMessage() );
56.
57.      }
58.
59.      }
60.
61.
```

For updates, the document key (doc_key) must be known. The value of the current document key is stored in the doc_key attribute of the session object as an Integer object reference. This object reference is retrieved and converted into its integer value and stored in a local integer variable on line 8.

On lines 11 through 16 the values of the knowledge_base DAO are set to the corresponding parameter values from the input form. On line 17, the entry_date for the knowledge_base record is set to the current date as stored in the session object attribute entry_date. Beginning on line 19, the knowledge_messages table is prepared for the update operation that occurs at line 23. The processing for the table that stores the keywords for the messages (base_keys) begins on line 28. Since there is no primary key for this table and to simplify the update logic, it is *updated* by deleting all existing rows for the document key and inserting the values that have been returned by the input form into the table. The deletion is accomplished by the calls made on lines 28 and 29, and the code on lines 31 through 45 are used to insert the new values.

On lines 38 through 54 various exceptions are caught. These exceptions are processed by creating and throwing a new exception, which contains information on where the failure occurred and appends the message text from the message that was caught. This exception will be caught in the doUpdate method, which will in turn throw the message back to the JSP, which will forward page processing to the `ErrorPage.jsp` page (as indicated by the `page` directive `errorpage` attribute on the JSP). (Note that the implementation shown here does not use transactions, which could potentially leave the database in an inconsistent state if one or more of the update operations fails.)

deleteKBRecs Method

The `deleteKBRecs` method is responsible for deleting all references to a specified message in the discussion group database. The method only needs the document key to the message to accomplish this, but for consistency it receives both the `request` and `session` objects as parameters.

```
1.    // delete this knowledge_base record and all of the related records
2.    public void deleteKBRecs( ServletRequest request,
HttpSession session ) {
3.    int doc_key;
4.
5.
6.    try {
7.
8.    doc_key = ((Integer) session.getAttribute( "doc_key"
)).intValue();
9.
10.    // knowledge_base
11.    knowledge_baseDAO.loadDAO( doc_key );
12.    knowledge_baseDAO.deleteDAO( );
13.
14.    // knowledge_messages
15.    knowledge_messagesDAO.setDoc_key( doc_key );
16.    knowledge_messagesDAO.deleteDAO();
17.
18.    // base_keys - the keywords for our message
19.    base_keysDAO.setDoc_key( doc_key );
20.    base_keysDAO.deleteDAO();
21.
22.    }
23.    catch (SQLException e) {
24.        System.out.println( "SQLException caught in
KnowledgeBaseFacade.deleteKBRecs(): " + e.getMessage() );
25.        throw new Exception( "Database exception in
deleteKBRecs." + e.getMessage() );
```

```
26.    }
27.    catch (Exception e) {
28.        System.out.println( "Exception in
KnowledgeBaseFacade.deleteKBRecs(): " + e.getMessage() );
29.        throw new Exception( "Database exception in
deleteKBRecs." + e.getMessage() );
30.    }
31.
32.    }
33.
```

The first step is to extract the document key for the message to delete. This is accomplished on line 8, where the document key (doc_key) is retrieved from the session object. The Object reference returned by the session object is cast as an Integer reference (its *real* type) and then the reference resulting from that cast is used to call the intValue method to return a primitive integer value. This integer value is stored in a local variable and is then used throughout the method to reference the message being deleted.

On line 11 the loadDAO method of the Knowledge_baseDAO class is used to load the message header for the document key passed to the method. Once the DAO has been set to this document key, the deleteDAO method is called to delete the referenced message document from the knowledge_base table.

On lines 15 and 16 the knowledge_messages table, which is used to store the text of the discussion group message, is processed. On line 15 the setDoc_key method of the knowledge_messages DAO is called to set the document key to the value of the document key that is passed. On line 16 the knowledge_messages records for that document key are deleted using the deleteDAO method.

On lines 19 and 20 the base_keys table, used to store the keywords for a discussion group message, is processed. The Base_keysDAO.setDoc_key method is called to set the document key to that of the message to be deleted. Once this has been set, the deleteDAO method of the DAO can be called to delete all references to the message in the base_keys table.

Error Page: ErrorPage.jsp

The ErrorPage.jsp page is, as the name implies, used to handle exceptions that are thrown on various JSP in the application. This page displays a message concerning the error and provides links through the page footer that allow the user to return to the main page (see Figure 10.13).

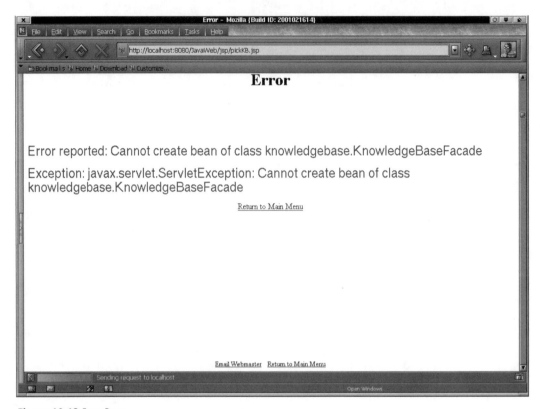

Figure 10.13 Error Page

As shown in the following code listing, this page does little more than display the error message as contained in the `exception` object and then displays output for the `exception` object by printing the object (which will eventually call the `toString` method on the object). A link in the middle of the page allows the user to return to the menu page. An JSP `include` page directive is used to include the `footer.txt` file (which contains a page footer used throughout the discussion group application) into the page.

```
<%@ page isErrorPage="true" %>
<html>
<body bgcolor="#FFFFFF">
<head>
<title>Error</title>
</head>
</body>
```

```
<br>
<br>
<center>
<H1>Error</H1>
</center>
<br>
<br>
<br>
<br>
<font face="helvetica,sans-serif" size=+3 color="red">
<p>Error reported: <%= exception.getMessage() %>
<p>
<p>Exception: <%= exception %>
</font>
<center>
<a href="menu.shtml">Return to Main Menu</a>
</center>

<br>
<br>
<br>

<%@ include file="footer.txt" %>

</html>
```

Using the JSP include Directive: Inserting a Page Footer

It is not uncommon to include a footer on an HTML page. This footer would probably include links to other sites that may be of interest to the user of your site. The insertion of the `footer.txt` file for the JSP include provides an example of just such an approach.

```
<center>
<br>
<br>
<br>
<br>
<font size=-1>
<a href="mailto:webmaster@nowhere.com">Email Webmaster</a>
   <a href="menu.shtml">Return to Main Menu</a>
</font>
<center>
```

The file `footer.txt` is inserted at the bottom of most of the pages in the discussion group application. Using this file provides a consistent look for the application, and, although it appears trivial in this example, on larger projects with more complex pages, this could save a significant amount of work by allowing some portion of duplicated code to be shared among developers.

The text in this files contains HTML and provides a link to the menu page as well as a link to send email to a specified email address. (This is done using the URL `mailto` as the reference for the link.)

Summary

In this chapter we examined JSP in practice. Sections in the chapter reviewed many of the design issues and principles that had been laid out in previous chapters. We provided examples of how to implement these design principles with a detailed code example for an application that delivers a discussion group system. This system uses numerous JSP pages which provide examples of a form-based login process that uses a database, the creation of dynamic HTML tables based on database content, and update and delete operations on multiple related tables. To make the discussion clear and thorough, JSP were presented and discussed and the Java code called within the pages was also discussed in detail.

Coming Up Next

In this chapter we left coverage of the lower-level database access, the creation and execution of SQL statements, to data access objects. These DAOs, as well as the lower-level database utility class (`DBUtil`), manage the database interaction for this sample application. These DAOs and the `DBUtil` class will be discussed in detail in the next chapter.

DATABASE ACCESS WITH JAVABEANS

Introduction

To improve the modular structure of the code, the application shown in Chapter 10 made use of several Java design patterns to manage the specifics of database access: *Database Access Objects* (DAOs) and *Value Objects*. DAOs encapsulate the details of database access, providing *coarse-grained* or record-at-a-time access to the database tables. Value Objects encapsulate the structure of the data being accessed and effectively represent the records being used. Both types of objects were used consistently throughout the application to model access to the database tables and the data records within those tables and are shown and explained in detail in this chapter.

To provide further modularity, a database utility class was used to isolate the low-level database access activity and remove the responsibility for these operations from the business methods that must retrieve and update data. This allows the specifics of database activity to be left to the utility class and shared effectively among the various objects that use the class.

(As of this writing the PostgreSQL JDBC driver did not provide connection pooling. By isolating the database activity in this class, connection pooling could be added with little pain since the DAOs would not need to be aware of the change; only the database utility object would require a change.)

In this chapter we provide samples of the database access code used in the sample application. Note that not all DAO and Value Object classes are shown since the same basic pattern is repeated throughout.

Data Access Objects Description

The DAO is intended to encapsulate database access and provide a means of shielding the business object from the details of this access. As stated previously, such an approach provides code sharing, and since the DAO is shared among various business objects, localizes any changes that may be required (and are not at all uncommon) for database access.

These DAOs are tightly coupled with corresponding Value Objects for the tables with which they interact. In one set of examples, the class members to store values from the table are stored in a Value Object that is a class member. In another example, data values from the table are stored in primitive data types within the class.

The DAOs used in the sample application from Chapter 10 use a design structure that contains a set of standard methods to read and write data to the database. To optimize performance, the database queries are prepared before being used by the business methods that call these methods. These prepared queries are retained and used when the business methods accessing the DAOs request data. Each DAO retains its own connection to the database through a reference to a DBUtil object that is a private instance member of the DAO. (The DBUtil object actually contains the JDBC Connection reference, not the DAO.)

All DAOs contain methods to set the DAO to the values within a Value Object or to return the values of the DAO in a Value Object. This structure provides an easy-to-use, efficient means of using the DAO and interacting with the database. The use of a single method to set a DAO or retrieve values from the DAO simplifies the interface between the business methods using the DAO and reduces the amount of communication required (the friction) between the objects.

The methods used in the DAO are listed in Table 11.1. These methods are shown and explained in the following sections.

Simple DAO: CategoryDAO

The code that follows provides an example of a simple DAO to perform the database access for the category table. Using the methods shown above in conjunction with calls to the database utility class, this DAO will encapsulate the

Table 11.1 Standard DAO Methods

Method	Description
`Get<propertyName>()`	Retrieves the class property (member) with the name <propertyName>.
`Set<propertyName>()`	Sets the value of the class property (member) variable of name <propertyName>.
`public void createPreparedStatements()`	Creates the prepared SQL statements used to provide the low-level database access.
`public void insertDAO() throws SQLException`	Executes the prepared SQL statement to perform the insert operation in the database. This requires setting the correct parameter values in the SQL statement from the class attribute values (the current state of the DAO).
`public void deleteDAO()`	Executes the prepared statement to perform the delete operation. This requires setting the correct prepared statement parameters from the class attribute values (the current state of the DAO).
`public void loadDAO ( String category )`	Used to load the DAO from the database. The parameter passed is the primary key and will be used to select the row from the database.
`public void loadDAO ( CategoriesVO vo )`	Used to load the DAO from the contents of the Value Object.
`public void setVO ( CategoriesVO vo )`	Used to set the Value Object the values con tained in the DAO.
`public void updateDAO()`	Updates the database using the current values of the DAO attributes.

details of the database access for the category table and effectively shield the business methods from these details.

```
package knowledgebase;
1.
2.      import javax.servlet.*;
3.      import java.util.*;
4.      import java.sql.*;
5.
6.      import db.*;
```

```
7.
8.    public class CategoriesDAO {
9.
10.   // private members
11.   private String category;
12.   private String description;
13.
14.   // hold query strings
15.   private String insertStmtStr;
16.   private String updateStmtStr;
17.   private String deleteStmtStr;
18.   private String selectStmtStr;
19.   private String selectCategoryListStr;
20.
21.   // hold prepared statements
22.   private PreparedStatement insertStmt;
23.   private PreparedStatement updateStmt;
24.   private PreparedStatement deleteStmt;
25.   private PreparedStatement selectStmt;
26.   private PreparedStatement selectCategoryListStmt;
27.
28.   DBUtil dbutil;
29.
```

In the following sections we cover this code sample in detail, describing the parameters, the code it executes, and return values and exceptions for each method. This example will provide an understanding of the basic structure of a DAO and the methods it should contain. Following this example, a more complex DAO is shown.

Import Statements and Declarations

As shown in the code example, the DAO class contains a number of import statements to make a small number of packages available to the local namespace. Following these import statements, class attributes are declared. Two members, the category and the description, are declared on lines 11 and 12 to hold the values or state of the DAO. (An alternative approach is to declare a corresponding Value Object, for example a CategoryVO instance, to carry the value of the DAO.)

A number of Java String types are then declared on lines 15 through 19 to hold the SQL statements that will be used to create the prepared statements. JDBC-prepared statements are then declared on lines 22 through 26 to hold the prepared SQL statements that will be used to provide database access. These class attributes will be used in the `createPreparedStatements` method to prepare the SQL statements used by the DAO.

Get and Set Methods

As shown in below, a number of `get` and `set` methods are then declared to retrieve and set the class members of the DAO. As would be expected, the `get` methods retrieve the data element requested and the `set` method sets the element requested.

```
1.    ...
2.    // getXXXX methods
3.    public String getCategory() {
4.        return this.category;
5.    }
6.
7.    public String getDescription() {
8.        return this.description;
9.    }
10.
11.   // setXXXX methods
12.   public void setCategory( String category ) {
13.       this.category = category;
14.   }
15.
16.   public void setDescription( String description ) {
17.       this.description = description;
18.   }
19.   ...
```

Preparing the Statements for CategoryDAO

The DAO must perform a number of standard functions: load, update, insert, and delete data in the database. A set of standard methods is declared to perform these functions as shown in the code sample below. These methods should use a consistent naming convention to improve readability and understanding.

```
1.    ...
2.    // standard DAO methods
3.    public void createPreparedStatements() {
4.
5.    try {
6.    insertStmtStr = "insert into categories( category, descrip-
tion) values (?,?)";
7.    insertStmt = dbutil.createPreparedStatement( insertStmtStr
);
8.
9.    updateStmtStr = "update categories set description = ?
where category = ? ";
10.   updateStmt = dbutil.createPreparedStatement( updateStmtStr
);
11.
12.   deleteStmtStr = "delete from categories where category =
?";
13.   deleteStmt = dbutil.createPreparedStatement( deleteStmtStr
);
14.
15.   selectStmtStr = "select category, description from cate-
gories where category = ?";
16.   selectStmt = dbutil.createPreparedStatement( selectStmtStr
);
17.
18.   selectCategoryListStr = "select category, description from
categories";
19.   selectCategoryListStmt = dbutil.createPreparedStatement(
selectCategoryListStr );
20.
21.   }
22.   catch( Exception e) {
23.
24.      System.out.println("Exception in
categoriesDAO.CreatePreparedStatement(): " + e.getMessage() );
25.
26.   }
27.
28.   }
29.   ....
```

The first of the standard methods presented, and one of the most important, is the createPreparedStatements method. This method will create corresponding prepared statements for each of the SQL statements that

must be executed for the DAO. Within this method the DBUtil class method createPreparedStatement is called. This method (shown later in this chapter) executes a JDBC prepareStatment method and returns the results as a JDBC PreparedStatement. This PreparedStatement reference is stored as a member variable of the DAO class. This process of setting the SQL statement string and using this string to create the prepared statement is repeated for each of the database operations the DAO must execute. This includes the expected select, insert, update, and delete operations which operate on a single row. But this particular DAO also includes a set of statements on lines 18 and 19 to retrieve multiple rows which are returned as a Collection object containing a list of categories. A getCategoryList method in this class is used to execute this query and capture the results. All calls to the dbutil object (a reference to an instance of the DBUtil class) throw an SQLException and all calls within the createPreparedStatements method are performed within a try/catch block which catches and reports any exceptions thrown.

Update, Insert and Delete Operations

The following methods are used to perform the update, insert, delete, and select operations for the DAO. Each of these methods sets parameter values needed to execute one of the prepared statements that was created in the createPreparedStatements method, then executes the prepared statement and stores results in the internal members (attributes) for the DAO class. Since the methods use the values of the internal members of the DAO (the class attributes/parameters), they do not need to receive method parameters to perform their function.

updateDAO Method

The updateDAO method is used to perform update operations for the DAO.

```
1.     public void updateDAO() throws SQLException {
2.
3.         updateStmt.setString(1, getDescription() );
4.         updateStmt.setString(2, getCategory() );
5.         updateStmt.executeUpdate();
6.
7.     }
```

This method will execute the SQL statement that was prepared in the `createPreparedStatments` method, as shown below.

```
...
updateStmtStr = "update categories set description = ? where cat-
egory = ? ";
...
```

This statement requires two parameters to be set: the `description` column and the `category` column in the SQL `where` clause. The `PreparedStatement` that contains this statement is used to set these parameters using the `PreparedStatement.setString` calls on lines 3 and 4. Then the `executeUpdate` call on line 5 is used to perform the update operation. Should any of these operations throw an exception, the exception would be thrown by the `updateDAO` method to the calling method.

JDBC Method Index References

Unlike virtually all of the Java API, the JDBC methods use indexes that count from 1 instead of 0. This may appear confusing at first but probably reflects the underlying SQL-based relational databases with which JDBC must interface with. (In the database world, columns in a select statement are generally referred to by their ordinal position, so that the first column in the list would be referenced as 1, not 0.)

insertDAO Method

The next method shown is the `insertDAO` method used to insert a new row into the database.

```
1.    public void insertDAO() throws SQLException {
2.
3.        insertStmt.setString(1, getCategory() );
4.        insertStmt.setString(2, getDescription() );
5.        insertStmt.executeUpdate();
6.    }
...
```

This method must set the parameters shown in the statement below: the category and the description.

```
insertStmtStr = "insert into categories( category, description)
values (?,?)";
```

As shown in the method listing on lines 3, and 4 the `PreparedStatement.setString` method is used to set the parameters corresponding to the category and description parameters. Then on line 5, the `PreparedStatement.executeUpdate` method is called to perform the update operation. Should the update operation fail, an `SQLException` would be thrown by the `PreparedStatement` operation, and the `insertDAO` method would throw the exception to the calling method.

deleteDAO Method

The next method shown is the `deleteDAO` method used to delete a row from the database.

```
1.
2.    public void deleteDAO() throws SQLException {
3.
4.         deleteStmt.setString(1, getCategory() );
5.         deleteStmt.executeUpdate();
6.
7.    }
```

The row deleted is the row the corresponds to the value of the internal class members of the DAO, specifically the row that matches the primary key of the DAO class. In this case, the primary key is the `category` field and the value of the internal category member is used to set the category parameter for the `PreparedStatement` update operation as shown on line 4. On line 5, the `executeUpdate` method of the `PreparedStatement` class is called to perform the delete operation. Should the delete operation fail for any reason and throw an SQLException, the `deleteDAO` method would throw an exception to the calling method.

loadDAO Method

The `loadDAO` method is used to load the DAO with values from the database.

```
1.    public void loadDAO( String category )   throws SQLException
{
2.
3.    selectStmt.setString(1, category );
```

```
4.      ResultSet rs = selectStmt.executeQuery();
5.
6.    if ( rs.next() ) {
7.     setCategory( rs.getString(1) );
8.     setDescription( rs.getString(2) );
9.    }
10.
11.   }
12.
```

The method is overloaded to accept either a string representing the category record to load or a category Value Object. The method accepts a string representing the category. The prepared select statement used to perform the select accepts a single parameter, the category to select.

```
. . .
selectStmtStr = "select category, description from categories
where category = ?";
. . .
```

Once the category has been set with the setString method, the PreparedStatement.executeQuery method is called to retrieve the row and return the results in a ResultSet.

The first call to the ResultSet.next method will return false if no rows have been found. If rows have been returned, the first call to this method will return true and set the pointer to the first row, where the results can then be retrieved using the getXX methods

The ResultSet.next method is called in a conditional statement on line 6. If the statement tests true (indicating there are rows), the setCategory and setDescription methods are called on lines 7 and 8 to retrieve the column values from retrieved by the select statement. If no rows were found, the internal values are not set (and retain their previous values or the default class member values).

The overloaded version of the loadDAO method shown below takes a Value Object as a parameter and sets the DAO members to the corresponding values stored in the Value Object (not from the database). The calls to setCategory and setDescription on lines 3 and 4 retrieve the values from the Value Object and set the internal members of the DAO to those values.

```
1.    public void loadDAO( CategoriesVO vo ) {
2.
```

```
3.      setCategory( vo.getCategory() );
4.      setDescription( vo.getDescription() );
5.
6.    }
```

Using these methods, the database could be updated to values stored in a Value Object by executing a series of calls. The `loadDAO` method for the DAO could be called passing the Value Object to use as a parameter, thus setting the DAO to the values stored in the Value Object. The `updateDAO` method for the DAO could then be called to update the database with those current values.

Using Value Objects: The setVO Method

The `setVO` method is used to set a Value Object passed as a parameter to the current values stored in the DAO. The `set` methods of the Value Object are used on lines 3 and 4 to set the members of the Value Object to the members of the DAO.

```
1.
2.    public void setVO( CategoriesVO vo ) {
3.
4.    vo.setCategory( this.getCategory() );
5.    vo.setDescription( this.getDescription() );
6.
7.    }
```

Division of Responsibilities Revisited

Having the DAO return an entire record rather than making a large number of calls to retrieve each element of the data record individually represents a *coarse-grained* approach to data retrieval. This approach further defines the division of responsibilities for these data objects, making the DAO responsible for manipulating the database and leaving the responsibility for the fine-grained retrieval of data fields to the Value Object.

This approach provides even better performance improvements when using application servers with Enterprise JavaBeans (EJBs), where the DAO would be an Enterprise JavaBean (running on the business tier) and would require network communication via RMI to access any method in the EJB.

Where Is the getRecord Method?

Note that there is no explicit `getRecord` method in this DAO implementation. Since the client is expected to hold a reference to a Value Object, a combination of a call to the `loadDAO` method followed by a call to `setVO` method would provide the same results as a `getRecord` method. The code sample below provides an example.

```
...
CategoryDAO categoryDAO = new CategoryDAO();
CategoryVO categoryVO = new CategoryVO();
...

// load the DAO from the database for the "System" category
categoryDAO.loadDAO( "System");
// set our Value Object from the DAO
categoryDAO.setVO( categoryVO );
// use our Value Object
System.out.println( "Category: " + categoryVO.getCategory() + " -
" +
                              "Description: " +
catgoryVO.getDescription() );
...
```

Although these calls could be combined into a single `getRecord` method, this separation of responsibilities provides more flexibility and provides a clearer approach.

Producing a List of Records: The getCategoryList Method

The `getCategoryList` next method is used to populate a drop-down list box of categories on the `inputKB.jsp` page. The code in this method demonstrates the retrieval of a set of records by a DAO.

```
...
1.    public Collection getCategoryList() throws SQLException {
2.    Vector v = new Vector();
3.    CategoriesVO vo = null;
4.
5.    ResultSet rs = selectCategoryListStmt.executeQuery();
6.
7.    while ( rs.next() ) {
```

```
8.              vo = new CategoriesVO();
9.              vo.setCategory( rs.getString(1) );
10.             vo.setDescription( rs.getString(2) );
11.             v.add( vo );
12.     }
13.
14.    return v;
15.
16.    }
. . .
```

The `getCategoryList` method retrieves a list of categories based on the execution of the SQL statement that has been prepared in `createPreparedStatements` (`selectCategoryListStmt`). The SQL statement for this operation does not contain a filter statement and retrieves all categories in the database.

```
. . .
selectCategoryListStr = "select category, description from cate-
gories";
. . .
```

This method begins by creating a local `Vector` object and a reference to a `CategoryVO` object. The `PreparedStatement.executeQuery` method is then executed on line 5 and a `ResultSet` is returned. A `while` loop is used to iterate through this `ResultSet` starting on line 7. For each iteration of the loop, a category Value Object (`CategoryVO`) is created and populated with the contents of the `ResultSet` iteration on lines 9 and 10. The Value Object is then added to the `Vector` on line 11. At the conclusion of the loop, the reference to the `Vector` is returned by the method (where it is implicitly cast as a `Collection` interface).

DAO Constructor

The constructor for the DAO needs to instantiate and initialize the class members. These class members include a `DBUtil` class member, which is created at line 5. The `createPreparedStatements` method is called at line 8. Calling this statement on object creation provides some performance benefits, since the queries will be prepared and ready before the methods requiring them are called.

```
1.      ...
2.      public CategoriesDAO() {
3.
4.          // create db wrapper
5.          dbutil = new DBUtil();
6.
7.          // create SQL prepared statements
8.          createPreparedStatements();
9.
10.     }
11.
12.     }
13.
```

There is no need to load database drivers or create database connections within this code; that housekeeping is localized and performed in the DBUtil class methods, discussed later in the chapter. If the DAO were using a Value Object internally (an approach not used in this example) that Value Object would instantiated here.

Value Object

The Value Object design pattern encapsulates the data record, containing class members or attributes that reflect the fields of the data record. A set of get and set methods is declared in the class to get values from the class members and set the class members to specific values. Although technically the Value Object is intended to be immutable (i.e., its value should not change) in a system design where these objects are going to be used to send a record to be inserted or updated in a database, set methods are virtually a requirement. (The alternative would be declaring a constructor that received parameters for all the fields in the record, which could become tedious for large records.)

Although this object design corresponds to a single table in a relational database, there is no requirement that that be the case. In fact, its design should represent the business domain being modeled and not the normalized or denormalized relational structure of the database. The following example shows the category Value Object declared as the CategoryVO class. The class declaration declares several local members with private protection.

```
1.      package knowledgebase;
2.
3.      // categories table value object
4.      public class CategoriesVO {
```

```
5.
6.    private String category;
7.    private String description;
8.    ...
```

In the code listing below the `get` and `set` methods for the Value Object are declared. The `get` methods are used to retrieve the corresponding class members and the `set` methods are used to set the values of the class members. In this example, no special treatment of the class members is required. In other cases, it may be necessary to validate the data being used to set a class member by a `set` method, or to manipulate or massage the data being returned by a `get` method.

```
...
// getXXXX
public String getCategory() {
    return this.category;
}

public String getDescription() {
    return this.description;
}

public void setCategory( String category ) {

   this.category = category;

}

public void setDescription( String description ) {

   this.description = description;

}

}
```

Database Utility Class: DBUtil

All the DAOs in the sample application, including the `CategoryDAO` shown previously, make use of a database utility class—`DBUtil`. This utility class is used to encapsulate the specifics of database access and to provide a set of convenience methods for database interaction. In the code used for this sample application, the standard JDBC driver for PostgreSQL provides access to the database resource, but this could easily be modified to use some other database driver, a `DataSource` connection, or a database pooling access class such as `PoolMan`.

The `DBUtil` class contains a number of methods to perform the housekeeping needed to access a database, such as loading a database driver and creating the connection needed to access the database. These methods are intended to simplify the process of interacting with the database by localizing these decisions and lowering the coupling of the client code (the DAOs) to the actual database being used. Should it become necessary to change the database location, use a different database driver, or change the process of managing connections, this could be changed in a single location rather than in each DAO used in the system. Table 11.2 identifies the methods used in this class and provides a description of each method.

Table 11.2 DBUtil Class Methods

Method	Description
`public void loadDriver()`	Loads the database driver for the class. The driver is currently retrieved from a local class member.
`public void getConnected()`	Creates a connection to the database (as identified in the driver URL).
`public void createDBStatement()`	Creates the internal JDBC statement object used by the class.
`public PreparedStatement createPreparedStatement ( String stmt )`	Creates a prepared SQL statement using the string parameter.
`public ResultSet executePreparedStatement ( PreparedStatement pstmt )`	Executes the prepared statement passed as a parameter. This is executed with the expectation that the statement being executed will return results.
`public int executePreparedStmtUpd ( PreparedStatement pstmt )`	Executes a prepared statement that is passed as a parameter. The statement is expected to be an update statement and an integer value of the number of rows updated will be returned.
`public ResultSet executeDBQuery ( String query )`	Executes a query as contained in the string parameter and returns the results in a `ResultSet`.

`public ResultSet getdbResultSet()`	Returns the internal `ResultSet` currently being used.
`public String getdbDriverName()`	Returns the name of the driver currently being used.
`public Connection getdbConnection()`	Returns the connection currently being used.
`public String getDbURL()`	Returns the database connection URL currently being used.
`public Statement getdbStatement()`	Returns the internal JDBC statement currently being used.
`public void setdbDriverName` `( String dbDN )`	Sets the database driver to be used by the object (should then call `loadDriver` and `getConnected` to establish the new connection).
`public void setOutputStream` `( PrintStream Out )`	Sets the output `PrintStream` for the class.
`public void setdbURL` `( String dbURL )`	Sets the database connection URL based on the string parameter passed.

The code behind the DBUtil class follows.

```
1. package db;
2.
3. import java.sql.*;
4. import java.io.*;
5. import java.util.*;
6.
7. public class DBUtil {
8.
9. String dbURL =
10. "jdbc:postgresql://localhost:5432/knowledgebase;user=puser;
password=puser";
11. String     dbDriverName = "org.postgresql.Driver";
12.
13. Connection dbConnection = null;
14. ResultSet  dbResultSet  = null;
15. Statement  dbStatement  = null;
```

```
16.
17. boolean driverLoaded      = false;
18. boolean Connected         = false;
19. boolean StatementCreated  = false;
20.
```

Imports and Class Member Declarations

The DBUtil class imports a number of packages to provide name space access to collections, JDBC methods, and java.io facilities. Following these import statements, a number of class members are declared. A database connection URL and a database driver name string are declared on lines 9 and 11, respectively, and are then initialized to the values needed for this application.

Required JDBC class references are declared on lines 13, 14, and 15 and will be used throughout the class. Following these declarations, several boolean flags are declared on lines 17, 18, and 19. These flags are used to determine whether or not the driver is currently loaded and whether or not the database connection has been established. Use of these flags in this convenience class is intended to provide some flexibility in use of the class. As the code will demonstrate, if the value of a particular flag is false, for example the database connection is not currently established, the getConnection method will be called to create the connection.

loadDriver and getConnected Methods

The loadDriver method shown below simply encapsulates the Class.forName call used to load the database driver. The driver name parameter provided to the forName method is the dbDriverName class member, which has been initialized to the name of the database driver to load, in this example, to the value "org.postgresql.Driver".

```
1.    public void loadDriver()  throws Exception {
2.         Class.forName( dbDriverName);
3.    }
4.
5.
```

```
6.     public void getConnected()   throws Exception {
7.
8.         if ( !driverLoaded ) {
9.         loadDriver();
10.        driverLoaded = true;
11.         }
12.
13.         dbConnection = DriverManager.getConnection( dbURL );
14.         Connected = true;
15.
16.    }
17.
```

The getConnected method that follows is used to obtain a database connection if one does not already exist. The code in this method first examines the driverLoaded flag. If the driver has not been loaded, the loadDriver method is called to load the driver and the driverLoaded flag is set to true. Once we are certain that the database driver has been loaded, we can create the database connection, which is done on line 13. On line 14 the Connected flag is set to true.

The createDBStatement method is used to create the JDBC Statement object used internally. The method first checks to determine whether or not a connection has been established. If there is no connection, the getConnected method is called. Once we are sure that the connection has been created, the createStatement method is called using the dbConnection member (a JDBC Connection reference) to create the statement (a JDBC statement reference).

```
public void createDBStatement() throws Exception {

    if ( !Connected )
        getConnected();

    dbStatement   = dbConnection.createStatement();

}
```

createPreparedStatement Method

The createPreparedStatement method is used to build a JDBC PreparedStatement from a string passed into the method. As with other methods in this class, it is tolerant of the lack of database connection and will create a connection if one does not exist (shown on lines 3 and 4). Once the connection has been made, the prepareStatement method of the JDBC Connection class is called to create the PreparedStatement object, which is then returned from the method. If this process throws an SQLException, it is in turn thrown to the calling method.

```
1.    public PreparedStatement createPreparedStatement( String
stmt ) throws Exception {
2.
3.            if ( !Connected )
4.                getConnected();
5.            return dbConnection.prepareStatement( stmt );
6.
7.    }
8.
```

executePreparedStatement and executePreparedStmtUpd Methods

The executePreparedStatement method shown below executes the PreparedStatement passed as a parameter. This method first checks to see if a database connection exists, and if it does not exists, it calls the getConnected method to create the database connection. Once the method code is sure that a connection exists, it calls the PreparedStatement.executeQuery method to execute the statement and returns the ResultSet as a return parameter.

The executePreparedStmtUpd performs a similar operation except that it expects the query being executed to be an update statement. Like the executePreparedStatement method, it takes a single parameter which is a PreparedStatement. If a connection to the database does not exists, it creates one and then executes the PreparedStatement update statement using the PreparedStatement.executeUpdate method and returns the integer result.

```
public ResultSet executePreparedStatement( PreparedStatement
pstmt ) throws Exception {

    if ( !Connected )
        getConnected();
    return pstmt.executeQuery();
```

```
}

public int executePreparedStmtUpd( PreparedStatement pstmt )
throws Exception{

    if ( !Connected )
        getConnected();
    return pstmt.executeUpdate();

}
```

executeDBQuery Methods

The executeDBQuery method shown in listing below executes a query string passed as a parameter and returns a ResultSet for the string executed. As with the other convenience methods, this method first checks to see that a connection exists, and if it does not exist, it calls getConnected to obtain a connection. The method then checks to determine whether or not the JDBC statement has been created for the instance. If the statement has not been created, it calls createDBStatement at line 9 to create the Statement object and then sets the statementCreated flag to true on line 10. At this point the method is ready to execute the query and at line 14 it executes the JDBC Statement.executeDBQuery method and stores the ResultSet reference returned in the dbResultSet class member. At line 16 it returns this same reference to the calling method.

```
1.    public ResultSet executeDBQuery( String query ) throws
Exception {
2.
3.        // make sure we are ready to do this
4.
5.        if ( !Connected )
6.    getConnected();
7.
8.        if ( !StatementCreated ) {
9.    createDBStatement();
10.        StatementCreated = true;
11.        }
12.
13.        // execute query
14.        dbResultSet    = dbStatement.executeQuery( query );
15.
```

```
16.          return dbResultSet;
17.
18.    }
19.
```

executeUpdDBQuery Method

The executeUpdDBQuery method shown below executes a database query passed in as a string parameter and returns an integer corresponding to the number of rows that have been updated by the method. This method also checks to determine whether or not we are connected to the database, and if not, calls getConnected to obtain the connection on lines. It performs the same function with the createDBStatement method, checking to see if the statement exists, and if not, creating the DB statement. Once everything is ready, the method calls the JDBC Statement.executeUpdate method to perform the update contained in the query that has been passed in. The integer result of this operation, which indicates the number of rows updated, is returned by the method.

```
1.    public int executeUpdDBQuery( String query ) throws
Exception {
2.
3.        // make sure we are ready to do this
4.         if ( !Connected )
5.     getConnected();
6.
7.         if ( !StatementCreated ) {
8.     createDBStatement();
9.     StatementCreated = true;
10.        }
11.
12.        // execute query
13.        int retVal   = dbStatement.executeUpdate( query );
14.
15.        // return number of rows updated
16.         return retVal;
17.
18.    }
19.
```

Get and Set Methods

A number of `get` methods are used in the DBUtil class to return the values of class members, essentially information about how the DBUtil object is being used and to allow use of the JDBC connection or JDBC Statement independent of the DBUtil class. These methods are shown below.

```
// Bean methods
public ResultSet getdbResultSet() {
     return dbResultSet;
}

public String getdbDriverName() {
     return dbDriverName;
}

public Connection getdbConnection() {
     return dbConnection;
}

public String getDbURL() {
     return dbURL;
}

public Statement getdbStatement() {
     return dbStatement;
}
```

Two `set` methods are used to set various members of the DBUtil class. A setdbDriver method is a public method available to set the database driver name. This method takes a string parameter for the name of the database driver and sets the internal member dbDriverName to this value on line 2. On line 3 the driverLoaded flag is set to false, which will force the driver to be loaded the next time a database operation is performed.

The setdbURL method can be used to set the URL or the connection string for the database connection. This method takes a string parameter for the database URL as shown on line 6. On line 7 the local member dbURL is set to the value of the parameter, and on line 8 the Connected flag is set to false to force the database connection to be remade the next time a database operation is attempted.

```
1.    public void setdbDriverName ( String dbDN ) {
2.    this.dbDriverName = dbDN;
```

```
3.        driverLoaded = false; // force new driver load
4.        }
5.
6.        public void setdbURL ( String dbURL ) {
7.        this.dbURL = dbURL;
8.        Connected = false; // force new connection
9.        }
10.
11.       } // end class
12.
```

Complex DAO: Knowledge_baseDAO

The CategoryDAO class shown previously was a simple, direct example of a Data Access Object. The category table contains only two columns, and inserts, updates, and deletes are simple database operations. The knowledge_base table, however, is more complex, containing a larger number of columns and additional queries to support filtered select statements (for the pickKB.jsp page).

A number of the methods in this class are very similar to the methods within the CategoryDAO class, so they won't be covered in detail in these sections, but they will be shown for completeness (and to avoid viewing fragmented pieces of code that don't seem to go together).

The Knowledge_baseDAO class is responsible for managing the database operations for the knowledge_base table. This involves not only simple select, insert, update, and delete operations with the table, but also handling queries filtered on keywords that have been stored with the message entries (in the base_keys table). These filtered operations require the passing of collections for the filter criteria and returning iterators or collections containing the results of the query. The getAll and getFiltered methods provide examples of this type of operation. We examine the Knowledge_baseDAO class next.

The Knowledge_baseDAO class shown below performs the same imports as the CategoryDAO class, providing the local namespace for a number of packages used in the class. These imports are followed by the declaration of class members on lines 12 through 21 to hold the elements of the knowledge_base table. On lines 27 through 40 class members are declared to hold the prepared statements used to provide the database operations for the DAO.

```
1.      package knowledgebase;
2.
3.      import javax.servlet.*;
4.      import java.util.*;
5.      import java.sql.*;
6.
7.      import db.*;
8.
9.      public class Knowledge_baseDAO {
10.
11.     // private members
12.     private int doc_key;
13.     private String doc_name;
14.     private String doc_location;
15.     private String post_user;
16.     private int link_doc;
17.     private int level;
18.     private String entry_date; // date
19.     private String date_submitted; // date
20.     private String category;
21.     private int base_doc_key;
22.
23.     // wraps JDBC methods
24.     DBUtil dbutil;
25.
26.     // string to hold SQL statements
27.     private String insertStmtStr;
28.     private String updateStmtStr;
29.     private String deleteStmtStr;
30.     private String selectStmtStr;
31.     private String selectAllStmtStr;
32.     private String selectFilterStmtStr;
33.
34.     // Prepared SQL statements
35.     PreparedStatement insertStmt;
36.     PreparedStatement updateStmt;
37.     PreparedStatement deleteStmt;
38.     PreparedStatement selectStmt;
39.     PreparedStatement selectAllStmt;
40.     PreparedStatement selectFilterStmt;
41.
```

Get Methods

The next code listing shows the `get` methods for the `Knowledge_baseDAO` class on lines 2 through 40. These methods do little more than return the DAO member their name implies. (Although these members are declared public, they are used primarily by local methods. Whenever possible, Value Objects are passed to and returned from the DAO, resulting in a cleaner, more convenient approach to managing these objects.)

```
1.    // getXXXX methods
2.    public int getDoc_key() {
3.       return doc_key;
4.    }
5.
6.    public String getDoc_name(){
7.       return doc_name;
8.    }
9.
10.
11.   public int getBase_doc_key() {
12.          return this.base_doc_key;
13.   }
14.
15.   public int getLink_doc() {
16.        return this.link_doc;
17.   }
18.
19.   public String getDoc_location() {
20.      return doc_location;
21.   }
22.
23.   public String getPost_user() {
24.     return post_user;
25.   }
26.   public int getLevel() {
27.        return level;
28.   }
29.
30.   public String getEntry_date() {
31.        return entry_date;
32.   }
33.
34.   public String getDate_submitted() {
35.          return this.date_submitted;
```

```
36.    }
37.
38.    public String getCategory() {
39.        return category;
40.    }
41.
```

Set Methods

The code listing that follows shows the set methods for the DAO on lines 2 through 42. As the names imply, these methods are responsible for setting the values of the internal class members of the Knowledge_baseDAO class. Although they are declared public, they are used primarily by the local methods of the class to work with Value Objects corresponding to the schema of the knowledge_base table.

```
1.
2.     // set methods
3.     public void setDoc_name( String doc_name ) {
4.         this.doc_name = doc_name;
5.     }
6.
7.     public void setDoc_key( int doc_key ) {
8.         this.doc_key = doc_key;
9.     }
10.
11.    public void setDoc_location( String doc_location ) {
12.        this.doc_location = doc_location;
13.    }
14.
15.    public void setPost_user( String post_user ) {
16.        this.post_user = post_user;
17.    }
18.
19.    public void setLevel( int level ) {
20.        this.level = level;
21.    }
22.
23.    public void setLink_doc( int link_doc ) {
24.        this.link_doc = link_doc;
25.    }
26.
27.    public void setBase_doc_key( int base_doc_key ) {
```

```
28.            this.base_doc_key = base_doc_key;
29.    }
30.
31.    public void setEntry_date( String entry_date ) {
32.          this.entry_date = entry_date;
33.    }
34.
35.    public void setDate_submitted( String date_submitted ) {
36.        this.date_submitted = date_submitted;
37.    }
38.
39.    public void setCategory( String category ) {
40.          this.category = category;
41.    }
42.
```

createPreparedStatement Method

Following the `get` and `set` methods in the `Knowledge_baseDAO` class
file, we encounter a number of the general-purpose methods of the class,
which are used to perform the database update operations the DAO must perform. The first of these we examine is the `createPreparedStatement`
method. This method is responsible for creating the prepared statements that
will be used to execute the queries for the DAO. The structure of the method
is to create the query string (storing the string in a local class member in case
it   needs   to   be   used   again)   and   then   calling
`DBUtil.createPreparedStatement` to prepare the statement and
return the result, a JDBC `PreparedStatement` object reference that will
be stored in a class member and used by the other methods.

```
1.    public void createPreparedStatements( ) throws Exception {
2.
3.    try {
4.        insertStmtStr = "insert into knowledge_base " +
5.                        "
(doc_key,doc_name,category,post_user,doc_location,link_doc,
level, base_doc_key, entry_date, date_submitted) values " +
6.                        " ( ?,      ?,         ?,          ?,
?,          ?,         ?,      ?,                 ?,           ? ) "
;
7.
```

```
8.        insertStmt = dbutil.createPreparedStatement(
insertStmtStr );
9.
10.       updateStmtStr = "update knowledge_base " +
11.                  " set doc_name = ?, " +
12.            "  doc_location = ?, " +
13.            "  category = ?, "   +
14.            "  post_user = ?, "  +
15.            "  level = ?, "   +
16.            "  link_doc = ?, "   +
17.            "  entry_date = ? "   +
18.               "  where doc_key = ? "   ;
19.
20.       updateStmt = dbutil.createPreparedStatement(
updateStmtStr );
21.
22.       deleteStmtStr = "delete from knowledge_base " +
23.               "       where doc_key = ?" ;
24.
25.       deleteStmt = dbutil.createPreparedStatement(
deleteStmtStr );
26.
27.       selectStmtStr = "select
doc_key,doc_name,category,post_user,doc_location,link_doc, " +
28.                  " base_doc_key,entry_date, date_sub-
mitted,level " +
29.                  " from knowledge_base " +
30.                  " where doc_key = ? ";
31.
32.     selectStmt = dbutil.createPreparedStatement(
selectStmtStr );
33.
34.       selectAllStmtStr = "select
doc_key,doc_name,category,post_user,doc_location,link_doc, " +
35.                  " base_doc_key,entry_date, date_sub-
mitted,level " +
36.                  " from knowledge_base " +
37.                  " order by doc_key, base_doc_key,
date_submitted, entry_date";
38.
39.       selectAllStmt = dbutil.createPreparedStatement(
selectAllStmtStr );
40.
41.       selectFilterStmtStr = " select " +
```

```
42.        " doc_key, doc_name,category, post_user, doc_location,
link_doc, " +
43.        " base_doc_key,entry_date, date_submitted, level " +
44.        " from knowledge_base " +
45.        " where base_doc_key in (" +
46.        " select knowledge_base.doc_key " +
47.        " from knowledge_base, base_keys   " +
48.        " where keyword in (?,?,?,?) and "   +
49.        " knowledge_base.doc_key = base_keys.doc_key ) " +
50.        " union "   +   // union query
51.
52.        " select "   +
53.        " knowledge_base.doc_key, doc_name,category, post_user,
doc_location, link_doc, " +
54.        " base_doc_key,entry_date, date_submitted, level " +
55.        " from knowledge_base, base_keys   " +
56.        " where keyword in (?,?,?,?) and " +
57.        " knowledge_base.doc_key = base_keys.doc_key " +
58.        " order by knowledge_base.doc_key, base_doc_key,
date_submitted, entry_date ";
59.
60.      selectFilterStmt = dbutil.createPreparedStatement(
selectFilterStmtStr );
61.
62.    }
63.
64.    catch (SQLException e) {
65.
66.      throw new Exception("SQLException thrown in
createPreparedStatements(): " + e.getMessage() );
67.
68.    }
69.    catch (Exception e)   {
70.
71.      throw new Exception("Exception thrown in
createPreparedStatements(): " + e.getMessage() );
72.
73.    }
74.
75.    }
76.
```

In the belief that a well-phrased nonprocedural SQL statement can replace a significant portion of procedural Java language code, a complex query is phrased on lines 41 through 57. The purpose of this query is to return the results that filter on an SQL `select` statement for the `base_keys` table to get records with the correct keywords and join those results with corresponding rows from the `knowledge_base` table.

This query is an SQL `union` of two queries. One query retrieves all base document keys for the keywords being used and a second query retrieves all document keys for documents that match the keywords being used. This resulting `union` query is sorted as document key, base document key, date submitted, and date last modified. Because a union query is used, duplicates will be filtered out of the query. This query is used to produce the filtered listing produced by the `pickKB.jsp` page (see Chapter 10).

Managing Self-Incrementing Keys: The insertDAO Method

The next method we encounter in the in the `Knowledge_baseDAO` class is the `insertDAO` method, which follows.

```
1.    . . .
2.    public int insertDAO( ) throws SQLException, Exception {
3.
4.    int doc_key = 0;
5.
6.    // set elements
7.    // set with 'sequence' on insert
8.    doc_key = generateDoc_key();
9.    insertStmt.setInt(1, doc_key );
10.   insertStmt.setString(2, getDoc_name() );
11.   insertStmt.setString(3, getCategory() );
12.   insertStmt.setString(4, getPost_user() );
13.   insertStmt.setString(5, getDoc_location() );
14.   insertStmt.setInt(6, getLink_doc() );
15.   insertStmt.setInt(7, getLevel() );
16.   insertStmt.setInt(8, getBase_doc_key() );
17.   insertStmt.setString(9, getEntry_date() );
18.   insertStmt.setString(10, getDate_submitted() );
19.
20.   int retval = insertStmt.executeUpdate();
21.
22.   return doc_key;
23.
24.   }
25.   . . .
```

26.

This listing performs an insert into the `knowledge_base` table, but unlike the previous insert operation into the `categories` table, this insert operation must manage a self-incrementing primary key, an integer column that is guaranteed to be a unique identifier for the table. Using the PostgreSQL database, a database `sequence` is used to produce this number. This `sequence` is a database object that retains an integer counter that can be queried and incremented to return a distinct integer number.

Since the `knowledge_base` table represents a parent table for a number of children tables (related records should not appear in these tables unless there is a corresponding record in this table), the primary key of this table, the `doc_key`, must be communicated to the method controlling the insert operation, the `insertKBRecs` method in the `KnowledgeBaseFacade` class, and then used to perform the insert of those records. Therefore, the `insertDAO` method must not only retrieve this unique integer and use it for the database insert operation, but must return this number to the calling method controlling the insert of the parent and child tables for the message.

This method begins by creating a local integer variable for the `doc_key` and initializing it to zero on line 4. A call is then made to the `Knowledge_baseDAO.generateDoc_key` method to generate the integer by reading from the sequence shown later in the section "`generateDoc_Key` Method." This key is then used to provide the values for the insert statement query shown below.

```
. . .
    insertStmtStr = "insert into knowledge_base " +
 " (doc_key,doc_name,category,post_user,doc_location,link_doc,
level, base_doc_key, entry_date, date_submitted) values " +
 " ( ?, ?, ?, ?, ?, ?, ?, ?, ?, ? ) "  ;
. . .
```

On line 9 of the listing, the document key (`doc_key`) that has been returned by the `generateDoc_key` method is used to set the document key parameter to be inserted into the table using the prepared insert statement (`insertStmt`). The remaining `set` statements on lines 10 through 18 are used to set the other parameters in the prepared insert statement.

Once all the parameters in the prepared statement have been set, the `PreparedStatement.executeUpdate` method is called at line 20. This method returns an integer value for the number of rows updated, which is ignored by this method. On line 22, the value of the document key used for the insert is returned by the method (to be used for the insert of values into the child tables of the `knowledge_base` table).

updateDAO Method

The `updateDAO` method is used to perform updates on the knowledge_base table.

```
1.     ...
2.     public void updateDAO( ) throws SQLException {
3.     // set elements
4.     updateStmt.setString(1, getDoc_name() );
5.     updateStmt.setString(2, getDoc_location() );
6.     updateStmt.setString(3, getCategory() );
7.     updateStmt.setString(4, getPost_user() );
8.     updateStmt.setInt(5, getLevel() );
9.     updateStmt.setInt(6, getLink_doc() );
10.    updateStmt.setString(7, getEntry_date() );
11.    updateStmt.setInt(8, getDoc_key() );
12.
13.    int retval = updateStmt.executeUpdate();
14.
15.    }
16.
```

This method uses the prepared statement shown below to update the database.

```
...
updateStmtStr = "update knowledge_base " +
            " set doc_name = ?, " +
        "   doc_location = ?, " +
        "   category = ?, "   +
        "   post_user = ?, "   +
          "   level = ?, "   +
          "   link_doc = ?, "   +
          "   entry_date = ? "   +
              "   where doc_key = ? "   ;
...
```

All columns except the primary key column (`doc_key`) can be be updated and must be set using the `PreparedStatement` set methods. These set methods are used on lines 4 through 11 to set the parameters using the internal values of the DAO as returned by the various `get` methods in the `Knowledge_baseDAO` class we are reviewing. On line 13, the `PreparedStatement.executeUpdate` method is called to perform the update operation. This method returns an integer for the number of rows updated, which is ignored by the updateDAO method. Any exception returned by the updateDAO method is thrown to the calling method.

deleteDAO Method

The next method in our journey through the Knowledge_baseDAO class is the deleteDAO method, shown below.

```
1.
2.    public void deleteDAO( ) throws SQLException {
3.
4.    deleteStmt.setInt(1, getDoc_key() );
5.
6.    int retval = deleteStmt.executeUpdate();
7.
8.    }
```

As the name implies, this method is responsible for the deletion of a knowledge base record and uses the following query statement:

. . .

```
deleteStmtStr = "delete from knowledge_base " +
              "            where doc_key = ?" ;
```

. . .

This prepared statement requires only one parameter to be set, which is set on line 4 of the code listing. On line 6 the PreparedStatement.executeUpdate method is called and returns an integer value representing the number of rows updated. As with the previous update examples, the value returned from the executeUpdate method is ignored and any exception thrown by the method is in turn thrown to the calling method, where it must be handled or thrown to yet another method.

loadDAO Method

The next method in the Knowledge_baseDAO class is the loadDAO method, a method responsible for loading the DAO based using the value of the parameter passed into the method. This method is overloaded in this class. One version loads the DAO from the database using the primary key parameter passed into the method, an integer representing the document key. The other version loads the DAO based on a Value Object passed into the method.

The version of the `loadDAO` method shown below loads the DAO from the database using the integer value passed into the method, a value representing a primary key for the `knowledge_base` table.

```
1.
2.     public void loadDAO( int doc_key ) throws Exception {
3.
4.     try {
5.
6.     selectStmt.setInt(1, doc_key );
7.     ResultSet rs = selectStmt.executeQuery();
8.
9.     if ( rs.next() )   {
10.
11.        setDoc_key( rs.getInt(1) );
12.        setDoc_name( rs.getString(2) );
13.        setCategory( rs.getString(3) );
14.        setPost_user( rs.getString(4) );
15.        setDoc_location( rs.getString(5) );
16.        setLink_doc( rs.getInt(6) );
17.        setBase_doc_key( rs.getInt(7) );
18.        setEntry_date( rs.getString(8) );
19.        setDate_submitted( rs.getString(9) );
20.        setLevel( rs.getInt(10) );
21.
22.    }
23.
24.    }
25.    catch (SQLException e) {
26.        System.out.println("SQLException thrown in
Knowlege_baseDAO.loadDAO(): " + e.getMessage() );
27.        throw new Exception( "Exception in
Knowlege_baseDAO.loadDAO(): " + e.getMessage() );
28.    }
29.
30.    }
```

The integervalue is used to set the single parameter in the prepared statement shown below.

```
. . .
    selectStmtStr = "select
doc_key,doc_name,category,post_user,doc_location,link_doc, " +
```

```
                    " base_doc_key,entry_date,
date_submitted,level " +
                    " from knowledge_base " +
                    " where doc_key = ? ";
```

. . .

This parameter is set on line 6 using the `PreparedStatement.setInt` method and the prepared statement is executed on the line 7 returning a `ResultSet` response.

The call to `ResultSet.next` on line 9 will return a `boolean` true if there are rows to be traversed in the `ResultSet`, and false if there are none, so the body of the `if` statement will be executed only if there is in fact a row to be processed. Since this method that asserts there is only one row to be found for the primary key passed (as should be the case), this assertion should not be a problem. A series of `set` methods for the `Knowledge_baseDAO` class are called on lines 11 through 20, which use calls to appropriate `ResultSet get` methods for the `ResultSet` returned by the `executeQuery` call on line 7.

Should the query fail to return any rows, the body of the `if` statement would not be executed and the DAO members would not be set. Although this may appear to be a problem, the manner in which this method is used precludes the failure of a select. This method is called from the `inputKB.jsp` page, which is in turn called from the `pickKB.jsp`. The `pickKB.jsp` page lists either all available messages or messages that have been filtered. In either case, the page lists only messages currently in the database, and the links that are provided with the listing contain references to the primary key for the listed item, so only valid primary keys are listed. This means that when this method is called within the message system application, we can assert that only valid primary keys will be used and we should never have a case where the query execution returns no rows. In the case that an attempt to execute the query generates an exception, a `catch` statement traps the exception, displays an error message, and throws an exception to the calling method.

Overloaded loadDAO Method

Since our design goal is to have the DAOs work with Value Objects, we would like the DAO to be able to accept a Value Object as a parameter and to set the internal parameters using the values in these value objects. The `loadDAO` method shown below accepts a Value Object as a parameter and then sets the class members of the DAO to those values. The operation of this method is fairly straightforward, with a series of `set` methods on lines 4 through 13 being used to set the values of the local members to the values of the Value

Object members for the Value Object passed in as a parameter. The Value
Object get methods are used to retrieve the values of that object.

```
1.
2.    public void loadDAO( Knowledge_baseVO knowledge_base ) {
3.
4.    setDoc_key( knowledge_base.getDoc_key() );
5.    setDoc_name( knowledge_base.getDoc_name() );
6.    setCategory( knowledge_base.getCategory() );
7.    setPost_user( knowledge_base.getPost_user() );
8.    setDoc_location( knowledge_base.getDoc_location() );
9.    setLink_doc( knowledge_base.getLink_doc() );
10.   setBase_doc_key( knowledge_base.getBase_doc_key() );
11.   setLevel( knowledge_base.getLevel() );
12.   setEntry_date( knowledge_base.getEntry_date() );
13.   setDate_submitted( knowledge_base.getDate_submitted() );
14.
15.   }
```

setVO Method

In continuing with our goal to use Value Objects and DAOs together, the next
method we examine, the setVO method, is used to set the value of a value
object to the internal values (the values of the class members) of the DAO as
shown below.

```
16.   // set ValueObject members from DAO
17.   public void setVO( Knowledge_baseVO vo ) throws Exception {
18.
19.   vo.setDoc_key( this.getDoc_key() );
20.   vo.setDoc_name( this.getDoc_name() );
21.   vo.setCategory( this.getCategory() );
22.   vo.setPost_user( this.getPost_user() );
23.   vo.setDoc_location( this.getDoc_location() );
24.   vo.setLink_doc( this.getLink_doc() );
25.   vo.setLevel( this.getLevel() );
26.   vo.setBase_doc_key( this.getBase_doc_key() );
27.   vo.setEntry_date( this.getEntry_date() );
28.   vo.setDate_submitted( this.getDate_submitted() );
29.
30.   }
31.
```

This method receives a Value Object parameter for a Knowledge_baseVO, a Value Object that reflects the elements of the knowledge_base table. A series of set methods are called for the Value Object on lines 19 through 28 using arguments that make calls to the get methods of the DAO to retrieve the values of the internal members of the DAO.

Database Access: Retrieving Multiple Rows with the getAll Method

The next method we examine is the getAll method, used to retrieve all knowledge_base records currently in the database. This method demonstrates a technique for retrieving multiple rows from the database and returning the results and is shown below.

```
1.
2.     // retrieve a collection of all knowledge_base record
ValueObjects
3.
4.     Iterator getAll() throws Exception {
5.     Vector v = new Vector();
6.
7.     try {
8.
9.     ResultSet rs = selectAllStmt.executeQuery();
10.
11.    while ( rs.next() ) {
12.
13.        Knowledge_baseVO vo = new Knowledge_baseVO();
14.
15.        vo.setDoc_key( rs.getInt(1) );
16.        vo.setDoc_name( rs.getString(2) );
17.        vo.setCategory( rs.getString(3) );
18.        vo.setPost_user( rs.getString(4) );
19.        vo.setDoc_location( rs.getString(5) );
20.        vo.setLink_doc( rs.getInt(6) );
21.        vo.setBase_doc_key( rs.getInt(7) );
22.        vo.setEntry_date( rs.getString(8) );
23.        vo.setDate_submitted( rs.getString(9) );
24.        vo.setLevel( rs.getInt(10) );
25.
26.        v.add( vo ) ;
```

```
27.
28.      }
29.
30.    }
31.    catch (SQLException e) {
32.        throw new Exception("SQLException caught in
knowledge_baseDAO.getAll(): " + e.getMessage() );
33.    }
34.
35.    // return the iterator for this collection
36.    return v.iterator();
37.
38.    }
39.
```

The getAll method will return an Iterator, a convenient Java object for moving through a set of object references. The object references to be returned will be references to Knowledge_baseVO objects, Value Objects that reflect the columns of the knowledge_base table. The method first creates a Vector to be used to store the results and then executes a PreparedStatement query on line 9 that contains no filter clause and will retrieve all rows from the database. The query executed on this line is shown below.

```
...
selectAllStmtStr = "select
doc_key,doc_name,category,post_user,doc_location,link_doc, " +
                    " base_doc_key,entry_date,
date_submitted,level " +
                    " from knowledge_base " +
                    " order by doc_key, base_doc_key, date_sub-
mitted, entry_date";
...
```

A while loop is started at line 11 to step through the results of the query. This loop creates a new Knowledge_baseVO Value Object on each iteration and then stores the values of the current row into this Value Object using the statements executed on lines 15 through 24. On line 26, a reference to the Value Object that has just been created and populated is added to the Vector object.

A catch clause on line 31 catches any exceptions that may be thrown and throws an exception to the calling method, providing a message that describes where the error occurred. The Iterator for the Vector that contains the

Value Object references is generated on line 36 with a call to the `iterator` method of the `Vector` class and is returned to the calling method.

generateDoc_key Method

The `generateDoc_key` method shown below is used to generate the unique integer value used to generate the document key (doc_key) for the `knowledge_message` table. This method uses the `DBUtil.executeDBQuery` method to execute a query string passed to the method. The query string used is hardcoded in this method to retrieve the output of the database function `nextval` for the argument `doc_key` on line 6. In the PostgreSQL database used with this application, this instructs the database engine to retrieve the next value from the `doc_key` sequence and to increment the `sequence` by one at the same time. Since this will be treated as a singleton transaction by the database, no other user will be able to retrieve that sequence value at the same time and we can be assured that we are retrieving a unique value.

```
1.
2.     private int generateDoc_key() throws Exception {
3.
4.     try {
5.
6.     ResultSet rs = dbutil.executeDBQuery( "select
nextval('doc_key')" );
7.     if ( rs.next() )
8.         return rs.getInt(1);
9.     else
10.        return 0;
11.    }
12.    catch (SQLException e) {
13.
14.        throw new Exception( "Error in doc_key generation: " +
e );
15.
16.    }
17.
18.    }
19.
```

Execution of the query will return a `ResultSet`, which we assert will retrieve only a single row. The `if` statement on line 7 tests the `ResultSet` for rows and if the `ResultSet` has rows, the value of the first and only column in that row, the unique integer value, is returned. If the `ResultSet` has not returned any rows, a 0 is returned, indicating that an error has occurred.

Note that the SQL statement to retrieve the self-incrementing value would need to be changed in the event that another database were used. Isolating this platform specific code as much as possible as was done in this example makes the process of managing this code that much easier.

getFilteredList Method

We will now look at the `getFilteredList` method which accepts a collection that contains the query criteria for the filtered list. This filtered list uses a set of keywords associated with the message to create and execute a query against the database for messages that use those keywords. Currently, this application is limited to four keywords per search.

This method begins by creating a new `Vector` which will be used within the method to accumulate the list of rows that match the filter criteria. The `criteria` parameter passed into the method is a `Collection`, so the `Iterator` method is available to create an `iterator` at line 7 and to use this object to step through the criteria values. Since a union query is used to produce the filtered list and the criteria values appear in the `where` clause for both queries, the same `Iterator` must be traversed twice, once at line 11 and again at line 17.

Once the query has been prepared it is executed at line 21 and the `ResultSet` obtained is used to control a loop on line 23. Within this loop a Value Object is created on each iteration (on line 25) of type `Knowledge_baseVO` and the values that are returned in the `ResultSet` row are stored in the Value Object. The Value Object reference is then stored in the `Vector` that was created at the start of the method (on line 3). This loop is used to capture the results for each row and store them in the value object on lines 27 through 36. On line 38 the Value Object itself is added to the `Vector`.

Several `catch` blocks are placed on lines 47 through 50 to catch any existing exceptions and to throw new exceptions. If all is well and no exceptions have been thrown, the `Vector` we have populated is used to produce an `Iterator`, which is returned by the method at line 53.

```
1.
2.    Iterator getFilteredList( Collection criteria ) throws
Exception {
3.    Vector v = new Vector();
4.
```

```
5.    try {
6.
7.    Iterator i = criteria.iterator();
8.    int n = 1;
9.    // currently, only store four search keywords
10.   // since using a Union statement with two queries we need
to set these keywords twice
11.   for ( n = 1; n < 5 && i.hasNext(); n++ )   {
12.        selectFilterStmt.setString( n, (String) i.next() );
13.          }
14.
15.   // set the next 4
16.   i = criteria.iterator();
17.   for ( n = 1; n < 5 && i.hasNext(); n++ )   {
18.        selectFilterStmt.setString( n + 4, (String) i.next()
);
19.          }
20.
21.   ResultSet rs = selectFilterStmt.executeQuery();
22.
23.   while ( rs.next() ) {
24.
25.       Knowledge_baseVO vo = new Knowledge_baseVO();
26.
27.       vo.setDoc_key( rs.getInt(1) );
28.       vo.setDoc_name( rs.getString(2) );
29.       vo.setCategory( rs.getString(3) );
30.       vo.setPost_user( rs.getString(4) );
31.       vo.setDoc_location( rs.getString(5) );
32.      vo.setLink_doc( rs.getInt(6) );
33.       vo.setBase_doc_key( rs.getInt(7) );
34.       vo.setEntry_date( rs.getString(8) );
35.       vo.setDate_submitted( rs.getString(9) );
36.       vo.setLevel( rs.getInt(10) );
37.
38.       v.add( vo ) ;
39.
40.     }
41.
42.     }
43.   catch (SQLException e) {
```

```
44.      System.out.println("SQLException caught in
knowledge_baseDAO.getFilteredList): " + e );
45.      throw new Exception("SQLException caught in
knowledge_baseDAO.getFilteredList(): " + e );
46.    }
47.    catch (Exception e ) {
48.      System.out.println("Exception caught in
knowledge_baseDAO.getFilteredList(): " + e );
49.      throw new Exception( "Exception caught in
knowledge_baseDAO.getFilteredList(): " + e );
50.    }
51.
52.    // return the iterator for this collection
53.    return v.iterator();
54.
55.    }
56.
```

Constructor for the Knowledge_baseDAO Class

Finally, we see the constructor for the Knowledge_baseDAO class, shown below. This constructor needs to perform some minor housekeeping to get the object ready for use. It needs to create an instance of the database utility class DBUtil, which it does at line 5. It then needs to see that all the SQL statements to be used are prepared, which it does at line 8.

```
1.
2.     public Knowledge_baseDAO() throws Exception {
3.
4.         // create our database helper
5.         dbutil = new DBUtil();
6.
7.         // prepare SQL statements
8.         createPreparedStatements();
9.
10.    }
11.
12.    }
13.
```

Value Object

An alternative approach to having a DAO use class members for retention of data values is simply to have the DAO carry an internal reference to a Value Object, what is effectively a *compositional* object-oriented relationship. This approach provides the ability to leverage the design of the Value Object within the DAO and thus gain access to any data validation logic that may already be in place in the Value Object. Additionally, since the DAO will be returning a Value Object, in many cases a reference to the internal Value Object could be returned, providing better performance than creating and passing a new Value Object instance as a return value.

The following example demonstrates this approach. The message_user table table is managed with the Message_userDAO, which, as it happens, contains an internal reference to a Message_userVO Value Object.

Message_userDAO Example

The following DAO code example is used to manage the message_user table, which stores information on the users of the message system. As with the previous Value Object examples, the class performs a number of import operations and then on lines 12 through 21 declares class members that will be used to store SQL statements to prepare and execute. On line 24 a reference to the database utility class DBUtil object is declared, and on line 27 a reference to a message_user table Value Object the Message_userVO class is declared. Since this will encapsulate the current state of the DAO, there is no need to declare internal class members to hold the current DAO state.

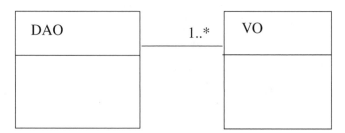

Figure 11.1 DAO and Value Object Relationship

```
1.
2.     package knowledgebase;
3.
4.     import java.util.*;
5.     import java.sql.*;
6.
7.     import db.*;
8.
9.     public class Message_userDAO {
10.
11.    // hold SQL statements
12.    private String insertStmtStr;
13.    private String updateStmtStr;
14.    private String deleteStmtStr;
15.    private String selectStmtStr;
16.
17.    // hold prepared statements
18.    private PreparedStatement   insertStmt;
19.    private PreparedStatement   updateStmt;
20.    private PreparedStatement   deleteStmt;
21.    private PreparedStatement   selectStmt;
22.
23.    // DB utility class
24.    DBUtil dbutil;
25.
26.    // internal Value Object
27.    Message_userVO message_userVO;
28.
```

createPreparedStatements

Since this DAO is being manipulated using a Value Object, specific get and set methods for the DAO members (as encapsulated in the Value Object) are not used. If the message_user table is being updated, a Value Object with the updated values would be passed to the setVO method and then the updateDAO method would be called.

The createPreparedStatements method creates the statements that will be used to perform the database updates for this class. This method is functionally similar to the createPreparedStatements method shown for the Knowledge_baseDAO DAO class, creating a separate JDBC PreparedStatement for each database select, update, delete, and insert statement used.

```java
// getXX methods

// setXX methods

// convenience methods
public void createPreparedStatements() {

try {

insertStmtStr = "insert into message_user( login, first_name,
last_name, location, date_submitted, last_login, pwd ) " +
                " values (?,?,?,?,?,?,?)";

insertStmt = dbutil.createPreparedStatement( insertStmtStr );

updateStmtStr = "update message_user set " +
                " first_name    = ?, " +
                " last_name     = ?, " +
                " location      = ?, " +
                " date_submitted = ?, " +
                " last_login    = ?, " +
                " pwd           = ? " +
                " where login = ? ";

updateStmt = dbutil.createPreparedStatement( updateStmtStr );

deleteStmtStr = "delete from message_user where login = ?";

deleteStmt = dbutil.createPreparedStatement( deleteStmtStr );

selectStmtStr = "select login,   " +
                " first_name," +
                " last_name," +
                " location, " +
                " date_submitted," +
                " last_login," +
                " pwd " +
                " from message_user where login = ?";

selectStmt = dbutil.createPreparedStatement( selectStmtStr );

}
catch (Exception e ) {
```

```
System.out.println("Exception in
Message_userDAO.createPreparedStatements(): " + e );

}
```

updateDAO Method

The updateDAO method uses the update statement that has been prepared in the createPreparedStatement method. The method makes a series of setString methods to set the prepared statement parameters on lines 4 through 10, but unlike the previous examples that used class members (attributes) to provide these values, this method makes calls to the get methods of the message_userVO Value Object that belongs to the class (it is a member of the DAO). On line 12 the executeUpdate method is called to update the database using the parameters that have been set on the previous lines. The executeUpdate method returns an integer value, but this value is ignored by this method.

```
}

1.
2.     public void updateDAO() throws SQLException{
3.
4.     updateStmt.setString(1, message_userVO.getFirst_name() );
5.     updateStmt.setString(2, message_userVO.getLast_name() );
6.     updateStmt.setString(3, message_userVO.getLocation() );
7.     updateStmt.setString(4, message_userVO.getDate_submitted()
);
8.     updateStmt.setString(5, message_userVO.getLast_login() );
9.     updateStmt.setString(6, message_userVO.getPwd() );
10.    updateStmt.setString(7, message_userVO.getLogin() );
11.
12.    updateStmt.executeUpdate();
13.
14.    }
```

insertDAO Method

The insertDAO method is used to perform insert operations for the DAO. As with the previous method, a series of PreparedStatement.setString methods are used to set the insert statement parameters on lines 4 through 10 using calls to the internal Value Object. On line 12, the executeUpdate method is called to perform the insert operation.

```
1.
2.    public void insertDAO() throws SQLException {
3.
4.    insertStmt.setString(1, message_userVO.getLogin() );
5.    insertStmt.setString(2, message_userVO.getFirst_name() );
6.    insertStmt.setString(3, message_userVO.getLast_name() );
7.    insertStmt.setString(4, message_userVO.getLocation() );
8.    insertStmt.setString(5, message_userVO.getDate_submitted()
);
9.    insertStmt.setString(6, message_userVO.getLast_login() );
10.   insertStmt.setString(7, message_userVO.getPwd() );
11.
12.   insertStmt.executeUpdate();
13.
14.   }
```

deleteDAO Method

The deleteDAO method sets a single parameter for the login field using the setString method. The method then executes the executeUpdate method to perform the delete operation for the login (the primary key for the message_user table) that has been used as the parameter for the prepared statement.

```
public void deleteDAO() throws SQLException {

deleteStmt.setString(1, message_userVO.getLogin() );

deleteStmt.executeUpdate();

}
```

loadDAO Method

The loadDAO method shown below is used to load the DAO with the appropriate values.

```
1.
2.    public void loadDAO( String login ) throws Exception {
3.
4.    try {
5.
6.    selectStmt.setString(1, login );
```

```
7.
8.    ResultSet rs = selectStmt.executeQuery();
9.
10.   if ( rs.next() ) {
11.
12.        message_userVO.setLogin( rs.getString(1) );
13.        message_userVO.setFirst_name( rs.getString(2) );
14.        message_userVO.setLast_name( rs.getString(3) );
15.        message_userVO.setLocation( rs.getString(4) );
16.        message_userVO.setDate_submitted( rs.getString(5) );
17.        message_userVO.setLast_login( rs.getString(6) );
18.        message_userVO.setPwd( rs.getString(7) );
19.   }
20.   else {  // no records found
21.        System.out.println("Message_userDAO.loadDAO(): no
records found.");
22.   }
23.
24.   }
25.   catch (SQLException e) {
26.        System.out.println("SQLException caught in
Message_userDAO.loadDAO() " + e );
27.        throw new Exception("Exception caught in
Message_userDAO.loadDAO() " + e );
28.   }
29.
30.   }
31.
```

This method is passed a single string parameter corresponding to the login.
The select statement shown below uses this login value as its parameter.

```
. . .
selectStmtStr = "select login,   " +
                " first_name," +
                " last_name," +
                " location, " +
                " date_submitted," +
                " last_login," +
                " pwd " +
                " from message_user where login = ?";

. . .
```

A `setString` method is used to set this value on line 6 and the `executeQuery` method of the `PreparedStatement` class is used to execute the `select` statement and returns a `ResultSet`. On lines 12 through 18 the values returned by the `ResultSet` are used to set the values of the internal Value Object, the `message_userVO` object. If no records are found, an error message is printed on line 21. Any exceptions thrown by any of the statements in the method are caught on line 25, an error message is printed, and a new exception is thrown.

setVO and the getVO Methods

The `setVO` method is used to set the internal Value Object equal to the Value Object reference being passed into the method. This method merely sets the internal reference to the object reference being passed into the method.

```
// set internal ValueObject
public void setVO( Message_userVO vo ) {

    this.message_userVO = vo;

}
```

The `getVO` method returns the reference for the internal Value Object. This simply returns the reference to the internal Value Object member.

```
...
// return the internal value object
public Message_userVO getVO() {
   return this.message_userVO;
}
...
```

DAO Constructor

The constructor for the `Message_userDAO` class performs some of the housekeeping chores that need to be performed before a `Message_userDAO` object can be created. It creates the internal `Message_userVO` object to be used by the class and then creates the `DBUtil` utility class used to interact with the database. Finally, it calls `createPreparedstatements` to create the prepared statements to be used to perform the database select, insert, update, and delete methods.

```
...
// constructor
public Message_userDAO() {

    // create our value object
    message_userVO = new Message_userVO();

    // create dbutil
    dbutil = new DBUtil();

    // create prepared statements
    createPreparedStatements();

}

}
...
```

Summary

In this chapter we examined several options for performing database access using JavaBeans. Specifically, we examined using several design patterns for database access: the DAO for encapsulating the details of database access for a specific table or set of tables, and the value object for encapsulating the structure of the table or tables.

The results of using these patterns were shown in this chapter. Several DAOs were shown, from a fairly simple DAO to a more complicated DAO. In each case, the responsibility of the DAO was to perform the low-level database access, the select, insert, update, and delete operations, using complete records. The role of the Value Object was to reflect the data record for the table being operated on by the DAO. In practice, this meant that the DAO would manipulate Value Objects as database records. Value Objects would be used to set the internal values of DAOs, and Value Objects would be returned by DAOs.

The DAOs did not access the database directly using JDBC. Database access was further abstracted into a database utility class named DBUtil. The DBUtil class, as shown in this chapter, managed the specifics of loading the database driver, connecting to the database, and wrapping the JDBC method to create prepared statements and execute queries.

Coming Up Next

In Chapter, the final chapter in the book, we focus once more on the infrastructure of the Web environment: the Apache server, the Tomcat JSP/servlet container, and the PostgreSQL database. Some additional topics are also covered, such as the use of Ant and deployment of Tomcat Web applications.

## CHAPTER 12

BRINGING IT ALL TOGETHER: THE COMPLETED APPLICATION

Introduction

In previous chapters we've shown how to create JSP and Java classes for the discussion group. We also discussed the Tomcat and PostgreSQL server in detail. In this chapter we detail how to deploy the Web application on Tomcat. We'll find that this involves not only placing the application code in the correct directories within the Tomcat server installation hierarchy, but creating one or more Java archives files with the correct contents. We'll show specifically how to configure the connection between the Apache and the Tomcat server, the settings required for the Apache `httpd.conf` file, and the configuration of the properties for the `mod_jk` workers.

For the PostgreSQL database, we've seen the Java code required to access the database. In this chapter we examine how to create the tables in the database and how to select the physical location for the database on the server.

The Goal

The goal of this book was to present the development of a Web site using Java technologies. We began by identifying the necessary components for a Java Web site: an HTTP server, a server to process the dynamic Web pages, and a database server. We have several configuration choices to choose among before we can build such a site. A single server application could be used to manage both the static HTML and server-side Java, or a separate server could be found to perform each function. Using separate servers provides some scalability improvements, spreading the application across multiple servers, and allows the specific benefits of each server to be leveraged. We chose separate servers: the Apache server to provide static HTML, the Tomcat server to provide server-side Java in the form of a JSP and servlet container, and the PostgreSQL database server to provide database services.

Although these servers all perform distinctly different functions, they do share many of the same attributes. They are all robust and have a rich feature set, they are open-source efforts and thus have a solid high-quality code base, and they are all free to use. Working with these choices, and in keeping with our goal to be a *complete* Web site book, we've discussed through the course of several chapters the installation and operation of each of these servers: the Apache server, the Tomcat server, and the PostgreSQL database.

Since JSP is our server-side scripting language of choice, we have covered JSP in detail, devoting well over 50 percent of the book to this significant Java technology. The basics of JSP were presented, several small sample applications were shown, and then a more complex, complete application was shown.

Now that we've covered all of pieces of our complete Web site, we'll discuss some of the practical approaches to using all of these technologies together. For us, that means using Apache, Tomcat, and the PostgreSQL database as servers and tools to build a single application.

Advantages of Using Multiple Servers

The TCP/IP ports below 1024 (1 through 1023 inclusive) are sometimes referred to as *well-known ports* and on many platforms (e.g., Unix) these ports are restricted and can only be accessed by certain users. Since Tomcat is a Java application and Java does not currently have the ability to switch user ids and access the well-known ports, Tomcat cannot generally access the well-known port for HTTP, port 80. Being written in native code, Apache can perform this function.

Using Apache with Tomcat and the mod_jk module to distribute requests to Tomcat also provides a facility for load balancing. The mod_jk module allows a set of servers to be defined with weights and can then distribute requests to these servers using a weighted, round-robin approach. With multiple servers we can allow each server to concentrate on what it does best. The

Apache server does an excellent job serving static HTML pages, and the Tomcat server does an excellent job managing dynamic content with Java Server pages. Allowing each server to do what it does best is only possible with the smooth communication between the two servers provided by the mod_jk module.

Apache and Tomcat Integration

For the Tomcat server to be able to work with the Apache server a communication channel must be opened and some agreed upon communication protocol needs to be established between the two servers. Apache communication with Java servers was originally provided for with the JServe, a Java servlet server/container, using an Apache loadable module named mod_jserv. Early in the Tomcat development cycle the mod_jserv module was used with Tomcat, but the use of SSL and other facilities required a more robust protocol. The mod_jk is now used for Apache-to-Tomcat communication, and this module supports both the ajp12 and ajp13 protocols.

The AJP (Apache Java Protocol, version 1.2) supports communication between the Apache and Tomcat servers. Whereas version 1.2 of the AJP protocol (ajp12) supported only a single request/response over a connection, the ajp13 protocol supports multiple request/responses and has support for additional functionality. Because of the expanded capabilities in its protocol, the AJP12 protocol provides superior performance over the ajp13 protocol and is thus the most common choice for Apache-to-Tomcat communication.

The History of Jserv

The Jserv project was an early attempt to implement the Java servlet specification and was not part of the Apache Software Foundation. GNU-JSP, also not an Apache project, attempted to implement the JSP specification as a servlet for Jserv. The Sun Java Webserver supported both servlets and JSP. Sun eventually turned over all Webserver sources to the Jakarta team (part of the Apache Software Foundation) and the Jakarta team merged Jserve, GNU-JSP, and the Java Webserver into the Tomcat application.

The mod_jserv Apache module originally provided communication between Apache and Jserve. To support SSL and provide additional capabilities (such as load balancing), a major rewrite was performed with the result being the mod_jk module.

Tomcat Request Interceptors

For this communication process to work, the Tomcat server must be listening for potential requests from the Apache server. When a request is detected, the Tomcat server must accept the request, process the request, and send an appropriate response. All of this work is accomplished in Tomcat using *request interceptors*. These request interceptors operate as separate threads within the Tomcat server and are directed to listen on specific ports for requests from the Apache server. Requests are configured with a port number which indicates which port it will use to listen for connections. When a request is detected, they must begin executing a specified protocol, currently either the ajp12 or ajp13 protocol (see Figure 12.1).

To provide communication between Apache and Tomcat, we need to be sure that request interceptor threads are started in the Tomcat server. This can be accomplished using entries in the server.xml file as shown below (for Tomcat version 3.3). (The server.xml file is explained in detail in Chapter 4 and Appendix A.)

```
<?xml version="1.0" encoding="ISO-8859-1"?>
<Server>

...

        <!- Apache AJP12 support. This is also used to shut down
tomcat.  ->
        <RequestInterceptor

className="org.apache.tomcat.modules.server.Ajp12Interceptor"
        port="8007" />
```

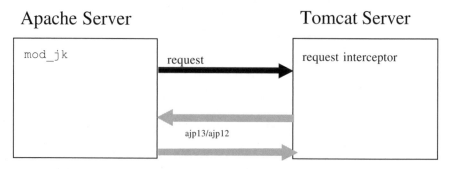

Figure 12.1 Apache-Tomcat Communication

```
        <!– Apache AJP13 support (mod_jk)      –>
        <RequestInterceptor

className="org.apache.tomcat.modules.server.Ajp13Interceptor"
        debug="1"
        port="8009" />

</Server>
```

These entries declare that interceptors will be created by the Tomcat server and will listen on port 8007 for the `ajp12` protocol and on port 8009 for the `ajp13` protocol. The class that will provide the interceptor is shown in the class attribute. (Unless you've written your own interceptor, this should be left as shown above.) A debug flag is provided to set the debug level.

The `mod_jk` module running within the Apache server makes use of workers. The workers will connect to one or more Tomcat servers and distribute work (in the form of requests) to those servers. These workers are configured using entries made in the `workers.properties` file, which contains a number of entries that control the runtime execution of the `mod_jk` workers within Apache. The entries that are of interest to us are shown in the listing below.

```
1.        . . .
2.
3.        worker.list=ajp12, ajp13
4.
5.        worker.ajp12.port=8007
6.        worker.ajp12.host=localhost
7.        worker.ajp12.type=ajp12
8.        worker.ajp12.lbfactor=1
9.
10.       worker.ajp13.port=8009
11.       worker.ajp13.host=localhost
12.       worker.ajp13.type=ajp13
13.
14.       worker.ajp13.lbfactor=1
15.       . . .
16.
```

On line 4 a list of workers is defined using the names for the workers, in this case workers named `ajp12` and `ajp13`, names that correspond to the protocol they are using, but are not required to (the naming is arbitrary).

On lines 5 through 7 a worker for the `ajp12` protocol is defined. The properties `port`, `host`, and `type` are used to declare the TCP/IP port on which the worker will listen, the host where the worker will listen, and the protocol type for the worker (currently set to either `ajp12` or `ajp13`).

On line 8 a load-balancing factor (`lbfactor`) is declared for the worker. This number must be greater than zero and is used to set a weight for the distribution of requests over the Tomcat servers available to Apache. The server with a lower weight will receive fewer requests than a server with a larger weight. Logically, then, a more powerful server should have a larger `lbfactor` than a less powerful server.

The load-balancing worker must also be declared and directed to load-balance the servers in the configuration, as shown below.

```
. . .
worker.loadbalancer.type=lb
worker.loadbalancer.balanced_workers=ajp12, ajp13
. . .
```

Although this example has defined both `ajp12` and `ajp13` workers, in production it is not necessary to run both, and given the performance and extended functionality benefits of running ajp13, this would be the preferred choice.

Load Balancing with mod_jk

Assume that a hardware configuration were available with three servers: a moderately powerful Sun server, a less powerful Dell server, and an even less powerful Compaq server. A single Apache server could distribute Tomcat server requests across these three machines using a `workers.properties` configuration, as shown below.

```
1.
2.    worker.list=server1, server2, server3
3.
4.    worker.server1.port=8009
5.    worker.server1.host=sun1
6.    worker.server1.type=ajp13
7.    worker.server1.lbfactor=60
8.
9.    worker.server2.port=8009
10.   worker.server2.host=dell1
11.   worker.server2.type=ajp13
12.   worker.server2.lbfactor=30
13.
14.   worker.server3.port=8009
```

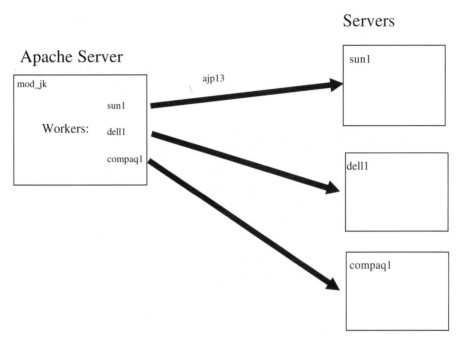

Figure 12.2 Apache-Tomcat Load Balancing

```
15.     worker.server3.host=compaq1
16.     worker.server3.type=ajp13
17.     worker.server3.lbfactor=10
18.
19.     worker.loadbalancer.type=lb
20.     worker.loadbalancer.balanced_workers=server1, server2,
server3
21.
22.
```

The workers in this configuration are assigned the names server1, server2, and server3 through the worker.list parameter on line 2. Of the three servers available, the server with the host name sun1 is the most powerful, and the worker assigned to this server on line 5 is assigned the highest load-balancing factor, a factor of 60 on line 7. On line 10 the worker server2 is assigned to the host dell1 and is given a load-balancing factor of 30 on line 12.

The least powerful of the servers available is the server host named compaq1. This server host is assigned to the server3 worker on line 15 and is assigned a load-balancing factor of 10. Using this configuration, the bulk of the requests passing through the Apache server and being dispatched by the `mod_jk` module will be sent to the `sun1` server approximately 60 percent of the time (60 divided by the total load-balancing factors for the module—100). Approximately 30 percent of the requests will be sent to the `dell1` server and approximately 10 percent of the requests will be sent to the `compaq1` server.

Telling Apache about JSP Pages

For Apache to work with Tomcat it must be able to recognize pages that should be processed by the Tomcat server. In the normal course of events, the Apache server processes a request, performs a set of of operations, and returns a response. As part of this request process, the Apache server must make a determination about how the request should be handled. In order to get Apache to communicate with the Tomcat server, the `mod_jk` module interjects itself into this evaluation process and intercepts these requests.

Entries or directives in the Apache configuration file control the way this evaluation process is performed. Specifically, certain directories or locations are mounted or identified as belonging to the Tomcat server, and all requests for those locations are directed to the Tomcat server. Alternatively, a file name extension can indicate that a file should be processed by the Tomcat server.

For the sample discussion group application, an Apache *location* is used to indicate that the request must be handled by Tomcat. A set of entries in the Apache configuration file `httpd.conf` (which are contained in a file named `mod_jk.conf` and then *included* into the `httpd.conf` file) provide this information to the `mod_jk` module. These entries effectively *mount* the location and direct Apache to process these locations through the `mod_jk` module.

```
. . .

JkMount /*.jsp  ajp13
JkMount /JavaWeb/* ajp13

. . .
```

Additional settings which usually accompany the `JkMount` directive are `Location` directives/containers which limit the access to the `WEB-INF` and `META-INF` subdirectories that will be created by the Tomcat server. An Apache `Alias` is also used to map the full location to a short name and to help obscure the true location of the Web site on the server. These entries as set for the sample application are shown below.

. . .

```
Alias /JavaWeb "/lin/local/jakarta/tomcat33/webapps/JavaWeb"

<Location "/JavaWeb/WEB-INF/">
    AllowOverride None
    deny from all
</Location>

<Location "/JavaWeb/META-INF/">
    AllowOverride None
    deny from all
</Location>
```

Using Apache to Provide Login Authentication Services

Since we would like to use Apache to manage authentication security for our application, we need to establish authentication for the directory which we do within an Apache `Directory` container , below.

```
1.       . . .
2.       <Directory
"/lin/local/jakarta/tomcat33/webapps/JavaWeb/jsp">
3.           Options Indexes FollowSymLinks
4.           AuthName "JavaWeb Realm"
5.           AuthType Basic
6.           AuthUserFile /home/tomcat/JavaWebUsers
7.           AuthAuthoritative on
8.           require valid-user
9.       </Directory>
10.
11.      . . .
12.
```

This entry is used to establish basic authentication for the directory identified on line 2. A realm named `JavaWeb Realm` is created on line 4 and identified as using `Basic` authentication on line 5. An authorization file is identified on line 6, and the authorization is identified as `Authoritative` on line 7. If this directive is turned "on," the module is authoritative and can reject the user if the login fails. (This directive could optionally turn `Authoritative` "off," which would not reject the user in the case of an invalid login; this would be done in the case where multiple modules are performing authorization and some additional module would be responsible for completing the authentication process.)

The fact that a valid user is required (the user must enter a correct name and password) is identified on line 8. The result of all of these entries is that when the user attempts to access the directory referenced on line 2 (or the `Alias` shown previously, which maps to that directory), they will be presented with a user name/password dialog box as shown in Figure 12.3.

Managing the User Login Process

As shown in Figure 12.3, the user login process involves the use of a login page which has one minor change from the example in Chapter 11. In the previous login example in Chapter 10, an HTML form was used to capture login information, and using the form post method, a JSP was used to process the login infor-

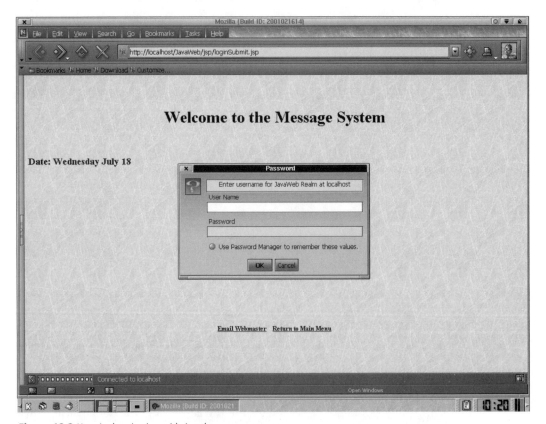

Figure 12.3 User Authentication with Apache

mation captured in the form. Since the user login information is no longer captured in an HTML input form, the new login submit page must recognize this change by calling a different method to handle the login process. On the new login submit page (loginSubmitRemote.jsp) the method used to process the login has changed from handleSubmit to handleSubmitRemote.

```html
<html>
<!- <body bgcolor="#FFFFFF"
background="/JavaWeb/img/bggradient.gif">  ->
<body bgcolor="#FFFFFF" background="/JavaWeb/img/bg2_grey.jpg">

<%@ page errorPage="ErrorPage.jsp" %>
<jsp:useBean id="loginFacade" class="knowledgebase.loginFacade"
scope="page" />
<center>
<h1>Login to Message List</h1>
</center>

<% loginFacade.handleRemoteSubmit( request, session ); %>

<br>
<br>
<b>Login Completed for user: </b> <jsp:getProperty
name="loginFacade" property="first_name" />   
<jsp:getProperty name="loginFacade" property="last_name" />
<br>
<b>Last logged in: </b> <jsp:getProperty name="loginFacade" prop-
erty="session_last_login" />
<br>
<br>
<br>
<a href="menu.html">Back to Menu</a>

</body>
</html>
```

The new method recognizes that the login information is no longer coming from an HTML form, as shown below. The reference accepts an HttpServletRequest as opposed to the ServletRequest parameter accepted by the handleSubmit method. The HttpServletRequest contains additional methods that allow it to access information about the HTTP server that has provided the request. One of these methods is the getRemoteUser method, which provides the name of the user as known to the HTTP server (assuming that the HTTP server has authenticated the user, which is exactly what we assume).

```
...
1.    public void handleRemoteSubmit( HttpServletRequest request,
HttpSession session) throws Exception {
2.
3.     // remote_user is our login
4.     String login = request.getRemoteUser();
5.
6.     // load the user information
7.     message_userDAO.loadDAO( login );
8.     message_userVO = message_userDAO.getVO();
9.
10.    // load the role for this user
11.    message_securityDAO.loadDAO( login );
12.    message_securityVO = message_securityDAO.getVO();
13.
14.    if ( message_userVO.getFirst_name() == null )
15.        throw new Exception( "Invalid user name." );
16.
17.        // a valid login
18.        // store session information about the user
19.        session.setAttribute( "first_name",
message_userVO.getFirst_name() );
20.        session.setAttribute( "last_name",
message_userVO.getLast_name() );
21.        session.setAttribute( "last_login",
message_userVO.getLast_login() );
22.        session.setAttribute( "location",
message_userVO.getLocation() );
23.        session.setAttribute( "login", message_userVO.getLogin()
);
24.        session.setAttribute( "role",
message_securityVO.getRole() );
25.
26.        // immediately update the database with the new last
login date
27.        message_userVO.setLast_login ( getCurrentDate(
"mm/dd/yy" ) );    // the new last_login date
28.        message_userDAO.setVO( message_userVO );
// update the database
29.        message_userDAO.updateDAO();
30.
```

```
31.    }
32.
...
```

The `handleRemoteSubmit` method begins by accepting two parameters: `HttpServletRequest` and `HttpSession`. On line 4, the `getRemoteUser` method is called to retrieve the "remote user" (the user the Apache server authenticated) from the request. The `getRemoteUser` method returns a string reference which is assigned to a local `String` variable. This variable is then used as a parameter to the `loadDAO` method of the `message_userDAO`, which will load the `message_user` DAO with the corresponding values for the user who has logged in. On line 8, a Value Object corresponding to the user record loaded by the DAO (and stored internally within the DAO) is retrieved. On line 11, the login string is used to load the `message_securityDAO,` and on line 12 a Value Object is retrieved from this DAO.

On line 14, a call to the `message_userVO.getFirst_name` method is made to determine whether or not the `First_name` member has been set (if it is set to the default value null, it has not been set). If the `First_name` has not been set, we know the validation has failed an exception is thrown.

If we reach line 17, we assert that we have a valid login and begin setting `session` attributes that we will use to carry the login information. On lines 19 through 24, session attributes are set for the login user's first name, last name, last login date, user's location, user's login, and the security role the user has been assigned.

The database record that tracks the user has a field for the last login date. Since at this point the user has completed a login, we update this record by setting the last login date for `message_user` Value Object on line 27 and then using this Value Object to update the `message_user` DAO (the message_user DAO will set its internal values to those of the Value Object), which is done on line 28. Once this is done, the `message_userDAO.updateDAO` method is called to update the database with the values of the DAO.

Integrating with the PostgreSQL Database

The examples in this book focused on using the PostgreSQL database as the database for the application, though in practice, any relational database could have been used. The database specifics have been isolated to a small set of classes: the DAOs and the `DBUtil` class, which further abstracts database operations. Using a different database would involve minor changes in these classes. In this section we assume the use of the PostgreSQL database (detailed in Chapter 3). The actual location of the database on the server is dictated by the setting of the PGDATA environment variable or by arguments passed to the PostgreSQL utilities and servers. The default location for the PGDATA database directory is /var/lib/pgsql/data.

The postmaster command is used to start the database and can take an optional "D" parameter to indicate the location of the database directory on the system. The postmaster command must use the "i" option to indicate that the database will listen on TCP/IP sockets for connections (the JDBC driver will use sockets). The command to start the database using the default connection would be as follows:

```
postmaster -i
```

The pgsql command is the basic tool used to access the database and perform database operations. This command accepts a "d" parameter for the name of database to access. To access a database with the name knowledgebase, the following command would be used:

```
pgsql -d knowledgebase
```

This will create an interactive command line interface to the database. It is useful to create a script of commands to perform a series of SQL statements such as the creation of a database. The pgsql command can accept a script on the command line using the Unix input shell script symbol, as shown in the following command:

```
pgsql -d knowledgebase < myScript.sql
```

This will cause pgsql to execute the contents of the script and then immediately exit upon completion.

Using a JDBC driver to access the PostgreSQL database, a URL is used to provide information on how to access the database. A sample database access URL for the discussion group system would be as follows:

```
jdbc:postgresql://localhost:5432/knowledgebase;user=puser;
password=puser
```

This indicates that the database to access is on the server localhost and is listening at port 5432. The string following the port number is the name of the database to access. The user and password are identified as puser, a user that has been created in the PostgreSQL database for the message system. (Alternatively, the DriverManager.getConnection could have been used to set the user name and password using the arguments `DriverManager.getConnection( URL, user_name, user_passwd))`.

The database driver loaded for access to the database is `org.postgresql.Driver`. The Java code used to load the JDBC database driver for the PostgreSQL database and then to connect to the database is shown below.

```
...
dbURL =
"jdbc:postgresql://localhost:5432/knowledgebase;
user=puser;password=puser";
Class.forName( "org.postgresql.Driver" );
dbConnection = DriverManager.getConnection( dbURL );
...
```

Creating the Database in PostgreSQL

Before creating a database in PostgreSQL, a database instance must be created with the `initdb` command as detailed in Chapter 3. This will create the area where the actual database can be created. Once the database instance is available, databases can then be created using either a client program such as `psql` or the `createdb` command and creating the database from the command line. The database will be created internally by PostgreSQL by creating a physical directory under PGDATA with the same name as the database and creating catalog tables to store information about the database objects. The syntax for the `createdb` command is as follows (for a more detailed description of this process, see Chapter 3):

```
createdb -a <authtype> -h  <server> -p <portnumber>
-D <location> [dbname]
```

The `dbname` parameter is the name of the database to create, and the `authtype` parameter indicates the authentication type to be used by the database. The `server` parameter is used to indicate the host name of the server to connect to for the database connection. The `portnumber` is the port number for the database connection, and the `location` is the location of an alternative directory for the database. The default is the PGDATA directory of the current database instance. This parameter affects the location of all database tables, including the system catalog tables.

All parameters are optional. If run with no parameters, the `createdb` command will attempt to create a database with the name of the user executing the command. To create the database for the message system application on the local host in the default data area (PGDATA), which expects the database to be named knowledgebase, the following command would be executed:

```
createdb knowledgebase
```

Schema Creation Script

A schema creation script is a useful mechanism for creating the database to use. The following SQL script provides the necessary SQL statements to create the message database and assign the correct permissions to the tables. The script uses a series of create table statements to create the tables used by the message system and then executes a number of grant statements to assign appropriate permissions for the message system user, who according to the database URL shown above, is a user named puser.

```
- create the tables

create table base_keys (   doc_key    integer,
                           keyword    varchar(50));

create table message_user ( login      varchar(20),
                            first_name varchar(30),
                            last_name  varchar(30),
                            location   varchar(50),
                            date_submitted date,
                            last_login date,
                            pwd            varchar(15));

create table message_security ( login  varchar(20),
                                role    varchar(20),
                                upd_date    date );

create table message_types ( message_type varchar(20),
                             description  varchar(50));

create table knowledge_messages ( doc_key    integer,
                                  message_txt  varchar(500),
                                  message_type char(10));

create table knowledge_base ( doc_key   integer,
                              doc_name   varchar(50),
                              doc_location   varchar(50),
```

```
                             level   integer,
                             category      varchar(50),
                             post_user     varchar(50),
                             date_submitted  date,
                             link_doc integer,
                             base_doc_key  integer,
                             entry_date     date);

create table categories ( category    varchar(20),
                           description varchar(30));

- grant permissions
grant select on knowledge_base to puser;
grant update on knowledge_base to puser;

grant select on knowledge_messages to puser;
grant update on knowledge_messages to puser;

grant select on categories to puser;
grant update on categories to puser;

grant select on message_types to puser;
grant update on message_types to puser;

grant select on base_keys to puser;
grant update on base_keys to puser;

grant select on message_security to puser;
grant update on message_security to puser;

grant select on message_user to puser;
grant update on message_user to puser;
```

Database roles could have been assigned and then users assigned to roles, but it is common practice to use a small set of database user ids for the application and map real users to one of these ids. With this approach, the user ids in the database effectively represent roles, and the real user (the user logging into the system) is mapped to one of those roles by the login process.

The sample application shown in this book, the discussion group application, provides the capability to map users to roles through the structure of the message_security table, which essentially maps a user login to a security role, but this is not used extensively in the current version of this application.

Using the createdb statement and a psql script that executes the SQL script shown above, the message system could be created. The following represents the statements that would be executed (assuming that the SQL script shown above is named `create_schema.sql`).

```
createdb knowledgebase
psql -d knowledgebase < create_schema.sql
```

This would create the database and the tables in the database but would not populate the `message_types`, `categories`, `message_users`, and `message_security` tables with the appropriate values. These tables would need to be loaded with values that make sense for the application to which the message system would be applied. (If the tables are not populated, the system would operate but not in any useful fashion.) For instance, a simple problem tracking system could have `message_types` of "Problem" and "Resolution" and could potentially have `categories` of "Software" and "Hardware." A general discussion group application for knowledge exchange for database systems could potentially have `message_types` "Message Post" and "Message Response" and could possibly have `categories` of "Oracle," "Sybase," "SQL-Server," and "Informix."

Deploying the Discussion Group Application in Tomcat

The Java Servlet 2.2 specification defined the specifics of a Web application: a collection of HTML pages, graphic images, JSP, servlets, and Java classes, and defined directories and a deployment descriptor that would contain information about the application. The Tomcat server conforms to this specification and therefore uses the directory structure defined there (see Chapter 4 for detailed Tomcat discussion). The directory structure specified is that of a *document root* directory for the application, effectively a home directory for the application. The collection of pages, images, and Java components that comprise the application all reside in subdirectories of that home directory. This document root directory is actually a subdirectory of the Tomcat `webapps` directory and is therefore `TOMCAT_HOME/webapps`.

For the message system application, the document root directory is named `JavaWeb` and contains the subdirectories shown in Table 12.1.

The JSP directory contains all the pages used by the application (which currently includes the HTML pages, but these could easily be moved to another directory). The `img` directory contains the various images. The `WEB-INF` and `META-INF` directories are for the use of the Tomcat server and should not be exposed to the users; we have established restrictions on access to these subdirectories using the Apache location container as shown previously in this chapter.

Table 12.1 JavaWeb Subdirectories

Directory	Description
jsp/	JSPs and HTML pages for the application
img/	Images used in generating the application pages
WEB-INF/	web.xml deployment descriptor and the Java classes written for the application (the JavaBeans and helper classes)
META-INF/	Additional information about the application

Using WAR Files

The servlet 2.2 specification also indicated that an archive file could be used to encapsulate the contents of the Web application and thus provide a more convenient mechanism for deploying the application. This archive file is named with the extension .war (an unfortunate acronym for "Web ARchive file").

The Tomcat server looks in the TOMCAT_HOME/webapps directory for applications to deploy. If a Web application archive (WAR) file is located in this directory, it will automatically be deployed by the Tomcat server when it starts. Using this approach, the message system application could be archived into a single archive file using the following command:

```
cd $TOMCAT_HOME/webapps
jar cvf JavaWeb.war ./JavaWeb
```

Since the jar command will automatically recurse a specified directory, this command will create an archive with the complete contents of the JavaWeb directory and all subdirectories. Given that our Web application is completely self-contained within the JavaWeb directory, this archive behavior is exactly what we want. Note that the WAR file is created from within the application directory, which is under the TOMCAT_HOME/webapps directory. Also note that the .war extension is required.

The result of this command is an archive file named JavaWeb.war. This WAR file should be placed in the TOMCAT_HOME/webapps directory of the production system. The application subdirectory (in this case it is named JavaWeb) need not be created (and to avoid confusion, should probably not be created).

When the Tomcat system is configured with the Auto Deploy option it will read any WAR file in the webapps directory (or the directory defined as the `docBase` of the context) and will deploy the application defined in the WAR file. In Tomcat 3.3 the `AutoDeploy` tag must appear in the `server.xml` file. This tag has the following syntax:

```
<AutoDeploy source="webapps" target="webapps" />
```

This tag instructs the Tomcat server to start the `AutoDeploy` module using the `webapps` directory as the directory where WAR files will be located and the `target` directory the directory where the applications will be deployed. (The current Tomcat implementation will unpack the WAR file into the target directory; later implementations may provide options not to unpack the file.)

Using ant with Tomcat Applications

The `ant` tool is a Java-build tool, an application written in Java to automate the build process. This tool is similar to the Unix `make` tool, which allows a build structure to be defined through a series of targets, dependency trees, and commands to execute to build targets. But unlike the `make` utility with its sometimes annoying syntax peculiarities, `ant` uses XML to define the build process, is easily extensible, and because it is built using Java, it is "cross-platform." The `ant` utility is an excellent adjunct to the Web application development process.

The development environment differs from the production environment with the inclusion of three directories: a `build` directory, an `SRC` directory and a `dist` (distribution) directory. The `build` directory is used to provide a location to store files that have been compiled and are ready to be packaged for production, and the `dist` directory is used to store the packaged files (in our case, a single package, the WAR file) ready to be moved to production. (*Note*: These examples were developed using `ant` version 1.3.) The `SRC` directory contains the JAVA source files.

build Directory

The contents of the `build` directory are shown below. This directory contains the subdirectories corresponding to the Java packages that are used in the message system application: the `knowledgebase` package, which stores the facade classes, the DAO, the Value Objects, and the `JSPCal` and `db` packages, which store utility classes used in the application.

Once the Java files have been compiled and placed in these directories, an archive will be created which will contain all the class files. This archive will then be placed in the `./WEB-INF/lib` directory, where it will be read by default and placed in the CLASS PATH for the Web application at runtime. The contents of the build directory are shown below.

```
./build
./build/knowledgebase
./build/knowledgebase/searchFacade.class
./build/knowledgebase/Message_typesVO.class
./build/knowledgebase/Message_securityDAO.class
./build/knowledgebase/Message_securityVO.class
./build/knowledgebase/loginFacade.class
./build/knowledgebase/Message_userVO.class
./build/knowledgebase/Message_userDAO.class
./build/knowledgebase/KnowledgeBaseFacade.class
./build/knowledgebase/Knowledge_messagesVO.class
./build/knowledgebase/Base_keysVO.class
./build/knowledgebase/Knowledge_baseVO.class
./build/knowledgebase/Knowledge_messagesDAO.class
./build/knowledgebase/Knowledge_baseDAO.class
./build/knowledgebase/CategoriesDAO.class
./build/knowledgebase/CategoriesVO.class
./build/knowledgebase/Base_keysDAO.class
./build/knowledgebase/Message_typesDAO.class
./build/JSPCal
./build/JSPCal/TagCal.class
./build/JSPCal/Cal.class
./build/db
./build/db/DBUtil.class
```

dist Directory

The `dist` directory will contain the compiled and packaged distribution for the application. For us, this is the `JavaWeb.war` file, which contains all the JSP pages, the HTML pages, the images, and the classes for the application. If placed in the `TOMCAT_HOME/webapps` directory, the application within this file will be deployed automatically by the Tomcat server. The contents of the `dist` directory are shown below.

```
./dist
./dist/lib
./dist/JavaWeb.war
```

src Directory

The `src` directory is used to store the source files for the application. Since we do not want these files to be part of the deployed version of the software (although they could be present), for security reasons we would prefer to deploy only the Java class files in the WAR file. To accomplish this, the source code for the application will be kept in this directory. The `ant` utility will be instructed to compile the source code here and place the resulting class files in the appropriate subdirectory of the `build` directory. The contents of the `src` directory are shown below.

```
./src
./src/db
./src/db/DBUtil.java
./src/db/DBUtil.class
./src/JSPCal
./src/JSPCal/TagCal.class
./src/JSPCal/TagCal.java
./src/JSPCal/Cal.java
./src/JSPCal/Cal.class
./src/JSPCal/CalBack.java.bak
./src/knowledgebase
./src/knowledgebase/Base_keysDAO.java
./src/knowledgebase/Base_keysVO.java
./src/knowledgebase/CategoriesDAO.java
./src/knowledgebase/CategoriesVO.java
./src/knowledgebase/Knowledge_baseDAO.java
./src/knowledgebase/KnowledgeBaseFacade.java
./src/knowledgebase/Knowledge_baseVO.java
./src/knowledgebase/Knowledge_messagesDAO.java
./src/knowledgebase/Knowledge_messagesVO.java
./src/knowledgebase/loginFacade.java
./src/knowledgebase/Message_securityDAO.java
./src/knowledgebase/Message_securityVO.java
./src/knowledgebase/Message_typesDAO.java
./src/knowledgebase/Message_typesVO.java
./src/knowledgebase/Message_userDAO.java
./src/knowledgebase/Message_userVO.java
./src/knowledgebase/searchFacade.java
./src/knowledgebase/README.txt
./src/knowledgebase/kb.txt
./src/samples
./src/samples/myBean.class
...
```

The `JavaWeb/img` directory is used to store the image or graphic files used to create the Web page. The `JavaWeb/jsp` directory is used to store the JSPs and HTML pages used by the application. The `JavaWeb/META-INF` directory stores additional information required by the application (and is not used in the application).

```
. . .
./JavaWeb
./JavaWeb/META-INF
./JavaWeb/img
./JavaWeb/jsp
./JavaWeb/WEB-INF
./JavaWeb/WEB-INF/web.xml
./JavaWeb/WEB-INF/classes
./JavaWeb/WEB-INF/lib
./JavaWeb/WEB-INF/lib/classes.jar
. . .
```

Providing ant with Instructions: The build.xml File

The `ant` build file is the basic instrument for providing instructions to the `ant` utility. This file is usually named `build.xml` and is located in the local directory where `ant` is invoked, but neither a specific location for the build file or specific name are requirements of the application. The `ant` build file uses XML tags to provide instructions on the build process. These tags can accept attributes and can have tag bodies. The `ant` utility allows multiple targets to be specified and allows build instructions to be provided for each target.

The `build.xml` file used in the discussion group application is shown below. The file begins with a series of property commands to set properties that will be used throughout the `build.xml` file. These properties are set primarily for the various directories used in the development environment, where `ant` must read the source files for compilation, and for the production environment, for which `ant` must provide a deployable WAR file. Lines 5 through 12 in this listing establish these directory names.

On lines 14 through 17 a `classpath` is established within a `path` tag. This path will be used throughout the application build process to manage Java's insistence on valid CLASSPATH settings. The path tag used on line 14 is an example of a tag that uses a tag body, in this case using a tag body that contains tags for a `pathelement`, a tag that defines the paths which will be contained in the classpath. As we shall see, this classpath will be referenced throughout the file using the `id` attribute set on line 14.

```
1.
2.    <project name="MyProject" default="dist" basedir=".">
3.
4.    <!- set global properties for this build ->
5.    <property name="classes" value="./JavaWeb/WEB-INF/lib"/>
6.    <property name="srcKB" value="./src/knowledgebase"/>
7.    <property name="srcDB" value="./src/db"/>
8.    <property name="srcUtil" value="./src/JSPCal"/>
9.
10.   <property name="appdir" value="./JavaWeb"/>
11.   <property name="build" value="build"/>
12.   <property name="dist"  value="dist"/>
13.
14.   <path id="project.class.path">
15.       <pathelement path="${classpath}"/>
16.       <pathelement location="./JavaWeb/WEB-INF/classes"/>
17.   </path>
18.
19.   ...
```

The next part of the `build.xml` file contains declarations for a series of targets. The first target declared is the `init` target, which contains a time stamp that allows time and date elements to be used throughout the build file. Additional targets are defined for each of the Java packages used in the message system application. These target tags all contain tag bodies with `javac` commands (see line 12) which instruct `ant` using tag attributes to build the Java code in the designated source directory (`srcdir`) and place the results in the destination directory (`destdir`). A tag within the target body instructs `ant` to use the designated CLASSPATH. As shown on line 13, the `classpath` tag allows a references id (`refid`) to be used which reference the class path defined in the preceding code segment. The Java compile commands issued by `ant` will compile the code using the appropriate directory structure (using the package directories) and place the results in a corresponding directory structure in the `build` directory tree.

```
1.    ...
2.
3.    <target name="init">
4.    <!- Create the time stamp ->
5.    <tstamp/>
6.    <!- Create the build directory structure used by compile ->
7.    <mkdir dir="${build}"/>
8.    </target>
9.
```

```
10.    <target name="compileKB" depends="init">
11.    <!- Compile the java code from ${src} into ${build} ->
12.    <javac srcdir="${srcKB}" destdir="${build}">
13.    <classpath refid="project.class.path"/>
14.    </javac>
15.    </target>
16.
17.    <target name="compileCal" depends="init">
18.    <!- Compile the java code from ${src} into ${build} ->
19.    <javac srcdir="${srcUtil}" destdir="${build}">
20.    <classpath refid="project.class.path"/>
21.    </javac>
22.    </target>
23.
24.    <target name="compileDB" depends="init">
25.    <!- Compile the java code from ${src} into ${build} ->
26.    <javac srcdir="${srcDB}" destdir="${build}">
27.    <classpath refid="project.class.path"/>
28.    </javac>
29.    </target>
30.
31.    ...
```

The next section of the `build.xml` file is shown below.

```
1.
2.     ...
3.
4.     <target name="libs"
depends="compileKB,compileCal,compileDB">
5.      <mkdir dir="${dist}/lib"/>
6.      <mkdir dir="${classes}"/>
7.      <jar jarfile="${classes}/classes.jar" basedir="${build}"/>
8.     </target>
9.
10.    <target name="dist" depends="libs">
11.    <jar jarfile="${dist}/JavaWeb.war" basedir="${appdir}"/>
12.    </target>
13.
14.    <target name="clean">
15.    <!- Delete the ${build} and ${dist} directory trees ->
16.    <delete dir="${build}"/>
17.    <delete dir="${dist}"/>
18.    </target>
19.    </project>
20.
```

In this section of the file, the Java `jar` command is used to create the library (JAR file) for the application. This is done on line 4, where the target block for the creation of the `classes.jar` file used in the message system is created. This target requires the Java source code in the package source code directories to have been compiled and is identified using the `depends` attribute on line 4 which references the target names for the targets identified in the preceding code segment. On lines 5 and 6 directories are created as needed for the distribution, and on line 7 the JAR file for the application is created.

On line 10 the distribution for the entire WEB application is created. This target depends on the creation of the `libs` target created on lines 4 through 8. The build command on line 11 shows a JAR file being created using the `jar` command, which will be executed from the directory specified by the `appdir` property (`./JavaWeb`).

The `clean` target on line 14 defines a set of commands that will be run to clean the `build` and `dist` directories. This target is executed only when specifically addressed in a `depends` tag or when called explicitly as an argument to the `ant` utility.

Using Auto Deploy with Tomcat

As mentioned previously, Tomcat applications can be deployed simply by placing an appropriate WAR file in the `TOMCAT_HOME`/webapps directory. This will create an application that will be read and interpreted at runtime, but each component of the application, specifically the JSP, will be recompiled the first time they are used in that session. This can create slow access for users who hit the site soon after the application has been deployed.

Optionally, Tomcat provides a facility for compiling all JSP in an application before they are accessed. Executing the `TOMCAT_HOME/bin/tomcat.sh` command using the `jspc` argument will instruct Tomcat to compile all JSP in a specified `webapps` directory. The syntax for this command is

```
tomcat.sh jspc -webapps JavaWeb
```

Note that with current versions of Tomcat (less than 4.x), this creates servlets that must then be entered in the `WEB-INF/web.xml` file in order for Tomcat to recognize the servlets. If you choose to deploy both compiled JSP files (compiled servlets) with entries for the servlets in the `WEB-INF/web.xml` file, note that Tomcat will not recognize the relationship between the JSP file and the servlet, and any changes to the JSP page will require that the JSP page be recompiled with the JSPC compiler and then the corresponding `.java` file compiled into the servlet class file for the JSP.

Although creating implementation servlets for the JSP does require some additional effort, this approach has the benefit of creating a smaller deployment footprint (only a servlet engine is needed) and will avoid the overhead of JSP page compilation (even though this should only happen once per server session).

Note that version 1.2 of the JSP specification requires that JSP containers support a `jsp_precompile` request parameter that provides a hint to the container to compile the page before it is requested. This request parameter will not be delivered to the page and the container could choose to ignore it. (Since there is demand for support of this feature, the expectation is that vendors will in fact provide servers that precompile the page.)

Summary

In previous chapters we discussed the individual components of our technical infrastructure: the HTTP server, the database, and the JSP/servlet container. We then proceeded to discuss our Java technology of choice for creating our dynamic Web content—Java Server Pages. We discussed JSP in general terms, reviewing the syntax of the tool and the basics of page development, and then provided a series of examples of JSP, first in a set of simple examples and then with a more complex example of a complete system.

Our goal in this chapter was to pull together all the examples and technology descriptions and discuss how to create and deploy an application, specifically our sample application, using Java server-side technologies. To that end we discussed using the Apache server with Tomcat and focused on the process of connecting these two servers using the `mod_jk` module. We examined once again the various directives that must be set to provide this link and reviewed how to use `mod_jk` to perform load balancing between multiple Tomcat servers.

We also discussed the creation of the database in PostgreSQL and how to execute a schema creation script.

Finally we discussed a build tool, `Ant`, that is useful in building Web applications.

THE TOMCAT 4.0 SERVER

Introduction

The Tomcat 4.0 server is the next-generation Tomcat engine. Tomcat 3.x and Tomcat 4.x both provide a servlet container and a JSP environment, with many of the same services. But Tomcat 4.0 differs somewhat in the underlying architecture of the engine.

Catalina is the name for the codebase for the Tomcat 4.0 server, a codebase different from the Tomcat 3.2/3.3 codebase. Catalina is the servlet container for the servlet 2.3 specification, and Jasper is the container for the JSP 1.2 specification. Catalina does not depend on the existence of Jasper and so could run as a standalone servlet container. Conceptually, the Tomcat server is an *engine* within which will operate one or more *containers*. These containers provide *services* for *contexts* within the containers.

Any JSP or servlet written within the scope of the JSP 1.1 and servlet 2.2 specification should run correctly under either Tomcat 3.2/3.3 or Tomcat 4.0. But Tomcat 4.0 is intended to provide additional extensibility and flexibility. In this appendix we describe Tomcat 4.0, its design goals, and how it has been architected to provide this extensibility. We also describe the components within this architecture and how they can be configured.

(Note that as of this writing, the Tomcat 4.0 server is in beta and so is subject to change. Although the final release is expected to track very closely the contents of this appendix, it is possible that some of the details may change by the time this book goes to press.)

Tomcat 4.0 Architecture

The Tomcat 4.0 architectural design is based on a set of interfaces that can support a variety of implementations. By using a well-designed set of interfaces for add-on components, developers can extend the functionality of the Tomcat server, an approach that provides better extensibility and interoperability for the server. For instance, the Tomcat 4.x server could be deployed as one of the following:

- Standalone HTTP-based Web server and servlet/JSP environment
- Server embedded within an application server
- Web-based interface for existing servers or embedded devices

These deployment environments are explained in more detail in the sections below.

Standalone HTTP Server and Servlet Container/JSP Environment

In this type of deployment, the Tomcat server will provide HTTP service for both static HTML documents and the dynamic content provided by JSP and servlets. Although this is technically possible with Tomcat 3.x (and is, in fact, used for that at many sites), more robust support for virtual hosts, logging, and enhanced performance and scalability are required to make this a feasible option for all sites.

Server Embedded within an Application Server

Application servers provide the ability to run distributable software components across one or more servers. These servers usually provide additional services, such as security, clustering, failover, scalability, and naming. These servers are robust and mature, and for the more active and secure sites, the use of these servers is generally considered a necessity. The Tomcat 4.x server has been designed so that it could be embedded into an existing application server, thus allowing the server to run in these secure, scalable environments.

Web-Based Interface for Existing Servers or Embedded Devices

The Tomcat server is compact and portable, and given the appropriate architectural design, could easily be embedded into a compact system. This would prove useful for existing server applications (e.g., firewalls or DBMS) or for embedded systems such as a router or X-10-based home automation).

Tomcat 4.0 Design Goals

The Tomcat 4.0 server was based on a design that had very specific goals for the development of the server. These goals were as follows:

- To provide extensible request processing
- To support diverse implementations
- To provide plug-in functionality

These design goals and how Tomcat 4.0 has sought to meet these design goals are described in more detail in the following sections.

Diverse Deployment Implementations

The Tomcat server should be able to operate in a variety of environments, from a standalone server to an embedded system. These environments can be distinctly different, having different requirements for security, logging, and request/response filtering. By building the Tomcat 4.0 architecture on a set of interfaces, the engine can be configured to support these diverse implementations by having the administrator choose from among various implementations of the interfaces, choosing the implementations that are appropriate for the deployment.

Plug-in Functionality

The Tomcat server should be highly configurable, allowing the administrator to choose which services or functions the server should provide. This has the potential to allow the administrator to restrict the activity of the engine and allow it to run with a smaller system footprint for a small site, or to have the server scale up to a large user load with load balancing and caching. By using an architecture based on interfaces that clearly define the contracts between services, and by adhering to the interface contract, Tomcat service components can be added or substituted as required and still work correctly with other components in the engine.

Extensible Request Processing

To support dynamic environments where more than one site may be hosted (using multiple *virtual hosts*), an architecture that supports extensible request processing is required. To manage these dynamic environments, request processing needs to be performed at several different levels within the server processing hierarchy. For instance, a request may be filtered and processed at the server level, at the virtual host level, or at the Web application level (through various application *contexts*). The Tomcat 4.0 *interceptor* architecture provides this capability.

The interceptor architecture provides this by using components that form a hierarchy of processing. Within this hierarchy, components are allowed to participate in the request/response processing of the engine. Using this approach, a request can be passed from the Engine to the Server, from the Server to the virtual Host, and from the virtual Host to an application Context with filtering being performed at appropriate locations along the way (see Figure A.1).

Interceptors can participate in request processing both before and after service processing. This mechanism has the potential to provide additional authentication services, to allow smoother integration into existing application servers, to measure site statistics, and to improve log processing.

Tomcat 4.0 Architectural Components

The Tomcat 4.0 architecture is comprised of three distinct families of architectural components within the server as follows:

- Communications adapter components
- Servlet container components
- Session management components

Communications adapter components are responsible for the management of communications with the server and its clients. They manage the request/response cycle for the Tomcat server and are the means by which the server communicates with the world at large. *Servlet container components* manage the servlet container, the set of services with which the servlet must run. All container components must implement the `Container` interface.

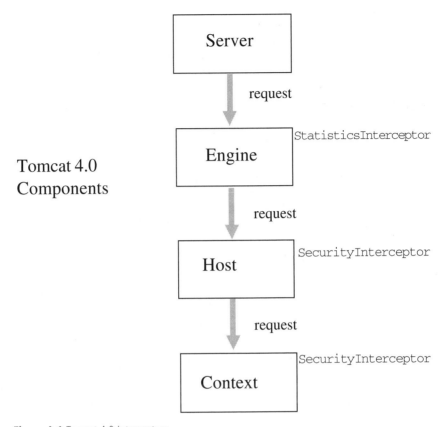

Figure A.1 Tomcat 4.0 Interceptors

This interface identifies a set of behaviors that allows *interceptors* to participate in request processing without having to make major changes in the container. *Session management components* provide management for all sessions running within the Tomcat server.

In keeping with the design goals for the the Tomcat 4.0 server, many components within these categories can be optionally selected and configured using a number of different attributes. In the following sections we detail these components and their configuration.

Tomcat 4.0 Components and Configurable Attributes

As with the Tomcat 3.0 server, the Tomcat 4.0 server uses an XML configuration file to identify and define configuration parameters for the server installation. Configuration parameters are XML tags or elements that correspond to the architectural components discussed previously. These attributes provide additional configuration information and options for the configuration parameter. Parameters can optionally have tag bodies which encapsulate additional configuration parameters that apply to the element, thus creating a hierarchy of configuration parameters.

For instance, an `Engine` configuration would use a `Engine` element as the outer tag, and within the body of the `Engine` tag would be configuration tags for `Server`, `Realm`, and `Logger`. The configuration for these parameters would, by nature of their location within the tag body for the engine, be considered part of the engine. Similarly, the engine could have one or more `Host` tags (considered part of the engine), and for each of these `Host` tags configuration parameters could be included for `Realm`, `Logger`, and `Context`. The `Context` tag could alternatively include configuration parameters for `Realm` and `Logger`.

The categories of components for the Tomcat 4.0 server are listed in Table A.1.

Table A.1 Tomcat 4.0 Component Categories

Component	Description
Connectors	Manages connections for the Tomcat 4.0 server; these are *communication adapter* components
Containers	Provides services for the servlet container, the logical processing environment for the servlet; these are *servlet container* components
Utility	Provides runtime utility functions for the server; these are considered *session management* components

The configuration elements and corresponding components under these categories are listed in the tables below. We explain the components in detail in later sections.

The `Connector` elements control connection components which operate inside the server engine. Currently, two connector components are available (see Table A.2).

Table A.2 Connector Components

Component	Description
HTTP/1.1	Configuration for the HTTP/1.1 connector
WARP	Configuration for the WARP protocol connector

The `Container` components (see Table A.3) represent processing environments within the server. These components generally deliver their functionality by encapsulating additional containers within their outermost container. For instance, a `Server` will contain a `Host`, which in turn could contain a `Context`. Within a given `Server`, multiple `Hosts` with multiple `Context` components could be declared.

Table A.3 Container Components

Component	Description
Server	Configures interactions with the Tomcat server
Service	Configures a service within the server
Engine	Configures an engine within the server
Host	Configures a host (virtual host) within the server
Context	Configures an application (context) within the server
Default	Configures a default context for the server

The `Utility` components (see Table A.4) provide utility services to the server. These include utilities to manage logging, provide authentication services, and perform other services.

Table A.4 Utility Components

Component	Description
Loader	Allows an alternative class loader to be defined
Logger	Logging facility to be used
Manager	Provides session management facilities
Realm	Identifies and configures authentication components
Resources	Provides resource management facilities
Valve	Identifies and configures filtering and processing resources

Tomcat 4.0 Configuring Components

The current implementation of Tomcat 4.0 (4.0b) has a number of component implementations available. In the following sections we provide details on the configuration of these components.

Server Component

The `Server` component represents the Tomcat container, and as such is the outermost configuration element. Within the server component resides one or more `Services` components. The `server` component supports attributes listed in Table A.5.

Table A.5 Server Component Attributes

Name	Description
classname	Class name that will be loaded for this component. The class must implement the `org.apache.catalina.Server` interface. The default class is `org.apache.catalina.core.StandardServer`.
port	Port where the server will listen for a shutdown command.
Shutdown	String that will be used to shutdown the server.

Service Component

The `Service` component is nested within an `Engine` component, the body of the `Engine` tag in the configuration file. This component accepts the attributes listed in Table A.6.

Table A.6 Service Component Attributes

Attribute	Description
classname	Class name that will be loaded for this component. The class must implement the `org.apache.catalina.Service`.
name	Display name of the service currently used in logging service activities.

Engine Component

The `Engine` component (see Table A.7) of the architecture represents the entire servlet container. A single `Engine` component is configured for each `Service` and will receive all requests from one or more engine components.

Table A.7 Engine Component Attributes

Attribute	Description
classname	Name of the class to be loaded for this component. The class must implement the `org.apache.catalina.Engine` interface.
defaulthost	Host to which requests from unidentified remote hosts will be directed.
name	Logical name of this component.

Logger Component

The `Logger` component saves information on the event, error, and debugging information concerning the operation of a component. A group of components can log information in the same location. A logger attached to an outer container will be used for all containers nested within that outer container. This container supports two attributes as shown in Table A.8, with verbosity levels as defined in Table A.9.

Table A.8 Logger Component Attributes

Attribute	Description
className	Name of the class to use for this component.
verbosity	Integer representing the amount of logging to perform, with a setting of 1 providing the least information and a 4 providing the most information (see Table A.9). Default (not specified) is 1.

Table A.9 Logger Component Verbosity Levels

Level	Description
0	Only fatal messages will be logged.
1	Errors are logged.
2	Warnings are logged.
3	General information on events and server activities is logged.
4	Debug information is logged.

Context Component

The `Context` component (see Table A.10) represents a Web application that is running on the server. The directory structure for the application should conform to that of the servlet 2.2 specification. Multiple context components can be specified within a `Host` component.

Table A.10 Context Component Attributes

Attribute	Description
`className`	The class to use for this component. The class specified must implement the `org.apache.catalina.Context` interface. If none is specified, `org.apache.catalina.core.StandardContext` will be used.
`cookies`	Set to `true` if the session id should be stored as a cookie in the client's browser. Set to `false` if you want to use URL rewriting.
`crossContext`	Set to `true` to have calls to `ServletContext.getContext` return information about other servlets running on the server. If set to `false`, `ServletContext.getContext` will return null. The default value is false.
`docBase`	The base or top-level directory for the context; all other directories are subdirectories of this directory.
`path`	The URL path to the application supported by this `Context`. All context paths within a specific `Host` must be unique. Note that within a `Host`, a blank path ("") must be specified to be used as a default context for the `Host`.

Table A.10 Context Component Attributes (cont.)

Attribute	Description
reloadable	Set to `true` if the server should reload the application if it detects changes in constituent classes of the application. Set to `false` if the server should not reload the classes of this application. (Usually set to `false` in production systems.)
wrapperClass	The wrapper class used by servlets in this context. The wrapper class must implement the `org.apache.catalina` interface. If no wrapper class is specified, the `org.apache.catalina.core.StandardWrapper` class will be used.
userNaming	Set to `true` if JNDI will be used by the server; set to `false` if JNDI will not be used.
override	Set to `true` to override the `defaultContext` configuration.

The standard implementation (`org.apache.catalina.Context`) of the server also supports the attributes listed in Table A.11.

Table A.11 Additional Context Component Attributes

Attribute	Description
Debug	Set to an integer value indicating the level of debug output, with higher numbers indicating additional debug output. The default value is 0.
WorkDir	The temporary work directory used by servlets within this context.

Host Component

The `Host` component represents a *virtual host* running within the server and is configured within an `Engine` element. The Tomcat server can functionally treat this server as though it were a distinct host environment. A virtual host can be running multiple applications each with its own context. At least one `Host` component must be declared within each `Engine` component declared in the `server.xml` file. The `Host` element accepts the attributes listed in Table A.12.

Table A.12 Host Component Attributes

Attribute	Description
AppBase	The directory where the applications for this host will be located. The attribute value may be either a full path name or a relative path name. The default value for this parameter is `webapps`. Applications are generally stored as `.war` files under this directory and are autodeployed by the Tomcat server (see Chapter 12).
ClassName	The class name to use for this component. The class must implement the `org.apache.catalina.Host` interface. If no class name is specified, `org.apache.catalina.core.StandardHost` is used.
name	The name of the virtual host as submitted on the host header of the incoming request. The evaluation of the name is not case-sensitive. This is a required attribute.

The standard implementation of the `host` component also supports the attributes listed in Table A.13.

Table A.13 Additional Host Component Attributes

Attribute	Description
debug	Set to an integer value indicating the level of the debug output, with higher numbers indicating additional debug output. The default value is 0.
unpackWars	Set to `true` to indicate that WAR files in the document base directory (`./webapp`) will be unpacked into a disk directory structure, or `false` if the application will be run from the WAR file. The default value is `true`.

Realm Component

The `Realm` component (see Table A.14) uses a database of name–password pairs to provide authentication services for a server. These authentication services include both password authentication and validation of security constraints. `Realm` would generally be attached to an outer `Host` container and would then be used for all nested containers, such as the `Host` or `Context` container.

Table A.14 Realm Component Attribute

Attributes	Description
className	The class used to provide `Realm` services. The class must implement `org.apache.catalina.Realm`. No single standard implementation exists; therefore, a class name must be chosen and this attribute is required.

There are currently two realms to choose from: `JDBCRealm` and `MemoryRealm`. These two alternatives are explained below.

JDBC Realm

The JDBC `Realm` allows a set of database tables to be used to provide authentication services for a security realm. As long as a database contains a table with user names and a table of corresponding roles for those names, and as long as the user name represents a primary key for the user names table and a foreign key for the user roles table, this authentication mechanism can be used.

The JDBC `Realm` uses the `org.apache.catalina.realm.JDBCRealm` class to implement the authentication realm. This configuration container for this realm accepts the attributes listed in Table A.15.

Table A.15 JDBC Realm Attributes

Attribute	Description
connectionName	Attribute requiredfor the database name to be used to establish the connection.
connectionPassword	Attribute required for the password to use when establishing the database connection.
connectionURL	Attribute required for the URL to use for the connection to the database; used in JDBC API to establish the connection.
digest	Name of the `MessageDigest` algorithm for encoding passwords; if blank, no encoding is used (the default).
DriverName	Attribute required for the fully qualified class name of the JDBC driver (the JAR file for the class must be accessible to the server).

Table A.15 JDBC Realm Attributes (cont.)

Attribute	Description
roleNameCol	Attribute required for the name of the column in the roles table, which contains the security role to be used in comparison tests.
userCredCol	Attribute required for the column name in the user table, which contains the user's password.
userNameCol	Attribute required for the column name for the user name in the user and user's roles tables.
userRoleTable	Attribute required for the name of the database table that contains the user's roles.
userTable	Attribute required for the table name of the users table.

User Table

The "user table" must have the user name as the primary key, meaning that there must be one and only one row for the user name in the table. This table must have a "user name" column that is identified by the userNameCol attribute for the realm and a "user credentials" column identified by the userCredCol attribute, which is encoded using the algorithm identified by the digest (MessageDigest) attribute.

The "user roles" table must have zero or more roles for each user. A primary key for this table is therefor a concatenation of the "user name" and "user role". (There can, of course, be alternate keys, but the JDBC Realm requires that 'user name' and "user role" identify a unique row.) A user may have no roles assigned, in which case they will not have a corresponding record in the "user roles" table. The "user roles" table must have a column as identified by the userNameCol attribute that identifies the user, and a role name column as identified by the userRoleCol attribute that identifies the role.

HttpServletRequest Security Methods

After a user has authenticated successfully, the Tomcat server will retain the information about the user and provide it when requested. The following methods of the HttpServletRequest interface will return the appropriate values.

• The getRemoteUser method will return the 'user name' of the user.

- The `getUserPrincipal` method will return a `java.security.Principal` object representing the user who has authenticated.
- The `isUserInRole` method, which takes a `String` argument for a role name to test, will return a boolean value indicating whether or not the user has authenticated for that role.

Memory-Based Realm

The memory-based realm reads an XML-formatted configuration file that contains user names and corresponding passwords and roles for the user. This information is then stored in memory, where it is used to authenticate users. This configuration directive supports the attributes described in Table A.16.

Table A.16 Configuration Directive Attribute

Attribute Name	Description
pathname	Path name to the configuration file (including the file name) for the realm. A relative path is supported and is considered relative to the CATALINA_HOME directory. Default is conf/tomcat-users.xml relative to CATALINA_HOME.

Configuration File

The configuration file for the `Realm` consists of one outer element named `<tomcat-users>` and one or more nested inner elements named `<user>`, one for each user. Each user element supports `<name>`, `<password>`, and `<roles>`, as explained in Table A.17.

Table A.17 Configuration File Attributes

Attribute	Description
name	Must be unique for the configuration file
password	Password for the user stored in clear text
roles	Comma-separated list of roles for the user

HttpServletRequest Security Methods

Once the user has authenticated successfully using the memory realm, permissions can be checked using the same `HttpServletRequest` interface methods as those outlined for the JDBC realm.

Single Sign-on Support

Different Web applications usually require separate authentication, so that at some sites a user may have to authenticate (enter a user name and password) several times if moving across applications. It is useful to be able to allow the user to enter a login once and have that login (and related security roles) recognized across all applications. This capability is optionally provided in Tomcat 4.0 through *single sign-on support*.

Single sign-on support is provided by making specific entries in the `server.xml` file. At the `<Engine>` or `<Host>` level in the configuration file, a `,<Realm>` element must be configured that identifies a database of user names and passwords (either through a JDBC Realm, Memory Realm, or some other appropriate mechanism). Using this approach, a `<Realm>` should not be configured inside a `<Host>` element, since this would invalidate the outer realm. A `<Host>` element should, however, include a nested `<Valve>` element, as follows:

```
<Valve class="org.apache.catalina.authenticator.SingleSignOn"/>
```

This entry defines the class that will provide a filter for access to this area of the Web site. The various Web applications linked by the single sign-on are not required to use the same authentication facilities.

The single sign-on support procedure uses client cookies to maintain the user's identity for the duration of the session. This implies some risk, since the user identity information is transmitted in plain text as part of the cookie. Although this approach to security is valid, the use of SSL encryption provides the best security over public networks.

DefaultContext Component

The `DefaultContext` element is used to describe various configuration components for the server and is nested within either an `Engine` or a `Host` element. If the default context is not going to be used, the `Context` element attribute override should be set to `true`. The attributes listed in Table A.18 can be set for this element.

Table A.18 DefaultContext Attributes

Attributes	Description
`cookies`	If this is set to `true`, cookies will be used to manage sessions (assuming that the client will accept the cookie). If set to `false`, URL rewriting will be used to manage sessions. The default is `true`.
`crossContext`	If set to `true`, the calls to retrieve the ServletContext will retrieve the context for other applications within the host. If set to `false` (for security purposes), attempts to retrieve the context will return null. The default value is `false`.
`reloadable`	If set to `true`, will automatically check the contents of the `WEB-INF/classes` and `WEB-INF/lib` directories to determine whether or not a class has been created after the server was started (and thus needs to be reloaded).
`wrapperClass`	The name of the implementation class for servlets within this Context. If not set, the default is used— `org.apache.catalina.core.StandardWrapper.`
`useNaming`	Set to `true` if the server is to enable the Java Naming and Directory Interface (JNDI).

You may optionally declare a number of elements for the `DefaultContext`, as listed in Table A.19.

Table A.19 Optional Elements for DefaultContext

Element	Description
`Loader`	Identifies a class loader for the Context
`Manager`	Manages the sessions associated with this context
`Resources`	Configures access to static resources associated with this context

Additionally, a `Lifecycle` listener can be defined within the context. This listener can listen for events such as the server stopping and starting on the `Context` and react to them. The `Listener` element must specify a Java class that implements the `org.apache.catalina.LifecycleListener` interface.

Valve Component

A `Valve` represents a Java class that is involved in the processing of a request and response within the container in which it is nested. The `Valve` component essentially represents a filter through which the request and response will be sent. The requests and responses passed to the filter are specific to the container within which it is nested, so that a `Valve` nested within an `Engine` will receive any request received by a `Connector` within the service within the `Engine`. A `Valve` nested inside a `Host` will only see requests received by the `Host` within which it is nested; requests sent to other hosts (virtual hosts) will not be received by the `Valve`. A `Valve` nested within a `Context` will only receive requests directed to the Web application specified by the `Context`; requests for other Web applications (`Context`) will not be seen.

Common implementations of `valves` would be to filter URLs or provide logging services. The attribute described in Table A.20 is available for the `Valve` component.

Table A.20 Valve Component Attribute

Attribute	Description
`className`	Attribute required to identify the class that will be used to manage the `Valve`. The class used must implement the `org.apache.catalina.Valve` interface.

A number of implementations for `Valve` are available:

- Access Log Valve
- Remote Host Filter
- Request Dumper

Access Log Valve

To use this `Valve`, the `classname` attribute must be set to `org.apache.catalina.valve.AccessLogValve`. The access log valve is used to create customizable log files to track page hits, session activity, and other pertinent statistics. This `Valve` can be contained within an `Engine`, `Host`, or `Context`. It will log activity for its container and all containers within its container. This container supports the attributes listed in Table A.21.

Table A.21 Access Log Valve Attributes

Attributes	Description
`directory`	Path name, either relative or absolute, of the directory that will be used to store the log files. Relative pathnames are considered relative to `CATALINA_HOME`. The default is `CATALINA_HOME/logs`.
`pattern`	String pattern that identifies how to format various information fields in the log record. If no pattern is specified, a common log format will be used.
`prefix`	Prefix that will appear at the front of the log file name. If not specified (with a zero-length string), the name `access_log` will be used.
`resolveHosts`	If set to `true`, will resolve the IP address of each client to get the domain name. If set to `false` (the default), the IP address will not be resolved (this will improve performance).
`suffix`	Suffix to be added at the end of each log file. If none is specified by using a zero-length string (the default), no suffix will be used.
`timestamp`	If set to `true`, log records will contain a time stamp. If not specified, log messages will not be time stamped.

Remote Address Filter

The remote address filter is a `Valve` used by setting the `classname` attribute for the `Valve` to `org.apache.catalina.valve.RemoteAddrValve`. It provides the ability to filter IP addresses based on one or more regular expressions. Specific addresses can be refused or allowed to continue based on these comparisons. This `Valve` can be contained within the `Engine`, `Host`, or `Context` containers and supports the attributes listed in Table A.22.

Remote Host Filter

To use the remote host filter `Valve` the classname attribute must be set to `org.apache.catalina.valve.RemoteHostValve`. This `Valve` allows the remote address of the request to be compared to one or more filter patterns to determine whether or not to accept the request. It should be

Table A.22 Remote Address Filter Attributes

Attribute	Description
`allow`	Comma-separated list of regular expression patterns that will be used to evaluate the IP address. Any IP address that matches these patterns will be allowed. If this attribute is specified and the IP address does not match, the IP address will be denied. If this is attribute is not specified, all IP addresses will be allowed.
`deny`	Comma-separated list of patterns to which the IP address will be compared. If the IP address matches one of these patterns, it will be denied access; otherwise (there are no matches), it will be permitted access. If this attribute is not specified, the address must match one of the patterns specified in the `allow` attribute.

declared within an `Engine, Host,` or `Context`. It will filter requests for its enclosing context and all `Contexts` within that `Context`. This `Valve` supports the attributes listed in Table A.23.

Table A.23 Remote Host Filter Attributes

Attribute	Description
`allow`	Comma-separated list of regular expression patterns that will be used to evaluate the host address. Any host address that matches these patterns will be allowed. If this attribute is specified and the host address does not match, the host address will be denied. If this attribute is not specified, all host addresses will be allowed.
`deny`	Comma-separated list of patterns to which the host name will be compared. If the host name matches one of these patterns, it will be denied access; otherwise (there are no matches), it will be permitted access. If this attribute is not specified, the address must match one of the patterns specified in the `allow` attribute.

Request Dumper

To use the request dumper `Valve` the `classname` attribute must be set to `org.apache.catalina.valve.RequestDumperValve`. This `Valve` dumps the HTTP headers associated with a request (before processing) and for the response (after processing). Logging will use the Logger of the associated container. This `Valve` can be contained within an `Engine`, `Host`, or `Context` and will be used for all nested Containers. It uses no additional attributes.

Catalina Connectors

The HTTP 1.1 connector is a connector implementation that supports the HTTP 1.1 protocol. This connector listens for a connection on a specified port and then forwards the request to an `Engine` for processing. One or more connectors can be created to send requests to one or more engines. This element is configured using a `Connector` element which is contained within a `Service` element.

The HTTP/1.1 `Connector` will start a given number of processor threads (`minProcessors`) and allocate these threads to incoming requests for the duration of the request. Should the number of requests exceed the number of processor threads, additional threads will be added up to a specified maximum number of threads (`maxProcessors`). The HTTP/1.1 `Connector` can be configured with the attributes listed in Table A.24.

Table A.24 Connector Attributes

Attribute	Description
acceptCount	Maximum queue length for connections. If connections arrive after the limit is reached, the connection will be refused.
address	IP address for listening for connections. If none is specified, the server will listen on all IP addresses associated with the host server.
bufferSize	Size of the buffer for input streams. If not specified, the default of 2048 bytes will be used.
className	Class name for the HTTP/1.1 implementation to use. The standard implementation is `org.apache.tomcat.connector.http.HttpConnector`.
debug	Debug level for logging where higher numbers will generate more detail. The default is 0.
enableLookups	Set to `true` to enable DNS lookups (the default) for calls to `request.getRemoteHost`. If disabled, the IP address of the remote host is returned.

Table A.24 Connector Attributes (cont.)

Attribute	Description
`maxProcessors`	Maximum number of processor threads that will be allocated for the connector. If not specified, the value of 20 will be used.
`minProcessors`	Number of processor threads that will be initialized when the connector is started.
`port`	TCP/IP port where the connector will listen for client connections. The default is port 8080.
`proxyName`	Value to be returned by calls to the `request.getServerName.` Useful for running the server behind a proxy server.
`proxyPort`	Port that will be returned by `request.getServerPort.` Useful for running the server behind a proxy server.

The HTTP/1.1 `Connector` can be run behind a proxy server and can provide SSL support if a valid socket factory is configured (see Table A.25).

Table A.25 SSL Socket Factor Attributes

Attribute	Descriptor
`algorithm`	Certificate encoding algorithm to use. The default value is SunX509.
`className`	Java class name of the SSL socket factory. If using HTTP/1.1, the `org.apache.catalina.net.SSLServerSocket Factory` class must be used.
`clientAuth`	This value is set to `true` if the client requires a valid certificate chain from the client. If set to `false`, the certificate chain is not required.
`keystoreFile`	Pathname of the keystore file. The default value is `.keystore` in the home directory of the user that is running the server.
`keystorePass`	Password to use to access the server certificate from the keystore file. The default is `changeit.`
`keystoreType`	Type of keystore file for the user certificate.
`protocol`	SSL protocol version. The default value is `TLS.`

ENTERPRISE JAVABEANS ARCHITECTURE

Enterprise JavaBeans Defined

If we consider applications to be composed of a set of components within our multitiered architecture, JSP and servlets are *Presentation Tier components*, components that are used to create Web pages (HTML). If a JSP is a component, an application is composed of one or, in most cases, more than one of these components. Our JavaBeans used to support these pages are also components, although we would not consider them Web tier components. Since they manage the business logic of the application we consider them *Business Tier components*.

The Java technologies we have used in this book, the JSP and JavaBeans, are adequate for a large range of applications. But they do have limits, and scalablity and fail-over represent two notable limitations of this technology. The *scalability* of an application represents the application's ability to handle an increase in use (see Figure B.1). For a Web site, use is generally represented by the number of concurrent users or the number of site page hits per some increment of time (day, hour, minute, second). Scalability is usually provided using a features known as *load balancing*, where a dispatcher can dispatch requests over one or more servers. Load balancing can be done using various algorithms, from a simple round-robin where requests are distributed evenly among all available servers, to a weighted average form of load balancing where requests are distributed among servers based on some statistical weight. Even more complex load-balancing algorithms will evaluate the system load on the available servers and factor that information into the distribution effort.

The *fail-over* capabilities of a site represent the ability of the site to survive a failure of some sort. Specifically, fail-over generally applies to the ability of session activity to survive the failure of one of the servers used to manage the site. Fail-over may be transparent, meaning that if the server on which the session is running fails, the other server will continue running the session transparently. This transparent fail-over may not always be the case; in some cases the user may have to reload a page or log in, but if the session information is retained, some degree of fail-over is provided.

The Tomcat server can provide scalability features using the `mod_jk` module and a weighted load-balancing algorithm. Using `mod_jk` and the `work-`

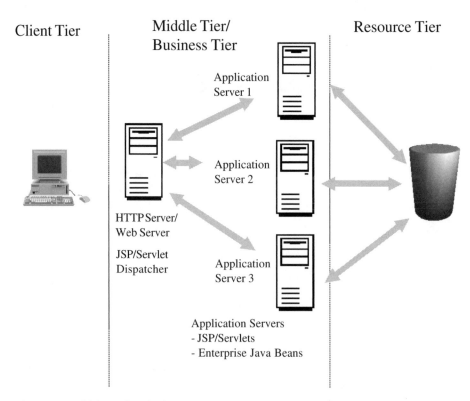

Figure B.1 Scalability with Multiple Servers

ers properties file, a load-balancing scheme can be implemented (see Chapter 12). This scheme will usually involve taking the entire Web application and distributing the application across multiple servers, but this approach is not required. An application could be divided into parts (e.g., modules or groups of modules) and the individual parts distributed across multiple servers, a form of *application partitioning*.

Enterprise JavaBeans (EJBs) extend this component architecture to the business tier components. Using EJBs, an application can be divided into components, which can be deployed and invoked and run across one or more machines. Like servlets, these components run within a *container* which provides an operating environment for the component. The container will manage the runtime execution of the component and provide security, transaction, and naming services. These EJB containers can also provide additional value-added services such as `Connectors` to allow connection to legacy database systems (mainframe DBs) and fail-over capabilities that allow EJB sessions to fail-over transparently to another machine.

The container is an abstraction that describes the services and environment provided for the component. An *application server* provides the container environment and additional services for the EJB. EJB components can easily be distributed and deployed and *clustered* across one or more servers running the same application server, allowing load balancing and fail-over to be provided.

Although this use of distributed software components is not new (CORBA components written in any language can provide most of these features), the ability to do it with a standard API and a standard cross-platform language is new. Many of the features but EJBs provide required custom development with other distributed components.

EJB Architecture

EJBs are deployed onto an application server and run within a container in that application server. The container provides *life-cycle management* for the EJB, which manages the EJBs in such a way as to use the resources of the engine (memory and CPU) as efficiently as possible. Part of this implementation can optionally (it's up to the application server vendor) be the use of EJB *pooling*. EJBs, which are implemented using Java classes, can be instantiated before use and kept in a pool. Then, when an EJB is requested by a client, it is simply retrieved from the pool and made available to the client, thus avoiding the overhead of object instantiation (for the EJB) at runtime (see Figure B.2).

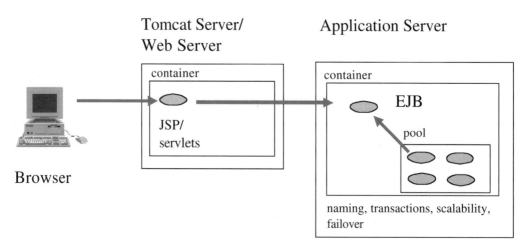

Figure B.2 EJB Pooling

The EJB container will also provide access to other features, such as naming services, security, and transactions. Optional features such as load balancing and fail-over are usually provided by the more robust application server vendors. Note that the scalability benefits of load balancing and the fail-over capabilities described earlier require the same application server to be installed on multiple machines in a clustered environment recognized by the application server. The application server vendor will usually provide tools to support the configuration and runtime management of this environment.

EJB Implementation

EJBs are easily implemented over existing Java classes and in fact were designed with that in mind. There are some restrictions; for instance, local machine resources (local files, TCP/IP ports) should not be accessed and the bean should not use multithreading. These restrictions make sense, however, when one considers that the EJB may need to fail-over or potentially migrate (for load balancing) in a clustered environment. Any bean that has migrated from one server to another would not find local resources available (e.g., files) nor would they find their threads, since threads are specific to the Java VM in which they are running.

There are two types of EJBs: *Session Beans* and *Entity Beans*. Each has specific benefits and is discussed in the following sections.

Session Beans

Session beans represent a session between a client and an EJB, a client conversational state. Using a service model, a client will request a service from the bean through some conversation and the bean will respond with a result. This communication between the client process and the bean may or may not require the EJB to retain state information between invocations.

If a session bean retains state between invocations, it is considered a *stateful session bean*. If a session bean does not retain state between invocations, it is considered a *stateless session bean*. Since a stateless session bean does not retain state between invocations, it should not use instance members or class members, as they will not be guaranteed to have sensible values, values specific to a client session, between invocations. In this vein, stateless session beans should receive a request, perform all work necessary to complete the request, and then return results for the request all within the space of the invocation (the method call).

Entity Beans

Entity beans represent a unique element in a persistent data store. They represent persistent data and in relational database terms are said to represent a row in a database table (or potentially, a unique record composed of a join across multiple tables). Since they represent a unique relation in a persistent data store, an entity bean is represented by a *primary key*, a unique representation for the entity bean. A primary key can be represented by one or more columns in the underlying table.

An entity bean does not need to be mapped into a relational database but could be mapped into a legacy database system or even a set of files, although the most common implementation is that of object-relational mapping, using the entity bean to represent some portion of a relational database. Entity beans must remain synchronized with the persistent data store. This is accomplished using a set of methods that must be implemented by the entity bean (methods defined in the entity bean interface). Specifically, the `ejbLoad` method is used to load the bean from the database, and the `ejbStore` method is used to synchronize the bean with the database. An entity bean developer can either write the code for the `ejbLoad` and `ejbStore` methods (and a few others), or the application server vendor can provide a tool that will write the code for these methods. If the developer provides the code for the entity beans database synchronization, the bean is using *Bean-Managed Persistence* (BMP). If the developer allows the application server tool to create the code for the Entity Bean persistence, the Entity Bean is using *Container-Managed Persistence* (CMP).

EJBs and Transactions

One of the services provided by the EJB container is transactional control. Transactions can be either controlled programmatically by the developer or controlled declaratively by the container. If transactions are controlled by the container, they are called *container-managed transactions* (CMTs) and are declared by making entries in a configuration file used to deploy the EJB application. If the transactions are controlled by programmatic instructions, they are called *bean-managed transactions* (BMTs). With Session Beans, transactions are optional, but with Entity Beans transactions are required. Furthermore, transactions with Entity Beans must use Container-Managed Transactions. Since Entity Beans are guaranteed to be synchronized with a persistent data store, they are considered transactional by nature.

Developing EJBs

What should be noted about EJBs is that an application server is required to develop and deploy these components. The Sun J2EE download from the Sun Web site includes a development version of an application server, but this is not considered appropriate for a production environment. Application servers range in price from nothing for open-source products (JBoss) to midrange prices for JRun and WebLogic, to the high range for IPlanet and WebSphere. (The Web site www.flashline.com has a very good application server matrix, which includes a comparison of application servers, their EJB compliance, their prices, and most important, user reviews.)

Note that not all application servers that support the development of EJBs are considered EJB compliant. Compliance is important in providing portability of EJBs, so that an EJB developed and deployed on the application server of one vendor can easily be deployed onto another application server vendor. (Developers are advised to look for application server compliance to the most recent EJB specification.)

Although simpler than previous distributed component development, EJBs require a very specific coding paradigm. Two interfaces must be coded for the EJB, and the actual bean class must implement a specific interface. Table B.1 elaborates on these details.

Table B.1 Bean Class Interfaces

EJB Type	Extend Interface	Implement Interface
Session bean	`EJBHome`	`SessionBean`
	`EJBObject`	
Entity bean	`EJBHome`	`EntityBean`
	`EJBObject`	

Client Access

Client application that access EJBs do not access EJBs directly; they access indirectly through a proxy object. A client application will use a naming service to look up the home interface (EJBHome implementation) for the EJB. Once the home interface object is obtained, it is used to access a remote object for the EJB. Then, using this remote object, the client application can interact with the EJB by calling the business methods of the EJB using the remote object. In this way, the client uses the EJB indirectly, via the remote object, as a *proxy* for the actual EJB (Figure B.3).

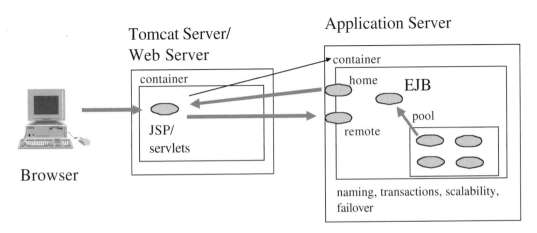

Figure B.3 EJB Communication

EJB Code Sample

EJBs require a specific development process. This process is required because of the nature of EJBs, where components must run within a container. Since the container must be able to communicate with the component, there are certain methods the component must implement in order to be able to work within the container.

The following code sample demonstrates the development of EJBs. In this example a simple Session Bean is created by implementing the SessionBean interface. Several SessionBean interface method implementations must be supplied, the most common of these being the ejbCreate method, which will be called by the container when the bean is created. The ejbActivate and ejbPassivate methods are called when the EJB is moved to the pool (ejbPassivate) and when the bean is retrieved from the pool (ebjActivate). The ejbRemove method is called when the bean is removed. Note that these EJB methods are not called directly by the client; they are called by the container based on actions initiated by the client.

```java
import javax.ejb.*;
import javax.naming.*;
import javax.rmi.*;


public class myBean implements SessionBean {
SessionContext sc;

// SessionBean interface methods

public void ejbCreate() { System.out.println("myBean.ejbCreate()
called."); }

public void ejbPassivate() { }
public void ejbActivate() { }
public void setSessionContext( SessionContext sc ) {
this.sc = sc;
}

public void ejbRemove() {}


// ** business methods
```

```
public String getData() { return "this string"; }

public String getCustData() {
CustRemote cr = null;
CustHome ch = null;
String retval = null;

try {
InitialContext ic = new InitialContext();

Object obj = ic.lookup("Cust");

ch = (CustHome) PortableRemoteObject.narrow( obj, CustHome.class
);
cr = ch.create();


retval = cr.getCustData();

}
catch (NamingException e) {

System.out.println("NamingException caught in getData(): " +
e.getMessage() );
throw new EJBException("naming exception");

}
catch (Exception e) {

System.out.println("Exception caught in getCustData(): " +
e.getMessage() );
throw new EJBException("naming exception");

}
finally {
return  retval;
}
}


}
```

Once the SessionBean method implementations are provided, a series of business methods are declared for the session bean. These methods have no specific restrictions other than those mentioned previously (no multithreading, no accessing local resources). Note that an additional restriction is that access to relational databases should be done using a `DataSource`, not through direct JDBC calls.

The `getData` method uses a lookup method call to access another EJB and is therefore a client to another bean. Other business methods in a Session Bean (not shown in this example) would perform business operations such as retrieving and updating database records and executing business logic.

EJBHome Interface

The `EJBHome` interface represents an implementation of the `Factory` design pattern. This interface essentially controls creation of remote objects for the EJB and allows the container to intercede in this process. The EJB developer must create a specific interface that extends the `EJBHome` interface as shown in the code below. A signature for the create method must be declared to return the type of the remote interface for the EJB.

```
import javax.ejb.*;
import javax.naming.*;
import java.rmi.*;

public interface myHome extends EJBHome {

public myRemote create() throws CreateException, RemoteException ;

}
```

It is the responsibility of the application server vendor to provide an implementation for this interface. This code process will occur during the deployment process.

EJBObject Interface (Remote Interface)

A remote interface must be declared for the EJB which extends the `EJBObject` interface. This interface must provide signatures for all the business methods in the EJB class that are to be accessed from the client to the EJB. As with the `EJBHome` interface, it is the responsibility of the application server vendor to provide an implementation for this interface during deployment. The deployment process will include a code generation process that will create the code necessary to implement this interface.

```
import javax.naming.*;
import javax.ejb.*;
import java.rmi.*;

public interface myRemote extends EJBObject {

public String getData() throws RemoteException;
public String getCustData() throws RemoteException;


}
```

Deploying the EJB

Once the interfaces and classes for the EJB have been declared, they must be *deployed* into the application server. This deployment process reads a deployment descriptor, an XML-encoded document that describes various properties of the EJB. These properties include but are not limited to transactional behavior, whether a session bean is stateful or stateless, or whether an entity bean is using CMP or BMP. The application vendor is expected to provide a tool that will perform the deployment process. The process will include reading the deployment descriptor, finding the classes and interfaces, generating implementation code for the interfaces, and making entries into the name server.

EJB Client Code

The client application for an EJB must obtain two object references to be able to access the EJB. The first reference it must obtain is the home object, the implementation of the EJBHome interface for the EJB. Once it has a reference to the home object, it can call the create method on the home object to receive a reference to the remote object, the implementation of the EJBObject interface that will provide a proxy to the actual EJB running on the application server.

The home object reference is usually found using the *name server,* provided as part of the J2EE compliant application server. The name server allows name–value pairs to be stored in a lightweight hierarchical database. J2EE specification provides that this name server will be provided by the application server vendor and that access to the name server will be provided using the Java JNDI (Java Naming and Directory Interface). The name–value pairs that can be stored in the name server include the ability to store references to objects as the *value*. Part of the deployment of an EJB application involves placing a JNDI lookup name and the object reference for the home interface.

In the code example that follows, a command line parameter is optionally passed in to provide the lookup name for the home interface. If a name is not supplied on the command line, a default name is supplied.

```
import javax.naming.*;
import java.rmi.*;
import javax.rmi.*;

public class testClient {

public static void main( String args[] ) {
myHome mh = null;
myRemote mr = null;

try {
String lookupName =null;

if (args.length > 0 )
   lookupName=args[0];
else
   lookupName = "myBeanJNDI";

InitialContext ic = new InitialContext();
System.out.println("InitialContext found. " );

Object obj = ic.lookup(lookupName);
System.out.println("myBean found. Performing narrow ... " );

mh = (myHome) PortableRemoteObject.narrow( obj, myHome.class );
mr = mh.create();
System.out.println("Customer Data: " + mr.getCustData() );

}
catch (Exception e) {
   System.out.println("Exception in main: " + e.getMessage() );
}
```

```
}

}
```

The usual process for an EJB client is to obtain an *initial context* using a call to the `InitialContext` method. This provides access to the name server and allows the `lookup` method to be called, passing a string that corresponds to the name for the home interface (as declared during the deployment process). The `InitialContext.lookup` method will return an `Object` reference that must be converted into the appropriate type for the home interface of the EJB. Because of the nature of the underlying communication mechanism for EJBs, the `PortableRemoteObject.narrow` method is used to convert the object reference to the type of the home interface.

Once the home interface has been obtained, a call can be made to the `create` method of the home interface. This method will return a reference to the remote object for our EJB. Once we have this remote object, we can make calls to the business methods of our EJB.

When to Use EJBs

Enterprise JavaBeans have their place in server-side development. For applications that require high scalability and some level of session fail-over capabilities, EJBs are a good fit. This would include sites with a heavy user load and/or the need for transactions to fail-over transparently to the end user. But for sites that don't have these requirements, the drivers for EJB use are less pronounced. EJBs also make it possible to create an application with components that can then be accessed fairly easily from remote locations. Using EJBs, a client application running on a modest hardware platform can access a complex, expensive processing routine, and through the architecture of EJBs, the processing routine will run on the remote hardware platform (where the EJBs are deployed). With this architecture, the resource-intensive processing will be done on the remote machine, which will have the hardware capability to manage the processing rather than on the modest client machine.

This architecture also allows IT a high degree of control of the development and deployment of component software. Since the EJBs will reside on a centralized platform, the IT department will have control over these machines and the development environment in general. Client applications, which could even be Web applications, can have a much smaller footprint, since they will not need to carry the complex code, which instead, will reside in the EJBs on the central server.

Over-Engineering with EJBs

It should be noted that EJBs are not a good fit for every application. In fact, there are a significant number of applications where EJBs are not needed and would represent overengineering. EJBs exact a cost in terms of both software and code development. EJBs require additional software to run, software that could prove expensive if some of the more robust high-end servers are selected. EJBs also require additional coding effort, since component interfaces must be written, beans must extend interfaces and provide implementations, and components must be deployed and retested and often redeployed when the components change (not unusual during development).

Enterprise Java Beans therefore exact higher development and production costs, which must be justified by the requirements of the application. For applications that do not have stringent fail-over requirements, can endure having a client restart a session if it fails, and do not have to scale up to 100,000 page hits per day with 3000 concurrent users, JSP and JavaBeans may be the preferred solution.

JDBC API

JDBC Application Programmer Interface

The JDBC Application Programmer Interface (API) is a standard Java API for accessing relational databases. This appendix will provide a brief overview of the use of the JDBC API, discussing the basics of loading the database driver, creating a connection, creating and executing an SQL statement, and iterating over the results of the query.

A Java programmer using JDBC uses primarily four classes, which enable the programmer to load a driver, connect to the database, create and execute a SQL statement, and examine the results. The interfaces that describe the classes used to perform these functions are as follows:

- `java.sql.DriverManager`: loads the JDBC driver and manages the database connection
- `java.sql.Connection`: connects to the database
- `java.sql.Statement`: manages an SQL statement on a connection
- `java.sql.ResultSet`: allows access to the results of an executed statement

A simple statement execution with Java would proceed as follows: A JDBC driver is loaded; a database connection is created from the driver; a statement is created from the connection; an SQL statement is executed using the statement and a result set returned; and the result set is used to retrieve additional rows and examine the data. The following code demonstrates this sequence of calls.

```
...
 try {
// load the JDBC driver
Class.forName ("org.postgresql.Driver");

String url =
"jdbc:postgresql://localhost:5432/knowledgebase;user=puser;pass-
word=puser";

// connect to the URL and return a Connection object
Connection con = DriverManager.getConnection (
                                    url, "", "");
// create a SQL statement
String qs = "select * from loadtest";
Statement stmt = con.createStatement();

// execute the SQL statement and return a
// ResultSet with results
ResultSet rs = stmt.executeQuery( qs );

// step through results in the ResultSet
boolean more = rs.next();
 while ( more  ) {

System.out.println( "Col1: " + rs.getInt( "col1" ) );
                more = rs.next();

    }
}
```

In this code fragment, a database driver is first loaded using the Class.forName method. This loads the JDBC-ODBC bridge driver and returns a reference to a Class object (which is ignored in this code). A URL for the database is then specified. The URL is composed of the character constant jdbc, a subprotocol, and a subname, as follows:

```
jdbc:<subprotocol>:<subname>
```

The subprotocol identifies a database connectivity mechanism that a number of drivers may support. The contents of the subname depend on the subprotocol. If a network address is to be used as part of the subname, the naming convention should follow that of standard URL names, with the subname named

```
//hostname:port/subsubname
```

Using this scheme, the URL for the PostgreSQL database would be

```
jdbc:postgresql://localhost:5432/knowledgebase;user=puse
r;password=puser
```

In this example, the `subprotocol` is postgresql for a PostgreSQL database driver, and `postgreSQL` is the `subname`.

Once the driver manager has been loaded, a `Connection` object is instantiated. The `Connection` class contains methods to control the database connection. From this object, objects can be instantiated to manage the SQL statements that are to be executed against the database. In this example the `createStatement` method in the `Connection` class is then used to create a `Statement` object.

The `Statement` object allows execution of SQL statements. Different methods are used to execute queries (`executeQuery`), updates (`executeUpdates`), and queries with parameters (`executePrepared`). When statements are executed that will return a series of results (such as an SQL select statement), a `ResultSet` object is returned to represent the series of rows and columns within the rows. This example shows the execution of the `executeQuery` method of the `Statement` class and subsequent execution of the next method of the `ResultSet` class to obtain data for each of the rows returned.

The commonly used classes identified and demonstrated in this code are an important part of using JDBC. These classes are used consistently throughout JDBC applications. Their usage is explained in more detail in the sections that follow.

java.sgl.DriverManager Class

The `DriverManager` class provides access to the JDBC facilities. The relationship between the `DriverManager` class, the `Connection`, `Statement`/`PreparedStatement`, and `ResultSet` classes is shown in Figure C.1.

Figure C.1 JDBC Class Relationships

When instantiated, the DriverManager object uses the system jdbc.drivers property to obtain a list of class names for the driver classes. The DriverManager attempts to load each of these driver classes.

Once the appropriate driver or drivers has been loaded, the DriverManager object manages the connections using that JDBC driver. The DriverManager.getConnection method will return a Connection object, which is then used to instantiate various Statement objects that produce Resultset objects when the Statement is executed. A given DriverManager can manage multiple connections, and multiple connections can support multiple statements, as shown in Figure C.2.

The DriverManager class is most commonly used to create connections to the database. This is accomplished using the getConnection method, as follows:

```
...
// connect to the URL and return a Connection object
Connection con = DriverManager.getConnection (
                                    url, "", "");
...
```

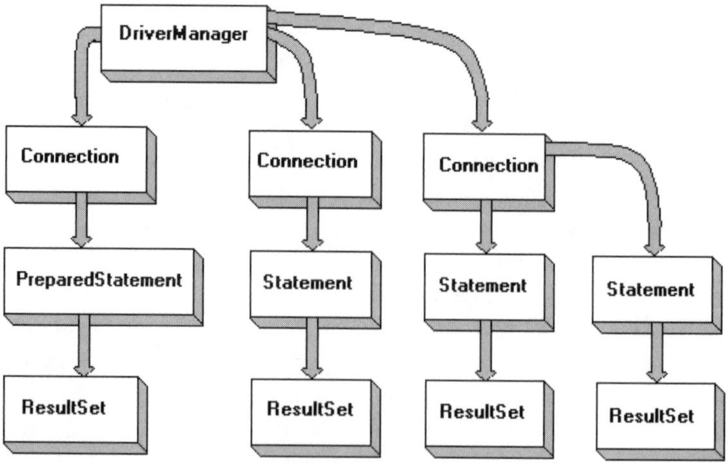

Figure C.2 Driver Manager and Multiple Connections

In this code fragment, the `DriverManager getConnection` method is called to create a `Connection` object. The `getConnection` method can be called with arguments for the database URL for the connection, the password, and the user name. Other variations of this method accept different parameters.

A number of methods are available in the `DriverManager` class to manage drivers. These methods register and de-register the driver, direct logging output, and set login timeout parameters.

Connection Class

An object of the Java `Connection` class represents a session with a database. Using a `Connection` object as a parameter, a `Statement` object can be created. This `Statement` object is then used to execute SQL statements and return a set of results.

A `Connection` can provide information about the tables in the database, the SQL grammar supported, the stored procedures available, and the general capabilities of the database connection using the `getMetaData` method.

AutoCommit in JDBC

Note that a connection is in `AutoCommit` mode by default. With `AutoCommit` set, each separate SQL statement executed is automatically committed to the database. To group a set of transactions together, the `AutoCommit` mode must be set off (using the `setAutoCommit` method) and the `commit` method must be used at the point that the transaction should be committed (or rolled-back) to the database. Methods are available to determine and set the `AutoCommit` state for a connection.

Table C.1 provides a description of the methods in this class. All methods throw an `SQLException`.

Table C.1 Connection Class Methods

Method	Description
createStatement()	Creates and returns a new Statement object
prepareStatement(String sql)	Creates a prepared Statement object for later reference in the program preparedStatement object
prepareCall(String sql)	Creates an object for calling a stored procedure; the CallableStatement class provides methods for managing IN and OUT parameters
NativeSQL(String SQL)	Converts JDBC SQL grammar into the database system's native SQL
setAutoCommit(boolean autoCommit)	Allows the default AutoCommit Mode of enabled to be disabled
getAutoCommit()	Retrieves the current state of the autoCommit mode
commit()	Commits all changes made since the previous commit/rollback and releases any database locks held by the Connection
rollback()	Rolls back any changes made since the previous commit/rollback and releases any locks held by the Connection
close()	Causes an immediate release of a Connection's database and JDBC resources
isClosed()	Returns true if the Connection is closed and false if the Connection is still open

java.sql.Statement Class

The Statement class is used to execute static SQL statements and to obtain the results from those statements. Only one ResultSet per Statement object can be opened at one time; if multiple statements are to be used at the same time, multiple Statement objects must be instantiated and used.

The Statement class is best used for an SQL statement that is executed only once and its results iterated through.

```
...
Statement stmt = conn.createStatement();
ResultSet rs = stmt.executeQuery( "select * from table1" );
...
```

As this code sample demonstrates, the Statement object is created via the createStatement method of the Connection class. Once created, the Statement object is used to execute a query statement that returns a ResultSet to represent the rows returned by the query. This ResultSet is then used to iterate through the results obtained by running the query.

The methods for the Statement class are listed in Table C.2. As with the methods described previously, these throw an SQLException when errors are encountered.

(*Tip:* If a statement is to be executed multiple times, it is better for performance reasons to use the PreparedStatement class to execute the SQL statement. A prepared statement is sent to the database engine to be parsed and optimized before being used. Therefore, each time the statement is executed, the overhead of parsing and optimization is eliminated.)

java.sql.ResultSet Class

The ResultSet class provides access to the data returned by the SQL statement that has been executed. The rows are retrieved in sequence, with the next method used to advance the cursor. A number of methods are available to retrieve the JDBC data types stored.

JDBC result rows can be retrieved only in a serial fashion; the result set cannot move to any previous rows.

```
...
// retrieve the set of results from the query
ResultSet rs = stmt.executeQuery(
                     "select * from table1" );
// position cursor before the first result element
boolean more = rs.next();
while ( more ) {
      System.out.println( "col1 value : " +
                            rs.getInt( 1 ) );
      // move to the next row
      more = rs.next();
  }
...
```

Table C.2 Statement Class Methods

Method	Description
executeQuery(String sql) ResultSet	Executes an SQL statement and returns the
executeUpdate(String sql)	Executes the SQL insert, update, or delete statement; returns the row count, or 0 for SQL statements that return nothing
close()	Releases a statement's database and JDBC resources
getMaxFieldSize()	Returns the MaxFieldSize limit, the maximum amount of data returned for any
column value	
setMaxFieldSize(int max)	Sets the MaxFieldSize limit
getMaxRows()	Gets the maximum number of rows that a ResultSet can contain
setMaxRows(int max)	Sets the maximum number of rows that a ResultSet can contain
setEscapeProcessing (boolean enable)	Sets escape processing for the driver on or off; if escape processing is on, the driver will do escape processing before the SQL is sent to the database
getQueryTimeout()	Retrieves the QueryTimeOut limit, which is the number of seconds the driver will wait for a statement to execute
SetQueryTimeout (int seconds)	Sets the QueryTimeOut limit
cancel()	Executed by one thread to cancel a statement being executed by another thread
getWarnings()	Returns SQLWarnings for the SQLStatement
clearWarnings()	Clears the warnings for this Statement
setCursorName	Defines the SQL cursor name (String name) that will be used by subsequent Statement execute methods
execute(String sql)	Executes an SQL statement that may return multiple results
getResultSet()	Returns the current result as a ResultSet
getUpdateCount()	Returns the current result of the update
getMoreResults()	Moves to an SQL statement's next result

This example shows the `Statement` object (`stmt`) being used to execute the query; the result of this action is returned as a `ResultSet` object representing the rows returned. The first time the next method is called, the `ResultSet` will be positioned at the first row of the set. Subsequent executions of the next method will position the `ResultSet` object to the next row in the set.

> Note that it is not an error to execute a query that doesn't return any rows. An empty `ResultSet` is indicated by a boolean false being returned from the first call to the next method. Testing and responding to this result provide a graceful method of managing an empty `ResultSet`, as shown in the following code.

```
. . .
ResultSet rs = stmt.executeQuery(
                    "select * from table1" );
   // position cursor before the first result element
   boolean more = rs.next();

   // if no rows found, print message and return
   if ( !more )
      System.out.println( "No rows returned." );
 . . .
```

Table C.3 lists the methods available in this class. Methods are available to move to the next row in the `ResultSet` and to retrieve columns by column index (integer number) or column name. Only methods to retrieve data by the column index are included in the table. The corresponding methods to retrieve data by column name merely receive a parameter for the column name as a character string rather than the integer column index shown in these methods.

PreparedStatement Class

Using JDBC an SQL statement can be precompiled and stored using an object reference. Once precompiled, this object will execute faster than a statement that is executed directly without the precompile phase.

A prepared statement potentially can have a series of parameters, sometimes called *placeholders*, which can be substituted for by actual values when the statement is executed. A series of methods are available to set these values.

. . .

Table C.3 ResultSet Class Methods

Method	Description
next()	Moves to the next row in the ResultSet
close()	Closes the current ResultSet
wasNull()	Reports whether or not the last column read had a NULL value
getString(int columnIndex)	Returns the value of the column index element as a string
getBoolean(int columnIndex)	Returns the value of the column index data element as a boolean data type
getByte(int columnIndex)	Returns the value of the column index data element as a byte
getShort (int columnIndex)	Returns the value of the column index data element as a short integer
getInt(int columnIndex)	Returns the value of the column index data element as an int
getLong(int columnIndex)	Returns the value of the column index data element as a long integer
getFloat(int columnIndex)	Returns the value of the column index data element as a float data type
getDouble(int columnIndex)	Returns the value of the column index data element as a double floating-point number
getBytes(int columnIndex)	Returns the value of the column index data elements as a series of bytes
getDate(int columnIndex)	Returns the value of the column index data element as a date
getTime(int columnIndex)	Returns the value of the column index data element as a time
BigDecimal getBigDecimal int index)	Returns the column at the index location as a (java.math.BigDecimal
BigDecimal getBigDecimal (String colName)	Returns the column at the index location as a java.math.BigDecimal
getTimeStamp(int columnIndex)	Returns the value of the column index data element as a time stamp
getAsciiStream (int columnIndex)	Returns the value of the column index data element as an ASCII stream

```
PreparedStatement stmt  = con.prepareStatement(
                 " select * from customers " +
                 " where lastname like ? " );
stmt.setString( 1,
        vectorParams.elementAt( 0 ).toString() );
   ResultSet rs = stmt.executeQuery();

. . .
```

This code sample demonstrates the creation of a `PreparedStatement` object. The `PreparedStatement` object allows placeholders (e.g., a question mark) to be placed in a query statement. Placeholders are used to substitute parameter values when the statement is executed. A number of set methods are available to set the values of parameters for various data types. In this example, the parameter is set using the `setString` method of the `PrepareStatement` class. The `executeQuery` method is then used to create a `ResultSet`.

An object used to store a prepared statement would be an instantiation of the `PreparedStatement` class. The methods in this class are described in Table C.4.

Table C.4 PreparedStatement Class Methods

Method	Description
`executeQuery()`	Executes a prepared SQL statement and returns the `ResultSet`
`executeUpdate()`	Executes a prepared SQL update statement and returns either a row count for the statement or a zero
`setNull( int parameterIndex, int sqlType )`	Sets a parameter to the SQL null representation for the data type
`setBoolean( int parameterIndex, boolean x )`	Sets a parameter to an appropriate value for the boolean data type at the parameter index
`setByte( int parameterIndex, byte x )`	Sets a parameter to an appropriate value for the byte data type at the parameter index
`setShort( int parameterIndex, short x )`	Sets a parameter to an appropriate value for the short integer at the parameter index
`setInt( int parameterIndex, int x )`	Sets a parameter to an appropriate value for the int at the parameter index
`setLong( int parameterIndex, long x )`	Sets a parameter to an appropriate value for the long integer at the parameter index

Table C.4 PreparedStatement Class Methods (cont.)

Method	Description
`setFloat( int parameterIndex, float x )`	Sets a parameter to an appropriate value for the float at the parameter index
`setDouble( int parameterIndex, double x )`	Sets a parameter to an appropriate value for the double number at the parameter index
`setNumeric( int parameterIndex, index`	Sets a parameter to an appropriate value for the numeric at the `Numeric x )` at the parameter index
`setString( int parameterIndex, String x )`	Sets a parameter to an appropriate value for the string at the parameter index
`setBytes( int parameterIndex, parameter index`	Sets a parameter to an appropriate value for the byte array at `byte x[] )` at the paramater index
`setDate( int parameterIndex, parameter index`	Sets a parameter to an appropriate value for the date at the `java.sql.Date x )` at the parameter index
`setTime( int parameterIndex, parameter index`	Sets a parameter to an appropriate value for the time object at `java.sql.Time x )` at the parameter index
`setTimestamp( int parameterIndex, java.sql. TimeStamp x`	Sets the parameter to an appropriate value for the time stamp variable at the parameter index
`setBinaryStream( int parameterIndex, java.io. InputStream x, int length )`	Sets the parameter to an appropriate value and size for the binary input stream at the parameter index
`clearParameters()`	Clears and releases the resources used by the current parameter values
`setASCIICodeStream( int parameterIndex, java.io. InputStream x, int length )`	Sets the parameter to an appropriate value and size for the ASCII input stream at the parameter index
`setObject( int parameterIndex, Object x, int targetSQLType, int scale )`	Sets the value of a parameter to the parameter (several variations of parameters are used to call this method; only one is shown here)

Mapping SQL Data Types into Java

With JDBC, data are retrieved from the database into `ResultSet` objects with correct data type mappings. This occurs automatically with JDBC and is the responsibility of the JDBC driver. It is when the data are retrieved from the `ResultSet` into member variables that data types must be mapped correctly. Various metadata methods are available to discover data types of returned columns if needed, but most applications will have data type knowledge and simply need to use the correct methods to retrieve the data.

The SQL data types do not map directly into Java data types, but this is not generally a problem. In some cases, a number of SQL data types can be mapped into a single Java data type. In other cases, there are several choices available for storing SQL data types in Java applications.

The reverse operation of storing Java data types in an SQL database involves using the same conversion rules in reverse. Once again, a number of options are available to the programmer for data storage. Table C.5 lists the SQL data types and the corresponding Java data types. Not all databases will store all these data types, and not all databases may use the SQL names for the same data type.

These data type mappings are discussed in more detail below.

SQL CHAR Data Type

The SQL CHAR data types all map into the Java `String` data type. Java has no fixed-length character string arrays; character string arrays in Java should be treated as `String` data types that can assume a variable length. There is, therefore, no need to distinguish between variable- and fixed-length character strings with Java. The SQL data types of CHAR, VARCHAR, and LONGVARCHAR all can be stored in a Java `String` data type.

SQL BINARY, VARBINARY, and LONGVARBINARY

SQL BINARY, VARBINARY, and LONGBARBINARY can all be expressed as byte arrays in Java. Because the LONGVARBINARY data type can be very large, JDBC allows the programmer to set the return value of a LONGVARBINARY to be a Java input stream.

Table C.5 SQL Data Types to Java Data Type Mappings

SQL Type	Java Type
CHAR	String
VARCHAR	String
LONGVARCHAR	String
NUMERIC	java.math.BigDecimal
DECIMAL	java.math.BigDecimal
BIT	boolean
TINYINT	byte
SMALLINT	short
INTEGER	int
BIGINT	long
SQL Type	Java Type
REAL	float
FLOAT	double
DOUBLE	double
BINARY	byte[]
VARBINARY	byte[]
LONGVARBINARY	byte[]
DATE	java.sql.Date
TIME	java.sql.Time
TIMESTAMP	java.sql.Timestamp

BIT Data Type

The SQL BIT type can be mapped to the Java boolean type.

TINYINT, SMALLINT, INTEGER, and BIGINT

The SQL TINYINT, SMALLINT, INTEGER, and BIGINT types can be mapped to the Java byte, short, int, and long data types, respectively.

REAL, FLOAT, and DOUBLE

The SQL floating-point data types of REAL, FLOAT, and DOUBLE can be mapped as follows: The REAL data type can be stored in a Java float data type, and the REAL and DOUBLE can be stored in a Java double.

DATE, TIME, and TIMESTAMP

SQL provides three date/time-related data types: DATE, TIME, and TIME-STAMP. The `java.sql.Date` class provides date and time information, but this class does not directly support any of the three SQL date/time data types. To accommodate these SQL data types, three subclasses were declared from `java.util.Date`: `java.sql.Date`, `java.sql.Time`, and `java.sql.TimeStamp`. The java.util.Date class can be used to store SQL DATE data, the java.util.Time class can be used to store SQL TIME information, and the java.sql.Timestamp can be used to store SQL TIMESTAMP data.

Transactions

A database transaction is a series of database updates that are grouped together as a single atomic update transaction. If any single update in the transaction fails, the remaining updates are rolled back; that is, their effect on the database is removed and any records they may have deleted or updated are restored to the state they were in before the transaction was started.

By default, JDBC classes operate in *auto-commit mode.* This means that each SQL statement executed is considered a separate transaction and a commit is made at the completion of the statement. To group a set of transactions together, the auto-commit mode must be disabled using the `Connection` class `setAutoCommit` method and passing the method a boolean `false` value.

With auto-commit disabled, an implicit transaction is always in place. An explicit commit can be made by calling the `Connection` method `commit`. Alternatively, a rollback can be made by calling the `Connection` method `rollback`. This rolls back the current transaction and restores the database to the state it was in before the start of the current transaction.

Various database-dependent isolation levels can be set. There are methods in the `DatabaseMetaData` class that can be used to learn the existing defaults in place in the current session, and methods in the Connection class that can be used to change the current isolation level.

CODE LISTINGS: CAL.JAVA AND TAGCAL.JAVA

Cal.java

```java
package JSPCal;

import java.text.*;
import java.util.*;
import java.io.*;

import javax.servlet.*;
import javax.servlet.jsp.*;

public class Cal {


// array for months
private static final String[] months = new
DateFormatSymbols().getMonths();

// array for days of week in string format
private static final String[] days = new
DateFormatSymbols().getWeekdays();
```

```java
// array for day abbreviations
private static final String daysAbbrev[] = new
DateFormatSymbols().getShortWeekdays();

// internal date
private int month;
private int day;
private int year;

private  String printHighLightColor = "grey";
//
private Calendar  mCalendar = null;  // internal calendar
private JspWriter mOut = null;         // response output stream

//
private boolean dateStringOnly = false;


// ***************************************************
// Bean methods

public void setMonth( int month ) {
  this.month = month;
}


public void setYear( int year ) {
  this.year = year;
  setCalDate();
}

public void setDay( int day ) {
    this.day = day;
}

public void setHighLightColor ( String color ) {
    this.printHighLightColor = color;
}

public void setDateString( boolean flag ) {
    this.dateStringOnly = flag;
}
```

```java
public void setCalDate() {
    // set to internal date
    setCalDate( this.month, this.day, this.year );
}

public void setCalDate( int month, int day, int year )
{
    mCalendar = new GregorianCalendar( year,  month, day );
}

public void setOut( JspWriter out ) {
    mOut = out;
}

public void setCalCurrentDate()
{
    mCalendar = new GregorianCalendar();

    setDay( mCalendar.get(Calendar.DAY_OF_MONTH ));
    setYear( mCalendar.get(Calendar.YEAR) );
    setMonth( mCalendar.get( Calendar.MONTH )+ 1 );
}

// getXXXX() methods


// return the Current date (month day, year) as a string
public String getCurrentDate() {

if ( mCalendar == null )
    setCalCurrentDate();

return months[ this.month ] +
               "   " +
          this.day +
          "," +
          "   " +
     this.year;
}


public String getCurrentDate( String format ) {
```

```java
// String s = DateFormat().getDateInstance().format(new Date());
if ( mCalendar == null )
    setCalCurrentDate();

if ( format.equals("mm/dd/yy") )
    return ( mCalendar.get( Calendar.MONTH ) + 1 ) + "/" +
            this.day + "/" +
            mCalendar.get( Calendar.YEAR );
else          // no other formats for now
    return null;

}

// ———————————————————————————-
public void printCal( JspWriter out ) throws ServletException {

Calendar cal = mCalendar;
String printAttr;

// set to the first day of the month
cal.set( Calendar.DAY_OF_MONTH, 1 );


// print the month in HTML table format

try {

// print the header
out.println("<H2> " +
                    months[ this.month ] +
                    "  " +
                    this.day +
                    "," +
                    "   " +
            this.year +
            "</H2>" );

out.println("<table border=3>");

// print the days of the week
out.print("<tr>");
for ( int n = 0; n <= 6; n++ )
    out.print("<td>" + daysAbbrev[n] + "</td>");
```

```
out.println("</tr>");

// print blanks up to the start day
out.print("<tr>");

// this is the day selected. let's highlight it with this dis-
play attribute
if ( this.day == 1 )
    printAttr = "<td bgcolor=" + '"' + printHighLightColor + '"'
+ ">";
else
    printAttr = "<td>";

if ( cal.get( Calendar.DAY_OF_WEEK) > 1 ) {

    for ( int x = 0; x <= ( cal.get( Calendar.DAY_OF_WEEK) - 1);
x++ ) {

        if ( x < ( cal.get(Calendar.DAY_OF_WEEK )-1) )
            out.print( "<td>" + "-" + "</td>" );
        else
            out.print( printAttr + "1" + "</td>" );

        if ( x == 6 ) {
            out.println("</tr>");
            out.print("<tr>");
        }
    }
}
else // day_of_week == 1 == 'Sunday'
    out.print( printAttr + "1" + "</td>" );

printAttr = "<td bgcolor=" + '"' + printHighLightColor + '"' +
">";

for ( int n = 2; n <= cal.getActualMaximum( Calendar.DAY_OF_MONTH
); n++ ) {

    if ( n == this.day ) // this is the day selected. let's
highlight it
        out.print( printAttr + n + "</td>" );
    else
        out.print( "<td>" + n + "</td>" );
```

```
      // print <tr> at end of week
      cal.set( Calendar.DAY_OF_MONTH, n );
      if ( cal.get( Calendar.DAY_OF_WEEK) == 7) {
        out.println( "</tr>" );
        out.print( "<tr>" );
      }
}

out.println( "</tr>" );
out.println("</table>");
}

catch (IOException e) {

    throw new ServletException("I/O Exception in Cal.printCal() "
);

}

}

}
```

TagCal.java

```
package JSPCal;

import java.text.*;
import java.util.*;
import java.io.*;

import javax.servlet.*;
import javax.servlet.jsp.tagext.*;
import javax.servlet.jsp.*;

public class TagCal extends TagSupport {


// array for months
private static final String months[] = new
DateFormatSymbols().getMonths();

// array for days of week in string format
```

```java
private static final String days[] = new
DateFormatSymbols().getWeekdays();

// array for day abbreviations
private static final String daysAbbrev[] = new
DateFormatSymbols().getShortWeekdays();

// internal date
private int month;
private int day;
private int year;

private  String printHighLightColor = "grey";
//
private Calendar  mCalendar = null;  // internal calendar
private JspWriter mOut = null;         // response output stream

//
private boolean dateStringOnly = false;

public int doStartTag() {

// use the current day as the default date
if ( ( mCalendar == null ) && ( this.month == 0 ) && ( this.day
== 0 ) && ( this.year == 0 ) )
   setCalCurrentDate();

if ( ( this.month != 0 ) && ( this.day != 0 ) && ( this.year !=
0 ) ) {
    this.month—; // GregorianCalendar expects 0 - based month
    setCalDate( this.month, this.day, this.year );
}

// set the default output stream to the JspWriter in the
pageContext
if ( mOut == null )
   setOut( pageContext.getOut() );

try {

// print the calendar
if ( !dateStringOnly )
    printCal();
else // print the current date as a string
```

```
    mOut.println( getCurrentDate() );

}

// **

// **
catch (ServletException e) {

  System.out.println("TagCal error: " + e.getMessage() );

}
catch (IOException e) {
      System.out.println( "IOException in TagCal: " +
e.getMessage() );
}


// the tag shouldn't have a body to process
return (SKIP_BODY);
}



// ****************************************************
// Bean methods

public void setMonth( int month ) {
  this.month = month;
}


public void setYear( int year ) {
  this.year = year;
}

public void setDay( int day ) {
    this.day = day;
}

public void setHighLightColor ( String color ) {

    this.printHighLightColor = color;
```

```java
}

public void setDateString( boolean flag ) {

    this.dateStringOnly = flag;

}

public void setCalDate() {
  setCalDate( this.month, this.day, this.year );
}

public void setCalDate( int month, int day, int year )
{
    mCalendar = new GregorianCalendar( year,  month, day );
}

public void setOut( JspWriter out ) {
    mOut = out;
}


public void setCalCurrentDate()
{

    mCalendar = new GregorianCalendar();

    setDay( mCalendar.get(Calendar.DAY_OF_MONTH ));
    setYear( mCalendar.get(Calendar.YEAR) );
    setMonth( mCalendar.get( Calendar.MONTH )+ 1 );

}

// getXXXX() methods


// return the Current date (month day, year) as a string
public String getCurrentDate() {

return months[ this.month ] +
                "      " +
            this.day +
                  "," +
```

```
                              "     " +
            this.year;
}


// ─────────────────────────────────────────
// this provides the widget to display a calendar in HTML table
format to the PrintWriter


public void printCal() throws ServletException {

if ( mOut == null )
    mOut = pageContext.getOut();

    printCal( mOut );

}

// ***   add functionality to highlight the current day if it is
in this month ****

// ─────────────────────────────────────────
public void printCal( JspWriter out ) throws ServletException {

Calendar cal = mCalendar;
String printAttr;

// set to the first day of the month
cal.set( Calendar.DAY_OF_MONTH, 1 );


// print the month in HTML table format

try {

// print the header
out.println("<H2> " +
                    months[ this.month ] +
                    "  " +
            this.day +
                    "," +
                    "   " +
            this.year +
```

```
                "</H2>" );

out.println("<table border=3>");

// print the days of the week
out.print("<tr>");
for ( int n = 0; n <= 6; n++ )
    out.print("<td>" + daysAbbrev[n] + "</td>");

out.println("</tr>");

// print blanks up to the start day
out.print("<tr>");

// this is the day selected. let's highlight it with this dis-
play attribute
if (  this.day == 1 )
    printAttr = "<td bgcolor=" + '"' + printHighLightColor + '"'
+ ">";
else
    printAttr = "<td>";

if ( cal.get( Calendar.DAY_OF_WEEK) > 1 ) {

    for ( int x = 0; x <= ( cal.get( Calendar.DAY_OF_WEEK) - 1);
x++ ) {

        if ( x < ( cal.get(Calendar.DAY_OF_WEEK )-1) )
            out.print( "<td>" + "-" + "</td>" );
        else
            out.print( printAttr + "1" + "</td>" );

        if ( x == 6 ) {
            out.println("</tr>");
            out.print("<tr>");
        }
     }
}
else // day_of_week == 1 == 'Sunday'
    out.print( printAttr + "1" + "</td>" );

printAttr = "<td bgcolor=" + '"' + printHighLightColor + '"' +
">";
```

```
for ( int n = 2; n <= cal.getActualMaximum( Calendar.DAY_OF_MONTH
); n++ ) {

    if ( n == this.day ) // this is the day selected. let's
highlight it
        out.print( printAttr + n + "</td>" );
    else
        out.print( "<td>" + n + "</td>" );

    // print <tr> at end of week
    cal.set( Calendar.DAY_OF_MONTH, n );
    if ( cal.get( Calendar.DAY_OF_WEEK) == 7) {
      out.println( "</tr>" );
      out.print( "<tr>" );
    }
}

out.println( "</tr>" );
out.println("</table>");
}

catch (IOException e) {

    throw new ServletException("I/O Exception in Cal.printCal() "
);

}

}

}
```

CODE LISTING: KNOWLEDGEBASEFACADE.JAVA

```java
package knowledgebase;

import javax.servlet.*;
import javax.servlet.http.*;
import java.util.*;
import java.sql.*;

import db.*;
import JSPCal.*;

public class KnowledgeBaseFacade {


// DAO
private Base_keysDAO          base_keysDAO;
private CategoriesDAO         categoriesDAO;
private Message_typesDAO      message_typesDAO;
private Knowledge_baseDAO     knowledge_baseDAO;
private Knowledge_messagesDAO knowledge_messagesDAO;


// VO
```

```
private Base_keysVO            base_keysVO;
private CategoriesVO           categoriesVO;
private Knowledge_baseVO       knowledge_baseVO;
private Knowledge_messagesVO   knowledge_messagesVO;
private Base_keysVO            base_keysVOArr[] = new
Base_keysVO[4]; // base keys for display

//
int doc_key;

String keyword[] = new String[4];

// general
String action;
String submitTitle;
String link_doc;

Iterator iterateKBList;

int rowsUpdated;

// defaults
String defaultMessageType = "Problem";
String defaultCategory    = "Operating System";


// ————————————————————————————————

// setXXXX
public void setDoc_key( int doc_key ) {
  knowledge_baseVO.setDoc_key( doc_key );
}

public void SetPost_user( String post_user ) {
    knowledge_baseVO.setPost_user( post_user );
}
public void setLink_doc( int link_doc ) {
    knowledge_baseVO.setLink_doc( link_doc );
}

public void setDoc_location( String doc_location ) {
  knowledge_baseVO.setDoc_location( doc_location );
}
```

```java
public void setDate_submitted( String date_submitted ) {
    knowledge_baseVO.setDate_submitted( date_submitted );
}

public void setMessage_txt( String message_txt ) {
    knowledge_messagesVO.setMessage_txt( message_txt );
}

public void setMessage_type( String message_type ) {
    knowledge_messagesVO.setMessage_type( message_type );
}

public void setKeyword1( String keyword1 ) {
    this.keyword[0] = keyword1;
}

public void setKeyword2( String keyword2 ) {
    this.keyword[1] = keyword2;
}

public void setKeyword3( String keyword3 ) {
    this.keyword[2] = keyword3;
}

public void setKeyword4( String keyword4 ) {
    this.keyword[3] = keyword4;
}

public void setRowsUpdated( int rows ) {
    this.rowsUpdated = rows;
}

public void setAction( String action ) throws Exception {

    this.action = action;
    setSubmitTitle( this.action );

    if ( action.equals("update") || action.equals("delete") ) {

        loadKnowledgeBase( knowledge_baseVO.getDoc_key() );

    }
    else // action='insert'
```

```java
            knowledge_baseVO.setCategory( "Hardware Failure" );

    // ** what about delete ... want to use a difft form maybe to
turn off input ??
}

public void setSubmitTitle( String submitTitle ) {
        this.submitTitle = submitTitle.toUpperCase() + " Record";
}

// increment the iterator and make the next knowledge_baseVO our
current VO
public void setNextKBVO( boolean val ) throws Exception {

try {

if ( iterateKBList.hasNext() ) {

        knowledge_baseVO = (Knowledge_baseVO) iterateKBList.next();

// debug
System.out.println("loading knowledge_base and related records
for " + knowledge_baseVO.getDoc_key() );

        loadKnowledgeBase( knowledge_baseVO.getDoc_key() );

    }
}
catch (Exception e) {
        System.out.println("Exception in
knowledgeBaseFacade.setNextKBVO(): " + e );
        throw new Exception("Exception in
knowledgeBaseFacade.setNextKBVO(): " + e );
}

}

// getXXXX
public String getEntry_date() {
    return knowledge_baseVO.getEntry_date();
}

public String getDate_submitted() {
    return knowledge_baseVO.getDate_submitted();
```

```java
}

public int getBase_doc_key() {
   return knowledge_baseVO.getBase_doc_key();
}

public int getDoc_key() {
    return knowledge_baseVO.getDoc_key();
}

public Iterator getCategoryList() {
 Iterator i = null;
 try {
   i = categoriesDAO.getCategoryList().iterator();
 } catch (SQLException e) {
     System.out.println( "SQLException in getCategoryList(): " +
e.getMessage() );
 }
 return i;
}

public Iterator getMessageTypesList() {
 Iterator i = null;
 try {
   i = message_typesDAO.getMessageTypesList().iterator();
 } catch (SQLException e) {
     System.out.println( "SQLException in getMessageTypesList():
" + e.getMessage() );
 }
 return i;
}

public String getDoc_location() {
    return knowledge_baseVO.getDoc_location();
}

public String getMessage_txt() {
    return knowledge_messagesVO.getMessage_txt();
}

public String getMessage_type() {
   if ( knowledge_messagesVO.getMessage_type() != null )
      return knowledge_messagesVO.getMessage_type();
   else
```

```java
        return defaultMessageType;
}

public String getPost_user() {
    return knowledge_baseVO.getPost_user();
}
public String getDoc_name() {
    return knowledge_baseVO.getDoc_name();
}


public String getKeyword1( ) {
    return this.keyword[0];
}

public String getKeyword2( ) {
    return this.keyword[1];
}

public String getKeyword3( ) {
    return this.keyword[2];
}

public String getKeyword4( ) {
    return this.keyword[3];
}

public int getLink_doc() {
    return knowledge_baseVO.getLink_doc();
}

public String getSubmitTitle() {
    return this.submitTitle;
}

public int getRowsUpdated() {
    return this.rowsUpdated;
}

public String getAction() {
    return this.action;
}

public String getCategory() {
```

```java
        return knowledge_baseVO.getCategory();
}

public String makeCategoryString( Object obj ) {
    return ((CategoriesVO) obj).getCategory();
}

public String makeMessageTypesString( Object obj ) {
     return ((Message_typesVO) obj).getMessage_type();
}

public boolean isDefaultCategory( String category ) {

// debug
if ( category == null )
    System.out.println("null category in isDefaultCategory");

  if ( category.equals( "Software Problem" ) )
    return true;
  else
    return false;
}
// test harness

public static void main( String args[] ) {
// test harness—not used in production since this is a JavaBean
try {
KnowledgeBaseFacade kbf = new KnowledgeBaseFacade();

// create a knowledge_messages record
kbf.knowledge_baseVO.setDoc_key( 1245 );
kbf.knowledge_baseVO.setDoc_name( "test document" );
kbf.knowledge_baseVO.setDoc_location( "New Jersey" );
kbf.knowledge_baseVO.setLevel( 2 );
kbf.knowledge_baseVO.setCategory( "Software" );
kbf.knowledge_baseVO.setLink_doc( 3333 );
kbf.knowledge_baseVO.setBase_doc_key( 5555 );
kbf.knowledge_baseVO.setPost_user( "Art Taylor" );
kbf.knowledge_baseVO.setEntry_date( "1/28/1958");
kbf.knowledge_baseVO.setDate_submitted( "2/28/2058");


// have the DAO load this object
kbf.knowledge_baseDAO.loadDAO(  kbf.knowledge_baseVO );
```

```
// update using the DAO
// kbf.knowledge_baseDAO.insertDAO();

// insert another one
// kbf.knowledge_baseVO.setDoc_key( 5465 );
// kbf.knowledge_baseVO.setDoc_name( "test again document" );
// kbf.knowledge_baseVO.setCategory( "Hardware" );

// have the DAO load this object
// kbf.knowledge_baseDAO.loadDAO(  kbf.knowledge_baseVO );

// update using the DAO
// kbf.knowledge_baseDAO.insertDAO();

// load the record for the first (1245) entry
kbf.knowledge_baseDAO.loadDAO( 1245 );
kbf.knowledge_baseDAO.setVO( kbf.knowledge_baseVO );

// dump the VO
System.out.println( " ** knowledge_baseDAO value: " );

System.out.println( "doc_key: " +
kbf.knowledge_baseVO.getDoc_key() + " - " +
kbf.knowledge_baseVO.getDoc_name() );


// knowledge_messages
kbf.knowledge_messagesVO.setDoc_key( 1245 );
kbf.knowledge_messagesVO.setMessage_txt( "this is a test mes-
sage");
kbf.knowledge_messagesVO.setMessage_type( "Problem" );

kbf.knowledge_messagesDAO.loadDAO( kbf.knowledge_messagesVO );
kbf.knowledge_messagesDAO.insertDAO();

kbf.knowledge_messagesDAO.setDoc_key( 4133 );
kbf.knowledge_messagesDAO.setMessage_txt( "this is a xxxxxx mes-
sage");
kbf.knowledge_messagesDAO.setMessage_type( "Solution" );
kbf.knowledge_messagesDAO.insertDAO();

kbf.knowledge_messagesDAO.loadDAO( 1245 );
kbf.knowledge_messagesDAO.setVO(  kbf.knowledge_messagesVO );
```

```
// base_keys

kbf.base_keysVO.setDoc_key( 1245 );
kbf.base_keysVO.setKeyword( "Operating System" );
kbf.base_keysDAO.loadDAO( kbf.base_keysVO );
kbf.base_keysDAO.insertDAO();

kbf.base_keysVO.setDoc_key( 4133 );
kbf.base_keysVO.setKeyword( "Software System" );
kbf.base_keysDAO.loadDAO( kbf.base_keysVO );
kbf.base_keysDAO.insertDAO();

kbf.base_keysDAO.loadDAO( 1245 );
kbf.base_keysDAO.setVO( kbf.base_keysVO );

System.out.println( "** base_keys: " );
System.out.println( kbf.base_keysVO.getDoc_key() + " - " +
kbf.base_keysVO.getKeyword() );


// categories
kbf.categoriesVO.setCategory( "Operating System" );
kbf.categoriesVO.setDescription( "Operating system problems." );
kbf.categoriesDAO.loadDAO( kbf.categoriesVO );
kbf.categoriesDAO.insertDAO();

kbf.categoriesVO.setCategory( "Hardware System" );
kbf.categoriesVO.setDescription( "Any hardware problem." );
kbf.categoriesDAO.loadDAO( kbf.categoriesVO );
kbf.categoriesDAO.insertDAO();


kbf.categoriesDAO.loadDAO( "Operating System" );
kbf.categoriesDAO.setVO( kbf.categoriesVO );

System.out.println( "** categories: " );
System.out.println( kbf.categoriesVO.getCategory() + " - " +
kbf.categoriesVO.getDescription() );


}
catch (SQLException e) {
```

```java
   System.out.println( "Exception thrown in KnowledgeBaseFacade: "
+ e );

}

catch (Exception e) {

   System.out.println( "Exception thrown in KnowledgeBaseFacade: "
+ e );

}

}

// ——————————————————————————

public boolean kbRecsHasMore() {
    return iterateKBList.hasNext();
}


// use a filter to retrieve the list of knowledge base records
public void setFilterKBRecs( ServletRequest request, HttpSession
session ) {

try {
     // filter criteria passed as a Collection in a session
object
     Collection filterCriteria
 = (Collection) session.getAttribute( "filter_criteria" );

  // debug
 System.out.println("setFilterKBRecs(): filter_criteria: " +
filterCriteria.toString() );

     iterateKBList                  =
knowledge_baseDAO.getFilteredList( filterCriteria );
}
catch (Exception e) {
    System.out.println("Exception in
KnowledgeBaseFacade.setFilterKBRecs(): " + e );
}
```

```
}

public void setFilterSelection( ServletRequest request,
HttpSession session ) {

try {
    if ( request.getParameter("type").equals("all") )
        setAllKBRecs( true );

    if  ( request.getParameter("type").equals("keyword") )
        setFilterKBRecs( request, session );
    }
    catch ( Exception e) {
        System.out.println("Exception in
KnowledgeBaseFacade.setFilteredSelection() : " + e );
    }
}


// load an internal collection of doc_key, doc_name, doc_location
records
public void setAllKBRecs( boolean val ) throws Exception {

iterateKBList = knowledge_baseDAO.getAll(); // get a collection
of ValueObjects for all knowledge_base records

}

public void insertKBRecs( ServletRequest request, HttpSession
session ) throws Exception {
boolean exceptionFlag = false;
int doc_key;

try {

// use the request to get the values for our VO members
knowledge_baseDAO.setCategory( request.getParameter( "category" )
);

knowledge_baseDAO.setDoc_name( request.getParameter( "doc_name" )
);
//knowledge_baseDAO.setLevel(  );
```

```
//knowledge_baseDAO.setPost_user( request.getParameter(
"post_user" ) );
//knowledge_baseDAO.setDoc_location( request.getParameter(
"doc_location" ) );

knowledge_baseDAO.setPost_user( (String) session.getAttribute(
"login" ) );
knowledge_baseDAO.setDoc_location( (String) session.getAttribute(
"location" ) );

// these parameters aren't in the form, they're stored in the
session object
knowledge_baseDAO.setLink_doc( ((Integer) session.getAttribute(
"link_doc" )).intValue() );
knowledge_baseDAO.setBase_doc_key( ((Integer)
session.getAttribute( "base_doc_key" )).intValue() );


if ( knowledge_baseDAO.getBase_doc_key() == 0 )
   if ( knowledge_baseDAO.getLink_doc() > 0  )
       knowledge_baseDAO.setBase_doc_key(
knowledge_baseDAO.getLink_doc() ) ;

knowledge_baseDAO.setDate_submitted( (String)
session.getAttribute( "date_submitted") );  // only set on ini-
tial insert
knowledge_baseDAO.setEntry_date( (String) session.getAttribute(
"entry_date" ) );

doc_key = knowledge_baseDAO.insertDAO();

//** should throw an execption if we get a 0 back from knowl-
edge_baseDAO.insertDAO

// knowledge_messages
knowledge_messagesDAO.setDoc_key( doc_key );
knowledge_messagesDAO.setMessage_txt( request.getParameter( "mes-
sage_txt" ) );
knowledge_messagesDAO.setMessage_type( request.getParameter(
"message_type" ) );
knowledge_messagesDAO.insertDAO();

// base_keys - the keywords for our message
base_keysDAO.setDoc_key( doc_key );
```

```java
base_keysDAO.setKeyword( request.getParameter( "keyword1" ) );
base_keysDAO.insertDAO();

base_keysDAO.setDoc_key( doc_key );
base_keysDAO.setKeyword( request.getParameter( "keyword2" ) );
base_keysDAO.insertDAO();

base_keysDAO.setDoc_key( doc_key );
base_keysDAO.setKeyword( request.getParameter( "keyword3" ) );
base_keysDAO.insertDAO();

base_keysDAO.setDoc_key( doc_key );
base_keysDAO.setKeyword( request.getParameter( "keyword4" ) );
base_keysDAO.insertDAO();
}
catch (SQLException e) {
    throw new Exception( "SQLException caught in
KnowledgeBaseFacade.insertKBRecs(): " + e );
}
catch (Exception e) {
    throw new Exception( "Exception in
KnowledgeBaseFacade.insertKBRecs(): " + e );
}
finally {
   // assume if we are here, we successfully updated the data-
base with this knowledge base record
   setRowsUpdated(1);
}

}

// perform the processing for the updKB.jsp page


// delete this knowledge_base record and all of the related
records
public void deleteKBRecs( ServletRequest request, HttpSession
session ) {
int doc_key;
boolean exceptionFlag = false;

try {

doc_key = ((Integer) session.getAttribute( "doc_key"
```

```java
)).intValue();

// debug
System.out.println("deleteKBRecs(): doc_key : " + doc_key );

// knowledge_base
knowledge_baseDAO.loadDAO( doc_key );
knowledge_baseDAO.deleteDAO( );

// knowledge_messages
knowledge_messagesDAO.setDoc_key( doc_key );
knowledge_messagesDAO.deleteDAO();

// base_keys - the keywords for our message
base_keysDAO.setDoc_key( doc_key );
base_keysDAO.deleteDAO();

}
catch (SQLException e) {
    System.out.println( "SQLException caught in
KnowledgeBaseFacade.deleteKBRecs(): " + e.getMessage() );
    exceptionFlag = true;
}
catch (Exception e) {
    System.out.println( "Exception in
KnowledgeBaseFacade.deleteKBRecs(): " + e.getMessage() );
    exceptionFlag = true;
}
finally {
    // assume if we are here, we successfully updated the data-
base with this knowledge base record
    if ( !exceptionFlag )
        setRowsUpdated(1);
}


} // —


// called by inputKB.jsp at the start of the input page
public void processParameters( ServletRequest request,
HttpSession session ) throws Exception {
Cal cal = new Cal();
int doc_key = 0;
```

```java
    // assert these parameters are always to inputKB.jsp which
will call this method
    if ( request.getParameter("doc_key") != null )
        setDoc_key( Integer.parseInt(
request.getParameter("doc_key").trim() ));

    // set action will load the DAOs and the value objects for the
knowledge_base (in loadKnowledgebase() )
    if ( request.getParameter("action") != null )
        setAction( request.getParameter("action"));

    if ( request.getParameter( "link_doc" ) != null )
        setLink_doc( Integer.parseInt(
request.getParameter("link_doc").trim() ));

    // add some of these to our session object, since they may not
be passed via the input form
    session.setAttribute( "doc_key", new Integer(
request.getParameter("doc_key")));
    session.setAttribute( "link_doc", new Integer(
request.getParameter("link_doc")) );
    session.setAttribute( "base_doc_key", new
Integer(request.getParameter("base_doc_key")));

    // store the dates as String ... let the database perform con-
version
    if ( request.getParameter("action").equals("insert") ||
         request.getParameter("action").equals("update")   )   {
        session.setAttribute( "entry_date", cal.getCurrentDate(
"mm/dd/yy" )); // date last changed
        knowledge_baseVO.setEntry_date( cal.getCurrentDate(
"mm/dd/yy" ));
    }

    if ( request.getParameter("action").equals("insert") ) {

        session.setAttribute( "date_submitted", cal.getCurrentDate(
"mm/dd/yy" )); // date first entered (submitted)
        knowledge_baseVO.setDate_submitted( cal.getCurrentDate(
"mm/dd/yy" ));

        // get the user name and location from the login informa-
```

```
tion stored in the session object
      knowledge_baseVO.setPost_user( (String)
session.getAttribute( "login") );
      knowledge_baseVO.setDoc_location( (String)
session.getAttribute( "location" ) );

      // if this is a threaded message, get the doc_name from
the base_doc_key record
      // since this is an insert, knowledge_baseVO has not been
loaded, so need to create a DAO to
      // get the base_doc_key
      if (
Integer.parseInt(request.getParameter("base_doc_key").trim()) ==
0  ) // no base_doc_key value passed
          doc_key = Integer.parseInt(
request.getParameter("link_doc"));          // use the link_doc
      else
          doc_key = Integer.parseInt(
request.getParameter("base_doc_key"));

      Knowledge_baseDAO baseDAO = new Knowledge_baseDAO( );
      baseDAO.loadDAO( doc_key );
      knowledge_baseVO.setDoc_name( baseDAO.getDoc_name() );

  }




  // if this is an update or delete, does the user have permis-
sion to do this
  if ( request.getParameter("action").equals("update") )
      if ( ((String) session.getAttribute("login")).equals( knowl-
edge_baseVO.getPost_user()) )
          return;  // the user that posted the message
      else
          if (( (String)
session.getAttribute("role")).equals("admin") )
              return; // this is the sysadmin
          else
              throw new Exception("You do not have permission to
perform this function.");
```

```
}

//
public void updateKBRecs( ServletRequest request, HttpSession
session ) {
int doc_key = 0;
boolean exceptionFlag = false;


try {

doc_key = ((Integer) session.getAttribute("doc_key")).intValue();

// use the request to get the values for update
knowledge_baseDAO.setDoc_key( doc_key );
knowledge_baseDAO.setDoc_name( request.getParameter( "doc_name" )
);
knowledge_baseDAO.setPost_user( request.getParameter(
"post_user") );
knowledge_baseDAO.setDoc_location( request.getParameter(
"doc_location") );
knowledge_baseDAO.setLink_doc( Integer.parseInt(
request.getParameter( "link_doc" )) );
knowledge_baseDAO.setCategory( request.getParameter( "category" )
);

// should not set the date_submitted, the date the message first
entered, on update
// but need to set entry_date - date last modified
knowledge_baseDAO.setEntry_date( (String) session.getAttribute(
"entry_date" ) );

// need to add base_doc_key to the form
//knowledge_baseDAO.setBase_doc_key( Integer.parseInt(
request.getParameter( "base_doc_key" ) ) ) ;


// knowledge_messages
knowledge_messagesDAO.setDoc_key(
 doc_key );
knowledge_messagesDAO.setMessage_txt( request.getParameter( "mes-
sage_txt" ) );
knowledge_messagesDAO.setMessage_type( request.getParameter(
"message_type" ) );
```

```
knowledge_messagesDAO.updateDAO();

// base_keys - the keywords for our message

// no true primary key in this table - it's just a list
// so delete all existing recs and then insert them again
base_keysDAO.setDoc_key( doc_key );
base_keysDAO.deleteDAO();

base_keysDAO.setDoc_key( doc_key );
base_keysDAO.setKeyword( request.getParameter( "keyword1" ) );
base_keysDAO.insertDAO();

base_keysDAO.setDoc_key( doc_key );
base_keysDAO.setKeyword( request.getParameter( "keyword2" ) );
base_keysDAO.insertDAO();

base_keysDAO.setDoc_key( doc_key );
base_keysDAO.setKeyword( request.getParameter( "keyword3" ) );
base_keysDAO.insertDAO();

base_keysDAO.setDoc_key( doc_key );
base_keysDAO.setKeyword( request.getParameter( "keyword4" ) );
base_keysDAO.insertDAO();

}
catch (SQLException e) {
    System.out.println( "SQLException caught in
KnowledgeBaseFacade.updateKBRecs(): " + e + " - " +
e.getMessage() );
    exceptionFlag = true;
}
catch (Exception e) {
    System.out.println( "Exception in
KnowledgeBaseFacade.updateKBRecs(): " + e );
    exceptionFlag = true;
}
finally {
   // assume if we are here, we successfully updated the data-
base with this knowledge base record
   if ( !exceptionFlag )
      setRowsUpdated(1);
}
```

```
} // updateKBRecs()


public void doUpdate( ServletRequest request, HttpSession session
) throws Exception {
int doc_key=0;

try {


// let's make sure we have a doc_key
if ( request.getParameter("doc_key") != null )
     doc_key = Integer.parseInt(
request.getParameter("doc_key").trim() );
else
  if ( session.getAttribute("doc_key") != null )
       doc_key = ((Integer)
session.getAttribute("doc_key")).intValue();

// if our doc_key is still 0 and this isn't an insert, throw an
exception
if (( doc_key == 0 ) && (
request.getParameter("action").equals("update")) )
     throw new Exception ("Invalid document key.");


// update can be an insert,update or delete operation
// check security before allowing an update

// user must be logged in to perform an insert
if ( request.getParameter("action").equals("insert") ) {
    if ( session.getAttribute("login") == null ) // the user has
not logged in
        throw new Exception("User must login to add a message.");
}

// if user is performing an update or delete, then
// this must be the user that posted the message
if ( session.getAttribute("login") == null ) // user has not
logged in
    throw new Exception("User must login to perform this opera-
tion." );

if ( request.getParameter("action").equals("update") ||
```

```
      request.getParameter("action").equals("delete") ) {
   if ( (!((String) session.getAttribute("login")).equals(
request.getParameter("post_user") )) ||
        (!((String) session.getAttribute("role")).equals(
"admin" ) ) ) {   // this is the sysadmin
      throw new Exception("User does not have permission to per-
form this function.");
   }
}

// security is ok, so perform the update
if ( request.getParameter("action").equals("insert") ) {
   insertKBRecs( request, session );
   return;
}

if ( request.getParameter("action").equals("update") ) {
   session.setAttribute("doc_key", new Integer( doc_key ) );
   updateKBRecs( request, session );
   return;
}

if ( request.getParameter("action").equals("delete") ) {
   session.setAttribute("doc_key", new Integer( doc_key ) );
   deleteKBRecs( request, session );
   return;
}

// if at this point, then we have not been passed a valid action
// log an error and throw an exception
System.out.println("knowledge_baseFacade.doUpdate() called with
invalid action: " +
                   request.getParameter("action"));
throw new Exception( "KnowledgeBaseFacade.doUpdate called with an
invalid action " +
                   request.getParameter("action"));

}
catch (Exception e) {
  System.out.println("Exception in KnowledgeBase.doUpdate(): " +
e );
  throw new Exception ("Exception in KnowledgeBase.doUpdate(): "
+ e );
}
```

```
} // end doUpdate()

// **********************************************

// load a knowledge base record with this record key
public void loadKnowledgeBase( int doc_key ) throws Exception {

try {


knowledge_baseDAO.loadDAO( doc_key );   // assert this has been
set previously
knowledge_baseDAO.setVO( knowledge_baseVO );


knowledge_messages(): calling " );
knowledge_messagesDAO.loadDAO( doc_key );
knowledge_messagesDAO.setVO( knowledge_messagesVO );
// debug
//System.out.println("loadKnowledgeBase-knowledge_messages():
completed " );

base_keysDAO.loadDAO( doc_key );
base_keysDAO.set4VO( base_keysVOArr );


setKeyword1( base_keysVOArr[0].getKeyword() );
setKeyword2( base_keysVOArr[1].getKeyword() );
setKeyword3( base_keysVOArr[2].getKeyword() );
setKeyword4( base_keysVOArr[3].getKeyword() );

}
catch (SQLException e) {
     System.out.println("SQLException thrown in
KnowledgeBaseFacade.loadKnowledgeBase(): " + e );
     throw new Exception("Exception in
KnowledgeBaseFacade.loadKnowledgeBase(): " +  e );
}
catch (Exception e) {
     System.out.println("Exception thrown in
KnowledgeBaseFacade.loadKnowledgeBase(): " + e );
```

```java
        throw new Exception("Exception in
KnowledgeBaseFacade.loadKnowledgeBase(): " +  e );
    }

}


// constructor
public KnowledgeBaseFacade() throws Exception {

// create DAO
base_keysDAO          = new Base_keysDAO();
categoriesDAO         = new CategoriesDAO();
message_typesDAO      = new Message_typesDAO();
knowledge_baseDAO     = new Knowledge_baseDAO();
knowledge_messagesDAO = new Knowledge_messagesDAO();

// create VO
base_keysVO           = new Base_keysVO();
categoriesVO          = new CategoriesVO();
knowledge_baseVO      = new Knowledge_baseVO();
knowledge_messagesVO  = new Knowledge_messagesVO();

}

}
```

KNOWLEDGE_baseDAO.java

```java
package knowledgebase;

import javax.servlet.*;
import java.util.*;
import java.sql.*;

import db.*;

public class Knowledge_baseDAO {

// private members
private int doc_key;
private String doc_name;
private String doc_location;
private String post_user;
private int link_doc;
private int level;
private String entry_date; // date
private String date_submitted; // date
private String category;
private int base_doc_key;
```

```java
// wraps JDBC methods
DBUtil dbutil;

// string to hold SQL statements
private String insertStmtStr;
private String updateStmtStr;
private String deleteStmtStr;
private String selectStmtStr;
private String selectAllStmtStr;
private String selectFilterStmtStr;


// Prepared SQL statements
PreparedStatement insertStmt;
PreparedStatement updateStmt;
PreparedStatement deleteStmt;
PreparedStatement selectStmt;
PreparedStatement selectAllStmt;
PreparedStatement selectFilterStmt;

// getXXXX methods
public int getDoc_key() {

   return doc_key;

}

public String getDoc_name(){

   return doc_name;

}


public int getBase_doc_key() {

    return this.base_doc_key;

}

public int getLink_doc() {

    return this.link_doc;
```

```java
}

public String getDoc_location() {

    return doc_location;

}

public String getPost_user() {

    return post_user;
}
public int getLevel() {

    return level;

}

public String getEntry_date() {

    return entry_date;

}

public String getDate_submitted() {

    return this.date_submitted;
}

public String getCategory() {

    return category;

}


// setXXXX methods

public void setDoc_name( String doc_name ) {

    this.doc_name = doc_name;

}
```

```java
public void setDoc_key( int doc_key ) {

    this.doc_key = doc_key;

}

public void setDoc_location( String doc_location ) {

    this.doc_location = doc_location;

}

public void setPost_user( String post_user ) {

     this.post_user = post_user;
}

public void setLevel( int level ) {

    this.level = level;

}

public void setLink_doc( int link_doc ) {

   this.link_doc = link_doc;

}

public void setBase_doc_key( int base_doc_key ) {

    this.base_doc_key = base_doc_key;

}

public void setEntry_date( String entry_date ) {

    this.entry_date = entry_date;
}


public void setDate_submitted( String date_submitted ) {
```

```java
        this.date_submitted = date_submitted;

}

public void setCategory( String category ) {

    this.category = category;

}


// convenience methods

public void createPreparedStatements( ) throws Exception {



try {

    insertStmtStr = "insert into knowledge_base " +
                    "
(doc_key,doc_name,category,post_user,doc_location,link_doc,
level, base_doc_key, entry_date, date_submitted) values " +
                    " ( ?,      ?,          ?,          ?,              ?,
?,          ?,      ?,                  ?,          ? ) "  ;

    insertStmt = dbutil.createPreparedStatement( insertStmtStr );


    updateStmtStr = "update knowledge_base " +
                    " set doc_name = ?, " +
             "  doc_location = ?, " +
             "  category = ?,  "   +
             "  post_user = ?, "   +
              "  level = ?, "   +
              "  link_doc = ?, "   +
              "  entry_date = ? "   +
                  "  where doc_key = ? "   ;

    updateStmt = dbutil.createPreparedStatement( updateStmtStr );

    deleteStmtStr = "delete from knowledge_base " +
                    "           where doc_key = ?" ;
```

```
    deleteStmt = dbutil.createPreparedStatement( deleteStmtStr );


    selectStmtStr = "select
doc_key,doc_name,category,post_user,doc_location,link_doc, " +
                    " base_doc_key,entry_date,
date_submitted,level " +
                    " from knowledge_base " +
                    " where doc_key = ? ";

    selectStmt = dbutil.createPreparedStatement( selectStmtStr );

    selectAllStmtStr = "select
doc_key,doc_name,category,post_user,doc_location,link_doc, " +
                    " base_doc_key,entry_date,
date_submitted,level " +
                    " from knowledge_base " +
                    " order by base_doc_key, doc_key, date_sub-
mitted, entry_date";

    selectAllStmt = dbutil.createPreparedStatement(
selectAllStmtStr );

    selectFilterStmtStr = " select " +
    " doc_key, doc_name,category, post_user, doc_location,
link_doc, " +
    " base_doc_key,entry_date, date_submitted, level " +
    " from knowledge_base " +
    " where base_doc_key in (" +
    " select knowledge_base.doc_key " +
    " from knowledge_base, base_keys   " +
    " where keyword in (?,?,?,?) and "   +
    " knowledge_base.doc_key = base_keys.doc_key ) " +
    " union "   +
    " select "   +
    " knowledge_base.doc_key, doc_name,category, post_user,
doc_location, link_doc, " +
    " base_doc_key,entry_date, date_submitted, level " +
    " from knowledge_base, base_keys   " +
    " where keyword in (?,?,?,?) and " +
    " knowledge_base.doc_key = base_keys.doc_key " +
    " order by knowledge_base.doc_key, base_doc_key, date_submit-
ted, entry_date ";
```

```java
    selectFilterStmt = dbutil.createPreparedStatement(
selectFilterStmtStr );

}

catch (SQLException e) {

    throw new Exception("SQLException thrown in
createPreparedStatements(): " + e.getMessage() );

}
catch (Exception e)   {

    throw new Exception("Exception thrown in
createPreparedStatements(): " + e.getMessage() );

}

}


public int insertDAO( ) throws SQLException, Exception {

int doc_key = 0;



// set elements

// set with 'sequence' on insert
doc_key = generateDoc_key();
insertStmt.setInt(1, doc_key );
insertStmt.setString(2, getDoc_name() );
insertStmt.setString(3, getCategory() );
insertStmt.setString(4, getPost_user() );
insertStmt.setString(5, getDoc_location() );
insertStmt.setInt(6, getLink_doc() );
insertStmt.setInt(7, getLevel() );

if (getBase_doc_key() == 0 ) // this is the base document
    insertStmt.setInt(8, doc_key );
else
    insertStmt.setInt(8, getBase_doc_key() );
```

```
insertStmt.setString(9, getEntry_date() );
insertStmt.setString(10, getDate_submitted() );

int retval = insertStmt.executeUpdate();

return doc_key;

}


public void updateDAO( ) throws SQLException {

// set elements
updateStmt.setString(1, getDoc_name() );
updateStmt.setString(2, getDoc_location() );
updateStmt.setString(3, getCategory() );
updateStmt.setString(4, getPost_user() );
updateStmt.setInt(5, getLevel() );
updateStmt.setInt(6, getLink_doc() );
updateStmt.setString(7, getEntry_date() );
updateStmt.setInt(8, getDoc_key() );

int retval = updateStmt.executeUpdate();

}

public void deleteDAO( ) throws SQLException {

// set elements
deleteStmt.setInt(1, getDoc_key() );

int retval = deleteStmt.executeUpdate();

}

public void loadDAO( int doc_key ) throws Exception {

try {

selectStmt.setInt(1, doc_key );

ResultSet rs = selectStmt.executeQuery();

if ( rs.next() )  {
```

```
        setDoc_key( rs.getInt(1) );
        setDoc_name( rs.getString(2) );
        setCategory( rs.getString(3) );
        setPost_user( rs.getString(4) );
        setDoc_location( rs.getString(5) );
        setLink_doc( rs.getInt(6) );
        setBase_doc_key( rs.getInt(7) );
        setEntry_date( rs.getString(8) );
        setDate_submitted( rs.getString(9) );
        setLevel( rs.getInt(10) );

    }


}
catch (SQLException e) {
    System.out.println("SQLException thrown in
Knowlege_baseDAO.loadDAO(): " + e.getMessage() );
    throw new Exception( "Exception in Knowlege_baseDAO.loadDAO():
" + e.getMessage() );
}


}

// set DAO members from ValueObject
public void loadDAO( Knowledge_baseVO knowledge_base ) {

setDoc_key( knowledge_base.getDoc_key() );
setDoc_name( knowledge_base.getDoc_name() );
setCategory( knowledge_base.getCategory() );
setPost_user( knowledge_base.getPost_user() );
setDoc_location( knowledge_base.getDoc_location() );
setLink_doc( knowledge_base.getLink_doc() );
setBase_doc_key( knowledge_base.getBase_doc_key() );
setLevel( knowledge_base.getLevel() );
setEntry_date( knowledge_base.getEntry_date() );
setDate_submitted( knowledge_base.getDate_submitted() );

}

// set ValueObject members from DAO
public void setVO( Knowledge_baseVO vo ) throws Exception {

vo.setDoc_key( this.getDoc_key() );
```

```
vo.setDoc_name( this.getDoc_name() );
vo.setCategory( this.getCategory() );
vo.setPost_user( this.getPost_user() );
vo.setDoc_location( this.getDoc_location() );
vo.setLink_doc( this.getLink_doc() );
vo.setLevel( this.getLevel() );
vo.setBase_doc_key( this.getBase_doc_key() );
vo.setEntry_date( this.getEntry_date() );
vo.setDate_submitted( this.getDate_submitted() );

}

// retrieve a collection of all knowledge_base record
ValueObjects
Iterator getAll() throws Exception {
Vector v = new Vector();

try {

ResultSet rs = selectAllStmt.executeQuery();

while ( rs.next() ) {

    Knowledge_baseVO vo = new Knowledge_baseVO();

    vo.setDoc_key( rs.getInt(1) );
    vo.setDoc_name( rs.getString(2) );
    vo.setCategory( rs.getString(3) );
    vo.setPost_user( rs.getString(4) );
    vo.setDoc_location( rs.getString(5) );
    vo.setLink_doc( rs.getInt(6) );
    vo.setBase_doc_key( rs.getInt(7) );
    vo.setEntry_date( rs.getString(8) );
    vo.setDate_submitted( rs.getString(9) );
    vo.setLevel( rs.getInt(10) );

    v.add( vo ) ;

 }



}
catch (SQLException e) {
```

```java
    throw new Exception("SQLException caught in
knowledge_baseDAO.getAll(): " + e.getMessage() );
}

// return the iterator for this collection
return v.iterator();


}

private int generateDoc_key() throws Exception {

try {

ResultSet rs = dbutil.executeDBQuery( "select nextval('doc_key')"
);
if ( rs.next() )
    return rs.getInt(1);
else

    return 0;
}
catch (SQLException e) {

    throw new Exception( "Error in doc_key generation: " + e );

}

}
// —-

Iterator getFilteredList( Collection criteria ) throws Exception
{
Vector v = new Vector();

try {

Iterator i = criteria.iterator();
int n = 1;
// currently, only store four search keywords
// since using a Union statement and the search is repeated, we
need to set these keywords twice
for ( n = 1; n < 5 && i.hasNext(); n++ )  {
    selectFilterStmt.setString( n, (String) i.next() );
    }
```

```
// set the next 4
i = criteria.iterator();
for ( n = 1; n < 5 && i.hasNext(); n++ )   {
      selectFilterStmt.setString( n + 4, (String) i.next() );
}

ResultSet rs = selectFilterStmt.executeQuery( );

while ( rs.next() ) {

    Knowledge_baseVO vo = new Knowledge_baseVO();

    vo.setDoc_key( rs.getInt(1) );
    vo.setDoc_name( rs.getString(2) );
    vo.setCategory( rs.getString(3) );
    vo.setPost_user( rs.getString(4) );
    vo.setDoc_location( rs.getString(5) );
    vo.setLink_doc( rs.getInt(6) );
    vo.setBase_doc_key( rs.getInt(7) );
    vo.setEntry_date( rs.getString(8) );
    vo.setDate_submitted( rs.getString(9) );
    vo.setLevel( rs.getInt(10) );

    v.add( vo ) ;

 }


}
catch (SQLException e) {
   System.out.println("SQLException caught in
knowledge_baseDAO.getFilteredList): " + e );
   throw new Exception("SQLException caught in
knowledge_baseDAO.getFilteredList(): " + e );
}
catch (Exception e ) {
   System.out.println("Exception caught in
knowledge_baseDAO.getFilteredList(): " + e );
   throw new Exception( "Exception caught in
knowledge_baseDAO.getFilteredList(): " + e );
}

// return the iterator for this collection
```

```
return v.iterator();

}

// —-



// Constructor
public Knowledge_baseDAO() throws Exception {

    // create our helper
    dbutil = new DBUtil();

    // prepare SQL statements
    createPreparedStatements();

}



}
```

INDEX

505

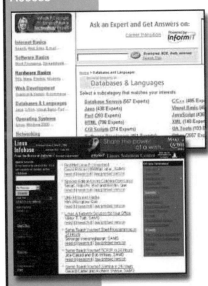